A Gardener's Guide to Florida's Native Plants

Florida A&M University, Tallahassee
Florida Atlantic University, Boca Raton
Florida Gulf Coast University, Ft. Myers
Florida International University, Miami
Florida State University, Tallahassee
University of Central Florida, Orlando
University of Florida, Gainesville
University of North Florida, Jacksonville
University of South Florida, Tampa
University of West Florida, Pensacola

A Gardener's Guide
to Florida's Native Plants

Rufino Osorio

University Press of Florida

GAINESVILLE · TALLAHASSEE · TAMPA · BOCA RATON

PENSACOLA · ORLANDO · MIAMI · JACKSONVILLE · FT. MYERS

Copyright 2001 by the Board of Regents of the State of Florida
Photographs copyright 2001 by Rufino Osorio
Printed in Hong Kong on acid-free paper

06 05 04 03 02 01   6 5 4 3 2 1

Library of Congress Cataloging-in-Publication Data
Osorio, Rufino.
A gardener's guide to Florida's native plants / Rufino Osorio.
p. cm.
Includes bibliographical references (p.).
ISBN 0-8130-1852-8 (pbk.: alk. paper)
1. Native plant gardening—Florida. 2. Native plant for cultivation—
Florida. I. Title.
SB439.24.F6 O86 2001
635'.951759—dc21 00-048823

The University Press of Florida is the scholarly publishing agency for
the State University System of Florida, comprising Florida A&M
University, Florida Atlantic University, Florida Gulf Coast University,
Florida International University, Florida State University, University of
Central Florida, University of Florida, University of North Florida,
University of South Florida, and University of West Florida.

University Press of Florida
15 Northwest 15th Street
Gainesville, FL 32611-2079
http://www.upf.com

To my mother, Trinidad Pagán,

and to the loving memory of my grandmother, Leonor Mendez de Pagán

About the Florida Native Plant Society

 The Florida Native Plant Society (FNPS) was organized in 1980 to promote the preservation, conservation, and restoration of the native plants and native plant communities of Florida.

Presently there are twenty-four local chapters throughout Florida, and if past trends are any indication, additional chapters are likely to be added in the future. Membership in FNPS is an invaluable resource for anyone with an interest in native plants and their cultivation. Attending the annual conference, as well as monthly meetings at local chapters, is a good way of meeting other growers, sharing plants, obtaining information on local sources of native plants, and participating in field trips to see native plants in natural habitats.

For additional information on FNPS membership and its benefits, visit the FNPS website at www.fnps.org or contact FNPS by regular mail or e-mail at:

FNPS
P.O. Box 690278
Vero Beach, Florida 32969-0278
(561) 562-1598
info@fnps.org

Our appreciation to the following chapters and individuals for their generous donations to this book:

Florida Native Plant Society
Doris and Bob Bareiss
Conradina Chapter
Eugenia Chapter
Heartland Chapter
Hernando Chapter
Lyonia Chapter
Martin County Chapter
Naples Chapter
Nature Coast Chapter
Palm Beach County Chapter
Pawpaw Chapter
Paynes Prairie Chapter
Pinellas Chapter
Suncoast Chapter

Contents

Acknowledgments

I offer special thanks to Nadja Chamberlain and Darla Fousek, two highly dedicated environmentalists who first proposed that I write this book. Their unwavering friendship, constant encouragement, and faith in this project helped me overcome many obstacles.

I owe a great debt to my friend Darrin Duling, the director of horticulture for the American Orchid Society and an extraordinary botanist and horticulturist. Darrin undertook an extremely thorough review of the initial manuscript and made significant contributions to the content of this book. Thanks are also due to the Preservation Foundation of the Palm Beaches for having the foresight to create Pan's Garden, which houses an outstanding collection of native plants and to which Darrin gave me complete access. In addition I extend heartfelt thanks to my friend Robert Hopper, a talented artist and landscape architect, and to Gil Nelson and Richard Wunderlin, noted authors who have extensively written about Florida's plants. They too reviewed the initial manuscript and provided many valuable suggestions and comments.

My thanks also go to Gloria Hunter, for reviewing the sections on woody plants and for so generously sharing with me plants from her garden. The mentor of many native plant gardeners, including myself, she is an avid birder and a pioneer in gardening with native plants.

Much gratitude goes to Richard Moyroud, the proprietor of Mesozoic Landscapes in Lake Worth, Florida, as well as one of the founders of native plant gardening in Palm Beach County and a tireless environmentalist and advocate of native plants. Richard was one of the earliest and staunchest supporters of this book.

I owe much to my gardening friends Amy Ferriter, Greg Phillips, Teri Ranaldo, Dale Steinmetz, and Tadziu Trotsky. Their native plant gardens have been and continue to be the sites for many interesting landscape innovations with native plants. Greg was especially helpful for sharing so many unusual and interesting plants with me as well as giving me access to his unique hammock garden and the several hundred Florida native plants growing there. Dale stands out for introducing me to the beauty of South Florida's native trees and shrubs.

I extend my thanks and appreciation to Donna Leone and Carl Terwilliger, proprietors of Meadow Beauty Nursery in Lake Worth. They were the source for many of the plants featured here and are responsible for introducing a wide variety of native plants into cultivation.

Finally, I would like to thank my mom, Trinidad Pagán, and my departed maternal grandmother, Leonor Mendez de Pagán. Their love and many sacrifices have sustained me throughout my life and I inherited my appreciation for the beauty of plants from them.

Introduction

Plants do not come with neat little labels proclaiming their origin, unfortunately. That being the case, *native* needs to be defined. In general, Florida botanists categorize a plant as native to the state if it was growing here on or before the date that Columbus arrived in the New World. Yes, this definition has some problems. However, it is widely accepted by Florida's botanical community and is the definition adopted here.

In the past, a rigid horticultural distinction was often maintained between native plants and non-native exotic plants. With few exceptions, natives tended to be relegated to informal gardens or to highly specific and frequently difficult garden situations, such as coastal gardens or wet areas. Recently, this has begun to change as a sizable number of native trees and shrubs have entered the commercial nursery trade and are finding widespread horticultural use, in both formal and informal landscapes. This book pushes this trend further and includes many types of native plants, not just woody ones, in its central premise: that Florida's native plants are wholly sufficient for realizing nearly any garden plan or landscape scheme that the home gardener may devise.

Basic gardening information and techniques, as they relate to native plants, are provided as a starting point. However, this is not a manual that will teach you how to garden. Instead, it is aimed at giving the growing requirements of native plants and their garden uses. Detailed information on gardening and landscaping techniques in Florida is now readily available, and no compelling purpose is served by repeating it here. By way of example, Schaefer and Tanner (1998) have written an excellent book on landscaping with natives, which makes an appropriate companion to the present work.

Although written specifically for Florida gardeners, this book does have wider application in neighboring states. Many of the plants included here have an extensive distribution outside Florida, and the information provided may prove useful to gardeners elsewhere in the southeastern United States.

Further, although intended chiefly as a horticultural guide for the home gardener, it also serves as a general introduction to Florida's native plants for anyone with an interest in the outdoors, such as birders and hikers. Information about natural growing conditions and flowering and fruiting seasons is useful in the field; the 350 plants profiled constitute 13 percent of all plants native to Florida and about the same number as in many field guides. Color photographs assist in plant identification, and many of the plants described are distributed widely within Florida and, as noted, beyond its borders.

Site Assessment

No single step is as important to the success of a garden as a thorough and well thought-out site assessment. Long before the first plant is placed in the ground, study the area where the garden will be situated as diligently as possible and pay close attention to the following factors.

Light

Closely observe the orientation of the sun with respect to the garden, not merely at one particular time of the day but throughout the entire day. Note carefully also the sun's changing orientation with the seasons. A site in southern Florida along a north-facing wall will be in full shade in the autumn, winter, and spring, but in the summer when the sun is high in the sky, it will receive several hours of full sun per day.

Water

Review the site with a careful eye as to how the changing seasons will affect soil moisture. Do not learn the hard way that a dry, well-drained site several feet from a roadside ditch may actually be underwater during heavy summer thunderstorms. A hardpan just below the soil surface will also result in a wet, flooded area during periods of heavy rain. If possible, try to observe how rain falls from and is directed by natural features and artificial structures such as buildings, driveways, and gutter downspouts.

Soil

Diligently examine the soil throughout the entire planting area. One home gardener discovered a large area of deep, pure sand in the middle of an otherwise ordinary lawn—a trench had been dug to repair a broken pipe and, upon completion of the repair, had been filled with sand. The only indication that this extensive area of sand was present was a slight yellowing and thinness to the grass. Frequently, construction rubble, such as limestone or pieces of concrete, is concentrated around the perimeters of buildings. Such rubble increases the alkalinity of the soil and may preclude the cultivation of acid-loving plants.

Access

Avoid placing plants where they will complicate access for home repairs and to utility easements. A particularly common problem in Florida is damage to plants during the tenting of homes for termite treatments. Plants too close to the house are adversely affected by the tenting. Also, bear in mind that various public employees, including postal carriers and electricity and water meter readers, must have access to your property. Make sure plants are not situated in their path.

Plant Survey

Do not undertake the construction of a garden without first conducting a thorough plant survey. Such a survey will identify native plants already on the site that should be preserved as well as noxious weeds or invasive pest plants that should be eliminated. If at all possible, try to enlist the aid of an experienced and knowledgeable member of your local chapter of the Florida Native Plant Society to assist in such a survey.

Site Preparation

At a minimum, site preparation should entail the removal of non-native plants and persistent weeds. Elimination of weeds is now greatly facilitated by the availability of modern herbicides with the active ingredient glyphosate. Glyphosate has numerous advantages as a weed killer, the chief of which is the specificity of its action. Glyphosate disrupts the photosynthetic metabolic pathway in plants and, therefore, has little or no deleterious effects on organisms other than plants. Indeed, glyphosate is less toxic than many common household products, including aspirin, salt, and baking soda. It is readily broken down in the environment by microorganisms into harmless compounds such as water and carbon dioxide, and it is not leached from the soil.

Glyphosate-based herbicides, however, are not perfect, and several of Florida's most pernicious weeds are highly resistant to glyphosate. Principal among these resistant weeds are bulbous *Oxalis* species and plants originating from deep, tough, under-

At the end of its first year, this native garden has minimal problems with weeds.

Aggressive, deep-rooted perennial sedges have ruined this wildflower garden due to inadequate site preparation.

ground rhizomes. Such plants often require multiple treatments, and if they are present, much patience and special effort will be required to eliminate them.

In spite of the efficacy and safety of glyphosate-based herbicides, many gardeners are loath to utilize chemical treatments of any kind whatsoever in their gardens. Various physical, nonchemical means are available as alternative means for the removal of existing vegetation. Such methods include hand-pulling, girdling, mowing, tilling, weeding with a variety of tools, and mulching with plastic film, newspaper, wood chips or similar materials.

Success with physical methods of clearing a site requires a thorough understanding of the life cycles of the weeds one is trying to remove. For example, annuals produce huge numbers of seeds that readily sprout following any disturbance to the soil. Once the land is cleared, the weed seeds should be allowed to germinate and then the plants can be destroyed. When a particularly large seed bank exists in the soil, several cycles of germination and subsequent destruction may be necessary. As with chemical treatments, weeds with deep subterranean rhizomes will require multiple treatments. If weeds are being smothered with a mulch such as plastic film or newspaper, the presence of bulbous or tuberous weeds will pose special problems since bulbs and tubers may provide a reserve of food to the plant that may last as long as two years or even longer.

Regardless of the method employed to clear and prepare a garden site, it is a good idea to allow a minimum of six to eight weeks to elapse during the growing season to see if any persistent perennial weeds make a reappearance and need to be retreated. Once these have been wholly removed, the planting of the garden may begin in earnest.

When preparing a site, take care to comply with all applicable regulations and laws. For example, some Florida counties have stringent zoning requirements that, with few exceptions, require a permit for clearing underbrush and for pruning, removal, or killing of trees.

Obtaining Native Plants

Acquiring native plants is now easier than ever, although it still takes some work to ferret out sources of some of the rarer and more unusual ones. The following sources for native plants are listed as a starting point.

Association of Florida Native Nurseries (AFNN)

AFNN publishes an annual *Native Plant and Services Directory* that lists member nurseries and the plants that each nursery sells. Their address is: Association of Florida Native Nurseries, P.O. Box 434, Melrose, Florida 32666-0434; (352) 475-5413. A complete listing of member nurseries and the plants they stock is also available on AFNN's World Wide Web page at www.afnn.org.

Florida Native Plant Society (FNPS)—State Level

Plants are not directly available from FNPS. However, an annual conference is held in a different part of Florida each year and there are usually six to ten native plant vendors present at the conferences. One never knows what will be available, but there are commonly some highly unusual and desirable plants for sale. Additionally, FNPS's quarterly magazine, the *Palmetto,* carries advertisements from a variety of native plant nurseries, including a few mail-order nurseries.

Florida Native Plant Society (FNPS)—Local Chapters

Most local FNPS chapters sponsor plant sales or raffles at their monthly meetings. Selections vary considerably from chapter to chapter and meeting to meeting. For additional details on the FNPS and to locate a local chapter near you, see the information provided in "About the Florida Native Plant Society" at the front of the book.

Although many of the larger and older native plant nurseries are members of AFNN, there are some very good native plant nurseries that are not. These are usually hard to find except through word of mouth from other FNPS members—another reason to join.

Other Sources

A variety of other sources are sometimes available for native plants. A few are listed here:

- I occasionally have mail-order Florida native plants or seeds available, especially the more unusual sorts. Check my World Wide Web page, Wildflower Nirvana, at www.wfnirvana.com for further details.

- Some colleges and universities with programs in horticulture or botany run nurseries that sell to the public. Native plants are usually available for sale at such nurseries.

- Environmental and nature centers and state and local parks often sponsor special Earth Day events at which native plants are offered for sale.

- Retail garden centers tend to offer a few native plants, especially the more popular trees and shrubs, and they may be able to procure rarer sorts if you ask.

- Botanic gardens often have plant sales or similar special events as fund-raisers, at which native plants may be available. See appendix 1 for a listing of botanic gardens in Florida.

Planting the Garden

The following general planting guidelines will assist gardeners in getting newly acquired plants off to a good start. These guidelines are applicable to all plants—wildflowers, trees, and woody shrubs.

- Bare-root plants or plants that have otherwise had their root systems disturbed should be planted while dormant during cool or mild weather.

- If possible, wait for a cloudy day or until the late afternoon to plant new acquisitions so that they will not be immediately shocked by the sun.

- Amending the soil prior to planting is usually not recommended. Plants that are placed in a spacious hole of rich, amended soil tend to produce excessive top growth and often develop poor root systems that fail to penetrate beyond the amended soil.

- Plants should be situated at the same level in the soil as occurred in the field or container.

- Large masses of circling roots in container stock should be slit lengthwise to stimulate lateral root production.

- If it is necessary to reduce top growth, this should be accomplished by thinning out rather than heading back if you wish to preserve the natural shape of the plant (see discussion of thinning and heading in the section on pruning in the next chapter).

- Unless there are prolonged periods of rainy weather, you will need to soak the ground thoroughly around the new plants immediately after planting and two or three times a week thereafter until they are established.

- After planting, lay a thick layer of organic mulch 2–4 inches deep around the new plants to conserve soil moisture and protect the roots from drying winds or high soil temperatures. Do not let heavy layers of mulch accumulate at the bases of woody plants, plants from sandy areas, or plants with fleshy stems.

An initial dose of dilute fertilizer to get the plants off to a good start is sometimes beneficial, but the routine fertilizing of native plants is *not* recommended, for the following reasons:

- Many native plants have evolved to extract nutrients maximally from poor sandy or rocky soils. When fertilized, they tend to grow too exuberantly and lose much of their character.

- By increasing the rate of growth, fertilizer increases the gardener's pruning chores and results in more garden waste to be added to burgeoning landfills.

- Fertilizer produces rapid spurts of soft, succulent growth that is less resistant to pests and diseases and, in trees and shrubs, results in weak wood that is prone to splitting.

- There is a class of soil fungi called vesicular-arbuscular mycorrhizal (VAM) fungi that form a beneficial symbiotic relationship with plants. When present in a plant's roots, VAM fungi have been shown to increase mineral and nutrient uptake, and they confer greater disease and drought tolerance to the plant. Fertilizer sometimes kills beneficial VAM fungi in the soil.

- Gardeners waste enormous quantities of fertilizer, and fertilizer runoff and leaching from the soil have far-reaching negative environmental consequences.

If fertilizers must be used, try to follow these guidelines:

- Use fertilizer only when absolutely necessary and only after you have identified a *specific* nutritional deficiency.

- Do not use general or all-purpose fertilizers. Use specially formulated fertilizers that will resolve the specific nutritional deficiency you have identified.

- Apply fertilizer in the smallest amount necessary and then do so only to the affected plants. Never apply fertilizer to the entire garden.

- Do not apply fertilizer toward the end of the growing season since lush new growth may not have sufficient time to harden before the onset of cold weather.

Maintenance

Native plant *restorations,* as opposed to gardens, usually do not receive further care beyond the initial establishment of the plants. However, if you have a garden, you will soon realize that while a garden may be low maintenance, it is never maintenance free. A myriad of activities comprise the maintenance of a garden, but most fall into just three broad categories: mulching, weeding, and pruning.

Mulching

A layer of organic mulch such as wood chips, straw, dried leaves, or pine needles is so beneficial that it may rightly be called the gardener's best friend. Principal benefits include the following:

- Mulch *suppresses weeds* in three ways. First, it physically smothers small or young plants of many weeds. Second, weed seeds that are near the soil surface, and that would normally germinate as soon as warmth and moisture allow, will not sprout if they are covered with a layer of mulch. Third, weed seeds that land on the surface of mulch tend not to germinate. These three effects combine to play an important role in easing the task of weeding the garden.

- Mulch *maintains soil moisture* in two ways. It breaks the force of heavy rains and allows more rain to enter the soil rather than escaping as runoff; and mulch slows down the evaporation of soil moisture during hot, sunny, or windy weather. By conserving soil moisture, mulch assists in the establishment of new plantings and cuts down on artificial watering.

- Mulch gradually breaks down and *improves the soil.* After two to three years of applying mulch, many soils develop a surface layer of rich, organic loam in which plants readily establish and thrive.

- Mulch is *utilitarian* and makes an excellent substrate for garden paths in informal gardens and, if edged with a decorative material such as brick, may be utilized to make paths even in formal gardens.

Although mulch is a boon to the gardener, there are two problems associated with it. Mulch made from chipped or shredded wood will form a waterproof layer if allowed to become bone dry. Avoid using such mulch in areas where there are no provisions for artificial watering during prolonged dry spells. Instead, use mulches such as dried leaves or pine needles, which will not compact into a tight, dry layer impermeable to water.

The second problem associated with mulch is more serious and affects the preservation of Florida's natural areas and native plants:

- There has been much concern over cypress mulch, since it is a nonrenewable resource that is being harvested from wild stands of bald- and pond-cypress.

- Concern is also being expressed over eucalyptus mulch and other mulches harvested from tree plantations, since natural areas are often destroyed in order to create such plantations.

- The recent explosion in the popularity of pine needle mulch is also troubling to many, since it has been found that harvesting pine needles, especially when done mechanically, destroys the wildflowers that grow beneath the pines.

In order to minimize negative impacts on natural areas and native plants, it is recommended that gardeners utilize wood mulch derived from melaleuca, a weedy pest plant. Melaleuca mulch is commonly sold in garden centers under the trade name of Enviro Mulch. Additionally, many tree-cutting companies and municipalities offer free wood mulch as a byproduct of garden waste and Christmas tree removal.

Weeding

When should a weed be removed from the garden? The instant it is noticed. This is the principal rule of weeding and gardeners should strive to adhere to it religiously. Annual and short-lived weeds are essentially seed factories. A single plant may produce hundreds or even thousands of seeds, and this will ensure trouble for the gardener for years to come. Very few gardeners realize just how long weed seeds can survive, and they are essentially little time bombs waiting to explode whenever the soil is disturbed. For example, Hall (1991) relates that seeds of common beggar's tick (*Bidens alba*) were recovered in 1987 from the ballast of the treasure ship *Nuestra Señora de Atocha,* which sank in 1622. When placed in a cup of fresh water, the 365-year-old seeds germinated and produced normal, healthy plants!

Long-lived perennial weeds tend to produce fewer seeds, but these plants often grow from storage organs such as tubers or have deep rhizomes. Once the organs are established, pulling up the aerial stems will not kill the plant. Indeed, this often serves only to stimulate the plant into even more vigorous growth. Either way, whether annual or perennial, it pays to remove a weed while it is still a young seedling. Learn to identify weeds during their earliest stages of growth and follow the admonishment to remove a weed the instant it is noticed.

Gardeners may be diligent about removing weeds from open areas of the home landscape where weeds are easily observed. However, one should not neglect to look for and remove weeds from less conspicuous areas such as hedges, the bases of low-branching trees or shrubs, or the middle of dense plantings. Weedy trees and shrubs pose special problems if they establish themselves in a hedge. If they go unnoticed, they may grow to a large size and then cannot be easily removed without damaging the hedge.

Another aspect of weeding that is frequently overlooked relates to self-sown seeds. Being wild plants, most natives do not have double flowers or other artificially selected traits that prevent seeds from forming. As a result, they often self-sow freely, and spontaneous seedlings will need to be weeded or thinned occasionally.

One of the most overlooked sources of weeds are the plants we bring to our garden. Many nurseries are overrun with weeds, and potted or field-grown material from such nurseries may well contain the unseen seeds, roots, or rhizomes of various weeds in the pot or in the root ball of the plant. If possible, quarantine potted plants to see if any weeds sprout in the pots. If they do, you should eliminate them before setting the plant out in the garden. Field-grown plants that are set directly in your garden should be carefully observed for any weeds that may pop up from the root ball, and these should be dealt with immediately so that they are not given the opportunity to spread to other parts of the garden.

Another overlooked source of weeds is fresh, uncomposted mulch. If the plants from which the mulch is derived were in fruit or had set seeds, the compost will be filled with viable seeds that may germinate in large numbers in your garden. Composting kills most seeds, and it pays to ensure that your mulch has been composted.

Pruning and Pruning Effects

Pruning is an essential form of maintenance in all gardens. By careful planning and plant selection, pruning may be minimized, but it can rarely be eliminated.

Pruning is frequently utilized as a tool for restricting or maintaining the size of an overly large plant. This is a misuse of pruning and is an indication that the wrong plant was selected for the place. Planting trees or shrubs in situations that they will eventually outgrow should be viewed for what it truly is: an error that often has long-lasting consequences beyond the life of the gardener who perpetrated it. With nearly three thousand plants native to Florida, at least one native plant can usually be found that is appropriate to a given location and that will not outgrow its allotted space.

There are numerous specialized pruning techniques and technical terms relating to them. By way of introduction, a brief summary of the most common techniques and terms follows.

Deadheading: Removal of a plant's spent flowers is known as deadheading and offers several benefits, especially in a formal garden setting. It improves a plant's appearance; inhibits disease; increases vigor and flowering by redirecting energy that would otherwise would have gone into seed production; and limits or eliminates the establishment of self-sown seedlings.

Coco-plum (*Chrysobalanus icaco*) is but one example of a native shrub suited for espalier and other formal pruning techniques

Disbudding: This involves removal of some of a plant's flower buds. By removing small side buds, the gardener directs more energy to the remaining flower buds, and the plant will produce fewer but larger flowers. This pruning technique is utilized to maximize flower size in plants that have been specifically bred to produce huge flowers.

Heading: Shortening stems or branches, but not removing them entirely, is referred to as heading. This technique stimulates the growth of dormant buds along the remaining portions of the stems and usually results in lush new growth and branching. The production of many new branches following heading tends to change the plant's shape; in contrast, thinning usually maintains the plant's natural shape.

Leader: A stem that forms the main axis of a woody plant is called a leader. When a plant has more than one leader, it is described as having multiple leaders.

Limbing Up: Also known as treeing up, limbing up refers to the removal of multiple leaders and/or lower branches of a shrub or shrubby tree to train it as a single-trunked tree. See the discussion under "scaffold limbs" for information on how the principal limbs of a tree should be arranged when it is limbed up.

Pinching: Consistent and regular removal of young shoots throughout the growing season is known as pinching, whether done with the hands or with a small tool. Pinching is regarded as one of the most efficient ways to remove suckers, shorten branches, and redirect growth with minimal disturbance or shock to the plant.

Root Pruning: Most home gardeners are unaware that roots, like any other part of a plant, may be pruned. This technique has two principal uses. Large shrubs and trees may be root pruned about one year prior to being moved in order to minimize damage at moving time. Root pruning may also be used to slow down the growth of an overly large or vigorous plant and is especially recommended for controlling the growth of robust, woody vines.

Root pruning is accomplished by plunging a sharp, long-bladed shovel into the ground in a circle around the plant. Hill (1986:34) recommends that evergreens have the circle cut just at the outer reach of the branches and deciduous trees have the circle cut just inside the spread of the branches but at least two feet from the truck. After root pruning, closely observe the plant to see if it is wilting excessively or if it becomes so loose in the ground that it is in danger of toppling in a strong wind. If such is the case, the top of the plant should be pruned so as to maintain a balance between its aerial and subterranean portions.

Scaffold Limbs: The major branches of a tree or large shrub are called the scaffold limbs. Ideally, scaffold limbs should form a 45°to 90°angle with the main axis or trunk.

Wax-myrtle (*Myrica cerifera*) and Simpson's-stopper (*Myrcianthes fragrans*) make elegant and ornamental hedges at Pan's Garden in Palm Beach, Florida.

Yaupon holly (*Ilex vomitoria*) is outstanding as a tall hedge at the entrance to Pan's Garden. It was originally clipped as a rectangle but was reshaped with an arch at the top in order to create greater visual interest and appeal.

Native plants are being used in many innovative ways, such as this buttonwood (*Conocarpus erecta*) trained as a standard.

Native plants are now appearing in unexpected places, like these pigeon-plum (*Coccoloba diversifolia*) standards at a car dealership along a busy commercial strip.

Limbs with smaller angles tend to be weak and are prone to splitting. The scaffold limbs should not be situated so that one is above another. Instead, they should be well separated and they should spiral around the main axis so that a higher scaffold limb does not directly shade a lower one. Some trees, such as gumbo-limbo (*Bursera simaruba*), paradise tree (*Simarouba glauca*), and many oaks, naturally tend to grow with wide-angled, spiraling scaffold limbs that are well separated from each other. If this is not the case, young trees should be trained and pruned to have such scaffold limbs to ensure both the health of the tree and the maximum strength of its limbs. Also, trees with scaffold limbs as described here are easy to climb and allow ready access to the crown of the tree. This is an important consideration when a tall, mature tree requires pruning or other treatment for pests or diseases.

Thinning: The removal of entire branches is referred to as thinning, and plants benefit from having exuberant tangles of branches and stems thinned occasionally. Thinning lets in light and air and is not merely an esthetic consideration. Increased light into the center of a plant directly inhibits the establishment of many plant diseases. Additionally, thinning a tree's crown makes it less likely to topple during wind storms and hurricanes, and it further inhibits disease by allowing the plant to dry more quickly after heavy rains. When done properly and judiciously, thinning preserves the natural shape of the plant, as opposed to heading, which often changes the plant's shape.

Tree-Topping: Removal of the top of a tree is known variously as tree-topping, beheading, or dehorning. It should be the pruning technique of last resort since it spoils a tree's appearance and may compromise its health. However, it is usually the pruning technique of first resort among utility tree-trimming crews dealing with trees that are growing into overhead utility wires.

Several decorative effects can be achieved by pruning. Some of the fancier ones have in the past been reserved for non-native plants, and there was a misconception that native plants were not amenable to the ornamental effects these techniques could produce. The recent explosion in native plant gardening has led to increased experimentation, and it is now clear that many native plants lend themselves to formal pruning effects. Some of these ornamental results cannot be achieved overnight; a number of years may be needed to train a plant gradually. Once completed, all of these pruning effects require continued periodic pruning for the life of the plant.

Espalier: Derived from the Old French word *aspau,* meaning a prop, espalier refers to the training of a plant in a two-dimensional plane by propping the young plant's branches along wires or stakes. This is a very formal effect and is especially useful when a plant is to be grown in a narrow space, such as along a wall.

Hedges: Healthy hedges add to the value of a property and have many uses, including producing privacy, demarcating boundaries, calming strong winds, and providing shelter for birds and small animals. Hedges may be trained in a variety of shapes so long as they are as wide or wider at the bottom than at the top. This is necessary to ensure that the lower branches receive sufficient light. Otherwise, the lower branches will tend to die out and spoil the appearance of the hedge. Formal hedges may be sheared back to just where new growth began for the season. For an informal hedge, remove the very oldest stems from the base of the plant each year and shorten overly long branches.

Pollarding: Severely cutting back all of the main branches of a mature tree is known as pollarding. It is often disparagingly referred to as "hat racking," since a pollarded tree resembles a giant hat rack. If pollarded on a regular basis, the truncated limbs develop club-shaped, knobby ends with a highly unnatural appearance that is out of place in most landscapes. If not pollarded at regular intervals, such trees tend to produce veritable thickets of elongated, weak branches that are prone to splitting during heavy winds or rains. Pollarding may also seriously compromise the health of certain trees. For all these reasons, many Florida municipalities have zoning codes that prohibit the practice.

Standards: Plants that are pruned to have a single straight principal stem with a ball-shaped crown are known as standards. Such lollipop-shaped plants provide an interesting accent in the garden, both elegant and whimsical. A wide variety of woody native plants may be trained as standards, disproving the misconception that natives are suitable only for informal or "wild" gardens.

Topiary: Shearing trees and shrubs into living sculptures, or topiary, requires persistent and dedicated pruning. Avoid the mistake of selecting a detailed and intricate shape for your topiary: it will be a maintenance nightmare and the details will be lost in the spurts of new growth between prunings. Also, topiary must be situated in open areas that receive equal light on all sides so that growth will be equally vigorous and dense on all sides.

When pruning your plants, follow these basic guidelines:

- Plants that have suffered a setback or damage to their root systems, such as during transplanting, should have top growth pruned by about one-third. This will give the plant a chance to develop a healthy root system capable of supporting its growth.

- Do not remove more than one-third of a plant's top growth when pruning. If a plant needs to be severely pruned, do this in a series of gradual stages.

- When shaping or directing the growth of a woody plant, do so while it is still young. Older plants have thicker branches that are more difficult to prune or that may be out of reach. Also, some plants heal poorly when large branches are removed.

- Cut back branches at an angle just above a bud. The bud should face the outside of the plant to avoid crossed branches or branches that grow into the plant's center or crown.

- Making a notch with a knife just above a dormant bud will stimulate its growth. If the notch is made below a bud, it will inhibit the bud from sprouting. A notch made below a shoot will restrain its growth.

- Never cut branches flush with the main stem. Instead, cut just beyond the ridge formed by the collar where the branch meets the main stem. Damaging the branch collar compromises a plant's ability to heal the pruning wound and fight disease.

- A host of fungal, microbial, and viral infections are readily spread in garden situations as a result of using unclean pruning tools. Avoid spreading disease by not using the same pruning tools on more than one plant without sterilizing them. This is easily accomplished by soaking your pruning tools in a solution of undiluted household bleach before using them on another plant.

Perhaps more than any other garden endeavor, pruning has the potential for serious accidents, injury, or death. Take care to follow all necessary instructions and precautions when using any pruning tool, whether manual, electric, or gas powered. The pruning of trees, especially where a ladder is necessary, should not be undertaken lightly, and if one is not experienced in this task, a professional should be employed to perform the job.

Propagation

This chapter provides an overview of general plant propagation techniques for the home gardener. Although this material is covered in a wide variety of books, it is briefly presented here because of the many important uses that can be made of propagated plant material.

First, many native plants are still not readily available. Thus, native plant enthusiasts often find themselves with just one or two plants of a particularly rare and coveted species. There may not be ready commercial sources for replacement, and if one loses the few plants in one's possession, it may be many years before another source is found. Under these circumstances, it is wise to propagate the parent plant in case disaster strikes. I often propagate my rarest plants and give the progeny to friends. Although this may seem generous, it is ultimately a form of insurance, since the friends then become a backup source for the plant should I lose my sole specimen. In this case I am following the old adage that the best way to keep a plant is to give it away.

A variety of native plants are beautiful on their own but spectacular when grown in large groups. Purchasing large numbers of plants, however, is sometimes prohibitively

There is a special joy to growing one's own plants from seeds; these are rusty staggerbush (*Lyonia ferruginea*) seedlings.

expensive. The solution here is to buy one or two starter plants, become familiar with propagation techniques, and then multiply your stock to whatever quantity is desired.

Many growers are aware that some of the more unusual and rarer native plants are available only through trade with other growers. Therefore, they try to keep on hand a few extra plants of particularly desirable species to use as trading material.

Another reason for increasing one's stock is the simple pleasure of caring for something and seeing it prosper. Many growers love to share the results of their propagation efforts, and garden visitors rarely leave without a handful of babies for their own garden. This is especially important with beginners, who benefit from the encouragement of being given a few starter plants to get them going down the road to becoming enthusiastic and dedicated native plant gardeners.

Yet a fifth use for propagated plant material is as sale or raffle plants at the meetings of local chapters of the Florida Native Plant Society. For many chapters, plant raffles are both the single greatest source of revenue and the principal draw in attracting members to meetings.

Vegetative Propagation

One of the chief benefits of vegetative propagation is the ability to produce additional plants that are identical in every way to the mother plant. If the original plant has some horticulturally desirable feature, such as pest resistance, a longer flowering season, or adaptability to pot culture, that feature is passed along to all its vegetatively propagated progeny. Moreover, it is not unusual for solitary garden plants to fail to set seed. Such a plant may be self-sterile or the gardener may have a plant of one sex and the species may have male and female flowers borne on separate plants. In such cases, vegetative propagation will serve as the only means of increasing the stock.

Stem Cuttings

Most people are aware that many plants may be propagated by taking a young but firm branch, trimming it to a suitable length, stripping the lower leaves, and placing the stem in a jar of water or a pot of moist soil or sand until it forms a good root system. To this I will add a few points to keep in mind:

- The importance of selecting a suitable branch or stem cannot be overemphasized. Choose a young, actively growing branch from which to make the cutting. Best results are obtained by selecting relatively firm, but not fully mature, stems.

- Avoid stems that are bearing flowers or flower buds. Often, cuttings taken from such stems will attempt to continue to produce flowers at the expense of a vigorous and healthy root system. If flowering material is the only material available to you, then remove every single flower and flower bud, no matter how tiny. You may be anxious to have your young plant blossom as soon as possible. However, the production of flowers by a young cutting will seriously weaken it and will adversely affect the production of a strong root system.

- Some plants are genetically programmed to flower during certain seasons. For example, some of our morning glories (*Ipomoea* species) flower in the autumn or spring whenever the days are short and the nights are long. It is hopeless to try to root cuttings during these flowering periods, since the cuttings will persist in producing flower buds rather than roots.

- If you root the cuttings in water, do not allow the roots to get longer than about one inch before you pot them up. Roots formed in water are not identical to those formed in soil. If you let them get too long, the young plant is set back while its root system adapts to growing in soil.

- Inexplicably, quite a few native plants refuse to root from cuttings placed in a glass of water. However, they will root if the cutting is placed in a small pot of moist sand or soil. Cuttings placed in pots of soil pose special problems since it may be difficult to keep the humidity sufficiently high. This can be resolved by carefully wrapping the pot with a small piece of clear plastic wrap, securing it with a rubber band around the pot and loosely twisting the top. The top is loosely twisted so that the ambient humidity is kept high but not so high that excessive condensation of water occurs. If you see water droplets condensing on the inside of the plastic wrap, loosen it at once; having the humidity too high may result in loss of the cutting to fungal or bacterial rot.

- In order to establish a healthy root system, the cutting needs to be actively photosynthesizing. Thus, in general, cuttings should be positioned where they will get bright light—but not so bright as to risk wilting them, since wilting for even a brief period sets cuttings back severely.

- Willows have been proposed as an organic alternative to rooting hormones. Willow branches placed in a glass of water quickly produce a robust root system. It is said that the water in which willow branches have rooted contains hormones from the willow's root system and that this water may be used to facilitate the rooting of more difficult cuttings. It is not clear if this has been scientifically validated, but since willow branches are often commonly available, one has little to lose by experimenting with this technique. Of course, one should avoid using branches of the Florida willow or the heart-leaved willow, as these are endangered species in Florida.

One form of vegetative propagation that is essentially unknown to cold climate gardeners is the propagation of plants from branch cuttings. In contrast to temperate woody plants, certain tropical plants may be propagated from large woody branches or even small trunks. Two well-known examples are coralbean (*Erythrina herbacea*) and gumbo-limbo (*Bursera simaruba*). One problem is that in their eagerness to produce as large a plant as possible in as short a time as possible, many gardeners, amateur and professional alike, are tempted to root very large branch cuttings. When propagating certain tropical woody plants from branch cuttings, remember the following points:

- Excessively large branches—that is, those larger than half an inch in diameter, often will not produce a root system that is in proportion to the above-ground portion of the plant. For the sturdiest root systems, and maximum wind and hurricane resistance, do not utilize large branches when making a branch cutting.

- Branch cuttings are usually made from side branches and the resulting plants tend to grow horizontally rather than vertically—evidently, a plant originating from a side branch is "programmed" to continue trying to grow as a side branch. Thus, gumbo-limbos grown from seed are tall, erect canopy trees, whereas those grown from branch cuttings tend to be short by comparison and to have a wide, spreading crown, never developing an upright central leader.

- If you want to grow a plant with an upright central leader from a branch cutting, then *plant the cutting sideways*. This way the growth buds that would normally have been side branches are now oriented to grow vertically. Usually, several vertical upright branches result when a branch cutting is planted sideways. Simply remove all of the new shoots except one, and you will get a plant that more closely resembles a seed-grown plant.

- For an interesting grouping effect, plant a branch cutting sideways. As already noted, usually several upright stems will develop. Leave two or three branches and you will have an instant "grove." These multitrunked plants have a lot of character and add considerable interest to the landscape, especially when grown as specimen trees in a formal or semiformal garden setting.

Root Cuttings

Cuttings derived from roots are seldom utilized for propagation by the home gardener. This is not surprising since in order to obtain cutting material, one must seriously disturb the plant, something most home gardeners are loath to do. In any case, it is commonly listed as a propagation method for just two native plants: orange milkplant (*Asclepias tuberosa*) and coneflower (*Echinacea purpurea*). If utilizing this method, select strong, thick, healthy roots, cut them into one-inch pieces, lay the pieces horizontally in pots, and lightly cover with soil. Vegetative buds generally appear in a few weeks.

Division

Division is probably the easiest method of plant propagation for the home grower. Why is it so easy? Because the plant has done all the work for you!

Division is rarely suitable for annuals or for excessively woody plants. However, it is eminently suitable for most clump-forming perennials. Many perennials start out as

How a plant is propagated can make a dramatic difference in its appearance. This gumbo-limbo (*Bursera simaruba*) was grown from a branch cutting. Note the short trunk and numerous horizontal branches. Contrast this plant with the seed-grown gumbo-limbo pictured on page 236.

a single, solitary growth. With age, the original stem produces basal side shoots and small to large clumps are the result. At first, the side shoots draw all of their water and nutrients from the mother plant, but eventually they form roots and for all intents and purposes become distinct plants. It is then a simple matter to sever a side shoot from the rest of the clump, carefully lift out its root system, and pot it up. In a few minutes, one has an "instant" plant. Potted divisions should be kept moist but not too wet and positioned in bright light but not full sun. Once they are established and actively growing, they may be treated like the mother plant from which they were derived.

Plants grown from divisions tend to be expensive, since it takes time for a mother plant to grow into a clump large enough to divide. However, division is one of the fastest methods of producing a mature flowering plant because the division already has both vegetative shoots and an established root system.

It is unwise to divide a sickly or dormant plant, and because division results in a disturbance to the plant, it is not recommended for that unique, one-of-a-kind and irreplaceable plant that took you ten years to obtain. If a division must be taken from such a plant, do it with care, use very sharp tools to sever the side shoot from the clump, and do so with as little disturbance as possible to the parent clump.

Some native perennials grow in very tight and compact clumps. It may be impossible to remove side shoots from such clumps without severely disturbing and damaging both the mother clump and the division. Often, the result is the slow death of the mother plant, usually from bacterial or fungal rot that establishes itself where the clump was damaged. One's hopes then lie with the division. However, often the division also dies, the plant becoming one more ignominious entry in one's life list of "plants I've killed."

Suckers

Side shoots borne below the ground and often growing horizontally some distance from the parent plant before upright, above-ground growth commences are referred to as *suckers.* If they arise from the roots, rather than from subterranean portions of the main stem, they are called *root suckers.* Like side shoots borne in a clump, suckers may be severed from the parent plant and treated in the same manner as a division.

Layering

Layering is, in principle, similar to taking cuttings but differs in that the stem is induced to form roots while it is still attached to the parent plant. There are two principal methods of layering.

In *air layering,* a branch is either partially girdled or else a small wedge extending about one-third the diameter of the stem is removed. In the latter case, a small pebble or piece of wood is inserted in place of the wedge to keep the cut portions from joining back together again. If the stem is girdled, be careful to scrape away just the bark and the green layer (the cambium) immediately below the bark; do not scrape away anything deeper than the cambium. The area that was girdled or cut is tightly wrapped with a ball of moist sphagnum moss, and this is carefully and tightly wrapped with plastic and aluminum foil. After three to four months, roots form where the stem was injured, and the branch is severed below the point where it was girdled or cut, resulting in what is essentially a large, rooted cutting.

Home gardeners who have tried air layering usually find they need several attempts before they are successful and master the technique. Since air layering is an involved process, most home gardeners give up before they have attained sufficient skill to succeed. Two things can go wrong. The first is that the girdled or cut area may form a callus and the two sections of the branch unite once again. If this happens, no roots will form. The second is that during the three to four months that it takes for roots to form, the ball of sphagnum moss may dry out. Again, if this happens the air layer will fail.

Air layering works only on plants with sufficiently large branches and is usually reserved for woody plants that cannot be propagated by any other means. Plants produced by air layering are expensive due to the time and skill involved. However, air layering allows one to produce big plants that reach maturity much sooner than plants produced from seeds or cuttings, which justifies the high cost for rare, unusual, or highly sought after species.

Much easier for the home gardener is *ground layering.* As in an air layer, a stem is injured by girdling or cutting into it. However, in a ground layer, a stem or branch that is close to the ground is selected. The injured portion is buried in the soil, or if it is too high off the ground, soil is heaped up around the injury. Then a rock or some other weight is placed over the branch to keep it from rising out of the mound of soil. If all goes well, roots are produced around the cut area and the branch is severed from the parent plant and potted up in the manner of a large rooted cutting. Many woody perennials and shrubby plants root naturally wherever low stems touch the ground or are buried by leaves. Such stems are essentially spontaneous ground layers, and they provide a quick and efficient means of propagating one's stock.

A clever variation of ground layering is to make a slit partly down the side of a plastic pot, position the pot next to a low branch that has been girdled or cut, and then insert the stem into the pot by way of the slit, so that the injured portion of the stem is inside the pot. The pot is then filled with soil and is watered in the same manner as any other potted plant. Eventually the pot fills up with roots, the stem is severed from the parent plant, and one has an already mature potted plant. In the tropics, hollow sections of bamboo as long as 5 feet (1.5 meters) have been utilized as containers in order to "ground layer" stems far above the ground.

Grafting

Grafting is seldom utilized in the propagation of native plants. Rarely, plants with highly specific soil requirements have been grafted onto more widely adaptable related species in order to grow them in areas to which they would otherwise not be suited. For example, scrub holly (*Ilex opaca* var. *Arenicola*) requires exceedingly deep and well-drained sand in order to grow well. However, it can be grafted onto the roots of dahoon holly (*Ilex cassine*), a species adapted to wet soils, thus allowing one to grow scrub holly in soils that would normally be too wet to support its growth. Of course, if one has wet soils, it is far easier, and more ecologically sound, to select native plants that are naturally adapted to growing in such soils.

Another specialized use for grafting is to save space in small gardens. Again, hollies are an illustrative example. In true hollies of the genus *Ilex,* the male and female flowers are borne on separate plants, and normally plants of both sexes are needed in order for the female plants to bear the brightly colored red berries so important in the plant's appeal. Where space is at a premium, one could graft a male branch onto a female plant, thus combining both sexes in a single plant. As in air layering, grafted plants are expensive because of the time and skill involved in consistently producing successful grafts, and the technique is best left to the professional nursery grower.

Seed Propagation

Seeds provide one of the cheapest methods of producing large numbers of plants. However, in order to succeed with seeds, one must have a legal source of seeds, the seeds must be viable, and they must germinate. The last part is often the rub, since many wild plants produce seeds with specific dormancy requirements, and if the dormancy requirements are not met, the seeds will die and rot before they ever germi-

Coralbean (*Erythrina herbacea*) seeds demonstrate the value of scarifying seeds with a hard coat. Both seeds were soaked in water for twenty-four hours. The scarified seed on the left has swollen from the absorbed water and will germinate in two to three days. The unscarified seed on the right was unaffected.

nate. Listed below are various tricks utilized by professionals, and easily adapted by the home gardener, to speed up the germination of recalcitrant seeds.

Scarification

Some of our showiest and horticulturally most desirable native plants occur in three families: the morning glory family, the hibiscus family, and the bean family. Besides being desirable and ornamental, nearly all members of these three families share another trait: seeds with a hard seed coat impervious to water. Under natural conditions, the hard seed coats are commonly broken down by the stomach acids of animals; by abrasion against rocks and stones when the seeds are rolled by wind or water; through breakdown of the seed coat by soil microorganisms; or as a result of exposure to intense, brief heat, such as during a wildfire, which cracks the seed coat. Seeds in which dormancy is the result of a hard seed coat are especially easy to germinate since one needs only two common and easily available tools to break their dormancy—a file and sandpaper.

Use a file carefully to scratch a small hole in the seed coat of large seeds in the bean, hibiscus, and morning glory families. Small seeds can be scarified by gently rubbing them between two pieces of fine sandpaper. The process is called scarification because you are "scarring" the seed by filing the small hole. Careful treatment is important. Filing too large a hole will injure the seed so that it rots before it has a chance to germinate. How can you tell if the seeds have been successfully scarified? Simply soak them in a cup of water for 24–48 hours. They should swell up to about twice their regular size or more. Those that don't swell need to be rescarified.

Once the seed coat has been scarified, the seeds can imbibe water and germination usually results in a few days. Often there is a dramatic improvement in germination over that of unscarified seeds, and germination rates measured in months may be shortened to two to seven days. This method is practically fail-safe for quickly and successfully germinating seeds in the bean, hibiscus, and morning glory families. Thus, members of these families are among the easiest of all plants to grow from seed, and they are highly recommended for beginners attempting to grow native plants from seed for the first time.

Stratification

Plants that originate in climates with a cold winter season often produce seed with a dormancy of a different kind from that provided by a hard seed coat. Such seeds freely imbibe water and become physiologically active. However, the seeds do not germinate until they have been chilled for a period of time and then exposed to warmer temperatures. The adaptive value of this type of dormancy is obvious: it prevents seeds from germinating before the onset of winter. Limiting germination to the spring means that the young plants have a lengthy period of warm weather to establish themselves before facing the rigors of their first winter.

Naturally, plants with seeds that require exposure to cold temperatures before they will germinate are more common in northern Florida. However, even in southern Florida, there are plants of northern affinity, such as red mulberry (*Morus rubra*), the seeds of which germinate more quickly or in greater numbers if briefly exposed to cool temperatures.

The process of treating such seed by exposing it to cold temperatures in the refrigerator is called *stratification*. In the past, this procedure was often made unnecessarily complex. The following two simple procedures are effective and involve little time and effort.

- Method 1: Place the seed to be stratified in a small container. Fill the container partially with water and let the seeds soak for about 12 hours, and then place the container in the refrigerator for several weeks. Remove the seeds and sow at once. Seeds obtained from plants coming from areas that experience extended hard freezes may be placed in the freezer and the seeds frozen in a block of ice. Occasionally, letting the ice thaw briefly and refreezing the container through several cycles of freezing and thawing further improves germination.

- Method 2: Place the seed on a moist paper towel in a plastic container with a lid. Seal the container with the lid and place in the refrigerator (*not* the freezer) for a few weeks. Proceed as above. If necessary, the container may be placed in the freezer to simulate a hard freeze. The advantage of this method is that once the container is removed from the refrigerator, the seeds do not need to be sown immediately. They can stay in the container with the moist paper towel until they germinate, and only those that actually germinate are potted up.

Fire

The prevalence of fire-dependent dormancy in the our flora is presently unknown; seeds of very few native plants have been tested for their response to fire. However, there are at least three species in which seed will not germinate without fire being present, and it would not be surprising if there were more. In *Kalmia hirsuta*, seeds will not germinate unless exposed to fire. Also, there occur in Florida two species of redroot (members of the genus *Ceanothus*) with seeds that have a small hole or pore filled by a waxy material. The heat of a fire melts the waxy plug, which allows the seed to imbibe water, and germination soon follows.

So how would one treat such seeds? Do you need to start a brush fire in your backyard? Luckily, nothing so dramatic is necessary. The following method has been successful:

- Sow the seeds in a pot of soil and water them thoroughly. Let the pot stand for 24–48 hours.

- Next, create a tube of aluminum foil and place it around the edge inside the pot. The foil will help contain and concentrate the fire as well as protecting the rim of plastic pots from the heat.

- Place a loose layer of coarsely shredded paper (such as facial tissues or toilet paper) about 1–2 inches high on the surface of the soil and put a match to it. *Be careful— the burning paper produces an intensely hot fire.*

- After the fire subsides, water the pot thoroughly so that the ash and other chemical by-products of the fire are washed into the soil or come in contact with the soil.

Remember, there are two distinct components to a fire: the heat, and the chemicals and gases produced by the combustible materials. Some fire-adapted seeds respond to the chemicals and gases produced by the fire and are not affected by the actual heat. It is only for these types that one has to use the method outlined.

For seeds that respond to the heat itself, such as those of *Ceanothus,* it is recommended that the seed be covered with very hot water (almost at boiling point) and the water be allowed to cool to room temperature. The seed is then potted up as usual. Incidentally, this method is often recommended for members of the bean family as an alternative to scarification, since it is far easier to pour hot water over a large number of seeds than to scarify each one by hand. The hot water causes the hard outer seed coat to develop tiny cracks, and the result is equivalent to scarification.

Double Dormancy

A few of our natives exhibit *double dormancy* and must be exposed to two or more periods of both warm and cold temperatures. Plants in this group have seed that may take up to two years to germinate and include many hollies (*Ilex* species), some of the viburnums, and most species of clematis. For this reason, when sowing the seeds of these plants, the pots of seeds should be kept a minimum of 24 months. Attending to a flat or pot of seeds for two years is a task that only the most dedicated of home gardeners will undertake, and one rarely sees plants in this group being propagated from seed.

The Ambient Method

Look at any garden book or magazine or horticultural catalog that covers the topic of seed germination and it will describe a more or less standard method of germinating seeds under controlled conditions:

- The seed is sown indoors.

- A regular photoperiod of 12–14 hours of light is maintained, often through the use of fluorescent lights.

- The seeds are kept at an even temperature of about 70° to 80°F, depending on the type of seed.

The method is effective for many traditional garden plants, but through trial and error, I have discovered that a large number of native plants have seeds that do not germinate under such conditions. People familiar with the standard method of seed germination often get unexpectedly dismal results when applying it to native plants. However, if the pots or flats of seeds are placed outdoors in a protected location, where they are subjected to the natural cycles of variation in temperature, sunlight, and moisture, the seeds germinate in one to four weeks without further treatment. This method, which I call the *ambient method* because the seeds are exposed to ambient environmental conditions, is especially effective when the seeds are sown in late spring or late summer. The seeds seem to respond to the change in season as spring turns to summer or summer turns to autumn, and often a high germination rate is achieved.

Finally, there are some native plants that defy germination efforts if they are in a pot or seed flat. Yet self-sown seed of the same plants may appear spontaneously in the garden, usually just below or near the mother plant and often in surprisingly large numbers. For these plants, the only way to propagate them is to let the parent plant go to seed in the garden and to pot up the spontaneous seedlings as they appear. It is not clear what the explanation is for this behavior.

Winter Annuals

For winter annuals, exposure to ambient environmental conditions is virtually essential, or they will not germinate. Winter annuals have an unusual life cycle: seeds germinate in the autumn (or late winter in northern Florida), and they grow quickly during cool weather. With the onset of warm weather, they produce large quantities of flowers and seed. By the time summer has arrived in full force, they have died down, leaving only their seed to repeat the cycle. In my experience, if the seed of winter annuals is maintained under controlled conditions, germination is usually very poor. When growing these plants from seed, generally the ambient method described produces the best results.

Counterfeit Natives

Errors are an inevitable part of human endeavors, and native plant gardening has its share. One of the most egregious is the cultivation of non-native plants as natives. These plants are "counterfeit natives," and once the mistake is made, it is difficult to correct. This error has many causes but more often than not it is due to one or more of the following.

Botanical Errors

Botanists may make mistakes that lead to the acceptance of a non-native plant as native by the general public. Generally, such errors are of two kinds. Botanists may misidentify a plant. An example of this occurred when a non-native, Old World blue porterweed (*Stachytarpheta urticifolia*), was identified by various Florida botanists as being the same plant as our native blue porterweed (*Stachytarpheta jamaicensis*).

Second, botanists sometimes find it difficult to identify the natural range of a given plant. Determining the natural range is complicated by several factors:

- Some plants have natural ranges that closely approach and may possibly include Florida. Sometimes it is difficult to tell if they are truly native or are merely escapes from cultivation.

- Some weeds and crop plants have a nearly cosmopolitan distribution due to their widespread dissemination by human activity, and their original ranges are no longer clear.

- Certain plants may have populations that include both ecologically conservative native strains and weedy non-native strains.

Misidentifications of non-native plants as native by professional botanists are fairly rare. However, as a result of confusion over natural ranges, there will always be some element of doubt regarding whether certain plants are native to Florida.

Errors by the General Public

Errors by the general public in identifying plants are fairly common and are usually due to:

- A lack of botanical training, especially with regard to distinguishing superficially similar plants.

- The tendency by some gardeners to confuse "xeriscape plant" with "native plant." These are, of course, two completely different concepts. A xeriscape is a landscape designed to conserve water by a variety of means but principally through the use of drought tolerant plants. Many native plants are indeed highly drought tolerant and are widely used in xeriscapes; however, gardeners must not conclude from this that *all* xeriscape plants are native since many non-native plants are also highly drought tolerant and sometimes used in xeriscapes.

- The tendency by some gardeners to confuse "commonly grown in Florida" with "native to Florida." Likewise, these are two different concepts.

Due to the propensity of gardeners to share plants with others, such misidentifications can lead to the widespread dissemination of non-native plants under the label "native." This is especially the case when a plant has a highly desirable trait; a number of non-native plants have been spread nearly throughout Florida under the guise of being native by butterfly gardeners for use as butterfly larval food and nectar plants. Some examples of non-native plants being spread as supposedly native butterfly garden plants are coral vine (*Antigonon leptopus*), fetid passion-vine (*Passiflora foetida*), and Old World blue porterweed (*Stachytarpheta urticifolia*).

Deception

As environmental awareness has grown among the general population, the status of a plant as native or non-native has become an increasingly important consideration in its purchase. More and more frequently, one can hear customers asking nursery proprietors if a particular plant of interest is native or not. Some nursery staff will readily and without compunction answer, "Yes, it's native" (regardless of whether the plant is truly native to Florida) if it will clinch the sale. Once purchased, the now mislabeled plant is often spread far and wide before the deception is finally uncovered.

The Reverse Problem

Occasionally, a native plant is incorrectly treated as non-native. Following are three examples of how native plants mistakenly come to be regarded as non-native:

- Taking the common name literally: Various native plants have common names with a geographical designation, such as Jamaican caper (*Capparis cynophallophora*) or Bahama-coffee (*Psychotria ligustrifolia*). Occasionally, beginners take these common names literally and believe that Jamaican caper is native *only* to Jamaica or Bahama-coffee is native *only* to the Bahamas.

- Taking the scientific name literally: Again, a variety of native plants have scientific names with a geographical designation, such as coinwort (*Centella asiatica*) or American hornbeam (*Carpinus caroliniana*). Such scientific names are indicative of where the first specimens known to botanists were discovered and are not meant to be an inclusive designation of the plant's total natural range. Thus, coinwort is indeed native to Asia. However, it is also widespread and native to the New World, including Florida. Likewise, American hornbeam was named on the basis of plants occurring in the general region of the Carolinas, but its natural range extends into central peninsular Florida.

· Weediness: Since many weeds are non-native, there is a tendency among some gardeners to overgeneralize and to regard any weedy plant as being non-native. This is incorrect and weedy tendencies alone cannot be used to determine if a plant is native or non-native.

Wildlife in the Garden

Appreciation of other occupants of the outdoors need not be limited to weekend jaunts, holidays, or vacations. With a little effort and planning, one can attract wildlife to a garden or yard for year-round enjoyment. Wild creatures, both small and large, engage in myriad activities, and it is fascinating to observe their bustling, animated lives—especially when doing so from the comfort of one's home. Additionally, they have two attributes that enhance their value to many outdoor enthusiasts. First, many wild animals combine attractive form with elegant colors, appealing to our esthetic sense. Foremost among these, of course, are butterflies and birds. Many other animals possess beauty of a more subtle nature, such as the elegant architecture of a snail's shell or the geometric regularity of the scales on a lizard or snake. Second, one should not underestimate the value of backyard wildlife in helping to maintain a healthy and balanced ecosystem. This is as important a consideration at home as it is in a national park. For example, my yard is filled with native plants that attract a considerable diversity of insects and birds. As a result, outbreaks of insect pests are minimal and are usually efficiently controlled by natural predators.

Wild creatures, like people, have three absolute requirements that must be met if they are to flourish: shelter, food, and water. If we are to attract them, the landscapes we create at home must supply these primal needs.

In the human world, shelter and food are wholly distinct categories, but this is not the case in the natural world. Why? Because plants are the principal structural components of natural environments, and plants provide both food and shelter. Our homes provide precious little by way of food—pray that you never have to eat your house! But this is not the case for animals. Think, for example, of caterpillars, for which shelter and food are one and the same plant, or birds, which may relish the fruits or insects to be found on the plants in which they nest or roost. The fact that plants provide both the structure and food for living communities leads to the first and most important principle for attracting wildlife to home landscapes: Plant as wide a variety of native plants as your home environment allows.

Look around your home and see how many microhabitats there are and how you might increase the value of those microhabitats to wildlife. Plant understory shrubs and wildflowers under large trees to create a cool, shady oasis for backyard wildlife. Many Florida homes have a swale somewhere along the perimeter of the property to aid in draining excess runoff from heavy rains. Considerable moisture usually accumulates in such swales during rainy periods, and they are the perfect spot for growing moisture-loving shrubs and wildflowers. Plants that like rocky, alkaline conditions will thrive near the foundation of the house since in many cases an accumulation of construction rubble is found there. And if you have a hot, dry, sunny area, consider a small planting of plants native to scrub or coastal situations. For best results, stick to native plants that naturally occur near your home. These will be the ones that are best adapted to your area and that will require the least watering.

Bear in mind that natural communities with a complex architecture have lots of niches, and the more niches there are, the greater the diversity of wildlife. It is no accident that the two most exuberant natural communities on earth, rainforests and coral reefs, are both communities of great structural complexity with innumerable niches to accommodate many kinds of animals. You can simulate the structural complexity of natural environments by planting many structurally different types of plants. Plant trees, shrubs, woody perennials, and wildflowers. At least one palm and conifer are native to every county in Florida, so be sure to include a palm or conifer native to your area. Don't overlook thorny plants; small animals love these because they can dive into such plants to escape predators. Thorny or spiny plants will not pose a problem if you place them in an out-of-the-way spot where they will not snag passersby. Try to plant in layers to maximize the structural complexity of your home wildlife habitat with groundcover plants, wildflowers and small shrubs in the bottom layer, midsized shrubs and large, robust perennials in the middle layer, and large shrubs and trees in the top layer. Florida has numerous native vining plants—as a final touch, grow a vine or two to weave through the plantings.

Utilize any or all of the following three techniques to increase further the amount of shelter for wildlife in your yard. Since many animals utilize tree hollows, putting up nest boxes will make your yard friendlier to wildlife. However, nest boxes need to be carefully designed to exclude aggressive species like squirrels, starlings, or house sparrows. Otherwise, such boisterous animals will monopolize the nest boxes. Nest boxes also need to be carefully placed to prevent easy access by predators, and they do need to be cleaned out periodically to avoid a buildup of parasites, which can seriously impair the health of nestlings. Smaller animals, such as many reptiles, require a layer of leaf litter on the soil as this not only provides shelter but also hides them from the eyes of bigger, hungry animals. So don't rake those leaves. They are the home to many little creatures, and they make excellent natural fertilizer to boot. Finally, you can construct a brush pile to provide additional shelter. This will shelter a wide variety of small animals and birds, which can utilize the brush pile to escape predators and as protection from inclement weather. To make a brush pile, first lay down a few large, heavy logs on the ground. Using the logs as a foundation, lay smaller logs, branches, and twigs to create a stable pile. The innumerable niches and spaces in the brush pile make it an ideal home for many backyard creatures.

Before leaving the subject of the physical environment, avid birders may want to consider creating a sand bed. This need consist of nothing more than a few square feet of fine, sandy soil kept free of encroaching vegetation. To prevent neighborhood cats from using the sand bed, which would ruin it for birds, place a small fence around it, such as the kind sold to set off flower beds. Many birds enjoy dusting themselves with fine sandy soil; it appears that such dust baths help keep birds free from parasites and otherwise serve to condition their plumage. In any case, there can be no doubt that the activity serves some important function in light of both the amount of time birds spend dust bathing and the frequency with which they dust bathe.

Food for your backyard inhabitants is directly or indirectly derived from the plants growing there. If you grow a diversity of plants, supplemental feeding of wild animals is neither recommended nor necessary. Wild animals, even the ones in your backyard, are indeed wild, and feeding of such animals is rarely beneficial. In some ways supplemental feeding may actually harm wildlife.

Providing animals with food other than that naturally occurring in the form of plants growing in your yard may accustom such animals to the presence of human beings, and animals that have lost their fear of people are in grave danger. Although you may never harm a wild animal, can you be absolutely sure that this is the case with your neighbors or your neighbors' children? Sadly, tame animals are easy targets for novice hunters who are eager to shoot something for practice. Additionally, tame animals often become a nuisance and their lives are seriously disrupted, or even terminated, when local animal control departments are called in to remove them. Further, tame wildlife can pose dangers for people either in being carriers of disease or when they bite or attack human beings in a painful reminder that no matter how tame they seem, they are indeed still wild animals.

The supplemental feeding of birds is an enjoyable hobby for many people. However, one should be aware that despite superficial appearances, it is not environmentally friendly, and it engenders many hidden costs that directly or indirectly harm birds or their habitats. Such costs include the farmland that is necessary to grow the bird feed; inputs of fossil fuels and other chemicals; and packaging and transportation of bird feed. Moreover, in many cases putting out bird feed tends to increase the populations of squirrels and of aggressive birds such as house sparrows, pigeons, crows, jays, starlings, blackbirds, and grackles. Although the supplemental feeding of birds may increase the *abundance* of birds, it rarely increases the *diversity* of bird species in a given area—and may actually cause bird diversity to decrease. These problems are not associated with bird food derived from plants growing on one's property. A neighbor who lives about four blocks away from me feeds birds, whereas I supply nothing except the seeds, berries, and insects to be found on native plants growing in my yard. We both have all of the same birds visiting our yards but with one important difference. In my yard there is a total absence of house sparrows and pigeons, and the number of egg and nestling thieves—squirrels, crows, grackles, blackbirds, and jays—that visit my yard is much smaller than in my neighbor's yard.

If you simply cannot forgo feeding birds, bear in mind that there are a number of specialty feeds that encourage visits by small, shy songbirds and discourage large, common, and aggressive birds. Aggregations of feeding birds will attract predators, especially cats and birds of prey, so situate your feeding station in an open area where such animals cannot sneak up on the birds. Of course, you will still need plenty of plants on your property for insects to feed on. Adult birds may flourish on a diet of bird feed, but insects are an important nutritional component for nestling birds and they usually need a diet high in insects to develop properly.

In addition to shelter and food, which are easily provided by growing a wide diversity of native plants, wild animals need a reliable and constant source of water. As an example, the small brown anole lizards that frequent many Florida yards are normally skittish; they rapidly scurry away when I go outside. However, if I am armed with a watering can and start to water any plants, they rapidly return to imbibe water droplets on foliage. Sometimes they abandon all caution and appear to be desperately thirsty. Nothing as elaborate as a garden pond is necessary in order to provide wildlife with water. If you want to keep it simple, you need do nothing more than provide a wide, shallow container that holds about half an inch of water. The container should be sufficiently shallow for all the water in it to evaporate in about two days or so. This is an important consideration since you do not want mosquitoes to breed in your backyard water container. Not only are mosquitoes a biting nuisance; they may also carry diseases, such as encephalitis and dengue. If you are an avid birder, you may want to set up a simple watering system that birds greatly enjoy. Arrange a water line so that it drips a drop or two of water every fifteen to thirty seconds or so into a wide, shallow bird bath. The dripping sound will attract birds from far and wide, and many will enjoy letting the water drops fall onto their backs as they bathe. Since this setup will maintain a constant level of water in the bowl, you will need to flush out the bird bath every few days to prevent mosquitoes from breeding in it.

As should be evident, creating and maintaining a home wildlife habitat can be a simple process. Just remember to plant and grow a wide diversity of Florida native plants. Such plants will provide both shelter and food for wildlife. Add a reliable and permanent source of water and you will be well on your way to creating a backyard Eden.

Pests and Diseases

All gardeners inevitably have to contend with an assortment of garden pests and diseases. Fortunately, experience has shown that if all other conditions are favorable for growth, most natives will survive and recover from such attacks without any intervention on the part of the gardener. When a native plant is repeatedly afflicted by pests or disease, this usually indicates that the plant is not suited to its present growing conditions (for example, the conditions are too windy, too dry, too wet, too sunny, too shady) or that the gardener's cultural practices are faulty. The solution lies not with a chemical spray but with replacement of the plant or a change in cultural practices. Sometimes a plant suffers recurrent damage from pests or disease because it lacks natural resistance. Such plants can be replaced with plants of the same species but only if one can find an alternate source with genetically different stock.

Garden Pests

Listed below are some common garden pests and simple, environmentally friendly ways of dealing with them:

- *Aphids* are easily dealt with a strong spray of plain or soapy water. However, a whole menagerie of animals preys on aphids, and if you leave aphids alone, their natural predators will do a good job of controlling them.

- *Borer* infestations may be cleared by removing all affected twigs and branches and disposing of them in a manner that prevents the borers from maturing.

- *Caterpillars* are easily dealt with by picking them off. Most native plant gardeners will tolerate a high degree of caterpillar damage since one cannot have butterflies without caterpillars, and caterpillars are an important component of the diet of many birds or their nestlings.

- *Flea beetles* are small, usually dark and shiny beetles that jump when disturbed. Organic gardeners recommend spraying a plant with water mixed with finely crushed garlic to repel them.

- *Lace bugs* are pests of many plants, including Geiger trees (*Cordia sebestena*) and azaleas (*Rhododendron* species). The larvae of some lace bugs are gregarious and unafraid. These are easily collected by picking off and discarding the leaves on which they are feeding. If they are a persistent problem on otherwise healthy plants, then those plants lack natural resistance and should be replaced with others obtained from another source.

- *Leaf cutter bees* produce mostly cosmetic damage and rarely harm plants. They should be left alone since they are important pollinators of many native plants.

- *Leaf miners* tunnel within the leaf tissue and are nearly impossible to kill with any material applied to the outside of a leaf. If only a few leaves are affected, picking them off and burning them will afford some control.

- *Lubber grasshoppers* are colonial feeders when young, and since they are poisonous and marked with warning coloration, they are slow moving and make mostly feeble attempts to escape when disturbed. Small infestations may be dealt with by scaring the young grasshoppers onto a hard surface and crushing them.

- *Mealybugs* are readily killed by touching them with a cotton swab soaked in rubbing alcohol. They are especially prone to attack a plant that is being grown in an overly dry or overly wet situation to which the plant is not adapted.

- *Scale insects* are enclosed in a waxy shell and are among the most difficult of insect pests to eliminate. If the plant is one that readily sprouts from the roots, severe infestations can be treated by cutting the plant to the ground and carefully discarding the affected plant material. Plants that do not readily sprout can be sprayed with soapy water or horticultural oil. In the past, horticultural oils were derived from petroleum. However, horticultural oils derived from soybeans are now available for the organic gardener.

- *Snails* may be picked off with a flashlight at night. Some gardeners set out saucers of stale beer into which the snails crawl and drown. Recently, African decollate snails (*Rumina decollata*) have been recommended for the biological control of brown garden snails. They should *not* be used in Florida, however, as there is insufficient information about how decollate snails may affect our endangered tree snails.

- *Spider mite* infestations are nearly always an indication of prolonged dry weather or poor cultural practices. Plants usually recover quickly with the onset of rainy weather or when cultural practices are improved.

- *Thrips,* like spider mites, are nearly always an indication that a plant is under stress due to either poor weather or poor cultural practices.

- *Whiteflies* are seldom a serious problem in native gardens. If necessary, they may be controlled by thoroughly soaking the lower surfaces of the leaves of affected plants with soapy water or horticultural oil.

- *Animal pests* such as armadillos, birds, cats, deer, dogs, opossums, raccoons, skunks, and squirrels often cause far more damage in the garden than any of the invertebrate pests already listed. Nuisance mammals may be trapped, but this is a short-term solution since it merely creates a void that will be filled by younger animals. Many different animal deterrents are on the market, but few are truly effective. In general, nothing is as effective as a good, solid fence, but of course even the best fence is no deterrent against birds or squirrels.

- *People* are not commonly regarded as pests, but they may be careless and heavy-footed when visiting the garden, resulting in substantial damage to plants. Older, well-established plants tend to recover even from severe trampling. Young plants, on the other hand, are seriously set back when crushed underfoot and often die as a result. The best way to prevent such damage is to supervise garden guests carefully, especially young children, and to have clearly marked paths for people to walk on. Also, be wary of a particularly insidious garden pest, the weeder. These are garden visitors who take the initiative of assisting you by removing weeds as they stroll the garden. As often as not, the "weeds" turn out to be the seedlings of desirable native plants with which the visitor is unfamiliar.

Diseases

Plant diseases may afflict native plants but they are usually not a major concern to the home gardener. The biggest exception is root rot, a malady caused by a number of fungi and bacteria. Symptoms include persistent wilting in spite of sufficient water, failure to thrive, dying back of large portions of the plant, or sudden death of the entire plant. Curing root rot is nearly impossible—by the time the first symptoms appear, it is usually too late to save the plant.

Root rot especially affects plants with a root ball growing in a moisture-retentive soil mix, as is commonly found in many nursery-grown potted plants. When placed into the ground, the soil mix may dry out more slowly than the surrounding soil, and even though the plant may be growing in a site that appears dry and well drained, its roots are growing in a pocket of constantly wet, stagnant soil. To avoid this problem, follow these steps:

- Remove the plant from its pot and gently shake off as much of the soil mix as possible.

- Dig a broad, shallow hole.

- Spread out the plant's roots so as to place them in close contact with the native soil.

- Fill in the hole and water thoroughly until the plant is established.

This treatment will set a plant back and makes it slightly more difficult to establish, but in the long run the plant produces a better root system, and the danger of root rot is greatly diminished.

Viral infections occasionally affect native plants, but they are frequently overlooked by gardeners. The symptoms of viral infection are similar to those produced by heavy infestations of aphids: deformed new growth and leaves. Unlike aphid damage, viral infections often produce crinkled foliage that may be discolored with pale streaks or spots. Presently there is no cure for plant viruses, and affected plants should be destroyed before they have a chance to infect other plants. Using pruning or cutting tools on more than one plant without disinfecting the tools in household bleach will readily spread viruses from one plant to another, as will touching other plants after handling a virused plant.

Prevention

Strive to prevent pests and diseases by following good cultural practices and carefully selecting plants adapted to your local conditions. Also, before buying a plant or accepting a plant from another grower, inspect it thoroughly for signs of pests and disease. Once you get a plant home, do not be too quick to set it in the ground. Quarantine it for at least a few days to ensure that no hidden pests or diseases have escaped your initial inspection. Take special care to inspect the plant at night, when pests that may be hidden during the day, such as snails, will manifest themselves. Finally, be willing to accept the fact that not every plant will thrive in your garden and that it is better to destroy a sickly plant than to let it serve as a focal point for pests or diseases that may spread to other plants.

Conservation

About 10 percent of our native plants are sufficiently rare to be afforded legal protection by the State of Florida. The basis for that protection is the Preservation of Native Flora of Florida Act, Section 581.185 of the *Florida Statutes*. The Division of Plant Industry in Florida's Department of Agriculture and Consumer Services has promulgated rules pertaining to the act and has prepared a list of protected native plants known as the Regulated Plant Index. A copy of the most current Regulated Plant Index may be obtained by writing to the agency:

Florida Department of Agriculture and Consumer Services
Division of Plant Industry
P.O. Box 147100
Gainesville, Florida 32614–7100
Telephone: (352) 372-3505

Of the 528 plants on the Regulated Plant Index, fifty-five have been afforded additional protection by the federal government as endangered or threatened plants.

For the most part, Florida law recognizes that plants belong to the landowner, and it is illegal to remove them or any parts, including seeds, without the landowner's permission. It is well to remember that *all* land in Florida is owned by someone, and there are no plants that are exempt from the requirement of obtaining the landowner's permission prior to their removal or removal of any of their parts.

A common misconception is that rare plants can be protected by cultivation in gardens. Unfortunately, this is rarely the case. The vast majority of gardens, and the plants they contain, are essentially destroyed once the gardener dies. Even in those few cases in which gardens survive the death of the gardener, there are factors that may make such plants scientifically worthless. Foremost among these are (1) lack of accurate records regarding provenance; (2) possible hybridization with close relatives also cultivated in the same garden; (3) exposure to plant pathogens such as fungi or viruses while in cultivation; and (4) conscious or unconscious artificial selection while the plants have been in the garden, such that they are no longer representative of wild strains of the same species. This is not to say that the cultivation of rare and botanically interesting plants by native plant gardeners is without its merits, but the preservation of the plant in perpetuity is rarely one of them. In the long run, only the preservation of suitable habitat that is maintained in its natural condition will safeguard the continued existence of Florida's endangered plants, and we need to appreciate and protect natural habitats if we are to ensure the long-term survival of many of our native plants.

The vast majority of plants listed in this book occur throughout a large portion of our state. Some plants occur in nearly every county in Florida. This raises a second issue relating to conservation: the preservation of local genetic forms. Scientists have expressed concern that the cultivation of native plants far from their original source will lead to the genetic homogenizaton or contamination of local populations of the same species.

This is not a trivial issue, and genetic variation in a single species may have important considerations for the gardener. For example, coco-plum (*Chrysobalanus icaco*) consists of several different forms somewhat analogous to human races. Coco-plums that grow along the coasts in sand dunes are dwarf, spreading plants that grow slowly to about 3–4 feet tall and are several times wider than they are tall. These coastal plants are highly adapted to local conditions and are salt tolerant. Inland coco-plums grow as large shrubs or small trees up to 15 feet high. These forms are not adapted to coastal conditions and do poorly if grown near the coast. Mixing of the two populations, by cultivating the inland form near the coast and vice versa, or by growing the two forms together in a nursery or garden, may lead to loss of the distinct identities of the two forms. Although this is not as serious a problem as the extinction of an entire species, it does constitute a form of "racial" or "cultural" extinction and results in the genetic and ecological impoverishment of Florida's wonderful botanic heritage. To avoid this problem, gardeners are urged to seek out nursery-propagated native plants derived from local stock and not to mix populations of the same species derived from widely different habitats or geographic areas.

Related to, but distinct from, the above concern is the growing of native plants outside their natural ranges. For example, sea-grape (*Coccoloba uvifera*) occurs in coastal dunes and maritime hammocks. Some gardeners have grown sea-grapes inland, away from coastal situations where they do not normally occur, and there is at least one report of sea-grapes having escaped into adjacent pinelands and exhibiting weedy tendencies there. When natives escape into natural areas where they do not normally occur, they become an incongruous or disharmonic element that is out of character with the local flora and can spoil the esthetic appreciation of such areas. Additionally, there is a remote but real chance that such escaped natives may alter the ecology of the habitats into which they escape.

The issue of natives escaping into new habitats is less of a problem in heavily urbanized regions, where there are few natural areas into which cultivated native plants can escape. It is a greater concern, however, in suburban and rural landscapes. For this reason, gardeners in such areas should be careful to select for their gardens native plants that are compatible with nearby natural areas. Gardeners should be especially cautious when utilizing Florida native plants that do not occur locally if such plants produce fruits or nuts that may be transported long distances by animals such as birds and squirrels.

In concluding these remarks on conservation, it is important to underscore that this book is intended to inform readers on the horticultural requirements of native plants as obtained from the commercial nursery trade, and under no circumstances should it be assumed that the inclusion of a plant in this book is license or encouragement to remove native plants or plant parts from the wild in any form, including spores or seeds.

The Plant Descriptions

The descriptions that follow are based mainly on my personal experience, although in many cases this has been supplemented by the observations of other growers. These descriptions are intended as general guidelines, and the information provided here does not guarantee horticultural success. Since it is impossible to anticipate every possible variable that may affect plant establishment and growth, gardeners need to adapt the horticultural information to their conditions and gardening practices. If something works, I urge you to stick with it even if it is contradicted by anything in the plant descriptions. For ease of reference, each description is organized the same way.

Scientific Name

Scientific names follow those used by Kartesz (1998). Occasionally, a long-standing and familiar scientific name is changed, either in adherence to the rules of the International Code of Botanical Nomenclature or else to reflect current taxonomic opinion. In such cases, the older name is listed as a synonym to assist readers who may be unfamiliar with the newer name. In a few instances, a multiplication sign appears between the genus name and the species epithet, as in *Sabal× miamiensis.* The multiplication sign signifies that the plant is a natural hybrid between two species.

Common Name

Common names generally follow those used by Kartesz (1998) or the Association of Florida Native Nurseries. Capitalization and hyphenation of common names follow the guidelines of Kartesz and Thieret (1991).

Common names are arbitrary and are not subject to the rule of authority. This results in three principal problems. First, two or more unrelated plants may have the same common name. For example, in Florida, Christmas-berry is a common name shared by two very different plants: *Crossopetalum ilicifolium,* a dwarf, prostrate shrub found in rocky pinelands, and *Lycium carolinianum,* a narrowly erect, fleshy-leaved shrub of salt marshes and salt flats. Second, common names are often taxonomically misapplied and cannot be relied upon to convey accurate taxonomic information. Good examples are pond-apple (*Annona glabra*) and gopher-apple (*Licania michauxii*), neither of which is related to the familiar apple of commerce. Creating further confusion is the fact that a plant may have more than one common name. Thus,

Quercus inopina has been variously called Archbold oak, inopina oak, sandhill oak, scrub oak, and unthought-of-oak. For all these reasons, it is necessary to utilize scientific names if one wishes to ensure accuracy and avoid equivocation.

Habit

The growth form, or habit, of many plants is easily categorized, but Florida has a fair number of highly variable plants that are difficult to pigeonhole. For example, depending on its genetic background and growing conditions, titi (*Cyrilla racemiflora*) may vary in habit from a tiny shrub less than 3 feet tall to a medium-sized tree 40 feet high. Gardeners need to be especially careful when selecting such plants to be sure of acquiring the form best suited for the proposed landscape.

Size

Plants are highly malleable as to their size and, like a plant's habit, this too is sometimes difficult to categorize. For the most part, the *average* size that a plant may be expected to attain under normal growing conditions and with good cultural practices is listed in the plant descriptions.

Season

It is a popular misconception, especially in central and southern Florida, that Florida has no seasons. This is untrue; the vast majority of plants have seasonal cycles of active growth and dormancy. As we move south to subtropical Florida, most plants are evergreen, but even these tend to follow highly seasonal growth cycles. Other horticultural attributes that follow seasonal cycles, such as flowering, fruiting, and autumn color, are also described in this section.

Maintenance

Many plants require periodic maintenance to look their best, especially in semiformal and formal gardens. In this section are brief notes on routine maintenance that may be required to keep plants looking neat and tidy. The section on pruning in the chapter on maintenance gives more detailed information on the role of pruning in plant maintenance.

Motility

Although we tend to think of plants as static and stationary organisms, this is far from being the case. Many plants are highly mobile and spread vegetatively by suckers or rhizomes that can cover large areas if allowed to do so. In addition, our native plants usually produce seeds, and it is not unusual for self-sown seedlings to establish themselves in suitable areas of the garden. The tendency for a plant to spread by these means is listed in this section.

Growing Conditions

A short sentence is provided on the growing conditions for each plant as it occurs in nature. For best performance and minimal maintenance, gardeners should grow the plants for which natural growing conditions closely match the conditions in their garden.

USDA Zones

The United States Department of Agriculture Plant Hardiness Zones are listed for each plant described. Note that the plant hardiness zones listed for each plant are those *in which the plant naturally occurs in Florida.* For best garden performance, grow plants that naturally occur in the plant hardiness zone in which you reside. However, it is a general rule of thumb that most plants can be grown one zone to the north or south of the zone(s) in which they occur in nature. Florida is divided into four USDA plant hardiness zones, three of which are further divided into subzones, for a total of seven zones: 8A, 8B, 9A, 9B, 10A, 10B, and 11. If no subzones are indicated, then the plant occurs throughout the entire zone. For example, a plant listed as occurring in Zone 9 occurs in both subzones 9A and 9B, but a plant listed as occurring in Zone 9B occurs only in that particular subzone.

Propagation

The section on propagation is not meant to be exhaustive and does not list every possible method of propagating a plant. Rather, it lists the methods most commonly and easily used with that particular plant. Being familiar with the concepts in the chapter on propagation is the way to get the most out of this section.

Comments

The comments section focuses on two aspects of the listed plant: a more detailed description of its ornamental qualities and information on its garden uses. For some species, additional information may also be noted, such as plant lore or traditional uses.

Ferns

In describing some of the more common and easily grown terrestrial ferns occurring in Florida, I have taken care to select a variety of species reflecting different habitats, from rather dry to wet and from shady to sunny. The ferns selected also range in sizes from diminutive to immense, to suit different landscape plans and garden sizes.

Although occurring in diverse habitats and having widely divergent appearance and growth form, all of the plants in this section are allied in reproducing from nearly microscopic spores rather than from seeds, as do flowering plants. A detailed discussion of their propagation from spore is beyond the scope of this book, but a simple and usually effective method based on twenty-four years' experience is presented here for interested readers who would like to try to grow ferns from spore. The method is known as the FFSTEW method (ferns from spore the easy way). Unlike nearly all other methods of growing ferns from spore, FFSTEW does not require sterilization or the cleaning of chaff from the fern spores.

- Fill small pots with a moist, nutrient-poor potting medium. Good choices include vermiculite, very fine seedling orchid mix (a combination of fine wood bark, fine charcoal, and fine perlite), or peat moss mixed with coarse sand. It does not matter which medium is selected as long as it has an extremely low nutrient content.

- Lightly sow the fern spore on the surface of the soil. There is no need to separate the spore from chaff.

- Gently moisten the pots by immersing them nearly to the rim in water.

- Place the pots in a clear plastic container to maintain high humidity and place the container in bright light but out of direct sunlight, as in an unobstructed north facing window. The lid on the container should be slightly ajar to allow some air flow.

- Examine the pots every two weeks with a 10× magnifying glass. When minuscule flecks of green are visible, the spore has germinated.

- Once the spore germinates, prepare an *extremely* dilute batch of fertilizer by thoroughly mixing one-eighth of a teaspoon of a balanced fertilizer in six cups of water. Very carefully water each pot of spore with a tablespoon or two of the fertilizer mix. If the fertilizer mix is too strong, a thick mat of algae, mosses, and/or liverworts will overrun the pots and you will have to start over again. (Note that fertilizers are prominently marked with three numbers somewhere on the package. These numbers indicate the percentage of the three most important plant nutrients: nitrogen, phosphorus, and potassium. A balanced fertilizer is one in which the three nutrients are present in the same proportion, such as 6–6–6, 10–10–10, etc.)

- The germinated spore will produce tiny heart-shaped growths. When these are about one-quarter of an inch in diameter, immerse the pots up to their rims in a container of water and let them sit in the water for 12 hours. Wait 3–4 weeks to see if the first true fern leaves have formed. If not, keep repeating the 12-hour water immersion every 3–4 weeks until they do.

- Throughout the entire process, the humidity must be kept high. However, if it is too high, it will be extremely difficult to acclimate the young ferns to ordinary garden conditions. This is why it is important to keep the lid of the container in which the pots of spore are held slightly ajar to allow the free flow of air.

Although growing ferns from spore is fairly straightforward once one gets the knack, it does require patience and close observation. Perhaps the most difficult part is showing restraint in fertilizing the medium, since most people tend to think that more is better. In my own case, it took about a dozen trials over a ten-year period before I was successful in raising a fern from spore to full maturity.

In addition to the ferns described in this section, four additional native ferns are discussed later. Three are epiphytes and are described in that section. The fourth is a miniature, floating aquatic, described in the section on aquatic plants.

1. *Acrostichum danaeifolium*

Common Name: Giant Leather Fern
Habit: Huge, erect fern with spreading fronds.
Size: About 8 feet high and 10 feet wide.
Season: Essentially all year but at its best just after new fronds mature in late spring or early summer.
Maintenance: Periodic removal of old fronds.
Motility: Forming large clumps from basal suckers; sometimes producing hundreds of young plants from spore in moist, open areas such as brick paths or sandy or rocky pond edges.
Growing Conditions: Swamps and marshes in both fresh and brackish water; Zones 8B–10.
Propagation: Spore; division.
Comments: Giant leather fern lives up to its common name—it is Florida's largest fern. As

such, it makes a bold statement in the home landscape and must be placed with care to allow it room for full development. A partly shaded, ample-sized, wet site is ideal. Under such conditions, plants reach an immense size and they lend a slightly eerie and very dramatic, primeval aspect to the landscape. They may also be planted along the edges of lakes and large ponds in both formal and informal settings. Many gardeners do not take into account its large ultimate size and giant leather fern is often consigned to a wet swale or the edge of a small pond, where it remains but a stunted shadow of its true self. A second species of leather fern, the golden leather fern (*Acrostichum aureum*), occurs in Florida, but it is an extremely rare plant that is seldom encountered in the wild.

2. *Adiantum capillus-veneris*

Common Name: Venus's or Southern Maidenhair Fern
Habit: Extremely elegant fern with pendant fronds and widely creeping stem.
Size: About 12 inches high.
Season: Foliage attractive all year.
Maintenance: Periodic removal of old fronds.
Motility: Moderately colonial; readily spreading from spore in moist, shady, rocky areas.
Growing Conditions: Well-drained, rocky but moist sites in dappled to full shade; Zones 8–10.
Propagation: Spore; division.
Comments: Widely scattered nearly throughout all of the world's warm temperate to tropical regions, southern maidenhair fern is also Florida's most widespread maidenhair fern, extending from Washington County in the Panhandle south to Miami-Dade County. In common with most maidenhair ferns, it greatly favors rocky, calcareous situations that are well-drained yet evenly moist. It makes an excellent pot plant if grown in wide, shallow pots of rich soil and quickly becomes a beautiful specimen plant. Although it requires neither lime nor rocks when grown in pots, it rarely prospers in garden settings if not set among limestone, and this is the best way of meeting its requirements for even moisture and perfect drainage.

3. *Asplenium platyneuron*

Common Name: Ebony Spleenwort
Habit: Small, clump-forming fern.
Size: About 12 inches high.
Season: Foliage attractive essentially all year but at its best in the spring when producing new fronds.
Maintenance: Periodic removal of old fronds.
Motility: No vegetative spread; very rarely may spread from spore.

Growing Conditions: Well-drained but moist sites in dappled shade; Zones 8–10.

Propagation: Spore; division.

Comments: In Hernando County, ebony spleenwort creates an attractive scene growing in rocky, limestone woodlands. Home gardeners may emulate such a setting since the delicate beauty of this little fern contrasts well with weathered rocks. However, limestone is not necessary for its successful culture; it grows well in acidic sandy soils, and large populations can be found in pine plantations (Nelson 1999). Ebony spleenwort produces two types of fronds, adding to its decorative value. The vegetative fronds form a loose, spreading rosette. From the center of the rosette, there arise larger, erect, spore-bearing fronds that more readily and effectively disperse the spores. Although seemingly very delicate, this is a tough little fern when well situated, and once established, it will tolerate considerable drought. It is also one of the easiest ferns to grow from spores if one is just beginning to learn how to grow ferns in this manner.

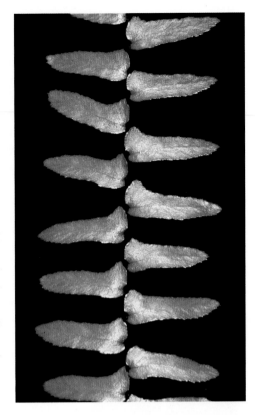

4. *Blechnum serrulatum*

Common Name: Swamp Fern

Habit: Moderate-sized to large colonial fern spreading by way of a widely creeping rhizome.

Size: 2½ to 3 feet tall, often taller in rich, moist, partially shaded sites.

Season: Essentially all year but most attractive when bearing young fronds, which are tinged in shades of maroon, pink, or burgundy.

Maintenance: Periodic removal of old fronds.

Motility: Unless restrained by larger plants, it will spread into all areas capable of supporting its growth; not suitable for formal situations or garden beds filled with small plants.

Growing Conditions: Moist sites in shade or partial shade; often grows in full or nearly full sun at the edges of swamps; Zones 8B–10.

Propagation: Spore; division.

Comments: Swamp fern is one of the most common ferns in central and southern Florida, and there is scarcely a swamp, cypress stand, or moist thicket where it does not occur. It is especially attractive when new fronds are being produced, as they are a striking bronze or mahogany red, contrasting pleasingly with the dark green of older fronds. However, this is a widely spreading fern that grows from an elongated, creeping rhizome. Thus, it is not suitable for planting among small and delicate plants. Otherwise, it is easily grown and adds variety and texture to garden settings. Perhaps because it is so common, it is scarcely ever available in native plant nurseries. This is surprising since it takes readily to cultivation and is easily propagated by division.

Special Note: Swamp fern is a large fern of the genus *Blechnum*. Do not confuse it with the genus *Blechum* (no "n"), a genus of non-native, small, weedy perennials in the same family as wild-petunias.

5. *Ophioglossum petiolatum*

Common Name: Long-Stem Adder's-Tongue
Habit: Diminutive fern with a unique, unfernlike appearance.
Size: Leaves 1–2 inches long, the fertile spike 2–3 times taller.
Season: Evergreen if conditions are mild and wet, going dormant during excessively cold, hot, or dry conditions.
Maintenance: Keep colonies free of fallen leaves or other organic material that might serve to harbor snails.
Motility: Colonial and spreading by subterranean adventitious buds that develop at the ends of the roots.
Growing Conditions: Moist sites in full sun to deep shade; Zones 8–10A.
Propagation: Division.
Comments: Most adder's-tongues are unusually difficult to cultivate, but the species listed here is a notable exception. Long-stem adder's-tongue sometimes occurs spontaneously among mosses growing along the north sides of buildings in urban yards. It also occasionally appears spontaneously in potted plants that are grown outdoors. It does occur in undisturbed natural areas, such as seeps, where it associates with a varied and rich assemblage of other native plants, but it is so tiny that it is usually overlooked in such situations. Its cultivation presents few problems except for snails, which relish its soft, succulent foliage and will decimate large colonies overnight.

6. *Osmunda cinnamomea*

Common Name: Cinnamon Fern
Habit: Large fern with long, somewhat spreading fronds.
Size: About 4 feet tall, sometimes taller, and usually as wide.
Season: Winter dormant in northern Florida, essentially evergreen southward; very attractive

in the spring when the new fronds are unfurling and again in early summer when the new fronds are fully mature.

Maintenance: Periodic removal of old fronds.

Motility: No vegetative spread; very rarely may spread from spore.

Growing Conditions: Moist to wet sites in full sun to deep shade; Zones 8–10.

Propagation: Spore sown immediately upon ripening; division.

Comments: The principal horticultural attribute of the cinnamon fern is its large size combined with an airy gracefulness. In garden situations, it should be placed in a sizable, moist site that is never allowed to dry out. If the site has dappled shade or the high shade of tall trees, so much the better. Under such conditions, truly immense and magnificent specimens are formed that become a principal focal point of the native wildflower garden. To add contrast, cinnamon ferns may usefully be combined with colorful wildflowers that like similar conditions, such as the brilliant red cardinal flower (*Lobelia cardinalis*) and the bright yellow bearsfoot (*Polymnia uvedalia*). If attempting to grow cinnamon fern from spore, bear in mind that unlike in most ferns, the spore of which may remain viable for several years, the spore of *Osmunda* species dies if not sown immediately upon ripening.

7. *Osmunda regalis* var. *spectabilis*

Common Name: Royal Fern

Habit: Large, erect, clump-forming fern.

Size: 3–4 feet tall and often as wide.

Season: Winter dormant in northern Florida, essentially evergreen southward; very attractive in the spring when the new fronds are unfurling and again in early summer when the new fronds are fully mature.

Maintenance: Periodic removal of old fronds; old clumps may be rejuvenated by being cut to the ground.

Motility: No vegetative spread; very rarely may spread from spore.

Growing Conditions: Moist to wet sites in full sun to deep shade; Zones 8–10.

Propagation: Spore sown immediately upon ripening; division.

Comments: From the scientific name of this fern, one would expect a plant of great beauty. The species name *regalis* means "regal" or "royal," while *spectabilis* means "showy" or "attractive." The royal fern does indeed live up to its name—it is among the most beautiful and elegant of all ferns. With age, royal ferns assume a stunning architectural or statuesque quality. The long, erect fronds are finely divided and this results in a surprisingly delicate effect for so large a plant. Its regal bearing is further enhanced by the colorful fronds, which change from a rosy burgundy hue when young to a silvery or grayish sea green at maturity. Like its relative the cinnamon fern, royal fern should be given plenty of space in a rich, moist site. Since the young fronds assume their richest color in bright light, the plants should be positioned where they will receive an hour or two of direct sunlight each day.

8. *Polystichum acrostichoides*

Common Name: Christmas Fern

Habit: Rather large, evergreen fern.

Size: 2½ feet tall.

Season: Attractive essentially all year, but most attractive when the new fronds are unfurling in the spring and again in late summer when they are fully mature.

Maintenance: Periodic removal of old fronds.

Motility: No vegetative spread; very rarely may spread from spore in cultivation.

Growing Conditions: Rich, moist woods; Zones 8–9A.

Propagation: Spore; division.

Comments: Christmas fern is a rather stout fern with thick, leathery fronds that are essentially evergreen. Thus, it was readily available to pioneer families as a source of decorative holiday greenery even in the severest winters. The large, dark green fronds make a strong statement and add a touch of elegance, as well as variety and texture, to the shady wildflower garden. In northern and central Florida, this fern makes a good companion for wildflowers such as jack-in-the-pulpit (*Arisaema triphyllum*), violets (*Viola* species), and wild columbine (*Aquilegia canadensis*)— the delicacy of the wildflowers perfectly complementing the strong lines of the Christmas fern. Throwing in a few well-chosen and strategically placed rocks will add the finishing touches to a charming garden scene.

9. *Pteris bahamensis*

Common Name: Pineland Brake; Bahama Brake

Habit: Medium-sized fern forming small to large clumps.

Size: Growing 12–24 inches tall and about as wide.

Season: Attractive all year but particularly showy when maturing a new crown of leaves in the spring.

Maintenance: Periodic removal of old fronds or cutting back of old plants to the ground.

Motility: None.

Growing Conditions: Rocky pinelands in full sun to light shade; Zones 9B–10.

Propagation: Spore; division.

Comments: Pineland brake is a well-behaved, elegant fern that grows in neat, tidy clumps. As

a result, it is well suited for both formal and informal gardens. Unlike many native ferns, it insists on bright light under ordinary garden conditions. Most native ferns either will not grow in full sun or, if they do, they require constantly moist soil. In nature, pineland brake occurs in habitats that have regular fires, which burn off the old fronds. In cultivation, the old and dead fronds persist for years, and a clump will look rather ragged after a while. The gardener can simulate the effects of fire by cutting back the entire plant to the ground in early spring. This rejuvenates the plant, and it responds by producing a crown of beautiful new fronds.

10. *Thelypteris hispidula* var. *versicolor*

Common Name: Stiff-Haired Maiden Fern

Habit: Midsized to large, slowly creeping fern.

Size: 12–18 inches, occasionally up to 36 inches in very rich, moist sites.

Season: Attractive all year if not exposed to strong sunlight, drought, prolonged cold spells, or frosts.

Maintenance: Periodic removal of old fronds.

Motility: Very slight vegetative spread from its short rhizome; sometimes aggressively spreading by spore into moist areas, including potted plants and rock work.

Growing Conditions: Moist, shady, calcareous sites; Zones 8–10.

Propagation: Spore; division.

Comments: This fern is common wherever moist soils with high levels of calcium occur. In nature, it is found on limestone outcrops and soils of oceanic origin that have an abundance of seashells. It also makes its appearance on artificial sites, such as the limestone rubble at the base of buildings where moisture accumulates and along rocky canal banks. In spite of being so abundant, it deserves a place in every garden that can accommodate it, since it is a resilient, easily grown fern that adds a touch of refinement to a shady site. Gardeners should note that this fern can become a weed in moist rock work and will assume a ghastly shade of pale, greenish yellow if exposed to too much sunlight.

11. *Thelypteris interrupta*

Common Name: Willdenow's Maiden Fern

Habit: Wetland fern with a creeping rhizome.

Size: Growing about 18–24 inches tall.

Season: Attractive all year.

Maintenance: Periodic removal of old fronds.

Motility: Spreading by way of its long, creeping rhizome.

Growing Conditions: Moist sites in full sun to full shade; Zones 8B–10.

Propagation: Spore; division.

Comments: Willdenow's maiden fern is a robust and beautiful fern for the wild garden, where it may be grown in either sun or shade. It is easily cultivated if given sufficient moisture and has sturdy, elegant fronds of beautiful dark green. The spore pattern on the lower surface of the fronds is distinctive and adds an interesting note as well as serving to identify the plant. Willdenow's maiden fern often occurs in wet meadows and swamps and may be utilized to add variety to a wet area in the garden or to beautify a wet ditch. The fronds arise from a widely creeping rhizome, limiting this fern's usefulness in formal garden situations somewhat unless its spreading tendencies are contained by other equally vigorous plants.

12. *Woodwardia virginica*

Common Name: Virginia Chain Fern

Habit: Large, widely creeping fern.

Size: 2–3 feet tall.

Season: Attractive throughout the growing season, dormant or essentially so during winter, especially northward.

Maintenance: Periodic removal of dead fronds.

Motility: Moderately spreading by means of its creeping rhizome; very rarely may spread from spore.

Growing Conditions: Wet sites in deep to light shade; Zones 8–10.

Propagation: Spore; division.

Comments: In its cultivation and garden use, Virginia chain fern is essentially identical to swamp fern (*Blechnum serrulatum*). The principal horticultural difference between the two is that Virginia chain fern produces a more delicate and airy garden effect. This is due to the fact that the primary lobes of the leaf of Virginia chain fern are deeply lobed (these are minutely toothed in swamp fern). A more technical difference lies with the pattern of the leaf veins. This is easily seen by holding up a leaf of Virginia chain fern up to a bright light, readily revealing the unexpectedly complex and almost geometrically regular pattern of veins.

Short-lived Wildflowers

Summer and winter annuals, biennials, and short-lived perennials are among the most colorful wildflowers native to Florida. These are plants that grow fast, flower early, set tremendous amounts of seed, and are short-lived. There is a price to be paid for enjoying their extravagant and colorful blooms. As the plants go to seed, they slowly wither, turn brown, and in formal situations must be removed to avoid an untidy eyesore. If they are grown in a meadow garden, the easiest solution is simply to mow the dying plants down after they have gone to seed.

More than any other group of native plants, the plants in this section are children of the sun. All will grow and flower in light shade and a few, such as innocence (*Hedyotis procumbens*), may be grown in nearly full shade. However, for best performance and maximum flowering, they require full sun for most of the day.

Some wildflowers included here are winter annuals, a group of plants common in desert and Mediterranean regions but unfamiliar to most eastern United States gardeners. Winter annuals germinate during cool temperatures in early spring or, in the deep South, in the autumn. They produce vegetative growth as long as cool temperatures prevail. Then, with the onset of warm weather, they flower and seed prodigiously. One must respect the requirements of these plants; attempts to cultivate them during the summer, as if they were ordinary garden annuals, are usually an invitation to failure.

For their continued existence in the garden short-lived plants are dependent on starting over from seed. Gardeners often report that these plants grew well for a season or two in their garden and then "disappeared." This is usually due to one or more of the following:

- The plants were removed at the first sign of withering, and this prevented the formation of seed for next year's crop.

- The gardener was overzealous in keeping the garden tidy and seedlings were weeded out.

- All parts of the garden were kept completely covered with a thick layer of fallen leaves or mulch, and there was no open ground where the seedlings could germinate and establish.

- The short-lived wildflowers were outcompeted or shaded out by long-lived wildflowers, shrubs, and trees.

13. Ageratum littorale

Common Name: Seashore Ageratum
Habit: Sprawling annual or short-lived perennial.
Size: 1 foot tall by 3 feet wide.
Season: Most attractive in middle to late spring; plants usually have a worn appearance by late summer.
Maintenance: Removal of older plants to allow self-sown seedlings to replace them.
Motility: Moderately spreading into suitable open areas by way of self-sown seed.
Growing Conditions: Moist or dry, often sandy, sites in bright light; Zone 11.
Propagation: Seed; cuttings.
Comments: Seashore ageratum is a distinctive and particularly attractive plant. The foliage is

bright green, smooth, and slightly succulent. The plant grows in a sprawling manner, and it may be utilized as a single specimen plant or planted in masses as a groundcover. The delicate flower heads are held on long stems well above the foliage, where they make an attractive display. The flower color, which is a distinctive shade of pastel blue, defies both verbal description and the effort to capture it on film. Essentially everblooming, attractive to butterflies, and easily propagated from either cuttings or seeds, this species is a valuable addition to the wildflower garden. Its only fault is a tendency to become susceptible to insect pests if grown in too shady or too dry a site.

14. Argemone mexicana

Common Name: Yellow Prickly-Poppy
Habit: Taprooted winter annual.
Size: 2½–3 feet tall.
Season: Early to mid-spring.
Maintenance: Removal of the plants, which die after setting seed in late spring.
Motility: Moderately spreading into open areas by way of self- sown seed.
Growing Conditions: Well-drained soil in full sun; Zones 8–11.
Propagation: Seed.
Comments: All parts of the yellow prickly-poppy, except the petals, are covered with sharp spines. Thus it is a difficult plant to handle with bare hands. In spite of this armature, it makes a lovely addition to the wildflower garden. Seeds germinate in cool weather in the autumn or early spring and form beautiful rosettes of an intense silvery

blue. With the arrival of warm weather, the rosettes produce elongated stems that bear large, bright yellow blossoms. These delicate, ethereal flowers form a striking contrast to the spiny, silvery leaves. Seed should be sown where plants are to grow since, as in all members of the poppy family, seedlings resent the root disturbance that accompanies transplanting. For variety, one may grow *Argemone albiflora,* a nearly identical plant that bears large, pure white flowers.

15. *Chamaecrista fasciculata* (Synonym: *Cassia fasciculata*)

Common Name: Partridge-Pea

Habit: Annual or short-lived perennial of extremely varied habit, sometimes erect, often spreading, or even prostrate, becoming woody and shrubby with age.

Size: Extremely variable from 1–4 feet tall, mostly as wide or wider than it is tall.

Season: Flowering in the summer and autumn in northern Florida, all year in southern Florida.

Fruit: Dark brown bean pod, the seeds eaten by birds.

Maintenance: Periodic removal of older plants to allow vigorous young seedlings to replace them.

Motility: Seed pods explosively hurl the seed upon maturity and spread it throughout open areas of the garden.

Growing Conditions: Dry to moist sites in light shade to full sun; Zones 8–10.

Propagation: Seed.

Comments: Partridge-pea is so remarkably variable that a host of different forms have been named as distinct species. Depending on the growing conditions and the plant's genetic background, its form may vary from erect, single-trunked plants that resemble tiny trees to densely branched, sprawling groundcovers. Although it is commonly seen with bright green foliage and clear yellow flowers, there also occur especially striking forms with red-tinged foliage and brilliant golden yellow flowers. The large, exotically shaped blooms, often with a contrasting red spot in their center, are perfectly set off by the delicate, feathery leaves. Its habitats are as varied as its growth forms, and it can be found from seasonally inundated pine flatwoods to the driest and sandiest scrub. Partridge-pea is extremely easy to grow. Scarified seed germinates in a few days and the young plants may begin to blossom in as little as three months. It excels when used as a quick filler between shrubs and trees in newly planted areas. This is certainly one of Florida's floral treasures and worthy of cultivation in every garden that can accommodate its modest needs.

16. *Coreopsis leavenworthii*

Common Name: Common Tickseed
Habit: Erect annual or short-lived perennial.
Size: 1½–3 feet tall.
Season: Especially attractive in the spring, but in cultivation, self-sown seedlings mature and flower nearly throughout the year.
Maintenance: Removal of plants that have spent themselves in flowering.
Motility: Moderately spreading into all moist, open areas of the garden by way of self-sown seed.
Growing Conditions: Moist sandy soil in full sun; Zones 8–11.
Propagation: Seed.
Comments: It is unfortunate that such attractive wildflowers as *Coreopsis* have the unattractive common name of tickseed. The plants have nothing at all to do with ticks; the name is based on a fancied resemblance of the seeds to ticks. The species is an attractive plant of exquisite charm and delicate form. In the spring, great patches of it may be found along roadside ditches, creating large swaths of brilliant yellow. After the "big

bang" in the spring, flowers are produced in smaller but still sizable numbers throughout the rest of the year. The plant is extremely easy to cultivate in just about any sunny patch of moist soil, and once established, it will come back year after year from self-sown seed.

17. *Crotalaria rotundifolia*

Common Name: Rabbit-bells
Habit: Taprooted annual or perennial with slender, profusely branching spreading stems.
Size: 6–8 inches tall, often much wider.
Season: Attractive essentially all year southward, becoming dormant in winter or nearly so northward.
Fruit: Attractive, diminutive, inflated black pods with loose rattling seeds.

Maintenance: Occasional removal of old seed pods and cutting back of older, larger plants.

Motility: Will gradually spread into moist, open areas throughout the garden by way of self-sown seed.

Growing Conditions: Regular or moist soil in full sun; Zones 8–11.

Propagation: Seed.

Comments: Rabbitbells is Florida's most common native species of *Crotalaria,* being found in a wide range of sunny situations, including disturbed sites. It is a delightful little plant that, in cultivation, forms extensive mats studded with small, bright yellow pea flowers. The charming little flowers are produced all year except during the depths of winter and extended dry spells. The seeds become loose at maturity and the inflated black pods rattle if shaken. The pods are rather large and add an additional charming note to this little plant. If possible, rabbitbells should be provided with several square feet of open ground in the garden where it may form a small groundcover without its diminutive charms being obscured by larger plants.

18. *Gaillardia pulchella*

Common Name: Indian Blanket; Gaillardia

Habit: Taprooted annual or perennial.

Size: 1–2 feet tall, usually 1½ times to twice as wide as it is tall.

Season: Spring through summer northward, all year southward.

Maintenance: Removal of spent flower heads to increase its lifespan and flowering; periodic removal of older plants.

Motility: Moderately spreads to sunny, well-drained sites by way of self-sown seedlings.

Growing Conditions: Well-drained sandy soil in full sun; Zones 8–11.

Propagation: Seed; cuttings.

Comments: Indian blanket is one of the most brightly and attractively colored wildflowers available to the native plant enthusiast. Fortunately, it is as easily grown as it is beautiful, and successful cultivation often requires nothing more than scattering seed in a suitably prepared area. Once established, plants tolerate very dry conditions and are essentially carefree as long as they are not subjected to poorly drained, wet soils or shading by taller plants. Indian blanket is especially adapted to coastal situations, where it contributes to a vibrant display of color along with such wildflowers as beach-peanut (*Okenia hypogaea*), beach sunflower (*Helianthus debilis*), and railroad vine (*Ipomoea pes-caprae* subsp. *brasiliensis*). The ray flowers (that is, the so-called petals of the flower head) exhibit considerable variation in color. Some plants have rays that are mostly red with a yellow tip, others are half red and half yellow, while still others are mostly yellow with a red base.

19. *Glandularia tampensis* (Synonym: *Verbena tampensis*)

Common Name: Tampa-Verbena

Habit: Sprawling short-lived perennial.

Size: 1½–2 feet tall and 3–4 feet wide.

Season: All year but tending to bloom most heavily in the spring.

Maintenance: Removal of spent plants that have flowered and seeded themselves to exhaustion.

Motility: Slowly spreading by self-sown seed.

Growing Conditions: Moist but well-drained soil in full sun; Zones 9–10A.

Propagation: Seeds; cuttings.

Comments: Tampa-verbena was unknown as a cultivated plant just a few years ago. However, it is now well established and common in the native plant nursery trade. This is not surprising. The plant itself has a sprawling growth habit and it makes an attractive groundcover. Contrasting with the foliage are the abundantly produced rosy pink flowers, and a large patch of Tampa-verbena in full bloom is a sight to behold. Additionally, it is readily propagated from cuttings, which root in a glass of water in about two weeks. It may also be propagated from seed, but germination may be erratic over a very lengthy period. Its increasing popularity in cultivation is ironic since it is declining in nature as a result of habitat destruction and, like beach-verbena (*Glandularia maritima,* described in the following chapter), it is on Florida's endangered plant list.

20. *Hedyotis procumbens*

Common Name: Innocence

Habit: Diminutive, mat-forming, short-lived perennial or winter annual.

Size: Forms a perfectly flat mat 3–6 inches wide, occasionally to 12 inches wide in cultivation.

Season: Flowering in late winter through spring,

extending into autumn southward; plants will disappear if conditions are hot and dry but reappear from self-sown seed when cooler, wetter weather returns.

Maintenance: None.

Motility: Slowly spreading by seed into moist, open areas.

Growing Conditions: Moist, often sandy, sites in full sun to shade; will grow in very dry sites as a winter annual; Zones 8–10.

Propagation: Seed; cuttings.

Comments: Although much of Florida rarely experiences severe winter weather, we do experience a distinct winter season with shortened days and cold temperatures that regularly dip to around 30°F in northern Florida, and with a resulting cessation of plant growth. Thus, it is a special joy to be greeted on late winter jaunts by innocence, an early flowering and aptly named little plant. The stems creep along the ground forming little carpets on moist, open ground. For a long period from late winter to late spring, the plant is studded with relatively large white flowers, occasionally tinged with a hint of pink. Cultivation is without problems except that some forms are reluctant to flower. Innocence is ideally suited, along with equally diminutive plants like twinflower (*Dyschoriste angusta*), dwarf-morning glory (*Evolvulus sericeus*), various star-grasses (*Hypoxis* species), pine pinklet (*Stenandrium dulce*), and lance-leaf violet (*Viola lanceolata*), for creating a miniature wildflower garden in a small patch of moist ground.

21. *Helenium amarum*

Common Name: Spanish Daisy; Bitterweed

Habit: Erect, taprooted annual with a densely branched crown.

Size: 1½ feet high.

Season: Spring, summer, and autumn.

Maintenance: Periodic removal of spent plants.

Motility: Moderately spreading by way of self-sown seedlings.

Growing Conditions: Open sunny areas, especially where sandy; Zones 8–10.

Propagation: Seed.

Comments: Spanish daisy is exceptional among Florida's species of *Helenium* for its annual growth habit, its occurrence in rather disturbed sites, and its thin, almost threadlike foliage. It is also unusual with respect to its growth form: it begins life as a single-stemmed plant but develops a densely branched crown at maturity. Although the bright yellow daisies are not particularly big, they make a colorful display since they are borne in great numbers, one at the tip of each of the many branches. In spite of its weedy tendencies, this is an attractive and showy wildflower. Since Spanish daisy quickly and abundantly flowers from seed, it is a good introductory annual wildflower for the beginning native plant gardener.

22. *Helianthus debilis*

Common Name: Beach Sunflower
Habit: Sprawling, groundcovering taprooted annual or short-lived perennial.
Size: 1–1½ feet tall and 3–4 feet wide.
Season: Summer in northern Florida, all year southward.
Fruit: Small kernels with an oily seed eagerly sought by birds and small mammals.
Maintenance: Periodic removal of spent plants.
Motility: Moderately spreading into suitable areas by seed.
Growing Conditions: Well-drained sandy soil in full sun; Zones 8–10.
Propagation: Seed; cuttings.
Comments: Beach sunflower is found in sandy coastal situations throughout Florida, where it makes a colorful and abundantly flowering groundcover. Except possibly for Indian blanket (*Gaillardia pulchella*), there is probably no other plant more suitable for dry, sandy, coastal situations that combines brilliant color over such a long season, freedom from pests, and ease of growth. Thus, it is not surprising that this sunflower has been enthusiastically taken up as an ideal xeriscape plant. Its only nemesis is poor drainage; if provided with too much water or too rich a soil, it slowly declines.

Special Note: Three subspecies of beach sunflower occur in Florida. In order to maintain the distinct identities and ecological roles of these subspecies, the different subspecies should not be grown together in cultivation and gardeners should ensure that the subspecies being cultivated is native to the locale (see Wunderlin 1998:633).

23. *Heliotropium angiospermum*

Common Name: Scorpion's-Tail
Habit: Fast-growing, erect or sprawling annual or short-lived perennial, becoming a small shrub in cultivation.
Size: Plant 1–3 feet tall and, in cultivation, as wide or wider than it is tall.
Season: Flowers produced all year except during extremely dry or cold periods.
Maintenance: Annual severe pruning to maintain a tidy appearance; complete replacement about every three years.

Motility: Produces self-sown seedlings, often abundantly under good conditions, but these rarely appear far from the mother plant.

Growing Conditions: Rather dry, often sandy or rocky soils, in full sun to partial shade; Zones 9–11.

Propagation: Seed; cuttings.

Comments: In nature, scorpion's-tail grows in rough, dry areas. As a result, the plants are nondescript with a weedy appearance, and the tiny white flowers are too few to attract any notice. But what a transformation when it is given a little care in cultivation! The annual weed becomes an attractive, densely leafy small shrub with a woody trunk 1–2 inches in diameter. The flowers, of course, remain as tiny as ever, but they are so abundantly produced that the plant takes on a quiet charm, and it attracts an amazing number of colorful and interesting insects, including a variety of butterflies. In spite of forming a woody shrub, it is still a short-lived plant and needs to be replaced every few years. However, this is not a problem since there are usually a few self-sown seedlings coming along that serve to replace the parent plant.

24. *Ipomopsis rubra*

Common Name: Skyrocket; Standing-Cypress
Habit: Erect, taprooted biennial or winter annual.
Size: About 3 feet tall.
Season: Flowering in summer (spring in annual forms).
Maintenance: Removal of spent plants.
Motility: Moderately spreading by way of self-sown seed.
Growing Conditions: Well-drained, sandy soil in full sun; Zones 8–9.
Propagation: Seed.
Comments: Skyrocket is one of our most spectacularly beautiful native wildflowers. Seeds germinate during cool, moist weather in the autumn and produce delicate rosettes of finely divided, ferny foliage. The rosette stage is fairly brief and the plants soon proceed to form nar-

row, elongated columns. At this point, they fancifully resemble dwarf, columnar cypress trees,
which accounts for the common name standing-
cypress. The typical, biennial form blossoms in
the summer, but annual forms that blossom in
early spring also occur. Skyrocket is a "big bang"
bloomer that produces a large quantity of flowers
in a very short time, resulting in a dramatic display. The flowers are an inch long and come in a
variety of brilliant shades of red or orange-red;
rarely a plant is found with pink, salmon, or pale
yellow flowers.

25. *Linaria canadensis*

Common Name: Toadflax
Habit: Erect, taprooted winter annual.
Size: 12–18 inches tall.
Season: Spring.
Maintenance: None.
Motility: Moderately spreading into dryish, sunny areas by self-sown seed.
Growing Conditions: Well-drained rather moist to very dry sandy soil in full sun; Zones 8–10.
Propagation: Seed.
Comments: Toadflax is essentially a little roadside weed. However, it lends a quaint and charm-
ing note to the informal wildflower garden, where it adds a temporary spot of color in early
spring. In spite of its common name, toadflax is not related to true flax in any way. Its affinities
lie with the common garden snapdragons, and a close examination of the flowers reveals that
their form is essentially that of a diminutive pink, lavender, or violet snapdragon. In cultivation,
toadflax presents no problems, and its establishment in a garden requires simply the scattering
of seed in suitable areas. For the most decorative effect, one should obtain seed from the largest-
flowered and most intensely colored forms available. Some forms of toadflax have tiny flowers
that tend to set seed without ever fully opening. Obvi-
ously, these forms lack horticultural merit and should
be assiduously weeded out.

26. *Lobelia feayana*

Common Name: Bay Lobelia
Habit: Creeping, mat-forming dwarf perennial.
Size: 6–12 inches tall.
Season: Early to late spring.
Maintenance: None.
Motility: Moderately spreading into moist areas by
self-sown seed.
Growing Conditions: Moist situations in light shade
to full sun; Zones 8B–10.

Propagation: Seed; cuttings; division.

Comments: Bay lobelia is a native wildflower of exceptional beauty and horticultural value. Coming into vigorous growth in the autumn, the sprawling little plants can cover sizable patches of moist open ground. In early January and continuing into late spring, they bear masses of small but showy flowers that vary from palest pastel blue to deep violet. Flower production is prodigious and it can color great stretches of moist ground with an intense blue haze. Occurring only in peninsular Florida and nowhere else on earth, the bay lobelia would have been a good candidate for John Thomas Howell's (1970:141) remarks with respect to the California-poppy: "In its abundance, this colorful plant should not be slighted: cherish it and be ever thankful that so rare a flower is common!"

27. *Lupinus diffusus*

Common Name: Skyblue Lupine

Habit: Large, erect to sprawling taprooted winter annual or short-lived perennial.

Size: 2–3 feet tall and as wide, sometimes wider.

Season: Spring.

Maintenance: Removal of spent plants.

Motility: Sparingly spreading by way of self-sown seed.

Growing Conditions: Well-drained, deep sandy soil in full sun; Zones 8–10.

Propagation: Seed.

Comments: Skyblue lupine is a refined wildflower of sublime beauty, its foliage covered with silky, intensely silvery white hairs. In the best forms, the coat of hairs is so dense that the plants are a brilliant, almost metallic white. In sharp but beautiful contrast to the silvery foliage are the large, abundantly produced spikes of elegant, pastel blue flowers. Seed should be sown in late spring or early summer where the plants are to grow since lupines are unforgiving of any root disturbance. With luck, the seed will germinate in the autumn, and if the winter rains are adequate, plants may bloom in their first spring. Northern strains are reported to be more or less reliably perennial. However, toward the southern portion of its range, skyblue lupine often behaves like an annual, with the entire plant drying up and dying after flowering.

28. *Melanthera nivea*

Common Name: Salt-and-Pepper; Nonpareil

Habit: Densely branched, erect to nearly prostrate annual or perennial.

Size: 1–4 feet and as wide, sometimes much wider than it is tall.

Season: All year.

Maintenance: Pruning of overgrown plants; removal of spent plants.
Motility: Moderately spreading by way of self-sown seed.
Growing Conditions: Moist to dry sites in full sun to part shade; Zones 8–11.
Propagation: Seed; cuttings.
Comments: The two common names for this plant are unusual. What

does this plant have in common with table condiments or small chocolate disks covered with white beads of sugar? Both names are based on the plant's flowers, which are pure white, accented by contrasting black anthers. The flowers are individually tiny but they are aggregated into dense heads and are surprisingly showy, especially when borne in large numbers on a well-grown plant. Their attractiveness is not lost on insects; flowering plants become a focal point for numerous and diverse insects. Salt-and-pepper is a remarkably variable plant, ranging in form from large, coarse roadside weeds to delicate, dwarf forms occurring mostly in natural habitats. The latter are especially attractive in garden settings and should be sought out for cultivation.

29. *Monarda punctata*

Common Name: Spotted Beebalm; Horsemint
Habit: Erect to spreading taprooted annual or short-lived perennial, sometimes biennial.
Size: 1½–3 feet, occasionally as high as 4 feet.
Season: Late spring through early autumn.
Maintenance: Yearly pruning of large, older plants; removal of spent plants.
Motility: Sometimes forming clumps by self-layering; occasionally spreading by way of self-sown seed.

Growing Conditions: Well-drained soil in light shade to full sun; Zones 8–10A.

Propagation: Seed; cuttings.

Comments: The chief horticultural interest of spotted beebalm lies in its flowers, which are borne in elongated spikes with conspicuous, leafy bracts. The white or pale creamy yellow flowers are variably marked with dark purple spots and are subtly attractive, especially when viewed at close range. However, what first attracts one's attention are the large, leafy bracts, which assume various shades of white, pink, and rose. The combination of white, speckled flowers and pink bracts is a particularly pleasing one and results in a dramatically different and attractive flowering plant. Since it blooms over a long period, and because the bracts are persistent, spotted beebalm provides color for many weeks. Large-bracted, intensely colored forms are especially attractive and should be sought out for garden use. In addition to the colorful flower spikes, spotted beebalm has leaves with a pleasingly pungent, oregano-like scent that has resulted in its use as a herb garden plant.

30. *Ocimum campechianum* (Synonym: *Ocimum micranthum*)

Common Name: Wild Basil

Habit: Erect, short-lived perennial becoming shrubby with age.

Size: 1–2 feet tall and wide.

Season: A summer annual northward or all year southward.

Maintenance: Periodic pruning of large, older plants; removal of spent plants.

Motility: Very slowly spreading by way of self-sown seed.

Growing Conditions: Moist but well-drained sites in part shade to full sun; Zones 10–11.

Propagation: Seeds; cuttings.

Comments: Although the majority of the forty or so species of basil occur in the Old World, one species is native to southernmost Florida. It is a remarkably widespread little plant, the natural range of which also includes the West Indies and Central and South America. Wild basil quickly forms a dense, shrubby mound of lime green foliage, studded at the tip of each branch with a spike of rosy purple flowers. The flowers are small, but very intricate, and merit careful study under a magnifying glass. As in all basils, the foliage is aromatic and possesses a warm, spicy fragrance reminiscent of allspice with a touch of camphor. Luckily, it is as easily grown as regular basil and is a plant that is sure to increase in popularity as an interesting and delightfully aromatic addition to herb gardens and wildflower gardens alike.

31. *Pectis linearifolia*

Common Name: Lemon Daisy
Habit: Dwarf annual forming dense mats of foliage.
Size: Up to 2–3 inches high and 6–18 inches across, depending on cultural conditions.
Season: Use as a summer annual northward, growing and flowering essentially all year southward.

Maintenance: Removal of spent plants.
Motility: Moderately to abundantly spreading to all parts of the garden capable of supporting its growth.
Growing Conditions: Sunny, moist, but well-drained sites free from larger plants; Zones 8B–10.
Propagation: Seed.
Comments: Both in the wild and in the garden, lemon daisy forms attractive, dark green little mats of very fine, linear foliage. Throughout the year, the mats are decorated with tiny yellow daisies. However, both the plant and the flower heads are too small to have much horticultural merit. Lemon daisy's true significance is in its foliage, which releases an intoxicating and refreshing citrus odor when crushed. The plant is edible and may be used whenever one wants to add to food a delicate citrus odor or flavor. It is easily established by spreading seeds in a suitable area, and once it gets going, it maintains itself through moderate self-seeding. It is important that self-sown seedlings not be weeded out, since mature plants tend to flower and seed themselves to death in just a few months.

32. *Poinsettia cyathophora*

Common Name: Wild Poinsettia
Habit: Erect annual or short-lived perennial.
Size: 1–2 feet tall (sometimes to 3 feet).
Season: Autumn in northernmost Florida, all year in southern Florida.
Maintenance: Removal of spent plants.

Motility: Moderately to aggressively spreading in open, sunny areas.
Growing Conditions: Full sun to part shade with average moisture; Zones 8–11.
Propagation: Seed.
Comments: Wild poinsettia is cultivated principally for the modified leaves that subtend the flowers. These leaves have a deep red basal blotch and are clearly reminiscent, though at a smaller and far less dramatic scale, of the Christmas poinsettia, to which this native wildflower is related. Wild poinsettia is an extremely variable plant, its growth form ranging from relatively open plants with thin, linear leaves to densely branched plants with broad, ample-sized leaves. Once established, plants tolerate considerable drought and maintain themselves by way of self-sown seedlings. Due to its ease of growth, long flowering season, and bright red color, wild poinsettia makes a welcome addition to native plant gardens. Additionally, its seeds are a great favorite of mourning doves, and it is useful for attracting these beautiful birds to the garden.

33. *Pyrrhopappus carolinianus*

Common Name: False Dandelion
Habit: Rosette-forming, taprooted annual or biennial.
Size: 1–2 feet tall.
Season: Spring.
Maintenance: None.
Motility: Moderately spreading by way of self-sown seed.
Growing Conditions: Moist, often disturbed areas in full sun; Zones 8–9A.
Propagation: Seed.
Comments: Looking very much like a large dandelion, this colorful native wildflower is nowhere near as perniciously weedy since it is an annual, whereas true dandelions are long-lived and persistent perennials. False dandelion is also more ornamental, bearing brilliant yellow flower heads much larger than do dandelions. Although often ignored because it is such a common roadside plant, it makes a splendid addition to the spring wildflower scene, where it lends a bright and cheery note at the end of winter. For the most ornamental effect, plants should be grown in large masses. Like many taprooted plants, false dandelion resents root disturbance of any kind. Thus, for best results, sow the seed where the plants are to grow in well-prepared ground.

34. *Rudbeckia hirta*

Common Name: Black-Eyed-Susan
Habit: Erect, taprooted annual, biennial, or short-lived perennial.
Size: 1–3 feet tall.
Season: Spring through autumn.
Maintenance: Pruning of large, older plants; removal of spent plants.
Motility: Moderately spreading by way of self-sown seed.
Growing Conditions: Wet meadows and moist, disturbed sites in full sun; Zones 8–10.
Propagation: Seed.
Comments: Black-eyed-susan is a much loved wildflower throughout the eastern United States. The plant itself is not particularly attractive, and all vegetative portions are covered with coarse, rigid hairs. However, few plants, native or otherwise, can compare with the brilliant floral display that these plants produce. And black-eyed-susans are among the easiest of all plants to grow, with the seeds germinating readily and the plants quickly maturing to flowering size. As is the case with so many other native wildflowers, the sturdiest, largest, and most abundantly flowering plants are produced from self-sown seed. Therefore, care should be taken to allow at least some of the flower heads to mature a seed crop for the next season's blooms.

35. *Sabatia grandiflora*

Common Name: Marsh-Pink
Habit: Erect, diffusely branched, taprooted annual.
Size: 1½–3 feet tall.
Season: Summer in northern Florida, all year in southern Florida.
Maintenance: None.
Motility: Slowly spreading by way of self-sown seed.
Growing Conditions: Wet, brackish, or freshwater sites in full sun; Zones 8–11.
Propagation: Seed.
Comments: Marsh-pink is noteworthy for its elegant growth form and large flowers of a beautiful and dazzling shade of dark rosy pink. It is,

however, a temperamental beauty with one chief obstacle to its widespread cultivation: the plant will not tolerate root disturbance. The best way of starting a colony is to sow seed in a moist sunny area. Plants may also be grown in pots in order to produce a large quantity of seed under controlled conditions. Seed should be sown on the soil surface since it is as fine as dust, and as with many members of the gentian family, the seed requires exposure to light in order to germinate.

36. *Salvia coccinea*

Common Name: Red Sage; Tropical Sage
Habit: Erect, short-lived perennial.
Size: 1½–2 feet tall, occasionally to 3 feet in cultivation.
Season: Summer and autumn northward, all year southward.
Maintenance: Deadheading to promote flowering rather than seed production; pruning of large, overgrown plants; removal of spent plants.
Motility: Moderately spreading to all areas of the garden capable of supporting its growth.
Growing Conditions: Well-drained soil in moderate shade to full sun; Zones 8–10.
Propagation: Seed; cuttings.
Comments: Red sage is an easily grown wildflower with sweetly aromatic foliage and brilliant red flowers irresistible to butterflies and hummingbirds. It is also one of very few southern Florida plants with boldly colored flowers that does well in the shade. For best effect it should be grown either as an isolated specimen, where its flowers will create a bright spot of color, or else in large, bold masses. In either case, plants need to be severely pruned occasionally for maximum production of vigorous, abundantly flowering growth. It self-sows, and spontaneous seedlings are usually healthier and more free-flowering than the carefully nurtured parent plants that one sets out into the garden. Because of its easy cultivation, ready propagation from seed, everblooming nature, and intensely colored flowers, this is a plant that belongs in every wildflower garden that can accommodate its simple needs. Horticultural forms with pink, white, or bicolored flowers are now readily available and serve to extend the color range of this species.

37. *Senecio glabellus*

Common Name: Cress-Leaf Ragwort; Butter-weed
Habit: Erect, taprooted winter annual.
Size: 3–36 inches, depending on growing conditions.
Season: Spring.
Maintenance: Removal of spent plants.
Motility: Moderately spreading to open, moist areas by self-sown seed.

Growing Conditions: Disturbed, moist sites in light shade to full sun; Zones 8–10.
Propagation: Seed.
Comments: Cress-leaf ragwort grows in both natural areas, such as marshes, riverbanks, and swamps, and in artificial sites, such as lawns and roadside ditches. It nearly always occurs where there has been some type of disturbance. The disturbance may be natural, as when a flood scours a riverbank, or it may be artificial, such as the periodic mowing of roadsides. In any case, it is a pioneer plant that soon dies out when longer-lived perennials and woody plants move in after the disturbance. Attempts to transplant all but the smallest seedlings usually fail; this plant must be started from seed. Fortunately, it is easily established by scattering seed in a suitable area. Although mostly ignored because it is so common, its easy cultivation and bright, perky yellow color in early spring make it a welcome addition to the natural garden.

38. *Trichostema dichotomum*

Common Name: Bluecurls; Forked Bluecurls
Habit: Taprooted annual or short-lived perennial, sometimes shrublike.
Size: 1–2 feet tall and at least as wide, occasionally up to 3 feet tall in cultivation.
Season: Late summer northward, extending into winter, late spring, and/or early summer southward.
Maintenance: Removal of older, spent plants.

Motility: Moderately to abundantly spreading by self-sown seed.

Growing Conditions: Well-drained, often sandy areas; Zones 8–10.

Propagation: Seed; cuttings.

Comments: In cultivation, bluecurls bear flowers sporadically from late summer to late spring, with the heaviest flowering usually occurring during the beginning of cooler weather in late summer or early autumn. The plants can grow into large, densely leafy shrubs 3 feet high by 4 feet wide and bear several thousand flowers during the course of a single flowering season. On cool autumn mornings, the sight of such a plant, with perhaps a hundred or more flowers open at once, is exceedingly attractive. The flowers quickly wilt in the heat of the day. Despite the flowers being short-lived, bluecurls is a charming addition to the native garden, where blue is a rare color and where the perky flowers help to attract bees, butterflies, and hummingbirds.

39. *Triodanis perfoliata* (Synonym: *Specularia perfoliata*)

Common Name: Venus's Looking Glass

Habit: Blue-flowered winter annual.

Size: Growing 4–8 inches tall.

Season: Flowering in late winter or early spring.

Maintenance: None; do not remove dried stems until seeds are mature to ensure plants the following year.

Motility: Spreading into open, sunny ground by seed.

Growing Conditions: Well-drained, often sandy soils in full sun; Zones 8–9.

Propagation: Seed.

Comments: Venus's looking glass is a quaint little winter annual, its attractive blue flowers adding a pleasing note to the garden scene at the end of winter. The flowers resemble tiny bells—not surprising since it is in the same family as bluebells and at one time was even classified as a bluebell in the genus *Campanula.* The flowers vary in color from lavender-blue to violet and provide a nice contrast to the yellow colors commonly found in many Florida wildflowers. An exceedingly similar plant, *Triodanis biflora,* also occurs in Florida and may be utilized in the same manner. The unusual common name is derived from the shiny, slightly flattened seeds, fancifully said to resemble a hand mirror.

Long-lived Wildflowers

Native perennial wildflowers are not the coddled and domesticated plants so readily available from retail garden centers and mail-order catalogs. Those plants have been specifically selected and bred for optimum performance in rich, well-drained loams with ample water and frequent fertilization. Our natives are wild plants, and when they are grown under such conditions, the results are often disastrous. The wet, overly rich soil encourages fungal and bacterial root rots that ravage the plants. Those that survive make excessive vegetative growth that is out of character for the plant and make it prone to insect damage.

Native perennial wildflowers should be grown under conditions that match as closely as possible their natural habitats. Most are extremely slow-growing while young or while getting established in the garden. This is not due to a weak constitution. Quite the contrary: they are laying the foundation to withstand harsh and severe conditions. That foundation consists, first and foremost, in a strong, sturdy root system. Beginning gardeners are often amazed at the extensive root systems that native perennials develop—often there are more roots underground than there is vegetative growth above ground. Not only are the roots extensive, they are usually also greatly thickened or arise from an enlarged underground stem. These adaptations are not surprising or accidental. After all, in their native habitats, the next fire, prolonged drought or hungry herbivore may be just around the corner. All of these may result in the complete destruction of the aerial portion of the plant, and the best chance for recovery lies in a strong root system with sufficient reserves to produce new vegetative growth.

Be patient with native perennials and realize that they cannot be hurried along with excessive water or fertilizer. Once they are established and have formed a good root system, growth is fairly rapid and they are long-lived plants that will reward you with their beauty for many years to come.

40. *Allium canadense*

Common Name: Wild Onion; Wild Garlic
Habit: Bulbous perennial.
Size: Forming small clumps 8–12 inches high.
Season: Flowering in the spring; often dormant in summer southward.
Maintenance: Remove and dispose of bulblets to prevent unwanted spreading.
Motility: Often weedy and rapidly spreading by way of bulblets.

Growing Conditions: Disturbed areas in full sun to light shade; Zones 8–9.

Propagation: Seed; bulblets; division.

Comments: Wild onion is native to Florida from the Panhandle south to central peninsular Florida. There are two distinct varieties. The more common one, *Allium canadense* var. *canadense,* is unmistakable since most of the flowers are replaced by tiny little bulbs technically known as bulblets. The few flowers that are present rarely, if ever, produce seeds. In spite of this, the plant is capable of rapid increase since every bulblet can produce a new plant when it falls to the ground. This variety is commonly found in areas with rich, moist soils, but it is easily grown under average garden conditions. A second variety of wild onion, *Allium canadense* var. *mobilense,* also occurs in Florida. It is less common and is characterized by a normal inflorescence consisting entirely of small pink flowers. Both varieties are edible and all parts of the plant possess a strong onion odor. The bulbs and bulblets may be used as one would use onions; the foliage may be utilized in the manner of green onion; and the flowers make an attractive edible garnish.

41. *Ambrosia hispida*

Common Name: Coastal Ambrosia

Habit: Sprawling groundcover that roots at the nodes.

Size: 6–12 inches tall and 3 or more feet wide.

Season: The foliage is attractive throughout the year.

Maintenance: Periodic pruning.

Motility: Will slowly spread by stems that root where they touch the ground.

Growing Conditions: Coastal beaches or dunes in full sun; Zones 9B–11.

Propagation: Cuttings; self-rooted stems.

Comments: Do not be put off by the fact that this plant is in the same genus as America's principal cause of hayfever, the ragweeds. Coastal ambrosia is not at all weedy and is in fact a beautiful wildflower adapted to harsh coastal conditions, including occasional salt spray, strong winds, and hot sun. Once established, it resents lush conditions, and if not provided with full sun and a lean, well-drained soil, it becomes prone to insect attacks, especially whitefly. The small, greenish flowers are frequently overlooked. This plant is grown instead for its attractive foliage and usefulness as a groundcover on coastal sites. The leaves are subtly aromatic, have a dense covering of silvery hairs, and are so finely lobed as to resemble lace. Fortunately, coastal ambrosia is rarely common enough to be a significant source of hayfever pollen.

42. *Angadenia berteri*

Common Name: Pineland-Allamanda
Habit: Erect perennial; occasionally taller older plants have very weakly twining stems.
Size: 1–2 feet tall.
Season: Flowering throughout the year in southernmost Florida; north of its natural range it flowers mostly in the spring and summer.
Maintenance: Light annual pruning.
Motility: Extremely slow spread by self-sown seed (seed is usually infrequently produced).
Growing Conditions: Moist but well-drained, often rocky soil in full sun; Zones 10–11.
Propagation: Seeds.
Comments: Pineland-allamanda is a delightful little plant that occurs in the rocky pinelands of southern Florida. Usually growing erect or nearly so, plants with longer stems are sometimes weakly twining at the stem tip. The plants have small, opposite, somewhat glossy leaves and, throughout a long period, produce bright yellow flowers about 1 inch long that greatly resemble miniature allamanda blossoms. The flowers are followed by linear capsules 2–4 inches long containing many plumed seeds. Cultivation presents no major difficulties. Seeds germinate within a week or two, providing an easy means of propagating this diminutive treasure.

43. *Aquilegia canadensis*

Common Name: Wild Columbine
Habit: Tufted perennial.
Size: 1–2 feet tall, occasionally to 3 feet in robust cultivated plants.
Season: Spring.
Maintenance: Occasional light pruning to remove old flowers and seed heads.
Motility: Can quickly spread to all parts of the garden capable of supporting its growth.
Growing Conditions: Dappled shade in rich, well-drained soil; Zone 8.
Propagation: Seed.
Comments: Wild columbine is one of the most exquisitely beautiful wildflowers native to Florida. Plants form small mounds of attractive ferny foliage that is pleasingly suffused with

burgundy when young, the color gradually changing to a soothing sea-green at maturity. Well-grown plants produce quantities of intricate, nodding flowers that are held well above the foliage on long, wiry stalks. Each flower consists of five red sepals and five yellow petals, the petals each bearing a prominent red spur filled with nectar. While attractive to human beings, the flowers are irresistible to hummingbirds. Plants benefit from morning sun, but hot, dry afternoon sun should be avoided. Although seemingly very delicate, wild columbine is a surprisingly tough plant if provided with evenly moist but well-drained soil. Listed as endangered in Florida, it is being propagated by several nurseries.

44. *Arisaema dracontium*

Common Name: Green Dragon
Habit: Erect perennial growing from an underground tuber.
Size: 1–2 feet tall.
Season: Flowering in early spring; fruit ripening in autumn.
Fruit: A large spike of brilliant red berries.
Maintenance: Essentially none.
Motility: Very slowly spreading by self-sown seed.
Growing Conditions: Rich, often wet woodlands in deep to partial shade; Zones 8–9B.
Propagation: Seed sown immediately upon ripening.
Comments: As with the related jack-in-the-pulpit, successful cultivation of green dragon

requires a rich, moist soil high in organic matter. Optimum results are achieved by growing the plants in a location sheltered from strong winds and receiving dappled shade during the spring but deep shade during the warm weather of summer. Green dragon is less well known to the public than jack-in-the-pulpit since its floral display is generally much less conspicuous. However, its oddly shaped leaf, which somewhat resembles a hand with seven to nine fingers, adds an unusual and exotic touch to the spring wildflower garden. Additionally, it equals jack-in-the-pulpit's autumnal display of dazzling, brilliant red berries.

45. *Arisaema triphyllum*

Common Name: Jack-in-the-Pulpit
Habit: Erect perennial growing from an underground tuber.
Size: 1–2 feet tall.
Season: Flowering in early spring; fruit ripening in autumn.
Fruit: A large spike of brilliant red berries.
Maintenance: Essentially none.
Motility: Very slowly spreading by self-sown seed.
Growing Conditions: Rich, often wet woodlands in deep to partial shade; Zones 8–10A.
Propagation: Seed sown immediately upon ripening.
Comments: Jack-in-the-pulpit is a member of the same plant family to which calla-lilies and anthuriums belong. Like those plants, it too has an attractive and unusual inflorescence. What many consider to be the flower is in reality a highly modified leaf subtending the inflorescence. It is this modified leaf that is the "pulpit" in which "Jack" sits. The flowers are tiny and are at the base of a thick spike (the spike of flowers is "Jack"). In the very best forms, the pulpit is dark purple marked with white stripes. Toward the southern end of this species' range, the pulpit tends to be almost entirely green with barely a hint of stripes. However, this is such a charming and interesting wildflower that even the rather drab green forms are well worth growing. After the early spring blooming period, it produces a second show in the autumn, by which time the foliage has died down for the winter: the thick spikes of green berries turn brilliant red.

46. *Asclepias humistrata*

Common Name: Pink-Veined Milkplant
Habit: Stout, erect or sprawling, tuberous-rooted perennial, mostly with a single stem.
Size: 1–2 feet long.
Season: Spring and summer.
Maintenance: Light annual pruning to remove older, dead stems.
Motility: Slowly spreading by seed into open, sunny areas.
Growing Conditions: Deep, well-drained sandy soil in full sun; Zones 8–9.
Propagation: Seed.
Comments: Many wildflower enthusiasts consider pink-

veined milkplant to have the most beautiful foliage of any milkplant native to Florida. The large, smooth leaves are an unusual shade of dark blue-gray or light violet-gray, accented by lavender or pink veins. The flowers come in a two-toned color scheme of pale rose or lavender combined with creamy white. Although interesting in their own right, the flowers are subordinate in beauty to the leaves. Indeed, the leaves are so attractive and unusually colored that pink-veined milkplant is worth growing as a foliage plant alone. It occurs only in deep sand in habitats with well-drained soil, such as scrub and sandy pastures and pinelands. In garden settings, poor drainage, heavy mulch, or too rich a soil leads to a quick and certain death.

47. *Asclepias perennis*

Common Name: Swamp Milkplant
Habit: Erect, perennial producing many-stemmed clumps.
Size: 1–2 feet.
Season: Spring through autumn.
Maintenance: Annual pruning of older, dead stems.
Motility: Slowly spreading by self-sown seed in moist areas free from larger, competing plants.
Growing Conditions: Riverbanks and swamps in deep shade to nearly full sun; Zones 8–9.
Propagation: Seed; Division.

Comments: Unlike many other milkplants, which grow best in full sun, swamp milkplant favors partly shaded, wet areas. It looks its best when protected from the hot sun, but it flowers more abundantly if it receives an hour or two of full sun each day. The small white flowers are individually insignificant, but they are produced in such great numbers that, en masse, they make an eye-catching display. Unopened flower buds are often tinged pink, and the visual effect of pure white flowers and pale pink buds is quite appealing. Beautifully contrasting with the flowers and further accentuating their brilliant whiteness is the smooth, dark green foliage. Swamp milkplant is fast becoming a favorite of wildflower and butterfly gardeners since it is attractive, readily propagated by seed or division, and easily cultivated. Indeed, if provided with good soil and constant moisture, seedlings begin to flower when only four months old.

48. *Asclepias tuberosa*

Common Name: Orange Milkplant; Butterfly Milkplant
Habit: Erect to sprawling, tuberous-rooted perennial.
Size: Stems 1½–2 feet long, occasionally longer.
Season: Evergreen in southernmost Florida, winter dormant northward; flowers borne spring through autumn.

Maintenance: Annual removal of older, dead stems.

Motility: Virtually none (unless many plants are grown together and much seed is set).

Growing Conditions: Well-drained, often sandy soil in full sun; Zones 8–10.

Propagation: Seeds; division; root cuttings.

Comments: Orange milkplant naturally occurs throughout all of Florida and may be grown and

enjoyed in every county of the state. It requires bright, open situations and favors deep, well-drained sandy soils. However, in southern Florida it grows in moist, rocky pinelands. Its presence in these southern pinelands, where it associates with numerous plants of West Indian affinity, is unexpected and surprising to those who are familiar with this plant as a prairie plant of the Midwest and Great Plains. Orange milkplant has become an exceedingly popular and beloved native wildflower, not just in Florida but throughout much of the United States. Its justifiable popularity is due to its long blooming season, immense attractiveness to butterflies, and the bright orange color of its flowers. The flower color closely matches that of an orange peel and, along with orange bachelor's button (*Polygala lutea*), is perhaps as true an orange color as is to be found in any Florida native plant.

49. *Aster adnatus* (Synonym: *Symphyotrichum adnatum*)

Common Name: Whipcord Aster; Scaleleaf Aster

Habit: Erect or spreading perennial.

Size: 1–2 feet tall and as wide or wider than it is tall.

Season: Autumn, winter, or early spring.

Maintenance: Annual removal of old, dried stems.

Motility: Moderately spreading by self-sown seeds.

Growing Conditions: Moist but well-drained sandy or rocky soil in light shade to full sun; Zones 8–10.

Propagation: Seeds; cuttings.

Comments: Whipcord aster has a very distinctive and unusual growth habit. It forms a wiry, open clump of long-branched stems that are clothed with very small and numerous leaves. The tiny awl-shaped leaves have their lower portion united to the stem, where their margins form two small wings along the stem. When not in bloom, the plant is scarcely recognizable as an aster and invokes much interest among native plant enthusiasts. Late in the year, and often into early spring as well, robust plants produce literally hundreds of flower heads, resulting in an attractive display. It readily adapts to cultivation as long as it is provided with full sun in an evenly moist but well-drained site, where it quickly becomes a specimen plant. Some forms of Walter's aster (*Aster walteri*) are similar to whipcord aster but the former appreciates more moisture.

50. Aster carolinianus (Synonym: Ampelaster carolinianus)

Common Name: Climbing Aster

Habit: Large, robust perennial producing numerous woody stems that climb over other plants and nearby supports.

Size: Stems elongated and climbing to 9 feet or more if allowed to do so.

Season: Late summer, autumn, and winter.

Maintenance: Annual removal of old flowering stems.

Motility: Slowly spreading by underground suckers; moderately spreading by self-sown seed.

Growing Conditions: Swamps and wet ground in deep shade to nearly full sun; Zones 8–10.

Propagation: Seed; cuttings; division.

Comments: Climbing aster is just the plant for those with wet soil and who despair of growing some of the showy asters of dry, sandy soils. It is unique among Florida's asters for its woody stems and vining growth habit. Well-grown plants form large masses of leafy stems with great quantities of flower heads borne at the end of each branch. In full bloom, it presents a strikingly lovely display that is as attractive to butterflies and other insects as it is to gardeners. Its cultivation presents no particular difficulties, and although naturally occurring in very wet situations, it adapts well to regular garden conditions. As with all asters, plants are unattractive when going to seed and should be severely cut back after flowering. Such treatment not only improves their appearance but provokes densely branched, vigorous new growth that results in better flowering. Elliott's aster (*Aster elliottii*) is another showy, robust aster that also grows in wet sites. It is an erect perennial that forms colonies by way of underground rhizomes and grows 3–5 feet tall. Elliott's aster may be utilized in areas where climbing aster's vining habit might be a problem.

51. *Aster concolor* (Synonym: *Symphyotrichum concolor*)

Common Name: Silvery Aster
Habit: Rigidly erect perennial.
Size: 1½–3 feet tall, depending on growing conditions and genetic form.
Season: Late summer, autumn, and winter.
Maintenance: Annual pruning of old, dried stems.
Motility: Moderately spreading by way of self-sown seeds.
Growing Conditions: Well-drained, sandy or rocky soil in very light shade or full sun; Zones 8–11.
Propagation: Seed.
Comments: Silvery aster is an exquisitely beautiful wildflower that favors dry habitats such as sandy oak hammocks and scrubby pinelands. The erect, wiry stems are clothed in attractive leaves that are densely covered with silky hairs of silvery gray. In autumn, the large flower heads are borne in a narrow, columnar inflorescence that greatly resembles in form the flower spikes of blazingstars (*Liatris* species). The flower heads come in distinct and pleasing shades of blue, violet, or pink, making this a very showy plant when in full flower. Fortunately, this desirable wildflower is easily grown if positioned in a bright spot with well-drained soil.

52. *Aster reticulatus* (Synonym: *Oclemena reticulata*)

Common Name: White-top Aster
Habit: Robust perennial producing numerous, stiffly erect, mostly unbranched stems.
Size: 3 feet (often taller, especially if growing among other plants).
Season: Spring and summer.

Maintenance: Annual removal of old, dried stems.
Motility: Moderately spreading by way of self-sown seed.
Growing Conditions: Moist pinelands and meadows; Zones 8–9B.
Propagation: Seed; division.
Comments: Whitetop aster produces flowers at the appropriate season regardless of its height at the time. Thus, as is the case in the pictured plant, if cut back just before the flowering season by fire (or by pruning in the case of cultivated plants), it will bloom while scarcely more than a few inches tall. However, if left undisturbed it develops into a tall, robust plant that produces an abundant display of pure white flower heads toward the top of the plant. Although strictly perennials, such well-developed specimens have a visual impact and landscape use similar to that of a small shrub. Most asters are difficult to identify, but whitetop aster is readily identified by its leaves, which are an unusual lime green, with the upper surface deeply impressed with a fine pattern of tiny veins.

53. *Berlandiera subacaulis*

Common Name: Florida Greeneyes
Habit: Rosette-forming perennial with a thick, tuberous taproot.
Size: 1–1½ feet tall.
Season: Spring through early summer in the north, nearly all year southward.
Fruit: Prominent green seed heads.
Maintenance: Periodic pruning of old, dried-up flowering stems.
Motility: Moderately spreading by way of self-sown seed.
Growing Conditions: Sandy or rocky, well-drained soils in very light shade to full sun; Zones 8B–10.
Propagation: Seed (germination usually very low).
Comments: Greeneyes is a true Floridian, native only to Florida, and an endearing wildflower. Its basal rosettes of distinctively lobed leaves, its attractive yellow flower heads with a prominent green disk, and its conspicuous green seed heads are a familiar sight in sandy areas. With age, the plants form sizable clumps that bear numerous flowers heads and make a spectacular show in the wildflower garden. Toward the northern part of its range, the flowers are borne mostly in the spring and summer, but in southern Florida it may be found in bloom nearly throughout the year.

54. *Bletia purpurea*

Common Name: Pine-Pink
Habit: Tuberous terrestrial orchid.
Size: 1–2 feet, the flower stalk often taller.
Season: Flowers in the spring; foliage dies back in the autumn and plant is dormant in winter.

Maintenance: Annual pruning of old flower stalks and removal of dead foliage as plant enters dormancy.

Motility: Slowly forms large clumps; can increase by seed under appropriate conditions.

Growing Conditions: Moist situations in full or nearly full sun; Zones 9B–11.

Propagation: Seed; division.

Comments: Pine-pink is unusual among our terrestrial orchids in that it is relatively easy to cultivate, the plants being tolerant of a wide variety of conditions and soil types as long as they receive adequate moisture and bright light. Indeed, it is so adaptable that plants have been observed growing in full sun on sandy pond margins. Under such conditions, the plants were stunted and yellowish-green but were actually increasing in numbers and flowering regularly. Pine-pink also differs from most terrestrial orchids in that it may be grown from seed scattered onto decaying organic matter, including wood mulch. At times it may grow from seed with such ease as to become a nursery weed of potted plants! Most forms of this species native to Florida are self-pollinating, sometimes going directly from flower bud to seed pod without the flower ever opening. Of course, forms that open their flowers fully are preferred for horticultural purposes.

55. *Campanula floridana*

Common Name: Florida Bluebell

Habit: Dwarf perennial with stems weakly supported by other vegetation or creeping along the ground.

Size: Stems are 12–16 inches long.

Season: Flowering in the spring; becoming more or less dormant in the summer.

Maintenance: None.

Motility: Will fill, by way of underground rhizomes, as large an area of moist, open ground as is available.

Growing Conditions: Moist situations in light shade to full sun; Zones 8B–10A.

Propagation: Seed; cuttings; division.

Comments: Florida bluebell has weak, sprawling stems, tiny leaves, and attractive dark blue to violet flowers that are rather large relative to the size of the leaves. It occurs as a native plant only in

Florida, where it grows in moist, usually sunny meadows and roadsides. Both in the wild and in cultivation, it makes an attractive companion to other native wildflowers that bloom in moist areas in the spring. In nature, it is most often found weakly clambering over other plants. However, if given room to itself, it will spread vigorously from underground rhizomes and form a dwarf groundcover gaily sprinkled with violet stars in the spring.

56. *Carphephorus corymbosus*

Common Name: Paintbrush
Habit: Robust, single-stemmed perennial arising from a basal rosette; forming large clumps with age.
Size: 3 feet.
Season: Flowering in late summer or autumn.
Maintenance: Annual removal of old flowering stems.
Motility: Will slowly form clumps; spread by seed is virtually nil (unless many plants are grown together and much seed is set).
Growing Conditions: Well-drained, often sandy areas in full sun; Zones 8–10A.
Propagation: Seeds; division.
Comments: In the vegetative phase, paintbrush consists of one or more rosettes of attractive, leathery leaves. Toward the end of summer, a single tall stem arises from the heart of each rosette and bears a prominent, flat-topped cluster of large, but surprisingly delicate, pink flower heads. The flowers contrast beautifully with native grasses, and paintbrush makes a splendid addition to the wild meadow garden. With each passing year, the number of rosettes increases and the floral display becomes more spectacular. Somewhat similar to paintbrush, but producing a far less dramatic floral display, is vanilla plant (*Carphephorus odoratissima*). It may be utilized instead of paintbrush in moist or wet sites and its foliage smells pleasingly of vanilla, especially when dried.

57. *Carphephorus paniculatus*

Common Name: Deer-Tongue
Habit: Single-stemmed perennial arising from a basal rosette.
Size: 2–3 feet.
Season: Autumn and winter.
Maintenance: Annual removal of old, spent flower stems.
Motility: Slowly forms clumps; spread by seed is virtually nil (unless many plants are grown together and much seed is set).

Growing Conditions: Sunny areas under moist to rather dry conditions; Zones 8–10A.

Propagation: Seed; division.

Comments: Deer-tongue's common name is derived from the shape of its basal leaves. This name provides no clue to the attractiveness of this interesting native wildflower. Vegetatively, it greatly resembles a smaller, more graceful version of paintbrush (*Carphephorus corymbosus*). However, all similarities end when it comes to the inflorescence. Whereas paintbrush has a wide, flat-topped cluster of soft pink flower heads, deer-tongue has an elongated, cylindrical spike of smaller, dark rose-pink flower heads. Older plants tend to produce sizable numbers of rosettes that form a solid green mat. Such plants are extremely attractive since each of the oldest rosettes will flower, resulting in an extensive and very showy display.

58. *Chamaesyce mesembrianthemifolia*

Common Name: Blue-Leaf Sandmat; Thick-Leaf Sandmat

Habit: Smooth, prostrate to erect, bluish or silvery green perennial with fleshy, slightly succulent leaves.

Size: Highly variable depending on growing conditions, from 1 to 12 inches high, nearly always at least as wide or wider than it is high.

Season: Evergreen; flowering from spring through autumn northward; all year southward.

Maintenance: None.

Motility: Slowly spreading into open areas in full sun from self-sown seed.

Growing Conditions: Rocky or sandy soil along coastal beaches above the high water mark; Zones 9A–11.

Propagation: Seed.

Comments: Blue-leaf sandmat is in the same family as, and is a distant relative of, the wildly flamboyant Christmas poinsettia. Yet there could not

possibly be a greater contrast between two plants. Our little native grows in a narrow strip between the high water mark on the beach and the edge of the foredunes. Here, where it is subjected to intense heat, relentless wind, blowing sand, and occasional salt spray, it makes its home. Beyond the fact that it thrives under such harsh conditions, its only other outstanding characteristic is its remarkably beautiful and intense blue-green or silvery green color. When given just a little shelter, a little extra water, and soil just a little richer, it forms attractive clumps of blue-green foliage about 8 inches tall and 12 inches wide. As such, it makes a decorative little specimen plant. It can also be massed to form a highly unusual and interesting groundcover.

59. *Chaptalia tomentosa*

Common Name: Sunbonnets
Habit: Mat-forming perennial.
Size: Rosettes up to 12 inches wide; flower stems 8–12 inches tall.
Season: Spring (winter and spring in southern Florida).
Fruit: Dandelion-like powderpuff.
Maintenance: Essentially none.
Motility: Very slowly forming a groundcover; very slowly spreading from self-sown seed.
Growing Conditions: Moist areas in light shade to full sun; Zones 8–10A.
Propagation: Seed; division.
Comments: The delightfully and appropriately named sunbonnets is one of the special joys of our moist pinelands when it flowers in the spring. The dark green leaves have minute callouslike teeth and form attractive rosettes that often cover large patches of ground. The rosettes are made more attractive by occasional partially upturned leaves that reveal their silky white lower surfaces. Small, pure white daisies are borne in early spring. Like sunflowers, they face the sun and follow its path across the sky. The plants often provide a second show by blooming in the winter after their summer rest. For the most attractive display, in cultivation they should be grown in sizable patches free from the competition of larger plants.

60. *Clematis baldwinii*

Common Name: Pine-Hyacinth
Habit: Erect to sprawling perennial, becoming multistemmed with age.
Size: Stems about 1–2 feet long, rarely longer if shaded by other plants.
Season: Flowering in sporadic bursts throughout the spring, summer, and autumn.

Fruit: A rounded head of seedlike fruits, each with a long, silky-plumed tail.

Maintenance: None in the wild garden; annual pruning of old stems in more formal situations.

Motility: Very slowly spreading by self-sown seed.

Growing Conditions: Somewhat dry to moist sites in light shade to full sun; Zones 8B–10.

Propagation: Seed (double dormancy, may take 1–1½ years to germinate); division; cuttings.

Comments: Pine-hyacinth is restricted to the moist pinelands of peninsular Florida and, in the graceful charm of its foliage and flowers, is among the most beautiful of native plants. The leaves are remarkably variable, their shape ranging from ovate or elliptical to pinnately divided into thin, linear lobes. These variations in leaf shape may often be found in the same colony or even on the same plant. The solitary, bell-shaped flowers range from almost white to lavender or purple and are pleasingly presented well above the foliage on long, unbranched stalks. Surprisingly, the flowers lack petals; the showy flowers are made up of four petal-like sepals. Although extremely slow-growing, pine-hyacinths live for

many years, the plants becoming larger and more beautiful with age. Propagation by seed requires much patience, since clematis seed often takes a long time to germinate. However, once germination occurs, the young plants will bloom when about six months old. Pine-hyacinths are not related to the true hyacinths, which grow from bulbs, but are instead in the same family as buttercups (*Ranunculus* species) and columbines (*Aquilegia* species).

61. *Cnidoscolus stimulosus*

Common Name: Tread-Softly

Habit: Erect to reclining, tuberous-rooted perennial, forming clumps with age.

Size: Growing to 12 inches tall, forming clumps as wide as or wider than they are tall.

Season: Deciduous northward, evergreen southward; flowering in the spring and summer northward, all year southward.

Maintenance: Annual pruning of old stems.

Motility: Rarely and very slowly spreading by way of self-sown seed.

Growing Conditions: Well-drained to somewhat moist, often sandy sites in full sun; Zones 8–11.

Propagation: Seed.

Comments: Tread-softly's common name is a warning to those who would stomp through this plant's habitat—all parts of the plant, except the petals, are covered with long, glassy,

stinging hairs! In spite of this formidable armature, it makes a lovely addition to the wildflower garden. The foliage is commonly lobed and in some cases the leaves are so finely and deeply divided that they resemble snowflakes. Additionally, some forms have leaves that are variously speckled or marked with silvery spots, which contrast attractively with the dark green of the leaves. These same dark leaves are a perfect foil for the brilliant, pure white flowers that are freely produced over a lengthy flowering season. Tread-softly will always remain a horticultural specialty item. However, as long as it is protected from shading by larger plants and provided with a sunny, well-drained site, it is an easily grown and long-lived wildflower for which the principal horticultural difficulty is finding a source of stock plants.

62. *Commelina erecta*

Common Name: Dayflower; Widow's-Tears
Habit: Sprawling, tuberous-rooted perennial.
Size: Stems 12–18 inches tall, occasionally longer, especially if shaded.
Season: Summer and autumn, but nearly all year in southern Florida.
Maintenance: None in the wild garden; moderate pruning a few times per year for a neater appearance in more formal gardens.
Motility: Moderately spreading in the garden by way of self-sown seeds.
Growing Conditions: Moist to very dry, often sandy areas, in full sun or part shade; Zones 8–10.
Propagation: Seed; division.
Comments: When not in flower, this is not a very distinguished plant since it is characterized by rather long, sprawling stems, sparsely clothed with a few dark green, linear leaves. However, when well-grown and in full flower, it is capable of making a most attractive display of conspicuous pale to dark blue flowers. The flowers are ephemeral, lasting only a few hours in the morning unless the weather is cool or cloudy, in which case they may sometimes last until early afternoon. Normally found in dry sandy areas

in full or nearly full sun, it adapts readily to cultivation, where it will grow even in damp, shady spots. A perfect companion for dayflower is roseling (*Cuthbertia ornata*). The two plants are in the same family, enjoy the same growing conditions, and look great together.

63. *Cuthbertia ornata*

Common Name: Roseling
Habit: Erect, deep-rooted, tough perennial but with a delicate appearance.
Size: Stems 12–18 inches tall.
Season: Spring, summer, and autumn.
Maintenance: Virtually no maintenance other than the occasional removal of an old stem.
Motility: Will very slowly spread by self-sown seed if a large seed crop is set.
Growing Conditions: Well-drained, sandy soil in full or nearly full sun; Zones 8B–10A.
Propagation: Seed; division.
Comments: Given that it is rarely available from native plant nurseries, we are fortunate that this graceful, charming, and attractive wildflower is easily grown from seed, germinating in about four to six weeks. As with many other wildflowers from dry habitats, young plants can be difficult to establish in the ground: if conditions are too wet, they will rot; if too dry, they fail to grow. .However, once they begin to put out new growth, they are far less touchy and are able to withstand extremely dry conditions as well as considerable moisture for short periods. A second species, *Cuthbertia graminea,* occurs in Florida and differs in its shorter stature and usually darker, rose-pink flowers.

64. *Dalea feayi* (synonym: *Petalostemon feayi*)

Common Name: Sandhill Prairie-Clover
Habit: Shrubby, mound-forming perennial.
Size: Plant 12–18 inches tall and about twice as wide.
Season: Flowering in spring and summer.
Maintenance: Occasional light pruning to keep it tidy.
Motility: None or nearly so in most garden situations.
Growing Conditions: Well-drained, often sandy soil, in full sun; Zones 8B–10.
Propagation: Seed.
Comments: This is one instance in which

the plant's common name clearly indicates how it should be grown in cultivation. "Sandhill" appropriately describes its preferred habitat: deep, well-drained sandy soil in full or nearly full sun. Yet, in spite of its specialized habitat preferences, it is relatively easy to grow as long as it is given perfect drainage and a warm, sunny spot. Scarified seed germinates within a few days, and once set out into the garden, the plants are mature and in full flower by their second spring—a time span of approximately fourteen months.

65. *Dicliptera sexangularis* (Synonym: *Dicliptera assurgens*)

Common Name: Six-Angle Dicliptera; False Mint
Habit: Erect, many-branched perennial.
Size: About 2–3 feet tall and nearly as wide.
Season: Flowering during the short days of autumn, winter, and spring.
Maintenance: Annual pruning to the ground of old plants or their removal to be replaced by self-sown seedlings.
Motility: Spreading to all parts of the garden capable of supporting its growth and sometimes weedy as a result of the abundantly produced self-sown seedlings.
Growing Conditions: Moist situations in full sun to deep shade; Zones 8–11.
Propagation: Seed; cuttings.
Comments: Six-angle dicliptera is often recommended for the novice gardener because of three characteristics. First, it is easily grown under a wide variety of conditions. Second, it is easily propagated by seeds or cuttings that root in short order. Last, it bears plentiful red flowers of an unusual shape that are attractive to hummingbirds. However, in addition to these good qualities, it has several bad ones. If not provided with ample moisture, especially when grown in full sun, the plants will be squingy, that is, small and stunted, with the foliage assuming an unattractive yellowish green color. Also, it is a rampant self-seeder that will thickly establish itself in moist corners of the garden. Thus, it is not recommended for new gardens where there is little competition and lots of open space. Two closely related plants, *Dicliptera brachiata* and *Yeatesia viridiflora* (formerly *Dicliptera halei*), have purple or pink flowers and occur in northern Florida. Aside from the difference in flower color, they are apparently horticulturally similar to *Dicliptera sexangularis*.

66. *Dyschoriste oblongifolia*

Common Name: Twinflower
Habit: Erect to sprawling, basally branched perennial forming a small groundcover when well grown.
Size: Stems 8–12 inches long, occasionally longer.

Season: Plant semidormant in winter; flowers borne from late spring through early winter, or all year southward.

Maintenance: Annual pruning of old stems.

Motility: Slowly spreading by underground rhizomes and/or self-sown seed.

Growing Conditions: Dry to moist, often partially sunny situations; Zones 8B–10A.

Propagation: Seeds; cuttings; division.

Comments: There are three species of twinflower in Florida, *Dyschoriste oblongifolia* being the largest and most ornamental species. Even though it is our most robust grower, it is still a small plant and should be grown in groups for best effect. The pale lavender flowers are about an inch in length and, as long as there is sufficient soil moisture, are borne throughout an extended period. The flowers are usually carried in pairs

near the tips of the stems, which accounts for the common name. Cultivation presents no problems whatsoever as long as the plants are not shaded out by taller plants. A vigorous, large-flowered form is presently being distributed by various Florida native plant nurseries and is the form most likely to be encountered in commercial trade. For a similar but more delicate effect, grow *Dyschoriste angusta* or *D. humistrata*. Both are diminutive plants, with the former growing in pinelands and the latter in swamps.

67. *Eryngium yuccifolium*

Common Name: Rattlesnake Master; Button Snakeroot; Button Eryngo

Habit: Perennial with leaves in a basal rosette.

Size: Rosettes about 12–24 inches high; flower stalks 2–5 feet tall.

Season: Leaf rosettes, which resemble a delicate agave, are attractive all year; flowers borne from late spring through the autumn.

Maintenance: Annual pruning of old flowering stems.

Motility: Occasionally spreading by seed into moist, open areas of the garden.

Growing Conditions: Moist, sunny areas free from larger competing plants; Zones 8–10A.

Propagation: Seed; division.

Comments: This unusual plant produces much incredulity among beginning wildflower enthusiasts. Although definitely a member of the carrot family, it bears an uncanny resemblance to a small

yucca or agave. The leaves are broadly linear, tapering to a sharp point, and grow in dense, stemless rosettes. In addition, the veins are parallel, exactly as is to be expected in a yucca or agave. Making the "disguise" complete, the edges of the leaves are sparsely provided with sharp bristles. However, unlike true yuccas and agaves, which are found in arid habitats, rattlesnake master favors moist habitats that are sometimes seasonally inundated, although it is also sometimes found in drier areas. The flower heads are borne on tall, erect stems held well above the foliage, and while each flower is insignificant, they are densely aggregated into attractive, white, rounded heads. Because of its interesting growth form, attractive foliage with silvery green tones, showy flower heads, and ease of cultivation, this is our most ornamental and horticulturally popular species of *Eryngium*. Previously, rattlesnake master was considered to be effective in treating the bites of venomous snakes; this explains the reference to snakes in two of its common names.

68. *Eulophia alta*

Common Name: Wild-Coco

Habit: Robust, tuberous-rooted, terrestrial orchid.

Size: Foliage to 3 feet high; flower stalk to 6 feet high.

Season: Flowering in autumn and winter; plant becoming dormant in spring and reappearing with the summer rains.

Maintenance: Annual removal of old foliage and flower stems just before going dormant.

Motility: Will slowly spread by seed if conditions are suitable.

Growing Conditions: Moist, usually sunny areas; Zones 9A–10.

Propagation: Seed.

Comments: Unlike the vast majority of orchids, wild-coco can reliably be grown from seed. The process is a simple one: merely scatter seed in late winter onto decomposing wood mulch in a moist part of the garden. Almost any type of wood will do; both eucalyptus and melaleuca mulch have been utilized for this purpose with much success. Initial growth is completely subterranean. The plants do not produce any foliage above ground until the middle of summer, at which time their growth is prodigious, especially if there are ample rains. If all conditions are to their liking, seedlings have been known to bloom in their second year, and occasionally even a one-year-old plant may attempt to produce a flower stalk. Surprisingly, in spite of the relative ease and speed with which this orchid may be grown from seed, it is very sensitive to disturbance and is extremely difficult to transplant. Thus, plants should be left to grow where they appear and should be moved only if absolutely necessary.

69. *Flaveria linearis*

Common Name: Yellowtop; False Goldenrod
Habit: Erect to sprawling perennial.
Size: Mostly up to about 2 feet tall and as wide as or wider than it is tall; some forms more erect and bushy and, in cultivation, grow to 3–4 feet tall or taller.
Season: Flowering mostly in the autumn and spring.
Maintenance: Annual pruning to remove old stems and flower stalks.
Motility: Slowly spreading by seed but solitary plants rarely, if ever, form viable seed.
Growing Conditions: Usually moist, open areas in full sun, or sometimes in dry, sandy sites; Zones 8B–11.
Propagation: Seed; cuttings.
Comments: Like many of our more common wildflowers, yellowtop is a vigorous and easily grown addition to the garden. In the wild, it often occurs in wet, sometimes mucky sites. However, it also occurs in dry habitats such as sand dunes, where it withstands prolonged dry spells. Plant habit varies from narrow-leafed, mostly sprawling forms that may be utilized as groundcovers to wide-leafed, subshrubby forms that, under ideal conditions, may grow to 5 feet tall or taller. Plants are splendidly beautiful when in full flower as a result of tiny but numerous brilliant yellow flower heads well displayed on sturdy stalks held above the foliage. Due to its ease of cultivation, ready propagation from cuttings, and pest and drought resis-

tance, yellowtop is highly recommended as a nearly fail-safe beginner's plant.
Special Note: This plant should be handled with care when it is being pruned. Several individuals have reported to me that its sap made their skin photo-sensitive and, upon exposure to sunlight, produced extremely painful blisters.

70. *Glandularia maritima* (Synonym: *Verbena maritima*)

Common Name: Beach-Verbena
Habit: Sprawling perennial that, in cultivation, roots along the stems as it spreads.
Size: Plant 6–8 inches tall and 24 inches or more wide.
Season: Heaviest flowering in the spring with sporadic flowers nearly all year.
Maintenance: None in a wild garden, light pruning in more formal gardens.

Motility: Spreading as a groundcover; casually self-seeding in open areas.
Growing Conditions: Well-drained soil in full sun; Zones 8B–11.
Propagation: Seeds; cuttings; division.
Comments: Beach-verbena is a sprawling groundcover native to coastal situations in peninsular Florida. It bears dark, glossy green leaves and a nearly constant procession of lavender flowers. The early forms first introduced into cultivation were fussy, short-lived plants that promptly died at the first sign of overwatering, yet failed to establish satisfactorily if kept too dry! However, there are now several forms that are reliably perennial and are rather easy to grow in moist but well-drained sandy soil in full sun. These forms are so vigorous that a single plant will readily carpet 1–2 square yards in a single growing season. Apparently, these vigorous forms are the result of inadvertent artificial selection of the original stock.

71. *Habenaria repens*

Common Name: Spider Orchid
Habit: Colonial terrestrial orchid.
Size: Flowering stems 12–18 inches.
Season: Flowering in the summer and autumn.
Maintenance: Occasional removal of old flowering stems.
Motility: Slowly spreading vegetatively by plantlets produced at the ends of the roots; may spread by seed if conditions are suitable.
Growing Conditions: Pond shores, moist grassy areas, and swamps in full sun to partial shade; Zones 8–10.
Propagation: Seeds; division.
Comments: Of the three terrestrial orchids listed in this book, this one is usually the most difficult to grow from seed. On the other hand, the plants themselves are among the easiest of terrestrial orchids to grow. They are tolerant of a wide variety of conditions and demand nothing more than continuously moist soil and freedom from larger, more aggressive plants. If these simple needs are met, a single plant will easily form a large clump of twelve or more growths in about eighteen months. Propagation is merely a matter of dividing the clumps into as many growths as one desires. The small, greenish white flowers are anything but spectacular. However, discerning gardeners welcome their appearance since they are fragrant at night, the best forms having a strong, sweet fragrance similar to that of jasmine.

72. *Helenium flexuosum*

Common Name: Sneezeweed
Habit: Erect perennial from a basal rosette of leaves, much branched above.
Size: Stems 2–3 feet tall.
Season: Flowering in summer and autumn, also in the spring southward.
Maintenance: Annual pruning nearly to the ground of old stems.
Motility: Slowly spreading by seed into moist, open areas, but solitary plants rarely form viable seed.
Growing Conditions: Moist sites in full or nearly full sun; Zones 8–10.
Propagation: Seed; division.
Comments: A reliable and easily grown native, sneezeweed is highly recommended for both the wildflower garden and the perennial flower bed. Plants grow from basal rosettes, from which arise much-branched flowering stems bearing numerous, relatively large, showy flower heads in an eye-catching combination of brilliant yellow and dark chestnut brown. Luckily, this very attractive plant takes readily to cultivation and its propagation is straightforward. It is at its best and most luxuriant in evenly moist soil in full or nearly full sun but will grow under average garden conditions and is tolerant of occasional drought once established. Seed germinates without special treatment, and if started early in the year, seedlings reach their full mature size and bloom in their first summer. As indicated by the common name, *Helenium* species indeed cause sneezing. However, hayfever sufferers have nothing to fear, for in order to induce sneezing, the flower heads must be dried, powdered, and inhaled as snuff.

73. *Helenium pinnatifidum*

Common Name: Glades Sneezeweed
Habit: Perennial from a basal rosette of leaves.
Size: Flower stems 12–24 inches tall.
Season: Flowering mostly in the spring, occasionally in the summer.
Maintenance: Periodic removal of old flower stems.
Motility: Slowly spreading by seed into moist, open areas but solitary plants rarely form viable seed.
Growing Conditions: Moist to wet sites in full sun; Zones 8–10.
Propagation: Seed; division.
Comments: Glades sneezeweed produces a very different horticultural effect than its

cousin *Helenium flexuosum* in the previous description. It too grows from a basal rosette, but there the similarities end. Instead of producing highly branched flowering stems with numerous bicolored flower heads, glades sneezeweed produces an unbranched stem bearing a solitary and very large yellow flower head. However, cultivated plants grown under rich conditions will bear branched flowering stems with up to a dozen or so flower heads. In spite of usually bearing so few flowers per stem, glades sneezeweed is capable of putting on a brilliant show if grown in large numbers, since it flowers over a long period and healthy plants are capable of producing numerous flowering stems. Glades sneezeweed is truly a wetland plant; if not grown in wet soil, it becomes weak and is prone to severe attacks by insects and snails. Savannah sneezeweed (*Helenium vernale*) is similar and has the same garden uses as glades sneezeweed.

74. *Heliotropium curassavicum*

Common Name: Seaside Heliotrope
Habit: Prostrate perennial with striking blue-green foliage; erect forms are sometimes encountered in the Tampa Bay area.
Size: Plant up to about 6 inches tall (to 12 inches tall or taller in erect forms), the stems spreading up to 16 inches.
Season: Evergreen; flowering in the spring and summer, or all year southward.
Maintenance: Occasional light pruning as required to maintain desired size.
Motility: Very rarely spreading by seed.
Growing Conditions: Usually moist, often brackish situations in sandy or rocky soil in full sun; Zones 8B–11.
Propagation: Seed (can be difficult to germinate); cuttings.
Comments: Seaside heliotrope is useful as a dwarf groundcover in coastal areas where salt spray, strong winds, and hot sun make gardening difficult. The plant is fleshy, smooth, and silvery blue in color and has small but brilliant white flowers that contrast well with the foliage. These traits combine to create a distinctive and ornamental effect different from that of most native plants and to make seaside heliotrope a good candidate for a native white or silver garden. It will adapt to average garden conditions, but rich soil and too much shade lead to poor growth and susceptibility to pests.

75. *Heliotropium polyphyllum*

Common Name: Pineland Heliotrope
Habit: Partly erect to completely prostrate perennial.
Size: Plant 6–12 inches tall (prostrate forms only 1–3 inches tall); stems 6–18 inches long.

Season: Flowering all year or, in northern Florida, only in the autumn.

Maintenance: Annual pruning to the ground in late winter or early spring in order to maintain a neat appearance.

Motility: Can slowly form large patches in cultivation from root suckers; very slowly spreading by self-sown seed.

Growing Conditions: Rather dry to moist soil in full or nearly full sun; Zones 8–11.

Propagation: Seed (can be difficult to germinate); cuttings.

Comments: Pineland heliotrope grows in a wide variety of habitats, including sandy coasts, prairies, flatwoods, and rocky pinelands. Occasionally, it is also observed along the drier, upland side of mangrove swamps, especially along the sunny edges where there has been some disturbance, such as from road building. In spite of having very small flowers, it is one of Florida's most gloriously beautiful wildflowers, for a single plant may bear hundreds, or even thousands, of snowy white or brilliant yellow flowers at one time. With just a little coddling in cultivation, magnificent specimens are formed that quickly grow to a large size and become a focal point of the garden. Moreover, the innumerable flowers attract a variety of nectar-seeking insects, including butterflies. Horticulturally, its principal flaws are that seeds are difficult to germinate and plants grow from a deep woody root system, making mature plants often difficult to transplant. Fortunately, cuttings are not too difficult to root, and the self-sown seedlings that appear now and then may readily be transplanted if this is done while they are still small.

76. *Hibiscus aculeatus*

Common Name: Pineland Hibiscus

Habit: Large perennial, seemingly shrubby but dying to the ground in winter.

Size: Plant 2–3 feet tall and at least as wide or wider.

Season: Flowers borne from late spring through autumn.

Maintenance: Annual pruning to the ground as the plant goes dormant in the autumn; seed pods can detract from tidy appearance.

Motility: Casually spreading by self-sown seed.
Growing Conditions: Moist sites in full sun to partial shade; Zones 8–9.
Propagation: Seed; cuttings.
Comments: Pineland hibiscus, sleepy hibiscus (*Hibiscus furcellatus*), and fairy hibiscus (*Hibiscus poepeggii*) are the native hibiscus best suited for average or even slightly dry garden conditions. With age, pineland hibiscus forms multiple stems from near ground level and assumes the aspect of a small, spreading shrub. However, it is a perennial that dies down in winter. Thus, one must take care with its placement and remember that it will all but disappear when dormant. Pineland hibiscus is easily distinguished from all other native hibiscus by its deeply five-lobed leaves and creamy yellow flowers with a dark purplish-red eye.

77. Hibiscus coccineus

Common Name: Scarlet Hibiscus
Habit: Large, stout, erect perennial.
Size: Stems 5–6 feet tall or taller if grown under very rich conditions.
Season: Flowering in late spring and summer; plant dormant in winter.
Maintenance: Annual pruning to the ground as the plant goes dormant in the autumn; seed pods can detract from tidy appearance.
Motility: Slowly spreading by self-sown seed in wet open sites.
Growing Conditions: Wet sites in full sun to partial shade; Zones 8–10.
Propagation: Seed; cuttings.
Comments: Scarlet hibiscus is one of the floral glories of the southeastern United States. The plant itself is attractive and distinctive with its smooth, hairless stems and leaves, foliage that is deeply divided into five sharply pointed lobes, and huge, brilliant red flowers. Of course, like all deep red flowers, it is extremely attractive to hummingbirds, and it is specifically adapted to attract these feathered jewels. In nature, it nearly always grows in very wet soils; it does poorly if planted in a hot, dry spot. Recently, an albino form has been introduced into cultivation. This form is wholly green, without any trace of red pigments in its stems or foliage, and bears striking pure white flowers.

78. Hibiscus furcellatus

Common Name: Sleepy Hibiscus
Habit: Large, erect perennial, some forms becoming woody shrubs.
Size: Plant 5–6 feet tall, the shrubby forms often as wide as tall.
Season: Flowering most of the year except during the height of summer.

Maintenance: Judicious pruning to keep it tidy; seed pods can detract from its appearance.

Motility: Producing few to abundant seedlings, usually close to the parent plant.

Growing Conditions: Dry to wet open sites in full sun or light shade; Zones 9B–10A.

Propagation: Seed; cuttings.

Comments: Sleepy hibiscus is a tropical species that occurs in southern Florida, the West Indies, and South America. Thus, it is not adapted to seasonally cold climates. It will grow year-round in southern Florida, eventually forming a large, coarse, woody shrub. Although usually growing in very moist or

wet soils, sleepy hibiscus is surprisingly drought tolerant, and plants have been observed growing quite happily in sandy, scrubby areas. Its common name is derived from its pendant, pink, funnel-shaped flowers. Like scarlet hibiscus (*Hibiscus coccineus*), sleepy hibiscus is adapted for hummingbird pollination; the inverted, bell-shaped flowers are probably an adaptation to facilitate access by hummingbirds but keeps other pollinators away.

79. *Hibiscus laevis* (Synonym: *Hibiscus militaris*)

Common Name: Halberd-Leaf Hibiscus

Habit: Large perennial, often shrubby but dying to the ground in winter.

Size: Stems 5–6 feet tall.

Season: Flowering in summer; dormant in winter.

Maintenance: Annual pruning to the ground as the plant goes dormant in the autumn; seed pods can detract from tidy appearance.

Motility: Producing few to abundant seedlings, usually close to the parent plant.

Growing Conditions: Wet sites in full sun to partial shade; Zones 8.

Propagation: Seed; cuttings.

Comments: Halberd-leaf hibiscus is a large, shrubby plant readily identified by its distinctively three-lobed leaves. The leaf bases bear a short lobe on each side, the two side lobes usually sticking out perpendicular to the elongated central lobe of the leaf. The large, exquisitely beautiful flowers vary from pure white to dark pink, with all color forms possessing a maroon "bull's-eye" in the center of the flower. Halberd-leaf hibiscus was long known as *Hibiscus militaris*.

The name was appropriate since the leaf shape closely resembles a halberd, a type of spearlike weapon utilized in early warfare.

80. *Hibiscus moscheutos*

Common Name: Rose-Mallow
Habit: Large, erect perennial.
Size: Stems 5–6 feet tall.
Season: Flowering in summer.
Maintenance: Annual pruning to the ground as the plant goes dormant in the autumn; seed pods can detract from tidy appearance.
Motility: Producing few to abundant seedlings, usually close to the parent plant.
Growing Conditions: Wet sites in full sun to partial shade; Zones 8–9.
Propagation: Seed; cuttings.
Comments: Rose-mallow is similar in habit and appearance to swamp hibiscus (*Hibiscus grandiflorus*). However, whereas the latter has pink flowers, rose-mallow has white or pale creamy yellow flowers with a dark maroon eye. Because of its large, very flat flowers, rose-mallow has been extensively utilized in hybridizing, and it is one of the principal parents of a striking line of dwarf, huge-flowered hybrid hibiscus cold hardy as far north as New York.

81. *Hibiscus poepeggii* (Synonym: *Hibiscus pilosus*)

Common Name: Fairy Hibiscus
Habit: Evergreen, subwoody perennial or dwarf shrub.
Size: Plant 2–4 feet tall, occasionally up to 6 feet tall.
Season: Flowering essentially all year.
Maintenance: Judicious pruning to keep its appearance tidy; removal of old, opened seed pods.
Motility: Producing few to abundant seedlings, usually close to the parent plant.
Growing Conditions: Full sun to part shade in moist soil; Zones 10–11.
Propagation: Seed; cuttings.
Comments: Florida's smallest hibiscus is a thoroughly charming, much-branched little shrub with tiny dark green leaves. The exquisite deep red flowers are pendant on fine stalks. Thus, a plant in full bloom is reminiscent of a diminutive Christmas tree

adorned with red ornaments. The flowers are followed by small capsules about the same size and shape as an olive, and these too lend an ornamental effect to the plant. The dry, opened seed pods are not very attractive and, when borne in large numbers, detract from the plant's tidy appearance. Readily adapting to cultivation, it will grow well under average garden conditions and has moderate salt tolerance. North of its natural range, it may be grown as an annual. This species also makes a perfect little pot plant and will flower freely in a 4- or 6-inch pot when only 12–18 inches tall.

82. *Hypoxis juncea*

Common Name: Yellow Star-Grass
Habit: Dwarf perennial growing from an underground, bulblike corm.
Size: Flower stems about 6 inches tall.
Season: Flowering from spring through autumn.
Maintenance: None.
Motility: None, or essentially none, under average garden conditions.
Growing Conditions: Moist, usually sandy sites in full sun; Zones 8–10A.
Propagation: Seed.
Comments: Yellow star-grass has leaves that are reduced to thin, wiry green threads and seem scarcely able to photosynthesize enough food to produce the relatively large, bright yellow flowers that are borne over a long period. Plants are self-sterile. Two or more genetically distinct clones must be cross-pollinated if seed is to be obtained. This is the most ornamental of Florida's five star-grasses, but because of the small size of the plants, it should be grown in fairly large groups for best effect. Yellow star-grass rarely, if ever, forms offsets from the bulbs. Thus it cannot be propagated by division, and seed is the only practical means of producing more plants.

83. *Iris hexagona*

Common Name: Dixie Iris
Habit: Large, rhizomatous perennial with erect fans of leaves.
Size: Plant about 3 feet tall, the flower stems taller.
Season: Flowering in the spring.
Maintenance: Pruning of old flower stems and seed pods.
Motility: Vegetatively forming large clumps; moderately spreading by seed in wet, open areas.
Growing Conditions: Swamps and wet meadows in full sun to partial shade; Zones 8B–10A.
Propagation: Seed; division.

Comments: Dixie iris is Florida's most widespread native iris, a large, bold plant accompanied by equally large and attractive flowers in a variety of blue shades. A white-flowered form is occasionally available from specialty nurseries. One of its common names, prairie iris, is somewhat of a misnomer since it is associated with a wide variety of habitats, including wet ditches, moist meadows, pond margins, and swamps. Its occurrence in swamps indicates that it will grow in shade. However, under shady conditions it is not nearly as free-flowering as when growing in full sun. As a consequence of its beautiful flowers and ease of propagation by division, it is readily available in the nursery trade and is extensively utilized in wetland restorations and as an accent plant in wet areas. Its only negative points are its short flowering season in the spring and its large ultimate size, the latter generally precluding its use in smaller gardens.

84. *Justicia angusta*

Common Name: Pineland Water-Willow
Habit: Erect perennial spreading by underground rhizomes.
Size: Stems about 12 inches tall.
Season: Flowering from spring through autumn.
Maintenance: None.
Motility: Slowly spreading by way of subterranean rhizomes.
Growing Conditions: Moist to wet soil in full sun or light shade; Zones 8–10.
Propagation: Seed; cuttings; division.
Comments: Pineland water-willow is a delightful wetland plant of delicate and graceful form. The upper axils produce elongated, loosely flowered spikes. The charming, exotically shaped flowers vary from white to deep lavender-pink and are marked with deeper purple and white. Plants are easily grown if provided moist soil, and they form loose colonies from underground rhizomes. Because of the rambling rhizomes, the plant is not suited for formal gardens, but it is perfect for the informal wildflower garden, wet ditches, and pond margins. Plants may be grown in pots, but sooner or later the rhizomes begin to circle the pot and new growths are then produced only along the rim of the pot.

85. *Lachnanthes caroliana*

Common Name: Redroot
Habit: Stout, erect perennial.
Size: Plants about 2–3 feet tall, the flowering stems about a foot taller.
Season: Flowering in summer and autumn.
Maintenance: Removal of old flowering stems and seed heads.
Motility: Colonial by underground rhizome and filling as large an area as is available to it.

Growing Conditions: Moist to wet situations in full sun to rather deep shade; Zones 8–10.

Propagation: Seed (sow immediately); division.

Comments: Redroot ranges widely in eastern North America, from Nova Scotia to southernmost Florida and east to Louisiana. Vegetatively the plant resembles an iris, but the peculiar greenish yellow flowers, which are loosely covered with whitish woolly hairs, quickly give away its true identity. It is easily cultivated in moist soil in both shade and full sun, and the plants are tough almost to the point of being indestructible. However, they will cover much ground because of the creeping rhizome and must be constrained in smaller gardens. Redroot is easily propagated by division of the rhizome or from seed. For best results, seed should be sown as soon as possible after maturity since it quickly becomes inviable. While not spectacularly beautiful, redroot is an easily grown addition to the wildflower garden; makes an unusual, fast-growing pot plant; and is useful in native plant restoration projects.

86. *Liatris chapmanii*

Common Name: Chapman's Gayfeather; Chapman's Blazingstar

Habit: Erect perennial growing from a tuberous root.

Size: Flowering stems 1–3 feet tall.

Season: Flowering in late summer and autumn.

Maintenance: Annual pruning of old stems nearly to the ground.

Motility: Spreading by self-sown seed, but solitary plants rarely form viable seed.

Growing Conditions: Sandy, well-drained soil in full sun; Zones 8–10.

Propagation: Seed.

Comments: Florida possesses fourteen species of *Liatris*, a moderately large group of showy perennials occurring in a variety of open, sunny habitats. Horticulturally, they may be divided into two groups: those that favor dry areas and those that favor moist or even wet sites. Chapman's gayfeather belongs to the former group and is highly recommended for gardens with well-drained sandy soils. The bright pink flower heads are individually small but are borne in such large numbers that this species produces a spectacular show in late summer or early autumn, especially when growing in large colonies. Like all blazingstars, it is easily propagated from its quickly germinating seeds and, with good cultural practices, reaches flowering size its first year.

87. *Liatris garberi*

Common Name: Pineland Gayfeather; Pineland Blazingstar
Habit: Erect perennial growing from a tuberous root.
Size: Stems 2–3 feet, up to 6 feet tall in cultivation if grown in too rich a soil.
Season: Flowering in autumn or early winter.
Maintenance: Annual pruning nearly to the ground of plants that have gone to seed.
Motility: Readily spreading by self-sown seed in open, sunny areas of the garden.
Growing Conditions: Well-drained but usually moist, often sandy soil, in full sun to light shade; Zones 9–10.
Propagation: Seed.
Comments: All species of *Liatris* make desirable garden subjects if given a level of soil moisture that matches that of their natural habitat. Pineland gayfeather is highly recommended for the beginning wildflower enthusiast since it is a highly adaptable species that is easily grown under a rather wide variety of garden conditions. It is equally at home in rocky pinelands and in somewhat moist sandy flatwoods. Its principal flaw is that, like all *Liatris,* it produces numerous disproportionately long and floppy stems if grown in too rich a site.

88. *Liatris tenuifolia*

Common Name: Grassleaf Gayfeather
Habit: Densely clumping perennial growing from a tuberous root.
Size: Basal clumps of leaves up to about 1 foot tall and usually as wide or wider, the flowering stems 2–3 feet long (or much longer in cultivation if grown in too rich a soil).
Season: Flowering in the summer, autumn, or early winter.
Maintenance: Annual pruning nearly to the ground of plants that have gone to seed.
Motility: Readily spreading by self-sown seed in open, sunny areas of the garden.
Growing Conditions: Well-drained but usually moist, often sandy soil, in full sun to light shade; Zones 8–10.
Propagation: Seed.
Comments: Grassleaf gayfeather has small flower heads and one of the narrowest inflorescences of any *Liatris* species. Therefore, it does not produce as spectacular a display as do some of our other blazingstars. It is still worthy of cultivation, however, on the basis of its interesting and unusual growth form. Like other *Liatris* species, it arises from a tuberous root, but it is distinct in its ex-

tremely narrow, grasslike leaves. Older, well-grown plants form large clumps of leaves that look much like clumps of grass. For the best effect, grow grassleaf gayfeather in large masses of at least one dozen plants and interplant it with true grasses. Its thin wands of pink flowers will provide a cheery and colorful accent among the golden browns, tans, and golds of the grasses' flowers.

89. *Lindernia grandiflora*

Common Name: Angel's-Tears
Habit: Dwarf, sprawling perennial forming a flat carpet of foliage.
Size: Plant only 1–2 inches tall but forming mats 6–24 inches in diameter.
Season: Flowering mainly in the spring, but sporadic throughout the year.
Maintenance: None.
Motility: Spreading by creeping stems that root wherever they touch the ground.
Growing Conditions: Moist ground in full shade to full sun; Zones 8B–10A.
Propagation: Seed; cuttings; division.
Comments: Angel's-tears is a sprawling little plant that will cover surprisingly large patches of moist, open ground. The white flowers have a greatly reduced upper lip, while the lower lip consists of three large lobes, each of which bears two dark blue or purple spots. The flowers are large for the size of the plant and are abundantly produced in the spring and more sparingly nearly throughout the rest of the year. The plant is not suitable for formal garden schemes because of its tendency to cover as much open ground as is available to it. However, it makes an ideal groundcover for an otherwise difficult but moist, sunny spot. Additionally, it makes an attractive little pot plant and has been used as a miniature hanging-basket plant.

90. *Lobelia glandulosa*

Common Name: Glades Lobelia
Habit: Stout, erect or reclining perennial.
Size: Stems 3–4 feet tall in full flower.
Season: Flowering mainly in the autumn but sporadically the rest of the year, especially southward.
Maintenance: Annual pruning nearly to the ground of old flowering stems.
Motility: Essentially none under typical garden conditions.

Growing Conditions: Moist or wet situations in full sun to partial shade; Zones 8–11.

Propagation: Seed; cuttings; division.

Comments: Glades lobelia is representative of a large number of Florida's lobelias: erect plants about 1–3 feet high with showy flowers about 1 inch long in shades of lavender, blue, or violet. Growing throughout the state, it may be distinguished by its leafy stems and linear leaves, often more than twelve times as long as they are wide. Like other members of the genus, it is easily grown from seed and will flower its first year if started early enough. It is an attractive plant that possesses much charm in its unusual form and the blue of its flowers. While it is often overlooked in the wild, large, older plants in cultivation may produce numerous stems bearing large quantities of flowers; in full bloom, it is splendid.

91. *Lygodesmia aphylla*

Common Name: Rose-Rush

Habit: Erect, nearly leafless perennial.

Size: Stems 18–24 inches tall.

Season: Flowering spring through summer, or into the autumn in southern Florida.

Maintenance: None.

Motility: Casually spreading by self-sown seed, but solitary plants rarely form viable seed.

Growing Conditions: Well-drained, usually sandy soil, in full sun; Zones 8–10.

Propagation: Seed.

Comments: In its very best forms, this is an unusually attractive and distinctive wildflower. Plants consist of a few tough, wiry, dark green, leafless or nearly leafless stems that bear pink, or rarely white, dandelion-like flower heads. Large-flowered, dark pink forms would be welcome additions to the wild garden; however, rose-rush will probably always remain a horticultural specialty item rarely available from nurseries. Although fresh seed germinates readily and grows well if given deep, well-drained soils, the plants do not always take kindly to pot culture. Additionally, if not in flower, a pot with a few wiry, leafless stems can scarcely be expected to have much appeal to the gardening public. In the garden, however, its growth habit is a decided bonus, since the stems merge into the background and the flower heads appear to float in the air.

92. *Lythrum alatum* var. *lanceolatum*

Common Name: Winged Loosestrife

Habit: Erect, much-branched, often shrubby perennial.

Size: Plant 2–3 feet tall and often nearly as wide or wider.

Season: Flowering in summer.

Maintenance: Annual pruning to keep it tidy.

Motility: Somewhat colonial by way of underground rhizomes; viable seed not usually formed by solitary garden plants.

Growing Conditions: Moist to wet soil in full sun or light shade; Zones 8B–10.

Propagation: Seed; cuttings.

Comments: At maturity, winged loosestrife forms a shrubby, much-branched perennial with small leaves and a large quantity of starry little pink flowers. Although individually small, they are borne in large numbers and produce a hazy pink effect that is simultaneously showy yet delicate and graceful. In full flower, the nectar-rich blossoms are tended by a large and varied assortment of colorful insects, a feature adding to the plant's usefulness and interest in the wildflower garden. If provided with moist soils, plants are easily cultivated, and they are thus eminently suitable for difficult garden situations such as wet ditches and pond margins.

93. *Mecardonia acuminata*

Common Name: Pixie-Foxglove

Habit: Dwarf perennial, erect when young but eventually sprawling with age.

Size: Plant about 6 inches tall and as wide or wider.

Season: Flowering all year whenever warm, moist conditions prevail.

Maintenance: None in the wild garden, otherwise periodic severe pruning to keep it tidy.

Motility: Colonizing moist, open areas by self-sown seedlings.

Growing Conditions: Moist to wet soil in full sun or light shade; Zones 8–11.

Propagation: Seed; cuttings; division.

Comments: Florida has a vast assemblage of small, overlooked, often trodden-upon little plants that are usually derisively dismissed as being only of botanical interest. However, many such plants turn out to be diminutive treasures that reward closer scrutiny and merit more extensive cultivation. One such plant is pixie-foxglove, an appealing and easily grown little member of the snapdragon family. At first growing rigidly erect, it soon spreads horizontally and makes a charming groundcover. Pixie-foxglove is also perfect for use as a pot plant with its tiny gray-green leaves spilling over the edge of a pot. The small, white, trumpet-shaped flowers with pale pink lines in the throat are produced nearly all year. Although pixie-foxglove occurs in moist sites or even in shallow standing water, it readily adapts to average garden conditions.

94. *Mimosa strigillosa*

Common Name: Sunshine Mimosa; Powderpuff
Habit: Prostrate, carpeting perennial.
Size: Plant 6–9 inches tall but covering many square feet.
Season: Flowering in spring and summer.
Maintenance: None.
Motility: Spreading by its widely creeping stems, which tend to root wherever they touch the ground.
Growing Conditions: Well-drained to moist soil in full sun; Zones 8B–10A.
Propagation: Seed; division.
Comments: In all respects except one, this is an exquisite and desirable ornamental of great charm and beauty. The foliage is divided into tiny leaflets of a lovely bluish green, and the leaflets are remarkably sensitive to disturbance, folding up within a second or two of being handled. The speed with which this is accomplished matches that of the commonly cultivated, non-native sensitive plant *Mimosa pudica*. The flower heads are intricate works of floral art. Rather large for the size of the plant, they consist of rounded pompoms of numerous prominent, bright pink stamens, each tipped with a bit of golden pollen. The visual effect of a large plant studded with dozens of these magnificent pink powderpuffs is stunning. Although it reaches its fullest development when growing on moist, sunny banks, sunshine mimosa is drought tolerant once established and will grow in rather dry, sandy areas. Propagation is easily accomplished since the tiniest piece of rooted stem will prove sufficient in starting another plant. In formal gardens, it does have one drawback: its creeping stems blanket large areas, and it is difficult to keep the plant within bounds in a small garden. The large trees with the common name of mimosa belong to a different genus (*Albizia*) in the same family; however, they are not at all closely related to members of the genus *Mimosa*.

95. *Opuntia humifusa*

Common Name: Prickly-Pear
Habit: Erect to more or less sprawling succulent perennial.
Size: Height extremely variable from 1 to 3 feet tall, the plants usually as wide or wider than they are tall.
Season: Flowering in the spring.
Fruit: Large, fleshy, many-seeded berry.
Maintenance: None.
Motility: None unless the pads are dislodged by garden visitors or animals.
Growing Conditions: Well-drained sandy soil in full sun; Zones 8–11.
Propagation: Seed; cuttings.

Comments: Perhaps because it is so common and "ordinary," Florida's most widespread and abundant native cactus is rarely cultivated except by the most ardent of native plant enthusiasts. This is regrettable since it is an easily grown, nearly indestructible plant with many horticulturally useful properties. First, of course, is its interesting growth form of spiny, succulent pads. In spring, these are adorned with remarkably large and beautiful flowers with silken petals in

shades of palest creamy yellow to dark intense golden yellow. For added interest, the flowers attract a range of unusually interesting and often colorful insects. Finally, late in the year the plants are adorned a second time, but now with highly ornamental fruit that ripens to various shades of pink to wine red, often with a purplish blush. As an added bonus, though care is needed to remove the barbed hairlike spines, the fruits are edible. For propagation one need merely bury the end of a pad lightly in sandy soil in full sun to start a new plant.

96. *Penstemon multiflorus*

Common Name: White Beardtongue
Habit: Tall, erect perennial arising from a basal rosette of grayish green leaves.
Size: Flowering stems 3–4 feet tall or taller.
Season: Flowering in the spring and summer.
Maintenance: Periodic removal of old flowering stems that have gone to seed.
Motility: Essentially none under most garden conditions.
Growing Conditions: Mostly well-drained soils in full sun or light shade; Zones 8–10.
Propagation: Seed; cuttings; division.
Comments: This is yet another native wildflower that is as suited to the wild garden as it is to perennial flower beds or cottage-garden-style borders. It can, however, be somewhat temperamental while becoming established in the garden and is rather easily lost if kept too wet or too dry. Luckily, after it is established, it tolerates a greater range of conditions. Best results are usually obtained by starting with young seedlings that can be acclimated to

your garden's conditions at an early age. Seed can be tricky and difficult to germinate, but one successful method is to scatter fresh seed onto well-prepared ground in late spring or early summer. With the onset of autumn thunderstorms and cooler weather, the seed germinates, and with little effort, a large number of seedlings may be produced. For smaller gardens, one may utilize southern beardtongue (*Penstemon australis*), a low-growing plant with purplish pink flowers.

97. *Peperomia obtusifolia*

Common Name: Broadleaf Peperomia; Baby-Rubberplant
Habit: Fleshy-leaved, groundcovering perennial with creeping stems.
Size: Plant about 6–9 inches tall but stems spreading to 12–24 inches long.
Season: Attractive all year as a foliage plant or groundcover; flowers inconspicuous.
Maintenance: Occasional light pruning to keep it within bounds.
Motility: Slowly spreading by creeping stems and eventually covering large areas.
Growing Conditions: Moist but well-drained sites in dappled shade; Zones 9B–10.
Propagation: Leaf cuttings; stem cuttings; division.
Comments: Broadleaf peperomia is commonly grown as a houseplant in the northern United States, but ironically, as a wild plant it is an endangered species in Florida. Along with the closely related *Peperomia magnoliifolia,* it has the largest leaves of any member of the genus and makes a beautiful groundcovering landscape plant. The large, glossy, deep green leaves are somewhat succulent and allow the plant to withstand significant dry spells. It prefers well-drained organic soils in partial shade. However, it will grow in dense shade and, if planted in a moist site, will also grow in full sun. Of course, it may be grown as a potted plant or houseplant and will tolerate much abuse and adversity.

98. *Phlox pilosa*

Common Name: Downy Phlox
Habit: Sprawling perennial.
Size: Plant 12–18 inches tall and twice as wide or wider.
Season: Heavy flowering in the spring; sporadic flowers produced into the autumn in cultivation.
Maintenance: Pruning old stems to the ground at the end of the summer.
Motility: None or essentially none under most garden conditions.

Growing Conditions: Well-drained soil in full sun to partial shade; Zones 8–9.

Propagation: Seed; cuttings; division.

Comments: The genus *Phlox* is one of North America's greatest gifts to the world of horticulture, and Floridians should count it as their good fortune that downy phlox, one of the most beautiful, easily grown, and adaptable species of phlox, is native to our state. Throughout the cool season, it forms sizable, groundcovering clumps of foliage. In the spring, the foliage is literally smothered under a mass of exquisitely beautiful flowers in various shades of pink. In the northern part of its range, the show ends there, but in southern Florida the plants continue to bloom, although with far less vigor, throughout the summer and into the autumn. By the time cooler weather returns, the plants look haggard and tired, ready to be cut back to the ground to start the process again for yet another season of glorious blossoms come spring.

99. *Piloblephis rigida*

Common Name: Wild-Pennyroyal

Habit: Spreading, densely branched, shrublike perennial.

Size: Plant 12–18 inches tall and about twice as wide or wider.

Season: Spring, sometimes with sporadic flowers in the autumn.

Maintenance: Light pruning to maintain tidy appearance; complete removal of old plants.

Motility: None, or essentially none.

Growing Conditions: Well-drained, but often moist soil, in full sun to light shade; Zones 8B–0.

Propagation: Seed; cuttings (these root with ease).

Comments: Wild-pennyroyal, the sole member of the genus *Piloblephis,* occurs only in peninsular Florida and on a few western islands of the Bahama archipelago. It is an attractive shrubby perennial with all parts of the plant having a strong minty fragrance and clothed with short, erect white hairs resulting in a hoary, grayish color. Its small leaves, densely branching habit,

and grayish aspect combine to produce an effect reminiscent of certain dwarf groundcovering conifers. The pale to dark pink (or rarely pure white or violet) flowers are attractively marked with tiny violet spots and are enjoyed by many insects, including butterflies. Currently, it has much popularity, both as a native xeriscape plant and as a herb garden plant tolerant of Florida's torrid summers. It will readily grow and flower prodigiously in a variety of garden situations so long it is in a sunny, well-drained spot. Its only fault is a tendency for the plants to exhaust themselves in cultivation and die out in a few years. Luckily, cuttings root with ease and serve as a convenient means of producing young plants to replace the parents.

100. *Piriqueta caroliniana*

Common Names: Morning-Buttercup; Piriquet; Piriqueta

Habit: Extremely showy, erect to sprawling perennial.

Size: Variable, the stems reaching 6 to 18 inches in length, depending on the form and growing conditions.

Season: Spring through autumn, or all year southward.

Maintenance: Pruning to the ground once or twice a year to maintain a tidy appearance.

Motility: Slowly spreading by subterranean rhizomes; moderately spreading by self-sown seedlings.

Growing Conditions: Moist to dry sites in full sun to very light shade; Zones 8–11.

Propagation: Seed; division; cuttings (these root in 7–10 days without special treatment).

Comments: This widespread and adaptable plant takes readily to cultivation. For the best effect, it should be grown in groups of several plants in moist but well-drained soil, in full sun, and without competition from larger and more aggressive plants. Three varieties are found in Florida and they may be distinguished by their habitat, growth form, and foliage. The typical variety (*Piriqueta caroliniana* var. *caroliniana*) is a hairless or nearly hairless plant growing in a wide range of open habitats, from moist flatwoods to rather dry, sandy areas. Growing in coastal sites is *P. caroliniana* var. *glabra,* a completely hairless plant with thickened fleshy leaves. The third form, *P. caroliniana* var. *tomentosa,* is usually found in well-drained rocky sites and is easily distinguished by its grayish leaves, which are densely covered with fine hairs. Piriquet is sometimes avidly eaten by caterpillars of the gulf fritillary (*Dione vanillae nigrior*), especially if their normal larval food plant, passion-vines, is not available.

101. *Pityopsis graminifolia* (Synonym: *Chrysopsis graminifolia; Heterotheca graminifolia*)

Common Name: Silky Golden-Aster
Habit: Highly variable clump-forming perennial, delicate or robust depending on the genetic form.
Size: Extremely variable, from 6 to 36 inches tall; old plants as wide as they are tall or wider.
Season: Silvery green foliage is attractive most of the year; flowering is variable but heaviest bloom tends to be in the spring and autumn.
Maintenance: Annual pruning of old stems.
Motility: Moderately spreading by seed, but solitary plants rarely form viable seed; some forms slowly spreading and forming loose colonies from underground rhizomes.
Growing Conditions: Dry to moist sites in light shade to full sun; Zones 8–11.
Propagation: Seed; division.
Comments: Silky golden-aster derives its name from the covering of soft, pure white hairs that clothe the plant. Some plants are so densely covered with these hairs that the leaves are silvery white and, in full sun, have a shiny, almost metallic look. When competition from other plants is high, silky golden-aster grows as a small plant with only one or two stems topped with several brilliant yellow flower heads. However, if given ample room to itself, as in some garden settings, it produces numerous stems to form large, dense clumps. Such plants are impressive in full bloom and spectacular when grown in large masses. Silky golden-aster is a particularly showy and easy-to-grow native wildflower and is highly recommended for the beginning native gardener. Fresh seed germinates readily, and if started in the spring, the young plants will flower by autumn, if not earlier.

102. *Polygala grandiflora*

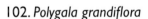

Common Name: Big-Flowered Candyroot
Habit: Erect to spreading perennial.
Size: Plant 8–12 inches tall.
Season: Flowering in spring and summer, or all year southward.
Maintenance: Annual pruning to maintain a tidy appearance.
Motility: Moderately spreading by self-sown seed.
Growing Conditions: Extremely variable but nearly always in open sunny situations; Zones 8–11.

Propagation: Seed.

Comments: This plant is a dwarf perennial with long spikes of purplish or rosy flowers. It is one of the more common species of *Polygala* and occurs in a wide variety of habitats throughout Florida, including such unlikely places as cracks in urban sidewalks. The specific epithet means "large-flowered." However, the flowers are less than half an inch wide—they are large only in relation to our other native *Polygala* species. Usually unfairly overlooked because it is so common, this one assumes a quaint and subtle beauty in the garden, where cultivated plants develop into large, many-stemmed clumps that may be in continuous bloom from earliest spring to late autumn, or even year-round in southern Florida. For an especially pleasing effect, combine the dainty and tiny rosy pink flowers of this species with the brilliant yellow flowers of *Coreopsis leavenworthii, Heliotropium polyphyllum,* or *Piriqueta caroliniana.* When crushed, the roots have a slight wintergreen fragrance, hence the name candyroot.

103. *Polygonella polygama*

Common Name: Showy Jointweed
Habit: Erect to sprawling perennial, depending on the form.
Size: Highly variable, 12–36 inches tall or taller, often as wide.
Season: Flowering in summer and autumn.
Maintenance: Annual pruning to remove old flowering stems.
Motility: Slowly establishing large colonies by self-sown seed in open sandy areas.

Growing Conditions: Well-drained sandy soil in full sun; Zones 8–10.
Propagation: Seed.
Comments: Ordinarily, this is a quiet little plant with subtly attractive grayish green or blue-green foliage but otherwise wholly lacking in horticultural interest. But what a transformation when it is in full flower! The tiny pure white flowers are individually insignificant,

but they are borne in such profusion that they look like patches of snow in the otherwise hot, sandy habitats that showy jointweed favors. Unfortunately, these are not easy plants to grow well in cultivation. They have a tendency to lose their roots in heavy, wet soils, yet, paradoxically, they can be difficult to establish if kept even a little too dry. Attempts are presently being made to introduce into cultivation plants from dryish pine flatwoods, in the hope that these will be more amenable to cultivation than the plants occurring in sand scrub.

104. *Polygonella robusta*

Common Name: Sandhill Wireweed
Habit: Erect or spreading perennial.
Size: Plant 15–24 inches tall and usually about as wide.
Season: Flowering in summer and autumn.
Maintenance: Annual pruning to remove old flowering stems.
Motility: Slowly establishing large colonies by self-sown seed in open sandy areas.
Growing Conditions: Well-drained sandy soil in full sun; Zones 8B–10A.
Propagation: Seed.
Comments: Sandhill wireweed puts on a remarkable and dazzling display in the autumn in moderately disturbed, open sandy situations. Under these conditions sizable colonies are formed, with each plant producing large, solid spikes of pristine white flowers that slowly and gradually age to palest blush pink or deep rose, depending on the plant's genetic background and the weather conditions. As with the preceding species, sandhill wireweed requires deep, sandy soil with perfect drainage. However, seed is abundantly produced and is reportedly not difficult to germinate. Thus, it is well worth the effort to try to grow if one can provide it with a suitable location in the garden.

105. *Pterocaulon pycnostachyum* (previously confused with and referred to as *Pterocaulon virgatum,* a name that applies to a different species)

Common Name: Blackroot
Habit: Erect or sprawling perennial growing from dark, tuberous roots.
Size: Plant 1–2 feet tall.
Season: Foliage attractive nearly all year; flowering in the spring, extending to autumn southward.
Maintenance: Annual pruning to improve appearance and remove old flowering stems.
Motility: Sparingly spreading by self-sown seed.

Growing Conditions: Well-drained sites, often disturbed, in full sun to deep shade; Zones 8–11.

Propagation: Seed.

Comments: Blackroot has a quiet, subtle charm. Certainly it does not possess showy flowers. Indeed, the peculiar spikes of creamy flower heads are much more odd than they are attractive. So why grow blackroot? For one thing, it is an easily grown and nearly indestructible wildflower that will thrive under a wide range of garden conditions from moist to rather dry and from shady to sunny. Biologically, it is interesting for its tuberous black roots, which allow it to survive prolonged periods of drought. Vegetatively, it is attractive and is worth growing for its foliage alone. The leaves have a velvety dark green upper surface that contrasts beautifully with the stems and lower leaf surfaces, which are densely clothed with a thick, feltlike mat of creamy white hairs. Thus, while not spectacular, blackroot is indeed useful in adding variety and texture to natural or wild gardens.

106. *Rhexia* species

Common Name: Meadow-Beauty

Habit: Erect, rhizomatous perennials.

Size: Plants growing 6–18 inches tall and forming loose colonies.

Season: Most species flowering from spring through autumn, essentially dormant in winter.

Maintenance: None in the wild garden.

Motility: Slowly spreading and forming sizable colonies by way of underground rhizomes.

Growing Conditions: Moist to wet, often acidic sites in full or nearly full sun; Zones 8–10A (combined range for all ten species native to Florida).

Propagation: Seed; division.

Comments: Florida has ten species of meadow-beauties, plants that are very aptly named indeed. All species are denizens of a variety of sunny, moist habitats, usually in acidic soils. The plants are graceful and attractive vegetatively and range from quaintly charming to spectacular when in flower. The blossoms are commonly some shade of pink or lavender, but one species has yellow flowers (*Rhexia lutea*) and two species occasionally have white flowers (*Rhexia mariana* and *Rhexia parviflora*).

107. *Rudbeckia nitida*

Common Name: Shiny Black-Eyed-Susan
Habit: Robust clump-forming perennial.
Size: Clump of foliage about 2 feet tall, the flower stems about twice as tall.
Season: Flowering in late spring or early summer, with sporadic flowers into autumn in cultivation.
Maintenance: Periodic removal of old flower stems.
Motility: Will spread by self-sown seed, but isolated plants rarely form viable seed.
Growing Conditions: Moist sites in full or nearly full sun; Zones 8B–9A.
Propagation: Seed; division.
Comments: Shiny black-eyed-susan is a distinctive species that produces a dazzling spectacle of highly ornamental golden yellow flowers in cultivation. The plants are tough, long-lived perennials that form large, robust clumps. In late spring, an established plant may produce numerous flowering stems, each bearing two to three good-sized brilliant yellow flower heads with a contrasting dark green disk that slowly changes to dark burgundy-brown with age. Although native to moist sites, the species adapts well to average garden conditions so long as it is situated in a bright spot and is given some water during prolonged dry spells. As in many perennial wildflowers, young plants are slow-growing and take about one year to become fully established. During this period, they are putting down a large root system; once this important task is accomplished, their above-ground vegetative growth speeds up greatly.

108. *Ruellia caroliniana*

Common Name: Wild-Petunia
Habit: More or less erect perennial.
Size: Plant variable in height, 6–15 inches tall depending on growing conditions.
Season: Flowering in early spring and extending at least into late summer southward.
Maintenance: Annual pruning to remove old stems.
Motility: Gradually spreading by self-sown seed.
Growing Conditions: Extremely variable, from moist, shady sites to dry areas in full sun; Zones 8–11 (including the closely related *Ruellia ciliosa* and *R. succulenta*).
Propagation: Seed; cuttings; division.
Comments: Wild-petunia is widespread throughout Florida,

occurring in remarkably varied habitats. The large showy flowers are commonly some shade of bluish purple, but white and pink forms occur with some frequency, sometimes intermixed in a single population. The plant is generally easy to grow in cultivation as long as it is provided with moist but well-drained soil in bright light. The seeds are explosively hurled from the capsules and are difficult to gather. However, cuttings root with ease and serve as a means of propagating select forms. Two closely allied species occur in Florida. Sandhill wild-petunia (*Ruellia ciliosa*) grows in areas with deep sand and is especially suitable for dry, sandy gardens. Trailing wild-petunia (*Ruellia succulenta*) occurs in rocky pinelands and is well-adapted to conditions in southernmost Florida.

109. *Sabatia calycina*

Common Name: Leafy Marsh-Pink
Habit: Much-branched dwarf perennial.
Size: Plant about 12 inches tall and wide.
Season: Flowering in the spring and summer.
Maintenance: Occasional pruning to remove old stems.
Motility: Slowly spreading by self-sown seed in moist areas.
Growing Conditions: Moist sites in deep shade to partial sun; Zones 8–10A.
Propagation: Seed; cuttings.
Comments: Leafy marsh-pink would not win a contest as the most ornamental of Florida's twelve species of *Sabatia*. However, it is a solidly perennial species and is among the easiest to grow, readily taking to cultivation if provided ample and continuous moisture. Flower color varies from white to clear, bright pink, and plants in full bloom have a wild and graceful charm that wins them much admiration. Additionally, the flowers are long-lived and are freely borne even by very young plants. Adding to its horticultural usefulness is the ease with which it may be propagated from cuttings. For successful cultivation, it does require continuously moist or wet soil in a lightly shaded position; plants tend to be short-lived and/or prone to a variety of pests when grown under hot, dry, sunny conditions.

110. *Salvia lyrata*

Common Name: Lyreleaf Sage
Habit: Perennial with leafy rosettes bearing spikes of blue or violet flowers.
Size: Rosettes to 12 inches across; flower spikes 12–24 inches or more tall.
Season: Flowering mostly from late winter to late spring.
Maintenance: Removal of old flower stems.
Motility: Abundantly self-seeding both in the wild and in cultivation.
Growing Conditions: Moist, often disturbed sites in partial shade to nearly full sun; Zones 8–10A.
Propagation: Seed; division.
Comments: Lyreleaf sage is a common wildflower with distinctive, vaguely violin-shaped leaves that are variegated with deep chocolate brown. The leaves are borne in basal rosettes,

from which nearly leafless spikes of blue or violet flowers arise. The flowers are attractive to butterflies and hummingbirds and often make a second appearance in the autumn after the main spring bloom. Although not nearly as colorful as red sage (*Salvia coccinea*), this species also deserves a place in every wildflower garden for its attractive foliage and abundantly produced flowers. Propagation is readily achieved by seed, with plants reaching flowering size in a few months.

111. *Sanguinaria canadensis*

Common Name: Bloodroot
Habit: Creeping colonial perennial.
Size: Plant about 12 inches tall, old plants eventually covering several square feet.
Season: Flowers in the spring; usually completely dormant by the height of summer.
Maintenance: None (or removal of old, yellow leaves in very tidy gardens as plant enters dormancy).
Motility: Slowly colonial by way of underground rhizomes.
Growing Conditions: Rich deciduous woodlands; Zone 8.
Propagation: Division.
Comments: At home in rich deciduous woodlands, bloodroot produces foliage and flowers early in spring and takes advantage of all the available sunlight before the tree canopy has leafed out and shaded the ground. The large solitary flowers have two sepals and eight to twelve pure white petals that frame numerous yellow stamens. In bloom, this ranks as one of the most beautiful wildflowers native to the United States, and a large, many-flowered clump is a breathtaking and exquisite sight. Forms with pink-tinged flowers have been described (forma *colbyorum*), as have double-flowered forms in which the stamens have been transformed into petals (forma *multiplex*).

The flowers are short-lived and quickly drop their petals when pollinated. Double-flowered forms have longer-lasting flowers since, lacking stamens, the flowers are sterile. Bloodroot is easily grown in either rich highly organic or clay soils as long as it is kept evenly moist, given abundant sunshine in early spring, and kept shaded later in the season. Once the plants go dormant in summer, they will withstand considerable drought. Propagation is easily effected by dividing the creeping rhizomes, which abundantly bleed an acrid, red-orange sap.

112. *Scutellaria arenicola*

Common Name: Scrub Skullcap
Habit: Erect leafy perennial arising from basal leaf rosettes.
Size: Plants 12–18 inches tall in flower.
Season: Flowering in late spring or early summer; often flowering again in the autumn.
Maintenance: Removal of old flower heads that have gone to seed.
Motility: Abundantly self-seeding in open ground.
Growing Conditions: Well-drained sandy soils in full sun; Zones 8B–10A.
Propagation: Seed.
Comments: Scrub skullcap is a species of the sand scrub and dry pinelands found only in the northern half of peninsular Florida. The leaves have deeply impressed veins and, when growing in strong sunlight, assume a deep burgundy-brown. The color seems to be richest and darkest just prior to flowering. The pale blue to lavender-purple flowers are large and showy. Cultivated plants branch profusely, and each branch bears flowers, the mass of flowers seeming too big for the amount of foliage that produced them. There is one "big bang" flowering in late spring or early summer, often followed by sporadic and less profuse flowering in the autumn. The urge to flower in early summer is so strong that even tiny seedlings will produce a few flowers at that time of the year. Unlike many other plants of sandy habitats, this species readily adapts to average garden conditions, although it is short-lived if kept too wet. For a similar plant that produces an identical horticultural effect in moist soils, try *Scutellaria integrifolia,* a closely allied species native to sandhills, flatwoods, and hammocks.

113. *Scutellaria havanensis*

Common Name: Tropical Skullcap
Habit: Dwarf clump-forming perennial.
Size: Plant about 3 inches tall and 8 inches wide with flowering stems to 8 inches tall.
Season: Flowering all year (but see Comments).
Maintenance: Annual pruning to the ground to maintain tidiness.
Motility: Slowly to abundantly self-seeding, depending on conditions.
Growing Conditions: Moist but well-drained soil in light shade to partial sun; Zones 10–11.
Propagation: Seeds; cuttings; division.
Comments: This is a charming, diminutive skullcap found in southernmost Florida and the West Indies. It is

a perennial that bears tiny, paired leaves up to 0.6 inches long. The stems are not held rigidly erect but instead spread in all directions, the whole plant scarcely reaching 3 inches in height. The flowers, which come in various attractive shades of purple or rosy pink, are produced year-round. However, the flowers develop fully only during the mild weather of autumn and spring. In summer, the flowers tend to set seed while still in bud, and normal flowers are rarely seen during hot weather.

114. *Silphium asteriscus*

Common Name: Starry Rosinweed
Habit: Stout erect perennial.
Size: Plant 2–4 feet tall in flower.
Season: Flowering in summer and autumn, or nearly all year southward in cultivation.
Maintenance: Annual pruning to the ground to remove old stems and flower stalks.
Motility: Rarely spreading by seed, if grown in large numbers and a large seed set is produced.
Growing Conditions: Well-drained soil in full sun to part shade; Zones 8–9.
Propagation: Seeds; division.
Comments: Starry rosinweed is yet another overlooked native with much horticultural potential. It is a tough, long-lived perennial that, throughout a prolonged period, bears large, highly attractive yellow daisies with a distinctive green disk. Well-grown robust plants in full flower are nothing short of spectacular, and they literally buzz with the frenzied activity of numerous interesting and unusual insects. As with nearly all of our long-lived perennial wildflowers, this one is slow to establish since it spends its first year producing a deep and extensive root system. However, after the root-establishing phase, it grows at a moderately fast rate. Presently, several forms are in cultivation in southern Florida, some of which appear to be better adapted than others to hot summers. However, except in severe dry or cold spells, all forms manage to produce flowers nearly every month of the year. Barestem starry rosinweed, *Silphium compositum,* is a horticulturally similar Florida plant in which the stems have greatly reduced leaves.

115. *Sisyrinchium angustifolium*

Common Name: Blue-Eyed-Grass
Habit: Dwarf clump-forming perennial.
Size: Plant about 6–12 inches, in cultivation usually as wide or wider than it is tall.
Season: Flowering throughout the spring.
Maintenance: Biannual pruning, in late spring to remove old flower heads and seed pods, and in the autumn to remove faded summer foliage.
Motility: Abundantly self-seeding in some situations, but solitary plants rarely produce viable seed.

Growing Conditions: Moist sunny areas; Zones 8–11.

Propagation: Seed; division.

Comments: This is perhaps the most attractive blue-eyed-grass native to Florida. It is highly variable, the most ornamental forms growing as dwarf compact plants with proportionately large, rounded flowers in rich shades of blue, purple, or violet. Albino forms with pure white flowers are also known, and these are just becoming available in the commercial nursery trade. Plants are essentially quiescent during hot summer weather and are in active vegetative growth during cool weather. Thus, they should be placed in the garden in the autumn or early spring so that they are fully established before the onset of hot weather. Dividing or otherwise disturbing the plants during the summer can be disastrous. Plants will tolerate surprisingly hot and dry conditions, although under such stress they become prone to attack by root mealybugs. Grow them in continuously moist soils in full sun for strong, sturdy, problem-free plants.

116. *Solidago odora*

Common Name: Sweet Goldenrod

Habit: Erect or decumbent perennial.

Size: About 12–24 inches tall in full flower.

Season: Flowers in summer and autumn and, in southern Florida, sometimes in the spring.

Maintenance: Annual pruning to remove old stems.

Motility: May spread from seed, but isolated plants rarely form viable seed.

Growing Conditions: Moist but well-drained soil in partial sun to light shade; Zones 8–9A.

Propagation: Seeds; cuttings.

Comments: Sweet goldenrod bears leafy stems with leaves that tend to curl in a distinctive manner. As a result, it is often possible to identify this species even when not in flower on the basis of the foliage alone. The leaves are dotted with tiny oil glands and are sweetly anise-scented when cut or bruised. This trait is unique among goldenrods. Because of its aromatic qualities, the species is being promulgated by herb garden enthusiasts, and it is reported that a fine tea may be made from sweet goldenrod. In the autumn, abundantly produced bright yellow flower heads result in a showy display. This species is widespread in the eastern United States and just barely enters peninsular Florida; however, it is being grown as far south as Palm Beach County without any problems. This is one of the most gardenworthy goldenrods native to Florida, its distinctive appearance, aromatic foliage, and brilliant autumnal bloom being a winning combination. Toward the south of its range, it is replaced by a nearly identical variety of the same species that lacks aromatic foliage (*Solidago odora* var. *chapmanii*), and care should be taken not to confuse the two.

117. *Solidago sempervirens*

Common Name: Seaside Goldenrod

Habit: Stout, rigidly erect perennial forming large clumps with age.

Size: Plant about 3–4 feet tall in full flower.

Season: Flowering in summer and autumn, sometimes also in the spring.

Maintenance: Periodic removal of old flowering stems.

Motility: Slowly forming clumps from underground rhizomes; will spread from seed, but isolated plants rarely form viable seed.

Growing Conditions: Moist to rather dry sites in full sun; Zones 8–10.

Propagation: Seeds; cuttings.

Comments: Seaside goldenrod is among the most striking and beautiful of all of Florida's goldenrods when growing in its natural habitat of coastal dunes and tidal marshes. Plants form solid sheets of brilliant gold that contrasts beautifully with the sand, the sea, and the sky. Thus, it is not surprising that the plant has been introduced into cultivation. It is rarely as attractive in gardens as it is in nature. This is generally due to its being grown under conditions that are too rich or too shady. As a result, the plants become giant masses of foliage with very sparse flowers. To duplicate the beautiful effect of seaside goldenrod growing wild, it should be grown hard in a rather dry site in full sun. This controls its natural tendency to spread by underground rhizomes, and the plants channel their energies into the production of flowers rather than foliage.

118. *Stenandrium dulce*

Common Name: Pine Pinklet
Habit: Dwarf perennial forming small basal leaf rosettes.
Size: Plant with rosettes about 1 inch tall and 1–4 inches wide, the flower spikes to about 6 inches long.
Season: Sporadic throughout the year except in extremely dry or cold weather.
Maintenance: None in the wild garden; removal of old flowering stems in more formal gardens.
Motility: Slowly spreading by way of self-sown seedlings.
Growing Conditions: Moist but well-drained soil in deep shade to full sun; Zones 9–10.
Propagation: Seed; division.

Comments: This genus of approximately thirty species is confined to the subtropics and tropics of the New World. The leaves grow in basal rosettes, from which are borne spikes of showy flowers. Pinklet, the only species in Florida, forms small rosettes in open ground and bears rather large pale to dark pink flowers from spring through autumn. It grows under a wide variety of conditions, from deep shade to full sun and from dry sandy soil to wet muck. Its one absolute requirement is freedom from competition, since it dies out when crowded by larger plants. In cultivation, it makes a delightful little pot plant, and in garden settings it will slowly colonize open ground.

119. *Stillingia sylvatica*

Common Name: Queen's-Delight
Habit: A woody perennial of few to many stems, dying to the ground northward, becoming evergreen and somewhat shrubby southward.

Size: Stems about 1½ feet tall, the plant 2–3 times as wide or wider.
Season: Flowers borne from spring through autumn whenever sufficient soil moisture allows.
Maintenance: None in the wild garden, light to heavy pruning to maintain tidiness in formal gardens.
Motility: Sparingly establishing self-sown seedlings near the parent plant.
Growing Conditions: Moist to rather dry, often sandy sites in full sun to light shade; Zones 8–11.
Propagation: Seed.
Comments: Queen's-delight is, admittedly, an acquired taste. It will not be supplanting impatiens at garden retail centers any time soon. However, for the wildflower enthusiast, it has many advantages. In garden trials in Palm Beach County, it has proven easy to grow and flowers in its

first year from seed. It grows relatively quickly and may be used as a single accent plant or in groups as a groundcover. The flowers are not showy, but they reward close inspection and bear large nectar glands that attract a variety of insects. Added to these features is an iron constitution, resistance to pests, and high drought tolerance. All in all, there is a lot to delight royalty in this unassuming little native.

120. *Stylosanthes biflora, S. calcicola,* and *S. hamata*

Common Name: Pencil-Flower
Habit: Diffusely erect perennial, becoming a flat, prostrate groundcover with occasional mowing.
Size: Up to 12–15 inches tall in natural habitats, or, if mowed, as low as ½–1 inch tall; at least as wide or wider than it is tall.
Season: Flowering all year whenever warm temperatures and adequate soil moisture allow.
Maintenance: None or, when used as a groundcover or lawn substitute, an occasional mowing.
Motility: Spreading by seed into open sunny areas.
Growing Conditions: Moderately moist to rather dryish areas in full sun or light shade; Zones 8–11 (combined range of all three species).
Propagation: Seed.
Comments: Florida has three species of pencil-flower, *Stylosanthes biflora, S. calcicola,* and *S. hamata*. Since they are distinguished on the basis of highly technical characters and are otherwise nearly indistinguishable, all three are here treated together. The plants are unassuming perennials growing from a woody rootstock that produces numerous spreading branches clothed with small leaves composed of three leaflets. The tips of the stems are adorned with tiny, bright yellow pea flowers, and a plant in full bloom is quaintly attractive. When growing on road shoulders, road medians, and empty lots, pencil-flowers tolerate both mowing and moderate foot traffic. They make a tough, pest-free, and highly drought tolerant alternative to a grass lawn, with the added bonus that they rarely require fertilizer (being legumes, they are able to fix atmospheric nitrogen with the aid of harmless root-inhabiting bacteria).

121. *Tradescantia ohiensis*

Common Name: Common Spiderwort
Habit: Erect, grassy-leaved perennial.
Size: Plant about 2 feet tall.
Season: Flowering from early spring through late autumn, most heavily in the spring.
Maintenance: Annual pruning to remove old stems, flower stalks and seed heads.
Motility: Abundantly self-seeding in open situations.
Growing Conditions: Dry to moderately moist but well-drained soils in full sun to light shade; Zones 8–9B.
Propagation: Seeds; division.

Comments: Extending from the Panhandle to southern Florida, common spiderwort is the widest-ranging species of *Tradescantia* in the state. Well-established plants form large clumps that bear numerous beautiful flowers over a long period. The flowers generally come in various shades of blue, but white- and pink-flowered forms are presently in cultivation. It is highly recommended for novice wildflower gardeners since the plants are nearly indestructible, pest-free, and easy to grow under a wide range of conditions. Except for the ephemeral nature of the flowers, which last only a few hours in the morning, and its abundant self-seeding, this wildflower is nearly perfect.

122. *Verbesina virginica*

Common Name: White Crownbeard; Frostweed
Habit: Tall, erect perennial.
Size: Plant 5–7 feet tall.

Season: Flowering in the summer and autumn.
Maintenance: Periodic removal of old seed heads; annual pruning to maintain neat appearance.
Motility: Moderately spreading by self-sown seed.
Growing Conditions: Well-drained to moist soil in moderate shade to full sun; Zones 8–10.

Propagation: Seed.

Comments: Like other large, robust perennial wildflowers, white crownbeard is considered an attractive component of natural communities by some gardeners and a coarse, weedy thing by others. Generally, it is attractive if grown hard under rather dry conditions in bright light. Not only does such treatment keep the plants short and compact; it also promotes heavier and better flowering. When grown with too much moisture or in too rich a soil, the plants grow huge and bear their flowers high above eye level, and they indeed have a coarse and unkempt appearance. In any case, this is a large, bold plant and it needs careful placement in smaller or more formal gardens. The oddly quaint and attractive white flowers are accented by contrasting black anthers; in full bloom, the plants are irresistible to a wide variety of insects.

123. *Viola lanceolata*

Common Name: Lanceleaf Violet
Habit: Small perennial with leaves arising from long, creeping rhizomes.
Size: Reaches 4–6 inches tall in the spring; leaves are often much longer later in the season.
Season: Spring.
Maintenance: Essentially none.
Motility: Casually spreading by underground rhizomes and seed in moist, open areas.
Growing Conditions: Moist soil in full sun to partial shade; Zones 8–10.
Propagation: Seed; division.
Comments: Longleaf violet is easily recognized by its elongated lanceolate leaves, which gradually taper at both ends. The sweetly scented flowers are pure white, with the lower petal attractively veined with purple. In the wild, this species produces rather large colonies since it grows from an elongated, stoloniferous rhizome. In cultivation, it is best to give it an open patch of ground free from competing plants in order to duplicate the effect. Longleaf violet makes a poor pot plant because new growth is produced in a circle around the edge of the pot as the rambling rhizome tries to escape the confines of its container. *Viola × primulifolia* is a very similar plant characterized by broader leaves with a rounded or heart-shaped leaf base.

124. *Viola sororia*

Common Name: Common Blue Violet
Habit: Small perennial with leaves arising from short, creeping rhizomes.
Size: Reaches 3–6 inches tall and about as wide or wider.
Season: Spring.
Maintenance: Essentially none.
Motility: Extensively spreading and occasionally weedy as a result of numerous self-sown seedlings.
Growing Conditions: Rich woodlands in partial to full shade; Zones 8–10A.
Propagation: Seed; division.
Comments: This is an aptly named little wildflower, for it is indeed Florida's most common violet. It is highly recommended for beginning wildflower enthusiasts for its ease of growth and freely borne spring flowers, which come in a wide variety of color forms from pure white to dark purple. However, be warned: it self-seeds with wild abandon, and this is not a plant for new gardens with lots of open spaces. Although it flourishes in southern Florida, most forms flower poorly there, probably as a result of not getting a sufficiently long or sufficiently cold winter rest. Such poorly flowering forms should be assiduously avoided by South Florida wildflower gardeners.

125. *Yucca filamentosa*

Common Name: Adam's-Needle
Habit: Stout perennial, the flower spikes arising from a basal rosette of leaves.
Size: Leaf rosette to about 2 feet tall and wide; flower stems 4–6 feet tall.
Season: Spring.
Maintenance: Annual removal of old flowering stems.
Motility: A few forms are sparingly rhizomatous, otherwise essentially none.
Growing Conditions: Well-drained sandy soil in full sun; Zones 8–10A.
Propagation: Seed.
Comments: Although mostly occurring in dry, sandy situations, Adam's-needle readily adapts to garden culture as long as it is provided with full sun and well-drained soil. The plant is easily raised from seed, and it grows with surprising speed, but it usually takes many years to begin flowering. It may be utilized in the same manner as agaves in

garden settings. However, it has many advantages over agaves, including its less fiercely spiny nature and smaller size. Additionally, unlike agaves, which die after flowering, yuccas continue to grow and will flower reliably year after year. Adam's-needle is perfect for providing a southwestern, desertlike touch to the native garden and it has a bold, architectural quality unmatched by most other native plants.

126. *Zephyranthes atamasco*

Common Name: Atamasco-Lily
Habit: Dwarf bulb with narrowly linear leaves.
Size: Flower stem to about 6 inches tall, the leaves to about twice as long.
Season: Late winter and spring, occasionally in the late autumn southward.
Maintenance: Essentially none in the wild garden; removal of old flower stems and seed pods in more formal gardens.
Motility: Slowly to moderately spreading by self-sown seed under suitable conditions.
Growing Conditions: Moist soil in full sun to partial shade; Zones 8–9B.
Propagation: Seed; division.
Comments: Atamasco-lily is a spectacular and free bloomer that will not disappoint the wild-flower enthusiast. Seedlings begin to bloom when about three years old and will put on a dazzling show either in a pot or in the ground. Its only fault is that, as in all rain-lilies, the flowers last only two or three days. However, plants grown in rich, moist soil in full sun will produce several flushes of flowers over a long period in the spring, compensating somewhat for the short-lived nature of the flowers. In southern Florida, the blooming season is even longer, with flowering commencing in the winter. Atamasco-lily is one of the great floral treasures of the southeastern United States and is highly recommended for every garden that can accommodate its needs.

Grasses

In gardening circles, the appreciation of grasses and grasslike plants has become a distinguishing characteristic of the sophisticated plants enthusiast. This is not surprising since grasses often have subtle charms that are not readily esteemed by novice gardeners. In spite of lacking gaudy flowers, many grasses are spectacularly ornamental for a variety of reasons: some are plants of such large size that they have a noble, almost architectural or sculptural quality, while many others are of interest because of their growth form and beautiful foliage, traits that make them useful for adding textural variety in the garden. Grasses may also be noteworthy for their ornamental flower and seed spikes, as these are often adorned by attractive awns or silky hairs. Last but certainly not the least of their special qualities, most grasses are both easily propagated and effortlessly cultivated.

Horticulturally, perennial grasses are divided into two principal groups: sodgrasses and bunchgrasses. The former produce elongated rhizomes, and when competing plants are eliminated, they will form a groundcover. Obviously, all of the cultivated lawn grasses are in this category. In contrast, bunchgrasses have such short rhizomes that new growth is formed in a close circle around the perimeter of the plant. Instead of forming a sod, the bunchgrasses tend to produce rounded clumps of varying dimensions. As such, they may be used in ways that would be unthinkable for a sodgrass, such as in flower beds, as accent plants, or in formal garden schemes. Of course, these two categories merely describe the ends of a continuum and there are grasses that do not fit neatly into either group.

Described here are some of our most common, readily grown ornamental native grasses. Some of them may seem far from appealing when growing in the wild. Yet in cultivation, they form dense, many-stemmed plants of great beauty. Some of these grasses naturally occur in wet areas, others in dry, sandy habitats. Fortunately, most are flexible and will tolerate quite a variety of soils with different moisture regimes. As for propagation, seed is the easiest method since many native grasses resent being divided, although there are exceptions to this rule. Nearly all of the grasses have seeds that germinate readily, some in as little as two days.

Our native grasses require a little care in order to maintain their most attractive appearance. Since their foliage is one of their principal assets, one should cut them back to within an inch or two of the ground once a year to remove old foliage. This may sound severe, but bear in mind that most of our grasses are fire adapted and they are actually rejuvenated by being cut to the ground periodically. This cutting back is best performed in late winter just before the plants begin their spring growth. Additionally, some of the grasses described here, especially the bluestems, can assume an ungainly and coarse aspect when going to seed. These should have the old flower stems cut back just before they go to seed.

The following brief listing of Florida grasses is by no means exhaustive, but it serves as a starting point for the gardener who wishes to explore the amazing horticultural potential of our native grasses. It also serves to provide the wildflower enthusiast with native alternatives to the foreign grasses that, thus far, have almost completely dominated the grass-growing craze currently sweeping the United States.

127. *Andropogon ternarius*

Common Name: Splitbeard Bluestem
Habit: Perennial grass forming large, dramatic clumps with age.
Size: Plant about 3 feet tall, 5–7 feet tall in flower.
Season: Flowering in the autumn.
Maintenance: Annual cutting back to the ground after flowering.
Motility: Moderately spreading by self-sown seed.
Growing Conditions: Growing in a variety of sunny, open, rather dry to somewhat moist habitats; Zones 8–11.
Propagation: Seed.
Comments: Splitbeard bluestem is a robust plant that, in good soil with adequate moisture, easily reaches 6 feet in height when in flower. Plants are often glaucous, a technical term that refers to foliage with a silvery blue, often waxy coating. The lax inflorescence is open and sways gracefully in the slightest breeze. Every branch terminates in a pair of spikes adorned with silky, silver awns. These are especially attractive when backlit, and their light color contrasts well with the darker greens and browns of woodland trees and shrubs, especially when the plant is growing along a woodland edge as in the accompanying photograph. Splitbeard bluestem occurs from the westernmost Panhandle to the Florida Keys. Thus it may be grown by wildflower enthusiasts throughout Florida and is an adaptable and readily grown native plant.

128. *Andropogon virginicus* var. *glaucus*

Common Name: Chalky Bluestem
Habit: Perennial grass forming large, dramatic clumps with age.
Size: 1–2 feet tall and about as wide, twice as tall when in full flower.
Season: Foliage attractive nearly all year; flowers borne in late summer and autumn.
Maintenance: Annual cutting back to the ground after flowering.
Motility: Moderately spreading by self-sown seed.
Growing Conditions: Moist but well-drained, often sandy soils in full sun; Zones 8–10.
Propagation: Seed.
Comments: Chalky bluestem is a common native bunchgrass of open areas. The typical form is rather nondescript, but there is an extremely attractive variety with highly ornamental foliage: *Andropogon virginicus* var. *glaucus.* All parts of this variety are covered with a dense silvery white waxy coating. The coating is nearly as white as chalk and is so thick that it may be scraped off, leaving a chalky residue on one's fingernails, obviously the reason for the plant's common name. In the wild, it is often found in highly acidic, very poor sandy soils in full sun. Under such conditions, the plant can scarcely be expected to achieve its full ornamental potential. However, it is quite striking in cultivation, where it forms large rounded clumps of intensely silvery white foliage. It is especially attractive when combined with vividly colored wildflowers such as black-eyed-susans (*Rudbeckia* species) and vernonias (*Vernonia* species). Chalky bluestem deteriorates badly as it goes to flower, and this is definitely a grass that should be cut to the ground annually.

129. *Ctenium aromaticum*

Common Name: Toothache Grass
Habit: Low, clump-forming perennial grass.
Size: Clumps are about 12–18 inches tall and at least as wide or wider, up to 3 feet high in flower.
Season: Flowering in the spring and summer.
Fruit: Spike of tiny flowers that curls into a spiral as the grains mature.
Maintenance: Light pruning to remove old flowering stems.
Motility: Very slowly and casually spreading by self-sown seed under suitable conditions.
Growing Conditions: Moist soil in light shade to full sun; Zones 8–10A.
Propagation: Seed.
Comments: Toothache grass is a low, densely clumping grass with dark green or bluish green foliage. Commonly found in moist or even wet areas, it has two principal points of interest.

The first is its flower spikes, which when fully mature and dried out form spirals reminiscent of a little pig's tail. The second is an aromatic compound found in its leaves, which when the leaves are chewed produces numbness in the mouth like that derived from novocaine, accounting for the common name of toothache grass.

130. *Dichanthelium* species

Common Name: Witch Grass
Habit: Low, clump-forming perennial grasses.
Size: Height variable depending on the species but usually 6–12 inches tall and as wide or wider.
Season: Foliage attractive nearly all year; flowering spring through autumn, or all year southward.
Maintenance: Essentially none.
Motility: Seeds often harvested by ants, the plants thus spreading widely throughout the garden.
Growing Conditions: The various species grow in nearly every terrestrial habitat of Florida; Zones 8–11 (combined range for all eighteen species native to Florida).
Propagation: Seed.
Comments: Often overlooked because they lack showy flowers, Florida's eighteen species of witch grass are surprisingly decorative and are useful for adding variety and texture to the wild garden. Although the individual species are distinguished on the basis of highly technical and recondite characters, the genus has a distinctive growth habit and is easily recognized. Witch grasses spend the winter as clumps of basal rosettes. With the arrival of warm weather, the rosettes produce branching stems, which, depending on the species and growing conditions, form loose to tight mats of grassy foliage. The genus is highly successful and the various species occur in widely varying habitats, including marshes, bogs, pond margins, flatwoods, hammocks, scrub, and sandhills. Thus there is at least one species of witch grass suitable for every gar-

den in Florida. However, they are best introduced into the garden after it is well established, since ants tend to spread the seed and self-sown seedlings soon pop up in every part of the garden capable of supporting their growth.

131. *Eragrostis elliottii*

Common Name: Elliott's Love Grass
Habit: Low, clump-forming perennial grass.
Size: Clumps 12–24 inches tall and at least as wide or wider.
Season: Foliage attractive all year; flowers heaviest in the autumn but produced nearly all year.
Maintenance: Annual pruning to ground level.
Motility: Very slowly and casually spreading by self-sown seed.
Growing Conditions: Moist, often disturbed sites in full sun or light shade; Zones 8–11.

Propagation: Seed.
Comments: Elliott's love grass is a small, fine-leaved bunchgrass that sports beautiful silvery blue leaves and masses of tiny flower spikes that create an attractive, almost cloudlike haze above the leaves. It is most commonly found on sandy soils, where it seems to tolerate both extremely dry and very wet conditions. In cultivation, the most spectacularly beautiful plants are produced in sunny open sites with well-drained but moderately moist soils. *Eragrostis spectabilis,* purple love grass, is similar in growth form to Elliott's love grass, but the innumerable tiny flower spikes create a striking reddish purple haze above the foliage.

132. *Muhlenbergia capillaris*

Common Name: Hair Grass; Muhly Grass
Habit: Robust, clump-forming perennial grass.
Size: Ultimate size variable from 1 to 4 feet tall and at least as wide.
Season: Foliage attractive year-round; heaviest flowering in the autumn.
Maintenance: Annual pruning to ground level to remove old flowering stems.
Motility: Casually spreading by self-sown seed.
Growing Conditions: Moist, open sites in full sun or light shade; Zones 8B–11.
Propagation: Seed.
Comments: Hair grass is surely one of Florida's great horticultural treasures and is among the loveliest of all ornamental bunchgrasses. It is often found on calcareous soils in full sun in areas that are seasonally moist yet subject to periodic drought. However, it is readily grown

under ordinary garden conditions. The leaves, which are thin to begin with, roll up into a very narrow, almost threadlike tube at maturity. Well-grown plants form spectacular nearly symmetrical hemispheres with large numbers of dark green wiry leaves. In bloom, the clumps produce tall stems of countless minute pinkish or purplish red flowers. The resulting effect of a reddish haze above the foliage is somewhat like that of a giant purple love grass. If possible, try to place hair grass where it can be backlit by the sun against a dark background. Situated in this manner, flowering hair grass becomes a stunning sight.

133. *Pharus glaber*

Common Name: Spirit Grass
Habit: Large broadleaved grass.
Size: Forming clumps 12–18 inches high and 18–36 inches wide.
Season: Foliage attractive all year; flowers insignificant.
Maintenance: None or occasional removal of old foliage.
Motility: None or essentially none in most garden situations.
Growing Conditions: Dappled to full shade in rocky woodlands; Zone 9A.
Propagation: Seed; division; ground layering.

Comments: Spirit grass resembles a dwarf clumping bamboo with attractive broad leaves and is equally at home in both formal and informal garden settings. The genus *Pharus* is unusual among grasses in that most of the species are specialized for growing in deep shade. Spirit grass is no exception, and its successful cultivation requires a moist but well-drained spot protected from both strong winds and hot sun. If all conditions are to its liking, it will adapt to early morning or late evening sun. Although rare in Florida, where it occurs only in Citrus and Polk counties, spirit grass is rapidly becoming established in cultivation since large, well-grown plants are extremely attractive and the plants are easily accommodated in formal gardens.

134. *Sorghastrum secundum*

Common Name: Lopsided Indian Grass
Habit: Robust, clump-forming perennial grass.
Size: Clumps 2–4 feet tall, flower spikes 4–6 feet tall.
Season: Flowering in the autumn.
Maintenance: Judicious annual pruning of old flowering stems; plants have died as a result of being severely cut back at the wrong time.
Motility: Occasionally and slowly spreading by self-sown seed.
Growing Conditions: Moist open sites in full sun to light shade; Zones 8–11.
Propagation: Seed.
Comments: Lopsided Indian grass is a noteworthy bunchgrass of singular beauty. Plants form large, rather loose clumps of little distinction. However, toward the end of summer and into the autumn, they produce dramatically tall spikes of numerous, extremely attractive flowers. The exterior of the bracts that enclose the true flowers are clothed in silky soft, golden brown hairs, and as a delightful contrast, one of the bracts of each flower bears a long, darker brown awn. The finishing touch is provided by the large yellow anthers. Thus, the total effect is that of a symphony of brass, mahogany, and gold. Like hair grass, Indian grass is at its best when the flower spikes are backlit by the sun.

135. *Sporobolus junceus*

Common Name: Pineland Dropseed
Habit: Clump-forming perennial grass.
Size: Clumps 1–3 feet tall and about as wide or a little wider.
Season: Foliage attractive all year; flowers from spring through autumn.
Maintenance: Annual pruning to the ground.
Motility: Slowly spreading into open sites by self-sown seed.
Growing Conditions: Moist to rather dry open sites in full sun; Zones 8–10.
Propagation: Seed.
Comments: Pineland dropseed ranks as one of the most beautiful and ornamental of all grasses. With age, plants form large, hemispherical clumps composed of hundreds of thin, wiry blades, these variously tinged in shades of

blue-green or silvery green. The plants are attractive at all stages of growth, from the first flush of new growth after being cut to the ground to the mature clumps sporting large numbers of flowering spikes in late summer and autumn. Appropriate for formal garden effects, pineland dropseed is also perfectly suited for the wild or meadow garden, where it makes an elegant foil for wildflowers.

136. *Tripsacum dactyloides*

Common Name: Eastern Mock Grama
Habit: Extremely robust, clump-forming perennial grass.
Size: Plants 5–10 feet tall, the flowering stems often 2–3 feet taller.
Season: Flowering from spring through autumn.
Maintenance: None to severe pruning, as appropriate.
Motility: Slowly spreading by self-sown seed under suitable conditions.
Growing Conditions: Wet situations in partial shade to full sun; Zones 8–10.
Propagation: Seed; division.
Comments: Eastern mock grama is the largest and most robust of all the grasses listed here. In nature it tends to form loose clumps, but in cultivation the clumps become dense as a result of the numerous growths it produces. Its flower spikes are borne in groups of two or three and resemble a three-toed bird's foot. The flowering stems are not particularly ornamental, but they lend an interesting accent to the plant as a result of their great height. Eastern mock grama is an excellent landscape plant for large estates, where it can be allowed to grow to its ultimate size of 6 feet or more. It is particularly well suited for growing along the edge of a pond and is probably the most dramatic and ornamental of our native grasses for such a situation. Although a grass of low, wet areas, it is very drought tolerant and, along with *Tripsacum floridana,* is becoming common as a xeriscape plant.

137. *Tripsacum floridana*

Common Name: Florida Mock Grama
Habit: Clump-forming perennial grass.
Size: Clumps to about 3 feet tall and at least as wide.
Season: Clumps attractive nearly all year; flowers borne spring through autumn.
Maintenance: None to severe pruning, as appropriate.
Motility: Slowly spreading by self-sown seed under suitable conditions.

Growing Conditions: Moist but well-drained sites in full sun to light shade; Zones 10–11.
Propagation: Seed; division.
Comments: Florida mock grama is a delightful miniature version of the preceding species, although the term "miniature" is relative, since *Tripsacum floridanum* quickly reaches 3 feet in height with a 4-foot spread. Florida grama grass has much narrower leaves than *T. dactyloides* and, as a result, produces a more delicate and airy effect in the landscape. This, in combination with its shorter stature, makes it a more appropriate choice for smaller gardens.

138. *Uniola paniculata*

Common Name: Sea-Oats
Habit: Large rhizomatous grass.
Size: Plant 3–6 feet tall.
Season: Flowering from spring through autumn.
Maintenance: None or essentially none.
Motility: Plants colonial with spreading, underground stems; rarely spreading by seed.
Growing Conditions: Deep sand of coastal dunes in full sun; Zones 8–11.
Propagation: Seed.
Comments: Nothing is as evocative of Florida's coastal shores as sea-oats waving against an azure sky. But think twice before reaching for the large showy seed heads to take with you as a memento of a day in the sun—it's illegal! Sea-oats plays a key role in stabilizing sand dunes and protecting beaches from erosion. The law against picking its seeds recognizes this important role. This large, noble, and handsome grass does not lend itself to cultivation away from maritime coasts. However, if you have beachfront property, planting sea-oats is a wise invest-

ment. After they are fully established (about six months after being set out), the plants are indestructible and will require no additional maintenance of any kind. And sea-oats will serve as a perfect foil for colorful wildflowers, such as the brilliant yellow beach sunflower (*Helianthus debilis*) and the cheery pink of the railroad vine (*Ipomoea pescaprae* subsp. *brasiliensis*).

Palms

Perhaps no other large, woody plants speak of the tropics more eloquently than palms, and Florida is fortunate in having eleven native species and one natural hybrid, all of which are highly ornamental and easily grown. Salt tolerance is moderate to high in our native species, and with few exceptions, they are extremely drought tolerant once established.

Another factor in their favor is the relative freedom from pests and diseases that native palms enjoy. However, ganoderma butt rot is a serious fungal disease that may afflict paroutis palm (*Acoelorrhaphe wrightii*), royal palm (*Roystonea regia*), cabbage palm (*Sabal palmetto*), and saw-palmetto (*Serenoa repens*). This disease, which is caused by a bracket fungus, can spread rapidly, persists in the soil, and is incurable. Serious insect pests include the royal palm bug (*Xylastodoris luteolus*), which may attack *Roystonea regia,* and palmetto weevils (*Rynchophorus cruentatus*), which attack cabbage palms and saw-palmettos. But native palms are rarely afflicted with pests or diseases unless they are severely stressed or are weakened by age.

The cultivation of quite a few non-native palms has been seriously affected, or in some cases nearly completely curtailed, by their susceptibility to mineral deficiencies and lethal yellowing. Fortunately, native palms are scarcely affected by these difficulties, although paroutis palm

Because of their slow growth rate and tough constitution, native palms, such as this Florida thatch palm (*Thrinax radiata*), make excellent pot plants.

occasionally suffers from manganese deficiency and royal palm may be affected by manganese or potassium deficiency. Symptoms of potassium deficiency "always occur first on oldest leaves and affect progressively newer leaves as the deficiency becomes more severe" (Meerow 1992:115). In contrast, the symptoms of manganese deficiency occur only on new leaves. These nutritional deficiencies are especially likely to occur on highly alkaline mineral soils, and it is perhaps best to avoid planting paroutis palms or royal palms in such soils. Our native *Coccothrinax* and *Thrinax* species would make suitable alternatives, since they naturally occur on alkaline sands and limestone outcrops. Lethal yellowing is an incurable disease caused by mycoplasmas. Fortunately, none of the native palms appear to be particularly susceptible to this inevitably fatal disease.

Our native palm species are extremely tough plants and highly tolerant of adversity. It is not surprising that far greater numbers are killed as a result of poor cultivation than as a direct result of insect pests, diseases, or poor climatic conditions. Overtrimming of the leaves by gardeners is perhaps the single greatest threat to cultivated palms, as so eloquently and succinctly stated by Meerow (1992:123):

> There is an unfortunate tendency for landscape maintenance workers to overtrim palms, removing perfectly good, green, functional leaves at the same time as dead or dying fronds are trimmed. The logic behind this practice, no doubt, is an attempt to lengthen the interval before trimming is once again necessary. The removal of healthy leaves is a disservice to the palm. . . . Overtrimming reduces the food manufacturing efficiency of the living palm and can result in sub-optimum caliper development at the point in the crown where diameter increase is currently taking place. There is also some evidence that overtrimming makes the palm more susceptible to cold damage.

Due to the anatomy of their vascular system and to their pattern of growth, palms can never be grafted or grown from cuttings. Also, palms do not possess bark; injuries to their trunks are permanent and will not heal over. Of our native species, paurotis palm and needle palm form clumps and may be grown from division. However, both species are well armed with spines, and for most homeowners, propagating any but the smallest of offsets is a troublesome and nasty business. All other native palms must be propagated from seed. Germination for most species is reported as taking two to three months but may take several months longer, while needle palms take at least six months or more.

139.
Acoelorrhaphe
wrightii

Common Name:
Paurotis Palm
Habit: Tall fan
palm forming
large, multi-
trunked clumps
with age.
Size: Trunks 20–
30 feet high, the
clumps at least
half as wide or
wider.

Season: Evergreen
and attractive all year, flowering and fruiting in summer and autumn.
Fruit: Numerous orange berries that ripen to black.
Maintenance: None if properly placed.
Motility: Slowly forms spreading clumps by production of new trunks from the bases of
older trunks.
Growing Conditions: Moist, often brackish wetlands of southernmost Florida; Zone 10A.
Propagation: Seed; division.
Comments: The paurotis palm is a tall, erect, clump-forming fan palm of very distinctive
appearance that grows in swamps and low wet areas in southern Florida, Mexico, Central
America, and parts of the West Indies. It clumps freely from the base; thus, unlike in solitary
palms, the principal stems are usually hidden by the leaves of shorter, younger stems produced at the perimeter of the clump. Well-grown healthy specimens present an attractive
solid mass of foliage from ground level upward, and a large clump seems more like a sculptural work of art than a garden plant. The leaves are bright green and are further distinguished
by a row of stout curved spines along each side of the petiole (leaf stalk). Large, many-
branched flower stalks are produced in the summer and are followed by black berries. Before
ripening, the berries are orange and provide an attractive accent, especially when contrasted
against the leaves or against a patch of blue sky. Given that the nature of this species is to form
large clumps and that its leaf stalks bear stout spines, it should be placed with care in the home
landscape, avoiding confined areas that it will eventually outgrow. If the spines pose a hazard
to passersby, the stems may be cleared, resulting in a pleasing and architectural outline.
Paurotis palm makes a magnificent specimen for large estates, parks, and botanic gardens,
and it is especially attractive when grown at the edge of a large pond in simulation of its
habitat in nature. In cultivation, one sees far too many specimens grown in parkways, high-
way medians, and tree islands in parking lots. These plants eventually outgrow such confined
areas and, when periodically cut back to keep them in check, they present a raw, ugly, and
mangled appearance.

140. *Coccothrinax argentata*

Common Name: Florida Silver Palm
Habit: Small palm with fan-shaped leaves and a solitary trunk.
Size: Very slowly growing to about 20 feet tall, the plants usually much shorter.
Season: Evergreen and attractive all year; flowering and fruiting in the spring and summer.
Fruit: Small black berries useful to wildlife.
Maintenance: Periodic removal of old leaves and flowering and fruiting stems.
Motility: None or essentially so under most conditions in cultivation.
Growing Conditions: Rocky pinelands in light shade to full sun; Zones 10–11.
Propagation: Seed.
Comments: Florida silver palm is an extremely ornamental fan palm, its rounded leaves deeply palmately divided. They have a bright green upper surface with a wonderfully contrasting silvery white lower surface. The silvery cast to the lower leaf surfaces results from a dense covering of scurfy hairs. Blowing in the breeze, the leaves alternately present their dark green and silvery surfaces, producing a most attractive display. This palm bears tiny white flowers that are followed by small black fruits, but neither the flowers nor the fruits have any particular ornamental value. Although the species is reported to grow up to 26 feet high, cultivated plants rarely reach even half that height, and in the wild, a 6-foot-tall plant may be a hundred years old. In one rocky pineland in Miami-Dade County, miniature forms occur that bear small leaves and are fully mature when only about 1.5 feet high. If these forms remain small in cultivation, they would make wonderful additions to even the smallest urban garden. Florida silver palm naturally occurs in rocky, well-drained pinelands and is salt tolerant and extremely drought tolerant.

141. *Pseudophoenix sargentii*

Common Name: Buccaneer Palm
Habit: Small palm resembling a miniature royal palm.
Size: Very slowly growing to about 10 feet tall in cultivation.
Season: Evergreen and attractive all year; flowering and fruiting all year.
Fruit: Large two- to three-lobed, orange-red berries.
Maintenance: Periodic removal of old leaves and old flowering and fruiting stems.
Motility: None.
Growing Conditions: Coastal thickets in full or nearly full sun; Zones 10–11.
Propagation: Seed.
Comments: Buccaneer palm grows slowly to about 10 feet tall, although heights of 23–26

feet are reported. It greatly resembles a dwarf royal palm and, like the royal palm, has a conspicuously swollen trunk, the degree of swelling varying in different individuals. Other similarities to royal palms include the tightly overlapping petioles that form a crownshaft and the pinnate leaf blades, which are divided into numerous segments and are borne in several ranks. However, in spite of the many outward similarities, buccaneer and royal palms are not at all closely related. The buccaneer palm's fruits are persistent, large, orange-red berries, these mostly two- to three-lobed, with each lobe corresponding to a seed. The species deserves a place in every garden that can accommodate it, for it has many horticulturally desirable qualities: small size, picturesque trunk, attractive foliage, extreme salt and drought tolerance, nearly complete freedom from pests and diseases, and brilliant fruits borne over a long

period. It has the drawbacks that it will not tolerate hard freezes, and except in southernmost Florida, it can be grown only in warm areas near the coast about as far north as Palm Beach County. Another drawback is its slow growth rate, although with today's smaller gardens, this may well be an asset. Wild plants were plundered for the horticultural trade, and this species is now endangered in Florida.

142. *Rhapidophyllum hystrix*

Common Name: Needle Palm
Habit: Small fan palm occasionally forming multistemmed clumps with age.
Size: Plant about 6 feet tall and about as wide.
Season: Evergreen and attractive all year; flowering in the spring, the fruit maturing in the autumn.
Fruit: Small reddish brown berries.
Maintenance: Periodic removal of old leaves.
Motility: None.
Growing Conditions: Understory of rich, moist woodlands; Zones 8–9A.
Propagation: Seed; division.
Comments: *Rhapidophyllum* is an interesting genus in the palm family with a single species. Along with *Sabal,* it is among the hardiest of native palms and may be grown as far north as Washington, D.C. With protection, it has survived Boston winters! In Florida, it occurs naturally from the Panhandle south to Highlands County. However, it may be grown throughout the state and there are

magnificent specimens in Miami-Dade County gardens. Needle palm is a fan palm with large, rounded leaves deeply divided into fifteen to twenty segments. It slowly grows to about 6 feet tall in cultivation, although old specimens growing in deeply shaded situations may get considerably taller. The leaf bases decay into long, needle-like fibers that persist on the stem for a long time. In spite of its formidable armature, it is an extremely attractive plant and worthy of wider cultivation. Although it is native to moist, shady sites in rich hardwood forests, young plants can be adapted to full sun and, once established, are extremely drought tolerant. With age, needle palms form clumps and may be propagated by division. However, the spiny stems make division of a large clump difficult. Flowers are inconspicuous, with male and female flowers usually borne on separate plants. The fruit is difficult to collect, and seeds are slow to germinate (at least six months). This species has been extensively collected from the wild for the horticultural trade, a practice that can no longer be condoned since needle palms are becoming widely and readily available from nursery-propagated stock.

143. *Roystonea regia* (Synonym: *Roystonea elata*)

Common Name: Royal Palm
Habit: Exceedingly tall and elegant palm with a single trunk.
Size: Trunks eventually reaching 80–131 feet in height.
Season: Evergreen and attractive all year; flowering and fruiting intermittently all year.
Fruit: Large dark purple berries.
Maintenance: Disposal of fallen fronds; large fruit crops can be a nuisance on pavement.
Motility: Occasionally spreading from self-sown seedlings.
Growing Conditions: Permanently moist swamps, the trunks emerging above the canopy into full sun; Zone 10.
Propagation: Seed.
Special Note: There is a long-standing and ongoing debate as to whether the royal palms originally found growing in Florida are the same species as those growing in Cuba. The Florida plants have commonly been treated as a distinct species, *Roystonea elata*. However, recent taxonomic research has resulted in it being lumped with the Cuban royal palm, *Roystonea regia*. Whether or not Florida royal palms are the same species as Cuban royal palms, the Florida plants represent a distinct population. Thus, care should be taken to preserve the genetic integrity of the Florida plants by keeping them isolated from Cuban forms (to prevent genetic swamping) and by keeping careful records, so that the Cuban plants are not sold as the Florida form.
Comments: At 80 feet high, the royal palm is one of the tallest palms in cultivation in the United States and is, by far, the tallest palm native to Florida. Long and Lakela (1971:242)

list its greatest height as an even more impressive 131 feet. Its trunk has a unique and distinctive appearance for it is extremely smooth and solid, appearing as if poured from concrete. Toward the base of the plant, the trunk manifestly bulges, adding a further note of interest to its appearance. Not to be outdone, the immense leaves are also of great beauty. The petioles (leaf stalks) are tightly united into a crownshaft that bears a crown of elegant dark green leaves at its summit. Considering their size, the leaves present a light and airy effect as a result of being divided into several hundred segments. Huge panicles of flowers are produced at the base of the crownshaft, where they be may viewed without any obstruction from the foliage. The panicles form masses of creamy white when in flower and gradually change to large masses of purple berries as the fruit matures. Due to its large size, this species is inappropriate for small properties, where it would be completely out of scale. Even individual leaves are very large; according to Tasker (1984:70), a single leaf from a mature plant "can weigh up to 100 pounds." The species has moderate to low drought tolerance and does not do well on poor, sandy soils. However, it does adapt readily to average garden conditions. Native to wet swampy areas in southernmost Florida, royal palm was formerly more widespread in peninsular Florida. It is not clear why its present range is so restricted, although severe freezes, overcollection, and habitat destruction have been advanced as possible explanations.

144. *Sabal etonia*

Common Name: Scrub Palmetto
Habit: Dwarf fan palm with a subterranean trunk.
Size: Plant 4–6 feet tall.
Season: Evergreen and attractive all year; flowering in the spring, the fruit maturing in summer.
Fruit: Small blackish berries.
Maintenance: Periodic removal of old leaves and old flowering and fruiting stems.
Motility: None or essentially none.
Growing Conditions: Sand scrub in full or nearly full sun; Zones 8B–10.
Propagation: Seed.
Comments: Scrub palmetto grows in dry pinelands and sand pine scrubs, where it withstands extremes of heat, sun, and drought. Like *Sabal minor*, scrub palmetto has a wholly subterranean stem. But it is distinguished from that species by its larger fruit (10 millimeters or more in diameter) and by the stringlike filaments that develop along the edges of the leaf segments, a characteristic that it shares with *Sabal palmetto*. Unlike many other sand scrub plants that defy cultivation under average gar-

den conditions, this species is as easy to grow from seed, and adapts to cultivation, as readily as our other species of palmetto. However, it must have well-drained soil. Of course, no amount of sun is too much for this species, although, if given excellent drainage, it will grow under partly shaded conditions. Scrub palmetto is one of the parents of *Sabal × miamiensis,* a natural hybrid with cabbage palm (*Sabal palmetto*).

145. *Sabal minor*

Common Name: Dwarf Palmetto
Habit: Mostly small fan palm with a subterranean stem.
Size: Usually 4–6 feet tall, taller in very wet, rich swamps.
Season: Evergreen and attractive all year; flowering in the spring, fruiting in the autumn.
Fruit: Small black berries.
Maintenance: Periodic removal of old leaves and old flowering and fruiting stems.
Motility: None or essentially none.
Growing Conditions: Shaded understory of rich, moist woodlands and swamps; Zones 8–9B.
Propagation: Seed.
Comments: Dwarf palmetto is similar to *Sabal etonia,* also growing to about 6 feet tall and having a subterranean stem. However, it is easily distinguished by its smaller fruit (5–8 millimeters in diameter) and leaf segments that lack stringlike filaments along their edges. Although it has a growth habit identical to that of *S. etonia,* it could not be more different in its habitat preference. Dwarf palmetto is a species of rich, moist to wet woodlands, where it often grows in dense shade. Yet, like all of our native palms, this species is highly adaptable; it will grow in full sun and has high drought tolerance once established. Additionally, it is very hardy, its natural range extending from southernmost Florida to coastal North Carolina. Extremely old specimens sometimes develop a short trunk above the ground, the trunk usually growing at a slight angle to the ground.

146. *Sabal palmetto*

Common Name: Cabbage Palm; Sabal Palm
Habit: Tall fan palm with a solitary trunk.
Size: Ultimately reaching 80 feet in height, but half that height is more typical.
Season: Evergreen and attractive all year; flowering in the spring, the fruit maturing in the autumn.
Fruit: Small black berries.

Maintenance: None in the wild garden; judicious pruning of the oldest leaves in formal situations.

Motility: Producing large numbers of self-sown seedlings if flowering stems are not pruned before the fruit matures.

Growing Conditions: Occurring in a wide variety of moist to moderately dry habitats in full or nearly full sun; Zones 8B–11.

Propagation: Seed.

Comments: Cabbage palm is the state tree of both Florida and South Carolina. It slowly grows to about 40 feet tall, very old plants reaching 60–80 feet in height. In Florida, it is a common sight and occurs in a wide variety of natural settings, where it may become a dominant species and form nearly pure stands. It also adapts readily to human disturbance and will grow from seeds lodged in the tiniest cracks in an asphalt parking lot or concrete sidewalk. In the past, it provided an edible delicacy sought after by epicures and useful as a survival food. With some effort, the central growing point can be removed and eaten as heart of palm, and it is from this practice that the common name is derived. However, removal of the central growing point results in the death of the palm, and the practice has been outlawed.

As is to be expected with such an abundant and widespread species, there is much natural variation. To most people, such variation is most obvious in the trunk. In some forms the trunk is clothed with the long-persisting basal remnants of the leaf stalks, forming what are referred to as "boots." The boots accumulate substantial amounts of organic detritus, and such palms are frequently home to a variety of epiphytes. In Florida, three species of ferns occur almost nowhere else except in the boots of cabbage palms: hand fern (*Ophioglossum palmatum*), golden polypody (*Phlebodium aureum*), and shoestring fern (*Vittaria lineata*). There is also a species of moss that is found nearly exclusively on the trunks of cabbage palms. Many other plants, including various non-epiphytic plants, may make their homes in cabbage palm boots, and plants as diverse as shiny blueberry (*Vaccinium myrsinites*) and grasses in the genus *Dichanthelium* have been observed growing on cabbage palms. In a West Palm Beach city park, an Australian eucalyptus (*Eucalyptus torelliana*) has even been found growing epiphytically on a cabbage palm. In other forms, the leaf bases tend to fall with the rest of the leaf; such trunks are smooth and support far fewer epiphytic plants. Occasionally, one can see sad cabbage palms from which the boots have been hacked off in order to give the trunk a smooth look. However, it is nearly impossible to remove all traces of the boots without damaging the trunk, and such palms generally look worse than they did prior to the hacking.

In addition to variation in the persistence of the boots, cabbage palms show much variation in size. In the rocklands of Miami-Dade County, there are dwarf forms that reach sexual maturity before an aerial trunk has developed and are hence confusingly similar to *Sabal etonia*. They slowly develop a trunk as wide as typical forms of cabbage palm but scarcely reach 6–10 feet at full maturity. There is some speculation that these forms are merely stunted as a result of the poor rocky soils on which they occur. However, typical cabbage palms do not begin to flower until the trunk is well developed. The fact that these forms flower while still barely more than a simple rosette of leaves indicates that they are genetically distinct. If they retain their dwarf habit in cultivation, they could make superb additions to small backyard gardens.

Cabbage palms are extremely useful for wildlife. They provide shelter; the flowers provide copious nectar for a wide variety of insects; and the fruits are eaten by many birds and mammals. This is certainly among our very toughest plants and has high salt, wind, and drought tolerance. Meerow (1992:87) lists palmetto weevils (*Rynchophorus cruentatus*) and leaf hoppers as major pests and ganoderma and graphiola false smut as major diseases. However, healthy, well-grown cabbage palms are rarely afflicted with these problems.

Cabbage palm is one of the parents of *Sabal × miamiensis,* a natural hybrid with scrub palmetto (*Sabal etonia*).

147. *Serenoa repens*

Common Name: Saw-Palmetto
Habit: Fan palm, the trunk subterranean or emergent and creeping or ascending.
Size: About 3–6 feet tall, but variable and reaching 20 feet under some conditions.
Season: Evergreen and attractive all year; flowering in the spring and fruiting in the autumn.
Fruit: Large berry varying from orange to nearly black at maturity.
Maintenance: Essentially none if properly situated; forms that sucker excessively may need pruning to maintain desired size. Do not plant where the spiny leaf stalks will prove a nuisance to passersby.
Motility: Slowly creeping and branching trunk will eventually outgrow any confined space; also spreading from self-sown seedlings.
Growing Conditions: Growing in widely varied habitats and conditions as long as the soils are not too rich; Zones 8–11.
Propagation: Seed.
Comments: Saw-palmetto is one of the most abundant and widely distributed palms native to Florida. It is generally a small palm 3–6 feet high with a tardily elongating, mostly creeping stem that forms clumps with age. It is one of our toughest native plants, with high salt and drought tolerance. In spite of its extremely slow growth, it has become one of the most common native plants in restoration work and in the horticultural trade. Young saw-palmet-

tos make charming additions to the home landscape, but care should be taken when selecting this palm. If not given full sun and very dry soil, it will eventually grow into immense clumps that are out of scale with most homes. The forms with silvery, blue-green leaves are especially apt to grow to large size. The flowers are individually small but are carried in large masses on a long stalk and add an interesting note. They are a favorite of bees, and saw-palmetto honey is highly esteemed. The flowers are followed by large orange-yellow to nearly black fruits that are edible but scarcely palatable.

148. *Thrinax morrisii*

Common Name: Brittle Thatch Palm
Habit: Small fan palm with a solitary trunk.
Size: Reported to grow slowly to 20–30 feet high, but usually less than 15 feet high, with a trunk diameter of 3–6 inches.
Season: Evergreen and attractive all year; flowering in the spring and fruiting in the autumn.
Fruit: Small white berries.
Maintenance: Judicious removal of old leaves and old flowering and fruiting stems.
Motility: None or essentially none in most garden situations.

Growing Conditions: Tropical hammocks in moderate shade to full sun; Zones 10–11.
Propagation: Seed.
Comments: Brittle thatch palm is an incredibly tough small palm often found in harsh coastal environments. In some places, it even grows in crevices on bare rock outcrops. Of course, it is able to take just about anything the home gardener can throw its way except severe cold and poorly drained wet soils. It may be utilized as a specimen or accent plant, and it makes a lovely addition to a hammock restoration, especially along the edge where it contrasts beautifully with a background of large shrubs or trees. Impeding its widespread use is the glacial speed with which it grows. Thus, this is not a palm for the impatient gardener. In the past, the stems were used for fence posts and the leaves were indeed used for thatch (Scurlock 1987) as well as to make utilitarian objects such as brooms. However, such uses have fallen away and this is now a rare plant.

149. *Thrinax radiata*

Common Name: Florida Thatch Palm
Habit: Small fan palm with a solitary trunk.
Size: Slowly reaching 20–30 feet high but usually much smaller in cultivation.
Season: Evergreen and attractive all year; flowering in the spring and fruiting in the autumn.
Fruit: Small white berries.
Maintenance: Judicious removal of old leaves and old flowering and fruiting stems.
Motility: None or essentially none in most garden situations.
Growing Conditions: Tropical hammocks in moderate shade to full sun; Zone 11.
Propagation: Seed.
Comments: Florida thatch palm shares all of the horticultural qualities of the brittle thatch palm but is generally a faster- and larger-growing plant. It is suitable for street use, as specimen plant, or for providing a tropical effect in the garden. If all other conditions are to its liking, it will grow in light shade, and it makes an interesting addition to the edge of a hammock garden, where its large, palmately divided leaves provide a pleasing contrast to the more common and typical hammock trees and shrubs, such as the stoppers, firebush, and gumbo-limbo.

Shrubs

The classification of woody plants into shrubs and trees is an artificial one, especially in Florida where warm temperatures allow many shrubby plants to grow into trees. The main criteria for including a plant in this section, rather than in the section on trees, were the tendency to grow with multiple trunks and the ultimate size reached. Woody plants that usually grow with a single trunk, even though sometimes rather small, were included in the tree section.

Many of the comments on pruning and pruning effects, addressed earlier in the chapter on Maintenance, are specifically applicable to shrubs and trees; some of the introductory remarks in the section on Trees, following this one, are also applicable to shrubs.

Florida has a wealth of woody plants since it is a transition zone between the warm-temperate region and the Caribbean Basin tropical region. Thus, many northern species reach their southernmost limit in Florida and many tropical species reach their northernmost limit here. Moreover, the state is rich in woody shrubs occurring in families that, to the north, consist mostly of annuals or perennials. The mint and verbena families are good examples of this phenomenon, which adds greatly to the diversity and richness of woody plants in Florida.

In addition to availability in the nursery trade and appeal of the flowers, selection criteria include attractive growth form, foliage, and/or fruit; fragrance of flowers; usefulness to wildlife; and ease of cultivation.

150. *Acacia pinetorum*

Common Name: Pineland Acacia
Habit: Dwarf spiny shrub.
Size: Reported as 9–12 feet tall, but forms in cultivation rarely exceed 4 feet in height.
Season: Flowering in the spring.
Fruit: Dark brown pods.
Maintenance: Judicious pruning as appropriate.
Motility: Essentially none under most garden conditions.

Growing Conditions: Moist (but well-drained) to rather dry soils in full sun or light shade; Zones 9A–11.

Propagation: Seed.

Comments: Few native shrubs are as enchanting as pineland acacia, a small plant of great charm and graceful beauty. If it never flowered, it would be well worth growing for its foliage alone. The leaves are divided into numerous tiny leaflets of a wonderful shade of bluish gray or grayish green, and this results in a delicate and airy effect. However, we are fortunate that it does flower for the blooms are rounded golden yellow pompoms that contrast beautifully with the foliage. The flowers have a strong, sweet fragrance, further adding to this plant's charm. On the negative side, the branches bear a pair of small, thin spines at the base of each leaf, but these pose relatively little danger since the plant is generally so low.

151. *Amorpha fruticosa*

Common Name: Bastard Indigo

Habit: Densely branched shrub.

Size: Plant 4–12 feet high and about as wide.

Season: Deciduous northward, more or less evergreen southward; flowering in the spring and summer.

Maintenance: None in the wild garden; judicious pruning of overly large, older plants in formal gardens.

Motility: Rarely spreading from seed; some forms throwing out suckers far from the parent plant.

Growing Conditions: Moist to somewhat dry sites, usually in light to moderate shade; Zones 8–10A.

Propagation: Seed (scarify).

Comments: This plant is well worth growing for its striking appearance when in full flower. At that time, the tips of every branch hold spikes of solidly packed, small, dark violet flowers. In some forms, the color is so intense as to appear almost black. Already we have a highly unusual flowering shrub, but it gets better. Contrasting with the dark violet of the petals are the stamens, each of which is tipped by a bright orange anther. The combination of violet and orange is attractive and quite unlike any other plant in our flora. Fortunately, it is an easy plant to grow, and it adapts readily to a wide variety of garden conditions. Since it usually occurs in moist sites in the wild, it does require consistent moisture in the garden, especially when first getting established. Occasionally, I run across plants growing on raised riverbanks high above the water line, where they are subject to drought at least occasionally. However, under such conditions, they are usually growing in partial shade.

152. *Amorpha herbacea*

Common Name: Southern Indigo-Bush
Habit: Dwarf, open shrub or shrubby perennial.
Size: Plant usually about 3 feet high and about as wide.
Season: Seasonally dormant or even dying back to the ground in colder areas; flowering in the spring and summer.
Maintenance: Occasional cutting back of old stems.
Motility: None or essentially none in most garden situations.
Growing Conditions: Well-drained, often sandy soils in very light shade to full sun; Zones 8B–10.
Propagation: Seed.
Comments: Southern indigo-bush may be used to good effect wherever the native plant gardener wants to create a colorful and enchanting scene in an area of rather dry, sandy, and sunny ground. From a stout rootstock are produced woody stems clothed in grayish green leaves. These are divided into small leaflets, giving the plant a light and airy effect. The tips of each stem produce elongated spikes of little pale pink or white flowers with contrasting light orange anthers. By combining southern indigo-bush with colorful wildflowers, such as pink downy phlox (*Phlox pilosa*), orange milkplant (*Asclepias tuberosa*), and brilliant yellow morning-buttercup (*Piriqueta caroliniana*), a sandy spot where little else grows can be brought alive with the beauty and color of native wildflowers.

153. *Amyris elemifera*

Common Name: Torchwood
Habit: Slow-growing small shrub or tree with a dense crown of attractive leaves.
Size: Slowly growing to 15–20 feet tall.
Season: Evergreen and attractive all year; flowering in the spring and autumn, the fruits ripening in summer or winter.
Fruit: Attractive deep purple berries about ½ inch long.
Maintenance: None.

Motility: Occasionally spreading by root suckers or self-sown seed.

Growing Conditions: Hammocks, usually in moderate to light shade; Zones 9A–11.

Propagation: Seed.

Comments: Torchwood is a native member of the orange family, but the citrus trees found in so many Florida yards are clumsy oafs compared to the delicate beauty and grace of torchwood. It is a small shrub with glossy, dark green leaves divided into three leaflets. Often the leaflets have a reddish-tinged midrib that further adds to their beauty. The leaflets tend to hang downward in a graceful manner and, when shimmering in a light breeze, present a very beautiful sight indeed. Torchwood, however, is not a plant to grow for showy flowers. The pure white flowers contrast nicely with the dark green foliage, but they are too small to put on much of a show. As if to make up for their small size, the flowers possess a lovely fragrance that has been likened to that of gardenias. In time, they are followed by beautiful purple or dark violet berries, showy and ornamental in their own right. Once established, the plants will take drought and cold weather in stride. It has been suggested that as a result of its slow growth and dense crown, torchwood may be a good candidate as a hedge plant. It may also be utilized in butterfly gardens since it is the larval food plant of several swallowtail butterflies.

154. *Ardisia escallonioides*

Common Name: Marble-Berry (often corrupted to "Marlberry")

Habit: Small shrub or tree.

Size: Highly variable, to about 3 feet northward, reaching 20 feet in southernmost Florida.

Season: Evergreen and attractive all year; flowers and fruits borne intermittently throughout the year.

Fruit: Small, black, single-seeded berries.

Maintenance: None.

Motility: Self-sown seedlings sometimes abundantly produced underneath the parent plant.

Growing Conditions: Generally an understory shrub in light to moderate shade; Zones 9A–11.

Propagation: Seed.

Comments: Commonly a shrub, or sometimes a small tree, marble-berry is an attractive native landscape plant. It is densely clothed in dark green leaves and bears at various intervals throughout the year branched clusters of small, fragrant white flowers that fairly seem to glow against the dark foliage. The flowers are followed by dark, one-seeded berries, these possessing a distinctive taste that combines both sweet and acidic elements. With selection for superior forms, this species may have potential as a minor fruit crop for the backyard gardener. As is the case with so many native plants, it is mostly overlooked by the landscape industry for far less attractive, and often intensely weedy, non-native plants. This is a shame since this versatile shrub will grow in both shady and sunny areas; is quite drought tolerant once established; and is of a sufficiently refined appearance to be used in even the most formal of garden landscapes. Additionally, it may be grown as a hedge or foundation plant that can be maintained at any preferred height and size by periodic trimming. The common name is usually corrupted to "marlberry," a misnomer since the plant never occurs in wet, marly situations.

155. *Argusia gnaphalodes* (Synonyms: *Tournefortia gnaphalodes; Mallotonia gnaphalodes*)

Common Name: Sea-Lavender
Habit: Highly distinctive mounding, silvery gray shrub.
Size: About 3–5 feet tall, usually much wider than it is tall.
Season: Evergreen; flowering and fruiting from winter through spring.
Fruit: White berries with a small black dot.
Maintenance: None.
Motility: Slowly spreading and forming large mounds from low branches that root as they are covered by sand.
Growing Conditions: Coastal sand dunes in full sun; Zones 9B–11.
Propagation: Seed; cuttings; ground layering.
Comments: Sea-lavender is a sad example of what happens to a plant that is highly specialized to live in an area also highly sought out by people as a place to build their homes and businesses. At one time, it was fairly common along stable beaches in southeastern Florida from the Florida Keys north to Palm Beach County, with outliers in St. Lucie and Brevard counties. But beachfront property is a hot commodity; development and concomitant erosion have lowered the population of sea-lavender to the point that it is now listed in Florida as an endangered species. Fortunately, a few nurseries are now propagating sea-lavender, and nursery-propagated stock is becoming available for beach restoration projects and as a landscape plant for gardeners with coastal properties. It may be grown in gardens with well-drained, sandy soil or in large containers of sand or gravel mixed with about 10 percent organic material by volume. Plants need to be kept moist until established but thereafter are extremely drought tolerant.

156. *Aronia arbutifolia* (Synonym: *Photinia pyrifolia*)

Common Name: Red Chokeberry
Habit: Stoloniferous low shrub with many ornamental features.
Size: Plant 6–10 feet high and 3–5 feet wide.

Season: Deciduous; foliage dark green and glossy, attractive from spring through summer, turning brilliant red in the autumn; white flowers borne in the spring; persistent fruits maturing in the autumn.

Fruit: Small, ornamental red berries, not relished by birds.

Maintenance: Do not plant where its suckering habit will be a problem.

Motility: Forming large colonies by way of underground suckers.

Growing Conditions: Rather dry to wet, often acidic, soils in full sun to light shade; Zones 8–9.

Propagation: Seed (stratify); cuttings; division; layering.

Comments: Red chokeberry is an attractive small shrub offering year-round interest. In the spring, the plants bear showy white flowers with beautifully contrasting maroon anthers. The foliage matures to dark green and leaves have a glossy upper surface. In the autumn, the leaves assume various shades of brilliant red or crimson, and in late autumn and early winter, the persistent red fruits provide interest. This plant is highly adaptable, tolerating both dry and wet sites. It is easily established by dividing the suckers and transplants well. For maximum flower and fruit production, as well as the best autumnal foliage, it should be grown in full sun, although it will also grow in light shade. The cultivar 'Brilliantissima' is an improved form that flowers and fruits heavily, has larger fruits, and bears intensely red autumnal foliage. However, it is probably not well adapted to Florida conditions, and it would be worthwhile to seek out superior forms from native Florida populations of red chokeberry.

157. *Asimina obovata*

Common Name: Scrub Pawpaw

Habit: Medium-sized to large deciduous shrub or small tree.

Size: Variable from about 6 to 12 feet tall and about two-thirds or more as wide.

Season: Foliage deciduous in winter; large numbers of flowers borne in late winter and spring when the plants are nearly leafless, the fruit maturing in late spring or early summer.

Fruit: Peculiar edible fruits resembling small, irregular yellowish green bananas 2–4 inches long.

Maintenance: None.

Motility: Occasionally spreading by seed in open situations if many plants are grown together and a large number of fruits are set.

Growing Conditions: Extremely well drained, deep sandy soils, in full or nearly full sun; Zones 8B–9 (also recorded from Zone 10).

Propagation: Seed; root cuttings.

Comments: Horticulturally, the effect of a scrub pawpaw in full flower is similar to that of a flowering dogwood or certain magnolias. Like all members of the genus *Asimina,* it may be grown in butterfly gardens as the larval food plant of the zebra swallowtail butterfly. In spite of its floral beauty, extreme drought tolerance, ability to thrive in deep sand, and utility in butterfly gardens, scrub pawpaw remains largely unknown and underutilized by gardeners. The species is stuck in a vicious circle: it is difficult to propagate, thus it is rare in nurseries; since it is rare in nurseries, there is little public demand for it; and since there is little demand, nurseries do not invest in research on how to propagate scrub pawpaw easily and efficiently, which brings us back to square one. In spite of this, it is available from time to time in the nursery trade and is worth any amount of trouble to locate a commercial source if one has the proper conditions in the garden for its successful cultivation.

158. *Asimina reticulata*

Common Name: Pineland Pawpaw

Habit: Small deciduous shrub.

Size: Variable depending on conditions, from 2 to 6 feet tall.

Season: Foliage deciduous in winter; flowering in spring, the fruit maturing in late spring or early summer.

Fruit: Peculiar edible fruits resembling small, irregularly shaped bananas 1–3 inches long.

Maintenance: None; plants may be pruned to the ground if necessary.

Motility: Occasionally spreading by seed in open situations if many plants are grown together and a large number of fruits are set.

Growing Conditions: Moist to dry, often sandy soils, in full or nearly full sun; Zones 8B–10.

Propagation: Seed.

Comments: During the last two decades, there has been an explosion in the availability of ornamental woody plants and vines from around the world, including from temperate Asia and the mountains of Mexico. Overlooked in this horticultural avalanche are the pawpaws, members of the genus

Asimina, with the greatest concentration of species found in Florida. This is quite unfair since some species, such as *A. incana, A. obovata,* and *A. reticulata,* are shrubs as spectacularly beautiful as are to be found anywhere in the world. The plants are "big bang" bloomers that produce quantities of large white flowers on leafless or nearly leafless branches in late winter or early spring. The two largest-flowered and showiest species are *A. incana* and *A. obovata.* These are plants of well-drained, deep sandy soils. Pineland pawpaw is almost as showy, but it is a smaller plant typically found in moist, sandy flatwoods, where it often survives periodic flooding. This quality extends the horticultural potential to native plant gardens where *A. incana* and *A. obovata* cannot be grown.

159. *Baccharis halimifolia*

Common Name: Groundseltree; Sea-Myrtle
Habit: Densely branched, small-leaved shrub; the male and female flowers on separate plants.
Size: Height variable from 3 to 12 feet, usually as wide or nearly as wide as it is tall.
Season: Evergreen southward, winter deciduous northward; flowers borne in the autumn.
Maintenance: Periodic judicious pruning, but only in formal gardens.
Motility: Freely self-seeding in moist, open ground, but only if both male and female plants are growing in close proximity.
Growing Conditions: Moist areas such as pond margins and ditches in full sun to moderate shade; Zones 8–10.
Propagation: Seed; cuttings.
Comments: Groundseltree is a small-leaved, freely branching shrub with profusely borne creamy white flower heads. Individual flower heads are insignificant, but a healthy plant in full flower has a certain curious charm and adds an interesting accent to the garden landscape. It is at its best in moist habitats, but the plants are drought tolerant once fully established. Groundseltree is also salt tolerant and often grows in coastal situations. Individual plants are either male or female, and the former are usually preferred in residential settings since female plants produce abundant soft, cottony seed masses that are blown by the wind into every corner of the home and yard. Additionally, a friend has opined that the male flowers are pleasingly fragrant. Plants may be propagated from seed or select forms may be propagated from cuttings. *Baccharis diocia* and *B. glomeruliflora* are closely related species with similar horticultural uses. A fourth species, *B. angustifolia,* has thin, linear leaves and is highly tolerant of both brackish and rocky, alkaline soils.

160. *Bumelia reclinata* (Synonym: *Sideroxylon reclinata*)

Common Name: Florida Bumelia

Habit: Dwarf, intricately branched, irregularly shaped, small-leaved shrub usually armed with sharp-tipped branchlets.

Size: Height variable from 1 to 15 feet depending on the form and growing conditions; as wide as it is tall.

Season: Deciduous or partially evergreen in winter; flowering in the spring and maturing fruit in late summer or autumn.

Fruit: Rather large, sweet, one-seeded berry maturing to dark purple or black.

Maintenance: None or light pruning in semiformal gardens.

Motility: Slowly colonial and suckering with age, rarely spreading by self-sown seed.

Growing Conditions: Moist to rather dry sites in full sun to light shade; Zones 8–11.

Propagation: Seed (sow immediately); root suckers.

Comments: Florida bumelia is an especially interesting dwarf shrub with three different botanical varieties. Depending on the variety, it may be 1–8 feet high, although an occasional plant may grow to 15 feet. All forms are delightful but never more so than when producing new foliage, the light green of which contrasts beautifully with the dark green of the older foliage. When in full bloom it is covered with fragrant, tiny white flowers. Plants are readily propagated from seed, which should be sown immediately after the sweet, edible fruits ripen, and from small but mature suckers that have developed a few roots of their own. The principal problem relating to this plant is its extremely slow growth. It is seldom available commercially since it takes an ample investment in time to raise it from seed or to get suckers to a marketable size.

161. *Bumelia tenax* (Synonym: *Sideroxylon tenax*)

Common Name: Tough Bumelia

Habit: Densely branched, irregularly shaped, small-leaved shrub or small tree usually armed with thorns.

Size: Variable, 4–20 feet tall, depending on the form and growing conditions, the smaller forms often nearly as wide as or wider than they are tall.

Season: Deciduous northward, evergreen southward; flowering in the spring, the fruit maturing in late summer or autumn.

Fruit: Rather large, dark purple or black, edible, one-seeded berry.

Maintenance: Occasional judicious pruning to maintain shape, but only in semiformal gardens; do not plant where its thorns will pose a problem.

Motility: Some forms tending to root sucker and forming thickets; self-sown seedlings are rare.

Growing Conditions: Well-drained, often sandy soils in full sun to moderate shade; Zones 8B–10.

Propagation: Seed (sow as soon as possible after the fruit ripens).

Comments: Tough bumelia is an intricately branched, often thorny shrub with small, dark green, glossy leaves, the undersides of which are thickly coated with a dense layer of silky hairs. Depending on genetic variation, the age of the plant, and the age of the leaves, the hairs may range from silvery white to a rich, dark cinnamon-brown. This makes tough bumelia an interesting and unusual garden plant that provides excellent cover for small animals in an increasingly cat-filled world. In the spring, it bears prodigious numbers of tiny, nectar-filled white flowers, and the plants come alive with the buzzing of numerous insects. Indeed, it is a veritable symphony of insect activity and is a marvel to behold at such times. By late summer or autumn, the dark, sweet, somewhat gummy berries mature and tough bumelia provides yet another bounty, but this time for birds and mammals. Its successful cultivation requires nothing more than a small open piece of ground with well-drained sandy soil. The plants are remarkably drought tolerant; even tiny seedlings may be established in the driest gardens without much difficulty.

162. *Byrsonima lucida*

Common Name: Locust-Berry
Habit: Dwarf, much-branched shrub or small tree.
Size: Height variable from 3 to 30 feet tall, depending on the form.
Season: Plant evergreen, attractive all year; flowers borne in late winter to early summer.
Fruit: One-seeded yellowish orange berry becoming yellowish brown at maturity.
Maintenance: None or essentially none.
Motility: Occasional self-sown seedlings, these usually appearing near the parent plant.

Growing Conditions: Moist but well-drained sites in rocky pinelands; Zones 10–11.

Propagation: Seed.

Comments: Locust-berry is attractive both vegetatively and when in flower. The leaves are borne in opposite pairs and are beautifully tinged in various shades of mahogany red when young. At maturity, they become dark green above with a contrasting silvery green lower surface. The rather small but abundantly-produced flowers are generally white, deepening to various shades of rose as they age. Thus, a plant in full bloom presents a subtle yet gaily decorative effect combining white, rose, and every intermediate color on the same plant. In spite of its many charms, it is not at all temperamental in its requirements as long as it is provided with well-drained soil and bright light. At its best with moderate moisture, it is nevertheless highly drought tolerant once established. Additionally, it may be grown in sheltered coastal situations.

163. *Caesalpinia pauciflora*

Common Name: Dwarf Caesalpinia

Habit: Small, prickly, vase-shaped or rounded shrub, the ends of the branches spreading or weeping.

Size: About 3–6 feet tall, usually wider than it is tall.

Season: Evergreen in its natural range, partially deciduous and semidormant in winter northward; flowering throughout the year whenever sufficient rain and warm temperatures allow.

Maintenance: None in the wild garden; for a neater appearance, may be lightly to severely pruned.

Motility: Rarely spreading from occasional self-sown seedlings.

Growing Conditions: Rocky pinelands and tropical hammocks in full sun to light shade; Zone 11.

Propagation: Seed (scarify).

Comments: For the most highly ornamental garden effect, grow dwarf caesalpinia in a sunny spot away from larger plants. Under such conditions, it develops a striking and highly pleasing compact form with numerous low branches gracefully arching from the central stem in a broad crown. The tips of the branches hang slightly for a delicate weeping effect. Contributing greatly to its charm are the leaves, which are divided into small leaflets in pleasing shades of grayish or silvery green. Its flowers open in the afternoon and are a bright, clear lemon yellow. They are rather small and are borne a few at a time, so the floral display is graceful and charming but not spectacular. The stems are prickly, but like everything else about this plant, the prickles are small and not too bothersome. In spite of its delicate appearance, this is an extremely tough plant that tolerates harsh coastal conditions as well as severe drought once established.

164. *Calamintha coccinea*

Common Name: Scarlet Calamint
Habit: Dwarf, stiffly erect shrub with few, wiry branches.
Size: Height varying from 1 to 3 feet.
Season: Evergreen to partially deciduous and semidormant in winter; flowering from early spring through late autumn.
Maintenance: Pruning of old flowering stems at the end of autumn.
Motility: None under most garden conditions.
Growing Conditions: Open, sandy sites in full sun; Zones 8–9.
Propagation: Seed; cuttings.

Comments: Scarlet calamint is a spectacular dwarf shrub most often found near the coast in dunes, scrub, and at the edges of hammocks. The flowers are larger than in any other species of *Calamintha* native to Florida, 1–2 inches long, and come in splendid shades of scarlet, red, or orange-red. Unlike our other species, which tend to produce a big show of flowers in either the spring or autumn, scarlet calamint produces flowers intermittently and in smaller numbers from early spring to late autumn. Large, well-grown plants with numerous branches and with each branch bearing three to four flowers produce a dazzling effect, making this one of

the most magnificently beautiful of all plants native to Florida. The brilliance of the red flowers is enhanced when they are contrasted with similarly showy and attractive yellow-flowered plants, such as pineland heliotrope (*Heliotropium polyphyllum*) or silky golden-aster (*Pityopsis graminifolia*). Of course, like all plants possessing nectar-rich, tubular red flowers, scarlet calamint is extremely attractive to hummingbirds.

165. *Callicarpa americana*

Common Name: American Beauty-Berry
Habit: Small to medium-sized shrub.
Size: Plants 4–6 feet high and about as wide.
Season: Winter deciduous in the north, evergreen southward; flowers borne spring through autumn (only late spring northward); fruit borne nearly all year southward (only late summer or autumn northward).
Fruit: Large numbers of highly ornamental amethyst-purple berries.

Maintenance: None in the wild garden; severe annual pruning nearly to the ground in late winter for a neat, tidy appearance.

Motility: Readily spreading by self-sown seed in moderately moist areas of the garden.

Growing Conditions: Somewhat moist to rather dry sites in full sun to partial shade; Zones 8–11.

Propagation: Seed; cuttings.

Comments: American beauty-berry has large, coarse, opposite leaves and bears abundant clusters of tiny but delicately attractive pink flowers. In the summer and autumn, the branches are laden with great quantities of amethyst-purple berries. These berries are the plant's most ornamental feature and they are among the most brilliant and beautiful fruits on any native plant. Since beauty-berry scarcely branches above the base, it should be severely cut back in late winter. This keeps it compact and results in vigorous young growth that flowers and fruits heavily. It is a useful shrub as it will grow under a wide variety of conditions, it begins to bloom and bear fruit while very young, the flowers attract butterflies, and the berries are eaten by birds, although sparingly so. It is readily grown from seeds or cuttings, with the latter producing plants of flowering size much sooner. An albino form with white flowers and pure white fruits, *Calliacarpa americana* var. *lactea,* is often encountered in the nursery trade. It is an interesting novelty, but its white berries become blemished with brown spots as they age.

166. Calycanthus floridus

Common Name: Sweetshrub; Strawberry-Bush; Carolina-Allspice

Habit: Small, rounded shrub with aromatic foliage, flowers, and fruits.

Size: Plants 4–7 feet tall, generally wider than they are tall.

Season: Deciduous in winter; flowering in the spring; autumnal foliage greenish yellow.

Fruit: An aggregation of small, dry, one-seeded fruits enclosed in a leathery receptacle.

Maintenance: None in the wild garden; prune after flowering to maintain desired size or shape.

Motility: None under most garden conditions.

Growing Conditions: Moist soils in rich woodlands; Zone 8.

Propagation: Seed (stratify 1–3 months); cuttings.

Comments: Sweetshrub is an often straggling or irregularly shaped plant of rich woodlands and stream banks in northern Florida, where it is rare and endangered. It is, however, available in the nursery trade, and cultivated plants have an attractive, dense, rounded growth habit if given

ample light and plenty of room. In spite of its woodland habitat, it is surprisingly adaptable and enjoys moderate popularity as an unusual landscape plant notable for having all parts pleasantly aromatic. The peculiar chocolate brown or maroon flowers are generally described as more curious or odd than showy. They make up for their somber color by their strawberry-like or spicy fragrance, which is especially pronounced in the evening. Horticulturally superior forms of sweetshrub are available in the nursery trade and include cultivars selected for shinier foliage, more compact growth habit, larger flowers, more intensely fragrant flowers, and/or flowers of unusual color (e.g., 'Athens' is a cultivar with yellow flowers). Although attractively aromatic, and having common names that hint at its being edible, sweetshrub is poisonous if ingested in sufficient quantities.

Special Note: Do not confuse this plant with *Euonymus americanus,* an unrelated plant that shares the common name of strawberry-bush.

167. *Capsicum annuum* var. *glabriusculum*

Common Name: Bird Pepper
Habit: Dwarf, densely and intricately branched, small-leaved shrub.
Size: Usually 1½–3 feet high and about as wide or wider.
Season: Evergreen and flowering and fruiting year-round except for extreme dry or cold spells.
Fruit: Pungent, tiny chile peppers, dark blackish green when immature and ripening to bright red.
Maintenance: None.
Motility: Sparingly spreading by bird-dispersed seed in open areas of the garden.
Growing Conditions: Moderately moist to rather dry sites in full sun to rather deep shade near the coast; Zones 8B–11.
Propagation: Seed (ambient method); cuttings.
Comments: Bird pepper, as this little plant is known, is the wild ancestor from which both our common sweet and chile peppers were derived. Native throughout a wide range in the New World tropics and subtropics, the variety listed here is sparingly found growing wild in peninsular Florida. It is a dwarf, densely branched shrub with tiny leaves and equally tiny, hot chile peppers. If not subjected to frost, it is everblooming and everbearing. Plants are extremely tough, usually pest and disease free, highly drought tolerant, and able to withstand cold temperatures well. It is reported, however, that Cuban brown snails greatly favor this plant, especially when it is young. The little peppers are fiery hot, yet are highly attractive to birds and are a special favorite of mockingbirds. Of course, they are completely edible and may be utilized in cooking. Plants are easily grown from cuttings, which root with ease. Propagation from seed is a different matter; the seeds germinate poorly unless they have passed through the digestive tract of a bird. Best results are obtained by utilizing the ambient method of seed germination.

168. *Ceanothus americanus*

Common Name: New Jersey-Tea; Redroot

Habit: Dwarf, open shrub, the stems arising from a large, woody, subterranean, tuberous caudex.

Size: Stems 2–4 feet high.

Season: Deciduous in winter, the stems often dying back to the ground; heaviest flowering in the spring, in cultivation intermittently flowering from late winter through late autumn.

Maintenance: Pruning of old branches in late autumn.

Motility: Very slowly forming clumps from the suckering underground woody caudex.

Growing Conditions: Well-drained, often sandy, sites in full sun to rather deep shade; Zones 8–9A.

Propagation: Seed (treat by pouring boiling water over them and letting them cool before sowing).

Comments: After the Boston Tea Party, it was considered unpatriotic for Americans to drink tea imported by the British. Thus, many turned to alternatives, one of which was the dried leaves of redroot. This use accounts for its other common name, New Jersey-tea. The plant springs up from a huge, subterranean woody stem known as a burl, and among the curses of the early settlers was clearing fields of redroot burls. This is an adaptation that allows redroot to spring back quickly after any adversity, including freezing winters, severe drought, or intense fires. Although individually tiny, the flowers are borne in small branched clusters from the tips of every branch, all of them opening more or less simultaneously to produce a showy display. The flowers are unusual among Florida native plants in that all parts, including the sepals, are pure white.

169. *Cephalanthus occidentalis*

Common Name: Buttonbush

Habit: Ornamental medium-sized to large shrub.

Size: Rounded habit to 10 feet tall and 8 feet wide (usually far smaller).

Season: Deciduous (very briefly so in southern Florida); flowering from spring to autumn.

Fruit: Rounded, persistent heads formed by the aggregation of numerous tiny fruits.

Maintenance: Occasional pruning to keep it tidy and control its size if desired.

Motility: Can form colonies from self-sown seedlings and root sprouts.

Growing Conditions: Swamps and margins of lakes and ponds in full sun to light shade; Zones 8–10.

Propagation: Seed; cuttings.

Comments: Buttonbush is easily grown in moist soils under a wide variety of conditions, although it is reported to dislike alkaline soils and is at its best in bright, sunny locations. Both the dried foliage and the flowers have a subtle, pleasing fragrance that has been likened to newly mown hay, and buttonbush is highly attractive to bees. The unusual flower heads, which consist of innumerable little florets packed into a small globe, are the plant's chief ornamental trait, and these are made more interesting by the protruding stamens. The dark green, often very glossy foliage is also highly ornamental, but it is often chewed by insects, especially toward the southern end of the plant's range. Seeds do not require any pretreatment before sowing, but their germination rate is low. Buttonbush may also be grown from cuttings, these taking about thirty days to root.

170. *Chionanthus pygmaeus*

Common Name: Pygmy Fringetree

Habit: Dwarf, suckering shrub or small tree.

Size: About 6–12 feet tall, depending on the form and growing conditions.

Season: Deciduous in winter; heavily flowering in the spring; fruits maturing in late summer.

Fruit: Purple plumlike fruits about 1 inch long.

Maintenance: None.

Motility: None under most garden conditions.

Growing Conditions: Deep, sandy and exceedingly well drained soil in full sun to light shade; Zone 9.

Propagation: Seed (may take one to two years to germinate).

Comments: Very few sights are as beautiful as this shrub or small tree in early spring when its branches are festooned with feathery clusters of fragrant, pure white flowers. The remarkably delicate floral effect results from the flowers' petals: there are four to each flower and they are divided into amazingly thin, threadlike lobes. In the wild, pygmy fringetree occurs only in sand scrub in central Florida. Usually scrub plants are among the most difficult to cultivate under ordinary garden conditions. However, this is not the case for pygmy fringetree, and we are fortunate that such a highly ornamental little plant adapts well to cultivation so long as it is provided with well-drained soil and bright light. White fringetree (*Chionanthus virginicus*) is a larger, more common plant of rich moist soils. It is also more widespread than pygmy fringetree, occurring from the Panhandle south to Sarasota County.

171. *Chrysobalanus icaco*

Common Name: Coco-Plum
Habit: Erect to spreading, densely branched and densely leafy shrub, sometimes a small tree.
Size: Spreading forms about 3 feet tall and many times wider; erect forms up to 15 feet tall.
Season: Evergreen and attractive all year; flowering and fruiting intermittently all year.
Fruit: White or dark purple, one-seeded, plum-like fruits 1–2 inches long.
Maintenance: None in the wild garden; annual pruning to maintain desired height and shape in formal gardens.
Motility: Self-sown seedlings establishing in the vicinity of the parent plant if fruits are not removed.
Growing Conditions: Growing under widely varied conditions from moist to dry and sunny to shady; Zones 9B–11.
Propagation: Seed; cuttings.
Comments: Coco-plum is a remarkably useful and attractive plant. In the wild, it is often found in coastal environments where it faces adverse

conditions, and it tolerates both salt and drought. In cultivation, it is easily grown, fast growing, and suffers remarkably few pests. It is beautiful enough to be utilized as a specimen plant, or plants may be grouped to create a boundary or a living fence. In the latter case, coco-plum may be left alone for an informal look or it may be trimmed into a formal hedge. In sandy coastal areas, it has been used to help stabilize dunes. The tiny flowers are inconspicuous but they are followed by rather large purple-black or white fruits. These are edible raw or may be made into preserves or jellies. The seeds have an oil-rich kernel and may also be eaten; it is reported that the Carib Indians strung them on sticks and burned them like candles. Have we exhausted all of the coco-plum's uses? Not quite: it has also been favored as a honey plant. Presently, there are at least three forms in cultivation in southern Florida: an all-green plant, a plant with new growth tinged burgundy red, and a dwarf creeping form found along coastal dunes and favored as a groundcover.

172. *Citharexylum fruticosum*

Common Name: Fiddlewood
Habit: Large, densely leafy shrub or small tree, with fragrant flowers, these either male or female and borne on separate plants.
Size: Slowly growing to about 12 feet tall with very old, large plants reportedly up to 30 feet tall.
Season: Evergreen; flowering and fruiting nearly year-round southward.
Fruit: Round, orange-brown berries borne on female plants.

Maintenance: None in the wild garden; judicious pruning to maintain tidy shape and appearance in more formal gardens.

Motility: Occasionally establishing self-sown seedlings, these usually around the mother plant.

Growing Conditions: Maritime and subtropical or tropical hammocks in full sun to moderate shade; Zones 9B–11.

Propagation: Seed.

Comments: Fiddlewood is a large shrub with so many desirable qualities that it is not easy to list them all. First, it is a nearly indestructible plant, highly drought and salt tolerant once established. Its branches are densely clothed with dark green glossy leaves that serve as the perfect backdrop for the hanging clusters of pure white, fragrant flowers, from which bees make a fine honey. Female plants bear rounded berries useful to wildlife. Fiddlewood rarely suffers from any pests, although an occasional plant may be attacked by scale. Severe infestations are best treated by cutting the plant nearly to the ground and disposing of the cut material. Fiddlewood vigorously sprouts after being pruned in this manner, quickly regaining its former size. As to the inevitable question of whether its wood is used to make fiddles, the answer is yes. Fiddlewood has hard, heavy, strong wood that is excellent for the manufacture of violins, guitars, and other musical instruments. However, once you see the full beauty of this plant, I doubt you will want to harvest its wood!

173. *Clethra alnifolia*

Common Name: Sweet Pepperbush; Summersweet

Habit: Small shrub with attractive dark green foliage and contrasting spikes of fragrant white flowers.

Size: Growing 3–8 feet tall and about two-thirds as wide or wider.

Season: Deciduous; flowering in early summer to early autumn; the autumnal foliage gold.

Maintenance: None or, in very formal gardens, light pruning to remove old flower spikes.

Motility: Tending to form tight thickets from its shallow, suckering root system.

Growing Conditions: Wet, acidic areas in full sun to rather deep shade; Zone 8 (also reported from Lake County in Zone 9).

Propagation: Seeds; cuttings; suckers.

Comments: Summersweet is a highly variable little shrub able to tolerate a wide variety of moist, shady conditions. For example, plants growing in highly sterile acidic sands in New Jersey have matured and flowered when only 4–10 inches tall! The dark green glossy leaves make it vegetatively attractive, and they nicely set off the 4- to 6-inch-long racemes of fragrant, pure white flowers, these being attractive to bees. In the autumn, the plants put on another show as the foliage assumes various shades of yellow or orange. Summersweet is surprisingly salt tolerant and is a good choice for a coastal garden if it can be given a sufficiently moist, shady spot. Choose a spot for summersweet carefully, since it is difficult to transplant and slow to recover after transplanting. There is now a fair range of cultivated varieties available, including one with dense, multiple flower spikes ('Anne Bidwell'); a plant with leaves speckled with white variegations ('Creel's Calico'); a dwarf plant that matures at 3 feet ('Hummingbird'); some with flowers larger than normal ('Paniculata'); and others with pale to dark pink flowers ('Pink Spire,' 'Rosea,' and 'Ruby Spice').

174. *Colubrina arborescens*

Common Name: Coffee Colubrina

Habit: Large, coarse-leaved shrub or small tree with an open crown.

Size: Height eventually to 20 feet or so, the crown half to two- thirds as wide.

Season: Evergreen; flowering toward late summer.

Maintenance: None or essentially none.

Motility: Occasionally establishing self-sown seedlings in the vicinity of the parent plant.

Growing Conditions: Tropical hammocks in full sun to light shade; Zones 10A and 11.

Propagation: Seed.

Comments: Because so much of Florida's population comes from northern cities, many people tend to think of tropical plants as being delicate, tender plants that require extensive coddling in order to thrive. However, nearly all of South Florida's woody plants of tropical affinity hail from low elevation, dry tropical forests, and they are remarkably tough and resilient plants. Coffee colubrina is a case in point. It is essentially pest-free, grows rapidly from seed into a large specimen, is extremely drought tolerant, and with a little shelter will grow in coastal situations. Although it does not get very tall and possesses a broad, open crown, its large attractive leaves cast considerable shade, and it has been utilized as a small shade tree in various countries in the tropics. The flowers are green and inconspicuous, but they attract a wide variety of interesting insects and are followed by three-seeded capsules bearing dark shiny seeds from which necklaces and similar ornaments may be made. Thus far, coffee colubrina has proven hardy as far north as coastal Palm Beach County, where it has survived temperatures into the low 40s. All in all, it is a useful, hardy plant that adds a distinctive touch to the native garden. Soldierwood (*Colubrina elliptica*) has smaller and more graceful foliage and may be utilized in more formal garden situations.

175. *Conradina canescens*

Common Name: False Rosemary
Habit: Dwarf, densely leafy and densely branched shrub with lightly aromatic foliage.
Size: Variable from 1 to 3 feet tall and about twice or three times as wide as it is tall.
Season: Evergreen; flowering profusely in the spring, in cultivation often with sporadic flowers from autumn through spring, especially when grown south of its natural range.
Maintenance: None.

Motility: None or essentially none in most garden situations, solitary plants rarely forming viable seed.
Growing Conditions: Deep, well-drained sandy soil in full sun; Zone 8.
Propagation: Seed; cuttings.
Comments: Conradinas are dwarf, densely leafy, and much-branched shrubs in the mint family, reminiscent of the aromatic, woody mints that occur in the Mediterranean region. However, conradinas are true natives, with the greatest concentration of species occurring in Florida. Apparently, all species except *Conradina canescens* are threatened or endangered as a result of habitat destruction since they grow in well-drained sandy areas that are favored by developers. *Conradina canescens* is easily grown if provided with well-drained soil in full sun and is readily propagated from either seed or cuttings. Plants tend to be short-lived and, after about three years, usually exhaust themselves by flowering and seeding to death. In spite of this short lifespan, plants grow with great rapidity and quickly form gnarled woody shrubs that look centuries old and have much character. Presently, two forms are in cultivation, one with dark grayish green leaves, the other with light silvery green leaves. The former is usually called the "green form" and it can form huge plants about 2½ feet high and 5–6 feet wide. It also appears to be longer-lived than is typical for most conradinas. The latter is usually referred to as the "gray form" and it is a smaller, short-lived plant. There is some speculation that they may represent different species. Both are spectacular "big bang" bloomers easily capable of producing thousands of flowers during a flowering season.

176. *Cordia globosa*

Common Name: Bloodberry
Habit: Small, densely branched and densely leafy shrub often growing in a symmetrical, rounded shape.

Size: Plant 4–9 feet high and usually as wide.

Season: Evergreen; flowering and fruiting year-round except during severe dry or cold spells.

Fruit: Small, brilliant red berries.

Maintenance: Occasional pruning to maintain desired shape and height, or none in the wild garden.

Motility: Numerous self-sown seedlings forming around and near the parent plant.

Growing Conditions: Tropical hammocks in nearly full sun to moderate shade; Zones 10–11.

Propagation: Seed.

Comments: Bloodberry has small, pale to dark, lime green leaves and begins to flower in less than a year from seed. The small white flowers are borne in dense, rounded heads about the size of a large marble, and they make an interesting but not particularly showy display. What they lack in ornamental value they make up with their abundant production of nectar, which is avidly sought by a wide variety of interesting and usually colorful insects, including various butterflies. The flowers are followed by red berries, but these are

too small to have much ornamental value. Because of its small leaves and densely branching habit, bloodberry makes an excellent native hedge plant and may be trimmed to nearly any desired height or shape. It is also useful for formal landscape effects, including standards.

177. *Crataegus marshallii*

Common Name: Parsley Hawthorn; Parsley Haw

Habit: Small, often multitrunked, shrubby tree, usually thorny and bearing deeply lobed parsley-like foliage, white flowers, and attractive fruits.

Size: Growing up to 20 feet tall but flowering and fruiting when much smaller.

Season: Deciduous; showy white flowers with red-tipped anthers borne in the spring; fruits ripening in the autumn.

Fruit: Small, apple-like, bright red berries attractive to wildlife.

Maintenance: None; do not plant where sharp thorns may be a problem.

Motility: Some plants suckering, especially where surface roots are disturbed.

Growing Conditions: Partially shaded understory of moist to wet woodlands; Zones 8–9A.

Propagation: Seed (scarify and/or stratify); cuttings; grafting.

Comments: Parsley hawthorn is an attractive small tree that deserves to be grown in every garden that can accommodate its one specific need: continuously moist soil. The deeply divided and lobed leaves do resemble parsley to a remarkable degree and create an elegant and refined appearance. They serve as a perfect foil for the beautiful spring flowers of pure white, accented by dark red anthers. In time, these are followed by tiny, edible, bright yellowish red apple-like fruits. In winter, when leafless, the plant is attractive for its exfoliating grayish brown bark. Of the native hawthorns that favor wet areas, parsley hawthorn has the widest distribution in Florida and is the one most readily available from native plant nurseries.

178. *Crataegus michauxii* (Synonyms: *Crataegus flava* (misapplied); *Crataegus lepida*)

Common Name: Michaux's Hawthorn
Habit: Large thorny shrub or small tree with an irregular crown, usually with the branches pendant and "weeping."
Size: Highly variable, from a few feet to 15 or 20 feet tall, the crown usually two-thirds or more as wide.

Season: Deciduous northward, partially evergreen southward; rather large white flowers borne in the spring; fruits borne in the autumn.
Fruit: Small, yellowish red apple-like fruits borne in late summer or autumn.
Maintenance: None; do not plant where its thorns may pose a problem.
Motility: None under most garden conditions.
Growing Conditions: Dry, well-drained sandy soils in full sun to light shade; Zones 8–9.
Propagation: Seed (scarify and/or stratify); cuttings; grafting.
Comments: Michaux's hawthorn has been the subject of much taxonomic confusion and in the past was referred to *Crataegus flava,* another species native to Florida but a rarer plant with a much more limited distribution. According to Wunderlin (1998:327), *Crataegus michauxii* is the only hawthorn in which the leaves have conspicuous and persistent dark glands, like tiny pinheads, along their margins. Toward the north of its natural range, this plant often has a distinctive growth habit with beautifully pendant branches. In some forms, this trait is so highly developed that the branches "weep" nearly or fully to the ground. Luckily, this attractive shrub readily adapts to average garden conditions if provided with well-drained soil and full sun. There is a dwarf, intricately branched form of this species in sand scrub with concomitantly tiny leaves, often no larger than a fingernail. This form is sometimes treated as a separate species, *Crataegus lepida.* The dwarf form is worth seeking out as a charming diminutive shrub suitable for even the tiniest garden.

179. *Crossopetalum ilicifolium*

Common Name: Christmas-Berry; Quailberry; Ground-Holly

Habit: Dwarf spreading or prostrate shrub.

Size: Plant rarely as much as 12 inches tall, but spreading and forming a groundcover 2–3 feet wide with age.

Season: Evergreen; flowering and fruiting all year except during prolonged cold or dry spells.

Fruit: Relatively large, highly ornamental red berries.

Maintenance: None or essentially none.

Motility: None in most garden situations.

Growing Conditions: Rocky pinelands in full sun to light shade; Zones 10–11.

Propagation: Seed.

Comments: Christmas-berry is a dwarf spreading shrub of delightful form. The small paired leaves are evergreen, bear three or four spiny teeth on each side, and have a marked resemblance to holly leaves. The tiny, greenish and inconspicuous flowers are followed by bright red berries and, together with the holly-like foliage, produce a highly ornamental effect. Although this plant is somewhat tolerant of shade, best growth is made in moist but well-drained soils in full sun. Propagation from seed is very slow, the main requirement being patience, since the seed may take eight or more months to germinate. However, germination rates of 33 percent within 10.5 weeks of sowing have been reported when the seeds are lightly nicked at one end (Brown 1995). Initial growth of young plants is slow, but with good culture they will begin to flower and bear fruit when eighteen to twenty-four months old and, by three years of age, can cover 2–3 square feet of ground.

Special Note: Do not confuse this plant with *Lycium carolinianum,* an unrelated plant that is also commonly known as Christmas-berry.

180. *Crossopetalum rhacoma*

Common Name: Rhacoma; Maiden-Berry

Habit: Small spreading to erect shrub.

Size: Slowly growing to 1½–6 feet tall, depending on the form and cultural conditions; low forms often much wider than they are tall.

Season: Evergreen; flowering and fruiting throughout the year except during prolonged dry or cold spells.

Fruit: Relatively large, brilliant red, one-seeded berries.

Maintenance: None or essentially none.

Motility: None in most garden situations.
Growing Conditions: Tropical pinelands and hammocks in full sun to moderate shade; Zones 9B–11.
Propagation: Seed.
Comments: Although described as an erect shrub or small tree in most references, rhacoma is variable and there exist low, spreading forms that make an excellent groundcover. All forms are attractive with many horticulturally desirable traits. The leaves are small and the plants present a graceful and refined appearance in cultivation. The tiny, inconspicuous flowers lack ornamental value, but they are followed by relatively large berries of intense red, and a well-grown plant in full fruit makes a beautiful accent in the garden. Additionally, rhacoma is generally pest- and disease-free, is highly drought tolerant once established, and grows well in coastal situations. It has a slow growth rate, but like its relative the Christmas-berry, in cultivation it too will begin to flower and bear fruit when only eighteen months to two years old.

181. *Croton humilis*

Common Name: Pepperbush
Habit: Dwarf shrub.
Size: Slowing growing to about 3 feet tall and nearly as wide.
Season: Evergreen; flowering all year except during prolonged cold or dry spells.
Maintenance: None.
Motility: Often spreading by self-sown seed in open areas of the garden.
Growing Conditions: Tropical hammocks in full sun to moderate shade; Zones 10–11.
Propagation: Seed.
Comments: Pepperbush is an unassuming little tropical shrub with subtle charms that slowly and quietly win gardeners over to it. One is perhaps first taken by its overall rounded and symmetrical shape. The dark green leaves are also notable: they have an odd quality to them resulting from a light dusting of tiny white, star-shaped hairs. The fact that pepperbush is a tough plant and can tolerate much adversity is an additional favorable feature. Last, there are the quaint little flowers borne at the ends of every branch. The flowers form little white starbursts that are conspicuous in contrast with the dark foliage. Both male and female

flowers are quaintly attractive, the male flowers being slightly more ornamental. The leaves and stems have oil glands and, when chewed, are initially flavorless. However, in a few minutes there develops a hot, lingering, peppery sensation in the mouth, accounting for the plant's common name.

Special Note: The plants commonly called crotons and featuring highly colorful variegated leaves are members of the genus *Codiaeum* and should not be confused with native plants in the genus *Croton.*

182. *Croton punctatus*

Common Name: Beach-Tea; Gulf Croton

Habit: Short-lived, small, silvery-leaved shrub naturally growing in a rounded, hemispherical shape.

Size: Height 1–3 feet and about as wide or wider than it is all.

Season: Evergreen southward, toward the north often an annual or short-lived perennial; flowering and fruiting all year southward but the flowers and fruits are insignificant.

Maintenance: None.

Motility: Casually establishing a few self-sown seedlings now and then.

Growing Conditions: Coastal dunes in full sun; Zones 8B–10.

Propagation: Seed.

Comments: Beach-tea is one of the most intensely silvery shrubs native to Florida. All parts of the plant are covered with minute silvery scales and star-shaped hairs. In full sun, certain forms look as if they are made out of aluminum or covered with silver paint. Beach-tea makes an excellent specimen plant in the garden and may be grown in front of dark-leaved plants for maximum contrast. It is also attractive when grown by itself on sandy soil, the metallic shine of the foliage then contrasting attractively with the matte sand. Of course, since it is native to coastal sand dunes, this plant revels in full sun, is impervious to wind and blowing sand, and tolerates occasional salt spray. On the negative side, it can be grown only where one can provide well-drained sandy soil, and it is wholly unforgiving of excessively wet, highly organic soils and of being shaded by other plants. Another silver-leaved croton (*Croton argyranthemus*) occurs in Florida. It is a winter-dormant, stoloniferous perennial native to sandhills and scrub.

Special Note: The plants commonly called crotons and featuring highly colorful variegated leaves are members of the genus *Codiaeum* and should not be confused with the native plants in the genus *Croton.*

183. *Cyrilla racemiflora* (Synonyms: *Cyrilla arida* and *Cyrilla parvifolia*)

Common Name: Titi

Habit: Shrub or small tree, developing with age a distinctive and striking architectural quality.

Size: Usually 12–20 feet tall and about as wide; dwarf forms occur that rarely exceed 6 feet in height.

Season: Deciduous northward, evergreen southward; flowering in the spring; brilliant autumnal foliage northward.

Maintenance: None or occasional judicious pruning to maintain desired shape or size.

Motility: Rarely spreading from seed, some forms slowly forming thickets by root suckers.

Growing Conditions: Swamps and bogs in full sun to rather deep shade, rarely occurring in scrub; Zones 8–9.

Propagation: Seed; cuttings.

Comments: For Floridians with suitably moist, acidic soil, titi makes a splendid specimen plant densely covered with rather small, dark green leaves. In the spring, the branch tips produce a new set of leaves and, immediately below the new leaves, elongated hanging spikes of small white flowers. A mature plant in full flower produces a highly ornamental effect. In the autumn, the foliage turns various shades of brilliant yellow veined with scarlet and orange. Titi is remarkable for its extremely wide morphological range; depending on the plant's genetics, habitat, and moisture level, it may vary from a dwarf shrublet barely 3 feet high to a medium-sized tree about 40 feet high.

184. *Dodonaea viscosa*

Common Name: Varnishleaf

Habit: Small to large shrub or small tree with slender stems, the leaves coated with a slightly sticky resin; sometimes the sexes separate and the plants then either male or female.

Size: Usually 6–12 feet tall at full maturity, up to 3 feet tall or so when grown in dry soil in full sun.

Season: Evergreen; flowers borne in spring and summer, the fruits borne in late spring to autumn.

Fruit: Inflated winged capsules, often brilliant red when young and maturing to pale chestnut brown.

Maintenance: None or judicious pruning to maintain desired size and shape.

Motility: Now and then spreading from self-sown seed if conditions are right.

Growing Conditions: Sunny, open sites near the coast, including dunes, pinelands, and hammocks; Zones 9–11.

Propagation: Seed.

Comments: Varnishleaf is a highly successful plant that occurs in tropical and subtropical coastal thickets throughout the entire world. This alone speaks of its tough, adaptable character. It has a wide distribution in central and southern peninsular Florida and has been recorded as far north as St. Johns County. A second species of varnishleaf occurs in the Florida Keys: *Dodonaea elaeagnoides*. It tends to have smaller leaves with a blunt tip and grows into a symmetrical, densely branched, rounded shrub; *Dodonaea viscosa* has larger, linear-elliptic leaves several times longer than they are wide and tends to grow as a somewhat irregular open shrub. The former is better suited as a specimen plant or in formal situations. Both are equally hardy plants, drought tolerant and salt tolerant, and suited for fence rows, hedges, and the wild garden in southern Florida. The flowers scarcely attract notice but they are followed by unusual, somewhat decorative three-winged capsules. In the very best forms, the young capsules are deep red with a glossy, highly varnished appearance, and such plants merit selective propagation. Occasionally, decorative purple-leaved plants appear in the nursery trade. These plants are said to originate from wild stock in New Zealand, and they temporarily lose their purple color during hot weather.

185. *Ernodea littoralis*

Common Name: Beach Creeper

Habit: Dwarf sprawling shrub with dark green shiny leaves.

Size: Highly variable depending on growing conditions, usually 1–2 feet tall and spreading 3–6 feet.

Season: Evergreen; flowers and fruits borne all year except during prolonged cold or dry spells.

Fruit: Small yellow berries.

Maintenance: None or judicious pruning to maintain desired size.

Motility: Can sparingly sucker from the roots; stems may root where they touch the ground; spreading by self-sown seed is rare or absent in most gardens.

Growing Conditions: Coastal dunes and edges of coastal hammocks in full or nearly full sun; Zones 9–11.

Propagation: Seed; cuttings.

Comments: Beach creeper is a tough, indestructible groundcovering shrub restricted to coastal sites in sandy or rocky areas close to the Gulf of Mexico or the Atlantic Ocean. The stems are widely spreading with a tendency to arch to the ground. When happily situated, it may cover fairly sizable areas, and it is being recommended as a groundcover for hot, dry, difficult areas. The leaves are an intense bright glossy green, giving the plant an extremely attractive appearance. With age, the leaves become tinged with yellow. The flowers and fruits are too small to have much ornamental value, but they do add an interesting note to this unusual native shrub. Borne throughout the year, the tubular flowers vary from white to pink and are followed by long-lasting yellow berries. Tip cuttings root readily and afford an easy means of propagation.

186. *Erythrina herbacea*

Common Name: Coralbean; Cherokee-Bean; Red-Cardinal

Habit: Prickly plant with oddly shaped three-part leaves; form highly variable, a perennial dying to the ground northward, a small erect or spreading shrub southward, becoming a sizable tree in southernmost Florida.

Size: Height variable from 3 to 24 feet, depending on form and growing conditions; low, shrubby forms usually as wide as they are tall, some forms sprawling and about twice as wide as they are tall.

Season: Dying to the ground in winter northward, a deciduous shrub throughout most of peninsular Florida, partially evergreen in southern Florida; heavily flowering in the spring, the fruits maturing in autumn.

Fruit: Brown bean pods 4–5 inches long, splitting open to reveal several brilliant red, but poisonous, seeds.

Maintenance: Northward, annual removal of stems that have died to the ground; southward, none or else periodic pruning to maintain desired height and shape; prune just after flowering since flowers are borne on the prior year's branches.

Motility: Self-sown seedlings occasionally establish near the parent plant.

Growing Conditions: Somewhat moist to rather dry hammocks in nearly full sun to rather deep shade, occasionally growing in dry, sandy areas in full sun; Zones 8–11.

Propagation: Seed (scarify); branch cuttings.

Comments: Coralbeans are tough plants that grow from greatly enlarged woody roots. As a result, they can withstand harsh conditions and severe insect attacks by going dormant and surviving on the reserves of food and water stored in the root system. The plants are prickly, the prickles sometimes extending even into the leaves along the principal veins. Leaves are divided into three leaflets, and coralbeans have a highly ornamental aspect due to their attractive, unusually shaped leaflets. The plants are spectacular when in full flower, the tips of nearly every branch bearing elegant, elongated spikes of large, tubular, brilliant rose, orange, or red flowers. The flowers, like all red tubular flowers, are irresistible to hummingbirds. Plants are easily propagated by scarified seed or by placing stems in the ground and keeping them moist. Erythrinas are attacked in Florida by the erythrina stem borer and leaf miners; depredations by these insects may disfigure the plant and result in poor flowering. Some forms of coralbean appear to be resistant to these pests, and these should be sought out for cultivation.

187. *Euonymus americanus*

Common Name: Strawberry-Bush; Hearts-A'-Burstin'

Habit: Weakly stoloniferous shrub with few erect or straggling green-stemmed branches.

Size: About 6 feet tall.

Season: Deciduous with attractive autumnal leaf color, occasionally weakly evergreen southward; flowers insignificant, borne in the spring or summer, fruit maturing in the autumn.

Fruit: Highly unusual five-lobed capsule with a warty outer surface, crimson at maturity and splitting open to reveal scarlet-skinned seeds.

Maintenance: None or occasional cutting back of wayward root sprout.

Motility: Slowly forming loose colonies with age; spread by self-sown seedlings uncommon.

Growing Conditions: Moist woodlands and stream banks in light to deep shade; Zones 8–9.

Propagation: Seed; root suckers.

Comments: Hearts-a'-burstin' is an unusual common name for an unusual little shrub. The plant has an odd pattern of growth, consisting of a few rigidly erect stems. Thus, it scarcely provides any cover for animals and, in most garden situations, tends to get "lost" among the branches and greenery of other plants. Nearly everything about hearts-a'-burstin' is some shade of green, including its branches and small flowers. However, in the autumn when goldenrods and asters are a riot of color, it too puts on a colorful, if more modest display. The fruit is a crimson capsule that splits open to reveal seeds covered with a scarlet skin. The seeds do not fall out but are persistent until plucked out by a bird or small animal. This is an enchanting plant, its allure increasing as one becomes more familiar with it, and its propagation entails nothing more than potting up young root suckers.

Special Note: Do not confuse this plant with *Calycanthus floridus,* an unrelated plant that shares the common name of strawberry-bush.

188. *Forestiera segregata*

Common Name: Florida-Privet
Habit: Large, densely leafy shrub with male and female flowers borne on separate plants.
Size: Usually 9–10 feet tall (rarely up to 20 feet tall), often nearly as wide as it is tall.
Season: Evergreen, sometimes deciduous northward; flowering and fruiting intermittently from spring through autumn but especially during warm, rainy periods.
Fruit: Female plants bearing one-seeded, blackish purple berries.
Maintenance: None or else judicious pruning to maintain desired shape and height.
Motility: Now and then spreading by bird-dispersed seed.
Growing Conditions: Growing in a variety of dry to wet habitats in full sun to nearly full shade; Zones 8B–11.
Propagation: Seed.
Comments: Florida-privet is distinct from all other species of *Forestiera* native to Florida in its evergreen leaves with an untoothed margin. Like so many other native plants, it is remarkably adaptable and may be grown in both shady and sunny situations in moist or dryish soil. Typically, its leaves are 1.2–2.4 inches long, but a distinctive, small-leaved variant also occurs in Florida (*Forestiera segregata* var. *pinetorum*). Both the regular and small-leaved forms make excellent, tough, pest-resistant garden plants. As a result of their stiff, densely leafy branches, Florida-privets make excellent hedge plants that may be trimmed to any desired height or shape. The typical form is favored where a large hedge is necessary for privacy, whereas the small-leaved form makes an excellent small hedge or specimen plant. Although the flowers are small and inconspicuous and lack petals, they are sweetly fragrant and provide abundant nectar for an assortment of insects.

189. *Garberia heterophylla*

Common Name: Garberia
Habit: Dwarf shrub in the daisy family.
Size: Mostly 1½–3 feet high and about as wide as it is tall; can grow up to 6 feet high in cultivation.
Season: Evergreen; flowering mostly in late autumn, occasionally also in the winter, spring, or summer.
Maintenance: None in the wild garden, otherwise pruning of old flowers and seed heads.
Motility: Usually none in most garden situations.
Growing Conditions: Exceedingly well drained, sandy soil in full or nearly full sun; Zones 8B–9.
Propagation: Seed.
Comments: Garberia is one of the few members of the daisy family in Florida that has a

woody, shrubby growth habit. It has a low spreading crown composed of woody branches arising near the base of the plant. These are clothed with grayish green leaves with a more or less rounded outline. The resulting shrub is interesting but rather coarse. In full flower, the tips of every branch bear large clusters of delicately graceful pink flowers. People are not the only ones delighted by a flowering garberia; butterflies of all kinds succumb to the nectar-filled flowers. As a result, this plant has been enthusiastically recommended for butterfly gardens with well-drained, sandy soil.

190. *Gossypium hirsutum*

Common Name: Wild Cotton
Habit: Large shrub, flowering and fruiting in about six months from seed.
Size: Reaching 6–12 feet tall and as wide as or wider than it is high.
Season: Evergreen; flowers and fruits borne intermittently throughout the year except during prolonged dry or cold spells.
Fruit: Large capsule splitting open to reveal a mass of white to brownish cotton, in which the seeds are embedded.

Maintenance: None or else judicious pruning to maintain desired shape and height; sometimes plants are weakly rooted and require staking.
Motility: Occasionally spreading by self-sown seeds.
Growing Conditions: Coastal hammocks and the drier landward side of mangrove swamps in full sun to moderate shade; Zones 9–11.
Propagation: Seed.

Comments: Wild cotton is among the easiest of plants to cultivate. Scarified seeds germinate readily when kept warm and moist, with the young plants beginning to flower in about five months. The flowers last only a single day, but they are produced throughout the year. They are a soft lemon yellow, fading to maroon-red as they age, and are followed by capsules that split open to reveal a rather large mass of cotton, in which the seeds are embedded. The cotton bolls persist on the plant for many weeks and lend a somewhat decorative effect. The cotton is markedly variable from plant to plant, some forms producing highly decorative and conspicuous pure white cotton of long, fine fibers and others producing a far less decorative brownish cotton of short, coarse fibers. Wild cotton is a coastal species that is equally at home in full sun near the beach and in the deep shade of coastal hammocks and mangrove swamps. Thus, it is readily adaptable to a variety of home garden situations.

191. *Guettarda scabra*

Common Name: Roughleaf Velvetseed
Habit: A rather open shrubby tree with stiffly ascending branches.
Size: Height variable, usually 10–15 feet tall but occasionally treelike and reaching 30 feet.
Season: Evergreen; flowering and fruiting intermittently all year, especially during warm, rainy periods.
Fruit: An odd, wine-red, dryish berry covered with soft, velvety hairs.
Maintenance: None or essentially none.
Motility: None or essentially none in most garden situations.
Growing Conditions: Hammocks and rocky pinelands in full sun to moderate shade; Zones 9B–11.
Propagation: Seed.
Comments: If you live in southern Florida and require a specimen plant of singular appearance, few are better suited than roughleaf velvetseed. First, it has a striking form and produces a narrow, open crown composed of rigidly ascending branches. The singular foliage is unlike anything else available in cultivation in Florida. The large leaves are borne in opposite pairs, have deeply impressed veins, and are a rich dark green. Their entire upper surface is covered with stiff hairs, giving them a sandpaper-like texture, yet, surprisingly, they are somewhat glossy. Young leaves are a rich burgundy brown and pleasingly contrast with the older foliage. Although the flowers are too small to put on much of a show, their white color, tinged with pale pink, makes a nice contrast against the dark foliage and they are delightfully fragrant at night. They are followed by burgundy red berries seemingly clothed in velvet. Roughleaf velvetseed is easily grown but it is slow-growing in comparison to most other native shrubs and demands a warm, well-drained sunny position.

192. *Hamamelis virginiana*

Common Name: Witch-Hazel

Habit: Large multistemmed shrub, usually about as wide as or wider than it is tall.

Size: Slowly growing to about 15 feet high.

Season: Deciduous; aromatic flowers borne in late autumn as the leaves begin to

fall; foliage becoming brilliant yellow in the autumn.

Maintenance: None.

Motility: None in most garden situations.

Growing Conditions: Rich, moist woodlands in partial shade; Zones 8–9A.

Propagation: Seed (double dormancy).

Comments: Witch-hazel is a robust, appealing shrub with three principal horticultural attributes. First, it has large, attractive leaves that resemble those of the unrelated hazelnuts but are less shiny. As such, it is perfect for planting in the understory to fill in open areas under taller trees. The remaining two attributes are borne together: spicy, aromatic flowers and brilliant gold autumnal foliage. The habit of flowering as the foliage is being dropped for the winter is an unusual one, and witch-hazel is certainly among the last plants to flower in much of northern and north-central Florida. Plants have no serious pests or diseases and may be grown in sun or shade, although they look better if grown in partial shade. Witch-hazels greatly resent transplanting and, for best growth, require rich, moist soil with a thick covering of mulch or leaves to provide a cool root run.

193. *Hamelia patens*

Common Name: Firebush

Habit: Densely branched and densely leafy large shrub or small tree.

Size: Highly variable, 3–5 feet tall and often dying to the ground in central Florida but becoming a large, 15-foot-tall shrub southward.

Season: Evergreen; flowering and fruiting throughout the year except during prolonged cold or dry spells.

Fruit: Small reddish berries ripening to blackish purple.

Maintenance: None in the wild garden, severe pruning to maintain desired shape and height in more formal gardens.

Motility: Spreading by bird-dispersed fruits.

Growing Conditions: Moist hammocks in nearly full sun to rather deep shade; Zones 8B–11.

Propagation: Seed; cuttings.

Comments: Firebush is an indispensable plant for the native garden in central and southern Florida. Even without a single flower, firebush attracts notice by its dark green leaves tinged in various shades of red or burgundy. The small tubular flowers, in varying combinations of yellow and red, are unlike those of any other plant native to the United States and lend the plant a highly exotic appearance. Firebush attracts butterflies and hummingbirds and is regarded as a premier butterfly nectar plant. It also appeals to an assortment of small animals and birds through its prodigious production of juicy berries. Plants grow rapidly, and cuttings will flower when only a few months old at a height of about 18 inches. In addition to its use in native and butterfly gardens, firebush is suitable as a specimen or accent plant, and because of its large size and rapid growth, it may be utilized as a screen. Firebush does not withstand freezing temperatures; it will die back to the roots. However, it readily sprouts back from the roots and will regrow to its former height in twelve to eighteen months.

194. *Hypericum hypericoides*

Common Name: St. Andrew's-Cross
Habit: Erect, dwarf shrub.
Size: Mostly 1–2 feet tall, usually about as wide as or wider than it is tall.

Season: Evergreen; flowering in the summer and autumn northward, all year southward.

Maintenance: None or essentially none if appropriately placed.

Motility: Spreading by seeds into moist areas; not suckering or very slow to sucker.

Growing Conditions: Wet or moist pine flatwoods in full sun to full shade; Zones 8–10.

Propagation: Seed.

Comments: The vast majority of hypericums are plants of wet sunny areas that do not do well in the shade. However, St. Andrew's-cross is an easily grown, highly adaptable little shrub that occurs in pine flatwoods, where it grows under a variety of conditions ranging from full sun to full shade. As such, it is one of the few hypericums that may be grown as an understory to tall trees, although the plant will be leggier and will produce fewer flowers than when grown in bright light. It has a long flowering season including the summer, a time when few understory plants are flowering. St. Andrew's-cross is admittedly not one of Florida's showier hypericums. Its flowers are rather small, soft, and pale yellow, and the four petals do not overlap to create a full effect. However, it is a plant of subtle charms that slowly grow on you, ensuring a place in the gardener's heart, as it grows and flowers well where few other plants will do so.

195. *Hypericum lissophloeus*

Common Name: Weeping St. John's-Wort; Smoothbark St. John's-Wort

Habit: Erect shrub with exceedingly fine needle-like foliage and beautiful weeping branches.

Size: Averaging about 6 feet tall and about half to two-thirds as wide.

Season: Evergreen; intermittently flowering from late spring through autumn.

Maintenance: None or essentially none if appropriately placed.

Motility: Amount of root suckering variable depending on growing conditions.

Growing Conditions: Pond margins in full sun to light shade; Zone 8.

Propagation: Seed.

Comments: *Hypericum lissophloeus* is not your typical St. John's-wort but is a small shrub that is full of surprises. First, it has a unique and interesting background as one of the rarest hypericums in the world: plants are known only from a few pond margins and sinks in Bay and Washington counties in Florida's Panhandle. Young plants have blackish

brown to almost black bark, such that the stems appear to have been fashioned from cylindrical pieces of charcoal. With age, however, the bark becomes smooth and silvery gray. Also unusual are the thin, wispy branches, which hang down to produce a lovely weeping effect. These are accented along the tips with rather large, golden yellow flowers with a boss of prominent stamens. All of these qualities combine to produce a superlatively beautiful native shrub. Fortunately, this remarkable plant is easily grown under average garden conditions and, once established, is quite drought tolerant. In the nursery trade it is sometimes confused with *Hypericum nitidum,* a similar plant characterized by thin bark that exfoliates in flakes or narrow strips.

196. *Hypericum myrtifolium*

Common Name: Myrtleleaf St. John's-Wort
Habit: Erect, dwarf shrub, often colonial by way of underground root suckers.
Size: Mostly 2–3 feet tall, usually about half to two-thirds as wide.
Season: Evergreen; intermittently flowering from late winter through autumn.
Maintenance: None or essentially none if appropriately placed.
Motility: Eventually forming colonies by root suckers.
Growing Conditions: Wet flatwoods and pond margins in full sun to light shade; Zones 8–10.
Propagation: Seed; root suckers.
Comments: Myrtleleaf St. John's-wort is distinguished by its broad, rounded leaves and large, highly attractive golden yellow flowers. Like so many wetland hypericums, it produces suckers, often at surprisingly long distances from the parent plant. Fortunately, it suckers sparingly, and in more formal garden situations the suckers may be easily pulled out in the autumn before they have fully rooted. It is likely that this ornamental plant will become more widespread in cultivation, especially as superior forms are selected and propagated.

197. *Hypericum reductum*

Common Name: Aromatic St. John's-Wort; Atlantic St. John's-Wort
Habit: A tiny, diffuse shrub when young, with age forming a more or less prostrate groundcover.
Size: Highly variable from 6 to 18 inches tall; taller forms up to about 3 times as wide as they are tall, short forms often very much wider than they are tall and forming a

groundcover.
Season: Evergreen; intermittently flowering from late spring through autumn, or flowering all year southward.
Maintenance: None or essentially none if appropriately placed.
Motility: None in most garden situations.
Growing Conditions: Exceedingly dry to somewhat moist sandy soils in full sun; Zones 8–10A.

Propagation: Seed.

Comments: All hypericums possess oil glands, but *Hypericum reductum* is exceptional in the large size of the oil glands present in its leaves. When the foliage is crushed, it releases a scent that varies from plant to plant but is usually likened to lemons with a hint of turpentine. It is an ideal little shrub for a well-drained sunny spot and, in cultivation, quickly becomes an extremely dense, solid mass of dark emerald green set off by the tiny golden flowers borne at the branch tips. Since it is a plant of sandhills and scrub, it always occurs in open areas in full sun with sandy soil. A similar species, *Hypericum brachyphyllum,* occurs in moist areas and is suitable for gardens that are too wet for *H. reductum.*

198. Hypericum tetrapetalum

Common Name: Blueleaf St. John's-Wort; Fourpetal St. John's-Wort

Habit: Dwarf shrub with blue-green foliage; some forms with multiple spreading stems, others with a single erect main stem.

Height: Erect forms mostly 2–3 feet tall; prostrate or spreading forms up to 1½ feet high and about twice as wide.

Season: Evergreen; intermittently flowering from late spring through autumn.

Maintenance: None or essentially none if appropriately placed.

Motility: Rarely or moderately spreading by root suckers.

Growing Conditions: Moist flatwoods in full sun to light shade; Zones 8–10.

Propagation: Seed.

Comments: Blueleaf St. John's-wort is a useful hypericum for average garden conditions. It is a shrubby plant, the habit of which may vary from spreading to erect. The spreading form makes an ideal groundcover, a single plant covering 3–4 square feet of ground in about one year in southern Florida (growth is slower with the shorter growing season in northern Florida). Erect forms make attractive specimen plants and in time form single-trunked, globe-shaped crowns. This is a very distinctive plant and one of our more easily recognized St. John's-worts because of its blue-green foliage and rather large, brilliant lemon yellow flowers. Its only horticultural flaw is the seed capsules, which are enveloped in large, conspicuous, leafy sepals that tend to detract somewhat from the plant's overall neat appearance.

199. Ilex verticillata

Common Name: Winterberry

Habit: Large multistemmed shrub.

Size: Grows up to 15 feet high and about as wide.

Season: Deciduous; flowers small, borne in spring; fruits maturing in the autumn.

Fruit: Small, long-lasting brilliant red berries.

Maintenance: None.

Motility: None in most garden conditions.

Growing Conditions: Moist woodland edges and swamps in Florida's Panhandle; Zone 8.

Propagation: Seeds (double dormancy, may take two years to germinate); cuttings.

Comments: Florida's five species of deciduous hollies generally occur in moist to wet habitats such as rich woodlands, along the banks of streams, and in swamps. Thus, female plants are especially useful for adding late season color in difficult, wet garden situations. Winterberry lacks noteworthy foliage and autumn color; however, it makes a brilliant show in winter when its leafless stems are festooned with ample quantities of bright red berries. Outside the Panhandle, gardeners may try sand holly (*Ilex ambigua*). Sand holly grows farther south to central peninsular Florida (USDA Zones 8–9), and it is our only native deciduous holly that is adaptable to dry, sandy soils.

200. *Illicium parviflorum*

Common Name: Yellow Anisetree

Habit: Large shrub or small tree with highly aromatic anise- or licorice-scented foliage.

Height: Growing up to 15 feet high but usually smaller, with a broad, densely leafy crown.

Season: Evergreen; bearing numerous, small pale yellow flowers in spring; fruits maturing in late summer or autumn.

Fruit: Unusual, star-shaped capsule.

Maintenance: None; may be pruned to any desired height or shape.

Motility: Rarely spreading by self-sown seedlings into moist, open areas.

Growing Conditions: Rich wet hammocks and swamps in partial to full shade; Zones 8B–9.

Propagation: Seed; cuttings.

Comments: Yellow anisetree is a rare plant native to rich, moist forests in six counties in north-central Florida. Yet, amazingly, it has proven to be an exceptionally tough, broadleaf evergreen amenable to a wide variety of landscape uses and situations.

Once fully established, it exhibits considerable drought tolerance and will grow under a range of light conditions from deep shade to full sun. Additionally, it is apparently pest- and disease-free, and the plants make excellent hedges or screens that may be pruned to any desired height or shape. However, like most broadleaf plants, it looks best as an informal hedge that is not pruned into a rigid geometrical shape. The small flowers are admittedly not very showy, but they and the subsequent star-shaped fruits do add a quaintly charming accent to the plant. The exquisitely fragrant foliage is not to be missed, and as a result this plant is being cultivated by Florida herb gardeners. Florida anisetree (*Illicium floridanum*) is a related plant restricted to the central and western Panhandle. It requires cool, moist, shady conditions, tends to be smaller, and has larger and showier maroon-red flowers.

201. *Itea virginica*

Common Name: Sweetspires; Tassel White; Virginia-Willow

Habit: Small to large suckering shrub.

Size: Height variable from 3 to 9 feet tall, depending on form and growing conditions; usually as wide as it is tall.

Season: Deciduous northward with brilliant autumnal foliage, weakly evergreen southward; heavily flowering in the spring.

Maintenance: None or essentially none if appropriately placed.

Motility: Colonial by way of underground suckering stems.

Growing Conditions: Swamps in light to deep shade or occasionally in full sun; Zones 8–10A.

Propagation: Seed; cuttings; divisions.

Comments: In its natural home of shaded swamps, sweetspires is usually sparsely branched and rather lanky. However, in cultivation it reveals itself to be one of the most strikingly beautiful of all shrubs native to the United States. When grown in moist soil in bright but not full sun, it is more compact and produces numerous branches that become thickly clothed in dark green leaves. In the spring, it becomes covered with long spikes of white flowers that shine brightly against the dark foliage. In northern Florida, autumn brings a second transformation as the leaves assume brilliant orange-red hues. In small gardens, root suckers may prove troublesome. However, if sweetspires is introduced into the garden after other plants are mature, competition from the others will keep its colonial tendencies in check.

202. *Jacquinia keyensis*

Common Name: Joewood
Habit: Densely leafy, shrubby tree with a wide, densely branched crown and fragrant white flowers.
Size: Very slowly growing to about 10 feet, although with great age it may reach 20 feet in height; the crown is about two-thirds or more as wide as the plant is tall.
Season: Evergreen; flowering and fruiting intermittently from spring through autumn, especially during warm, rainy periods.
Fruit: Round yellow berries.
Maintenance: None or essentially none.
Motility: None or essentially none in most garden situations.
Growing Conditions: Moist to dry limestone soils in full sun to deep shade; Zones 10–11.
Propagation: Seed.
Comments: Joewood makes an unusual and interesting specimen or accent plant with two important wildlife benefits: its wonderfully fragrant, nectar-filled flowers attract a wide variety of insects, and the rounded berries are favored by birds and other small animals. Like nearly all southern Florida woody plants with tropical affinities, it has an iron constitution and, once established, can take whatever heat and drought our weather throw at it. Since it often occurs in coastal habitats, including the drier landward side of mangrove swamps, joewood also has considerable salt tolerance. It is rare in the nursery trade since it is not an easy plant to propagate and has a very slow growth rate. However, it is such a rewarding plant as to be well worth the patience required to seek it out and to wait the requisite number of years before it is sufficiently mature to flower and bear fruit regularly. According to Stephen Mullins (1993), joewoods have adapted to the pattern of summer rains and winter drought, and they live in full sun on the ridges, and yet we still find them deep in the forest and occasionally only a few feet from high tide level near the mangroves, with their deeper roots most certainly in salt water. A remarkable plant indeed!

203. *Koanophyllon villosum* (Synonym: *Eupatorium villosum*)

Common Name: Shrub Thoroughwort
Habit: Shrub or small tree in the daisy family.
Size: Up to about 6 feet tall and half or more as wide.
Season: Evergreen; flowering heavily in the autumn and again in the spring.
Maintenance: None or else light to heavy pruning to maintain desired height and shape.
Motility: Spreading from self-sown seedlings in sunny, moist garden areas.

Growing Conditions: Rocky pinelands and tropical hammocks in full sun to light shade; Zone 10.

Propagation: Seed; cuttings.

Comments: Throughout most of the year, shrub thoroughwort is a quietly attractive plant with lime green foliage clothed with minute, whitish hairs. It is unusual among Florida members of the daisy family in being a shrub and, with age, it may even assume a treelike appearance. It appreciates sunny, open areas but also grows well in light shade and looks its best at the edge of a ham-

mock, where its light green foliage and pure white flowers contrast nicely against the dark green background of hammock trees and shrubs. Depending on weather conditions, plants flower in the autumn, winter, and/or early spring, when numerous little white flower heads are borne at the tips of every branch. The flowers are lightly but pleasantly fragrant and are a rich source of nectar to which every butterfly in the vicinity succumbs. While not a spectacular plant, shrub thoroughwort does make an unusual and interesting addition to the wildflower garden and is charming and attractive when in full flower. In addition to its use in the garden, the flowering branches are easily utilized as cut flowers, with a single plant providing abundant cutting material.

204. *Lantana depressa*

Common Name: Pineland Lantana

Habit: Variable from prostrate to erect, depending on the variety.

Size: Variable from 0.5 to 6 feet tall, depending on the variety; small, prostrate forms much wider than they are tall.

Season: Evergreen; essentially everblooming except during prolonged dry and cold spells.

Maintenance: None or judicious pruning to maintain desired height and shape.

Motility: Usually none in most garden situations.

Growing Conditions: Rocky pinelands and dry open areas in full sun to very light shade; Zones 10.

Propagation: Seed; cuttings.

Comments: Pineland lantana is native only to Florida, where it occurs in three distinct varieties. Two are tall plants with erect or arching stems that somewhat resemble, and form hybrid

swarms with, the non-native common lantana (*Lantana camara*). Thus far, these varieties of pineland lantana do not appear to be in cultivation. The third variety is a dwarf, prostrate shrub with glossy, dark green leaves, eminently suitable as a groundcover. It is also a striking ornamental with brilliant, golden yellow flowers borne in large quantities throughout the year. Plants with creamy white flowers are also known, and these are useful for the gardener seeking a white-flowered plant that can withstand Florida's sultry summers. Although easily propagated from cuttings and readily grown in moist but well-drained soil in full sun, pineland lantana is extremely susceptible to root nematodes in cultivation and rarely survives for more than eighteen months. In spite of this, it is so colorful and attractive, and flowers so freely and abundantly from an early age, that it may well be treated like an annual if necessary. With regard to wildlife value, its principal use is as a butterfly nectar plant. The plants do bear dark purplish blue berries, but these are too scantily produced to be of much use to birds and other small animals.

Special Note: Most plants of *Lantana depressa* in cultivation are hybrids; as a true, un-hybridized species, this one will probably go extinct in the near future due to genetic swamping from *Lantana camara*.

205. *Licania michauxii*

Common Name: Gopher-Apple

Habit: Dwarf, woody groundcover spreading over several square yards by underground stems.

Size: Mostly 9–16 inches tall but capable of covering many square yards with age.

Season: Foliage persistent and evergreen; flowers mostly borne in spring and summer, the fruits maturing in summer and autumn.

Fruit: Rather large at 1–1½ inches, the one-seeded, whitish plumlike fruits are relished by mammals and gopher tortoises; the fruits are sometimes described as having a "lovely fragrance."

Maintenance: None.

Motility: Colonial by its subterranean, rhizomatous stem.

Growing Conditions: Deep, sandy soils in sandhill and scrub in full sun; Zones 8–11.

Propagation: Seed.

Comments: Gopher-apple is an interesting plant useful for its strong constitution and ability to stabilize sandy areas. Its growth habit has often been likened to that of a large subterranean woody shrub with only its branch tips growing up out of the ground. This growth habit is similar to that of several oaks that also occur in dry, deep sandy habitats and is clearly an adaptation that allows gopher-apples to withstand prolonged drought, scorching sun, and intense fires. But this growth habit makes this plant essentially impossible to transplant. It must be established in the garden from containerized, seed-grown plants. Horticulturally, it is valuable as an indestructible groundcover impervious to drought and highly salt tolerant. Additionally, its flowers are attractive to many insects and its fruits are edible to every animal large enough to ingest them, including humans. Species of *Licania* occur throughout the tropics, some reaching tree size; one species, *Licania platypus,* is sparingly cultivated as an exotic fruit tree in California with the common name of sansapote.

206. *Lycium carolinianum*

Common Name: Christmas-Berry
Habit: Unusual small to large open shrub, with gray, usually stiffly ascending branches, which may bear occasional thorns.
Size: Variable from 3 to 10 feet tall, depending on the form and growing conditions.
Season: Evergreen, or deciduous if stressed by drought; flowering and fruiting intermittently with heaviest flowering in the autumn and heaviest fruit set in winter.
Fruit: Multiseeded, brilliant red, egg-shaped berries.
Maintenance: None or judicious pruning to maintain desired height and shape.
Motility: Essentially none under most garden conditions.
Growing Conditions: Growing in open saline situations, such as salt marshes, in full sun; Zones 8B–11.
Propagation: Seed; cuttings.
Comments: Among Christmas-berry's useful horticultural qualities is its ability to grow in moist, brackish areas where the choice of plants is severely limited, and it is eminently suited for coastal sites so long as it can be supplied with adequate moisture. However, it is a remarkably adaptable plant. A seedling established in a dry, scrubby site adjusted to these inhospitable conditions by going dormant in the heat of summer and growing in the winter when the weather was cooler. Although the flowers are not large, they are quaintly attractive in a pretty purplish blue rarely found in Florida native plants. Christmas-berry is at its most ornamental when laden with its brilliant, clear red berries, which contrast wonderfully with the fleshy, grayish green foliage. Various non-native species of *Lycium* have been sparingly cultivated by exotic fruit fanciers for their berries, but it is not known if it is safe to use our native Christmas-berry in this fashion.
Special Note: Do not confuse this plant with *Crossopetalum ilicifolium,* an unrelated plant that shares the common name of Christmas-berry.

207. *Lyonia ferruginea*

Common Name: Rusty Staggerbush
Habit: Erect, often straggly or contorted shrub or small tree, somewhat colonial by underground stems.
Size: Plant 6–9 feet tall, the crown about half as wide.
Season: Evergreen; flowering in the spring.
Maintenance: None or, in more formal gardens, removal of old seed heads and root suckers.
Motility: Almost never spreading by seed; usually colonial by subterranean, suckering stems.
Growing Conditions: Scrub and flatwoods in dry to somewhat moist soils in full sun; Zones 8B–10.
Propagation: Seed.
Comments: There is scarcely a stretch of scrub or flatwoods in all of Florida where one can hike without encountering rusty staggerbush or its close relative *Lyonia fruticosa*. On first acquaintance, it blends into the background, an unassuming little shrub of no particular significance. But on becoming more familiar with it, one realizes that it is a picturesque and charming little shrub with an irregular growth form and distinctive leaves with turned-under margins. New growth appears in flushes and is a tawny, yellowish brown contrasting beautifully with the older, dark green foliage. The small white flowers are quaintly attractive, faintly but sweetly fragrant of roses and shaped like little globes with a pinched mouth. In the garden, rusty staggerbush asks only for acid well-drained soil, a sunny spot, and nothing more. Unfortunately, it is seldom offered by wildflower nurseries. However if no commercial source is available, it may be grown from its dustlike seed, which germinates readily in a few weeks. Rusty staggerbush does not venture south of central peninsular Florida. However, southern Florida gardeners may utilize *Lyonia fruticosa*, a similar plant that extends south to Collier and Miami-Dade counties.

208. *Lyonia lucida*

Common Name: Fetterbush
Habit: Erect shrub forming colonies by underground stems.
Size: Plant 4–9 feet tall, the crown often nearly as wide.
Season: Evergreen; flowering in the spring.
Maintenance: None or, in more formal gardens, removal of old seed heads and root suckers.
Motility: Slowly colonial by subterranean, suckering stems.
Growing Conditions: Flatwoods and moist sites in full sun to partial shade; Zones 8–10.
Propagation: Seed.
Comments: Like the related staggerbush (*Lyonia fruticosa*), fetterbush is a common component of Florida's flatwoods. It is not a spectacular plant, but its subtle charms have a way of growing on you, especially in late winter and early spring when it is festooned with

quantities of pastel pink flowers. Forms with very pale, almost white flowers occur, but these are not nearly as attractive as the typical forms. Occasionally, one encounters plants with very dark pink, almost red flowers, and these are extremely striking. Cultivated plants are neat and trim enough to be used in foundation plantings so long as the soil is acidic. Fetterbush makes a wonderful addition to the wild garden, where it adds variety and texture. Impeding its widespread cultivation is the difficulty of propagating it vegetatively, but like staggerbush, it too may readily be grown from seed, which easily germinates without special treatment.

209. *Melochia tomentosa*

Common Name: Grayleaf; Teabush; Broomwood
Habit: Densely branched small shrub with small, greenish gray leaves and pink flowers.
Size: Plant 3–7 feet tall, one-half to almost as wide.
Season: Evergreen; blooming throughout the year but most heavily from late autumn through early spring.
Maintenance: None or judicious pruning to maintain tidy appearance.
Motility: Rarely spreading by self-sown seed.
Growing Conditions: Open, sunny situations in full or nearly full sun; Zone 10 (also reported from St. Lucie County in Zone 9B).
Propagation: Seed; cuttings.
Comments: Grayleaf has many attractive and useful horticultural qualities. First, perhaps, is the plant's graceful form, an open but densely branched small shrub with long, supple

branches that are gracefully pendent toward the apex. Equally appealing are the small, surprisingly delicate leaves. About an inch long, they are densely covered with gray-green or silver-gray hairs. As a result, the entire shrub is an unusually attractive shade of silvery gray and it is perfectly suited as an accent plant, especially if planted in front of plants with contrasting dark green foliage. Perfectly complementing the foliage are profusely borne, candy pink flowers with a pleasing light fragrance reminiscent of lilacs. The flowers are ephemeral, lasting but one day. However, they are renewed in such numbers and for such a long period that one scarcely notices their fleeting nature. A mature plant covered with hundreds of little pink stars beautifully contrasting against the silvery foliage is a splendid sight. It is also irresistible to a multitude of insects. Finishing off this long list of admirable traits are the ease with which it may be propagated from cuttings and a tough, enduring constitution that allows it to withstand considerable heat and drought.

210. *Myrica cerifera*

Common Name: Wax-Myrtle; Bayberry
Habit: Short-lived, densely branched and densely leafy dwarf to large suckering shrub with sexes on separate plants.
Size: Highly variable, from 3 to 25 feet, depending on the genetic form and growing conditions.
Season: Foliage evergreen; flowers inconspicuous, the fruits borne in late summer or autumn.
Fruit: Female plants bearing small, dry, one-seeded fruits covered with a waxy coating.
Maintenance: None in the wild garden, regular pruning when utilized as a hedge; periodic

mowing around the plant will control root suckers.
Motility: If left unchecked, will form thickets from the root suckers; spread by seed is rare.
Growing Conditions: Highly variable from wet to dry in full sun to partial shade; Zones 8–11.
Propagation: Seed; root suckers; cuttings.
Comments: Wax-myrtle is highly recommended for wildlife landscaping since it forms thickets that protect larger animals, and its much-branched, densely leafy crown provides cover for small animals. The waxy berries definitely do not appeal to people, yet they are highly sought after by a rather large number of birds. In more formal situations, wax-myrtle is recommended as a screen or as a hedge that may be trimmed to any size or shape. Its ability to adapt to both wet and dry situations, hardiness to cold, and salt tolerance make it suitable for many difficult gardening situations; wax-myrtle is often found as a foundation plant in urban landscapes otherwise devoid of native plants. Diminutive forms that grow only 3 feet high or less occur in the wild and are occasionally offered in the nursery

trade. Usually they are propagated from cuttings in order to avoid hybridization with normal-sized forms. The berries are covered with an aromatic waxy coating from which bayberry candles derive their scent. One can boil the berries in water and skim off the wax to make one's own candles. But be forewarned, it is a messy process, and a gallon of berries yields barely a single cup of wax. Wax-myrtles contain nitrogen-fixing bacteria in their roots and are said to improve the fertility of the soil in their general vicinity. In addition to all these useful features, wax-myrtles are the larval food source of the red-banded hairstreak butterfly, and it is reported that wax-myrtle "repels insects, particularly fleas, and for many years, was planted around southern homes to keep the fleas out. A sprig in a closet or drawer will keep cockroaches out." Scheper Interactives L.C. (1999).

211. *Ocotea coriacea* (Synonym: *Nectandra coriacea*)

Common Name: Lancewood
Habit: Short-lived, densely branched shrub or small tree with a broad oval or rounded crown.
Size: Reportedly growing to 25 feet tall but usually smaller.
Season: Evergreen; flowering in the spring, with the distinctive fruits maturing in late summer and autumn.
Fruit: A dark purple or black one-seeded berry held in a yellowish or reddish cup.
Maintenance: None or else light and judicious pruning.
Motility: No vegetative spread; sparingly to abundantly producing seedlings in the vicinity of the parent plant.
Growing Conditions: Tropical and coastal hammocks in full sun to full shade; Zones 9–11.
Propagation: Seed.
Comments: In natural communities, lancewood plays an important role. It is a pioneer species that quickly colonizes sunny, open areas following disturbances resulting from fierce storms or hurricanes. It then forms shade and serves as a "nurse plant," enabling other hammock species to establish themselves. In garden settings, it is valuable for its ornamental, dark green, glossy leaves, attractive form, and iron constitution. Once established, it is amazingly drought tolerant and will happily grow in full sun or deep shade. The tiny white flowers have no ornamental value, but they are attractive to a variety of insects and it is reported that lancewood, like its relative the avocado, is a good honey plant. The blackish purple fruits that follow are about the size of a small olive, each held in a yellowish or reddish cup. Cultivated plants often produce quantities of fruit; occasionally, these can be a nuisance when a jungle of baby lancewoods sprouts underneath the mother trees.

212. *Picramnia pentandra*

Common Name: Bitterbush
Habit: Extremely tough, shrubby tree with leaves divided into five to nine leaflets.
Size: About 10 feet tall at maturity and about half as wide as it is tall.
Season: Evergreen; flowering in the spring and fruiting in the summer and autumn.
Fruit: Female plants bearing rather large clusters of sizable one-seeded berries maturing from reddish to wine red or black.
Maintenance: None or else very light and judicious pruning.
Motility: No vegetative spread; producing seedlings in the vicinity of the parent plant.
Growing Conditions: Tropical hammocks in almost full sun to rather deep shade; Zone 10.
Propagation: Seed.
Comments: Bitterbush has three eminent horticultural properties. First is its ease of growth and tough, resilient constitution. It will grow in a wide variety of settings from sunny to shady and is highly drought tolerant. Second, it presents an overall graceful appearance and would not be out of place in the most formal garden. It is especially attractive when grown in small groups, and it may be planted in rows as a living fence or informal hedge. Third, bitterbush produces narrow, pendant clusters of fruits that ripen from green to red and finally black, these contrasting beautifully with the dark green foliage. In addition to its horticultural qualities, bitterbush has wildlife value that extends beyond the use of its fruits by various animals. Its flowers are not showy, but they are fragrant and are attractive to many insects. Since bitterbush is the larval food plant of bush sulphur butterflies (*Eurema dina helios*), it is a good choice for South Florida butterfly gardens.

213. *Pithecellobium keyense*

Common Name: Florida Keys Blackbead
Habit: Large shrub or small tree with leaves divided into four leaflets; branches tending to spread horizontally when growing in full sun, growing more erect when partly shaded.
Size: Variable, often 10 feet or less, but up to 20 feet or so in larger, erect-growing forms.
Season: Evergreen, the new growth attractively tinged with red or maroon; flowering in the spring, the fruits maturing in the summer.
Fruit: Odd, contorted bean pods that split open to reveal black seeds partly covered with a red, fleshy aril.
Maintenance: None or else occasional light pruning.
Motility: Occasionally establishing by self-sown seedlings, usually near the parent plants.

Growing Conditions: Shell mounds and coastal hammocks in full sun to partial shade; Zones 9B–11.

Propagation: Seed.

Comments: This shrubby plant forms thickets on sandy shores and dry coastal areas. It is a tough, widely adaptable plant with high salt and drought tolerance. However, in spite of its iron constitution, it has a rather delicate appearance. This results from its small leaflets and the highly attractive new growth tinged in various shades of red or burgundy. Also adding to the delicate effect are the ethereal, fragrant, white or pale pink flower heads. These are small rounded globes made conspicuous by the long, thin stamens. In addition to its landscape and ornamental values, Florida Keys blackbead is a useful plant for wildlife: its densely leafy branches provide cover for animals; the foliage serves as the larval food for the giant orange sulphur butterfly; and the black seeds, with a red fleshy covering that mimics a juicy berry, are eaten by birds. Although the plant is described as usually lacking spines, this trait is variable. Some populations are nearly as spiny as cat's-claw, *Pithecellobium unguis-cati,* another native and horticulturally similar plant with smaller leaflets but always armed with spines.

214. *Psidium longipes*

Common Name: Longstalked-Stopper

Habit: Usually straggling or prostrate shrub with small, dark green, glossy leaves.

Size: Mostly 1½–3 feet tall and wider than it is tall; occasional erect forms reportedly becoming small trees.

Season: Evergreen; flowering and fruiting intermittently throughout the year except during cold or dry spells.

Fruit: Small, black, many-seeded berries.

Maintenance: None or essentially none.

Motility: None in most garden situations.

Growing Conditions: Rocky pinelands and tropical hammocks in full sun to light shade; Zones 10–11.

Propagation: Seed.

Comments: Longstalked-stopper is not a true stopper—those are members of the genus *Eugenia*—but is instead a relative of the guava. It is an absolutely delightful little shrub with small, glossy, dark green leaves, the new growth pale green and contrasting with the older leaves. The small flowers have a subtle and quaint beauty and are conspicuous as a result of the numerous white stamens. In due course the flowers are followed by blackish purple berries about 0.4 inches wide containing many seeds. The plant occurs only in southern Florida but is being successfully grown at least as far north as Palm Beach County along the east coast. Forms commonly encountered in cultivation are low, spreading shrubs and make attractive, useful, and distinctive groundcovers both in tropical hammock restorations and in formal gardens. Propagation is easily effected by seed, which should be sown as soon as the fruits ripen. Seed germinates readily, but the plants are slow-growing when young.

215. *Psychotria ligustrifolia*

Common Name: Privetleaf Wild-Coffee; Bahama Wild-Coffee

Habit: Densely leafy large shrub or small tree with very dark green, glossy foliage.

Size: Plants growing 6–9 feet tall, about half to two-thirds as wide, dwarf forms as wide as or wider than they are tall.

Season: Evergreen; flowering and fruiting year-round except during prolonged cold or dry spells.

Fruit: Small, brilliant red berries.

Maintenance: None or else judicious pruning to maintain desired height and shape.

Motility: Some forms extensively root suckering and forming thickets; occasional self-sown seed-lings may appear around the parent plant.

Growing Conditions: Moderately moist tropical hammocks in partial shade; Zones 10–11.

Propagation: Seed; cuttings; root suckers.

Comments: Privetleaf wild-coffee forms a dense shrub when grown in full sun and, of all our wild-coffees, is the species best suited for formal garden effects. In the shade its growth is more open, and in its attempts to reach the light, it assumes the proportions of a small tree. Found in the Bahamas and the West Indies, it occurs in our range only in southernmost Florida, and its cold hardiness is yet to be fully tested. It has survived temperatures to 35°F (approximately 2°C) without harm at least as far north as Palm Beach County. An extremely compact form with very short leaf internodes was introduced into cultivation by Gann's Native Tropical Greenery, a nursery no longer in operation. This dwarf form naturally grows in a globular, rounded shape as wide as or wider than it is tall and makes an excellent hedge or foundation plant. However, if grown in rich, moist soil, the plants produce numerous root suckers.

216. *Psychotria nervosa*

Common Name: Wild-Coffee
Habit: Small shrub with distinctive highly glossy leaves with deeply impressed side veins.
Size: Plants growing 6–9 feet tall and about half to two-thirds as wide.
Season: Evergreen; flowering and fruiting year-round except during prolonged cold or dry spells.
Fruit: Rather large, conspicuous, dull red berries.
Maintenance: None or else judicious pruning to maintain desired height and shape.
Motility: Abundantly establishing self-sown seedlings near the parent plant.
Growing Conditions: Dry to moist hammocks in partial to full shade; Zones 8B–11.
Propagation: Seed; cuttings.
Comments: Wild-coffee is one of the most widely planted of all native shrubs. Its popularity is due to a variety of factors, foremost of which is the beauty of its foliage. The leaves are a rich shade of green with a glossy, almost varnishlike sheen. In addition, the veins are deeply impressed, resulting in a dramatic textural effect. In its overall growth form

and foliage, it is reminiscent of a gardenia, another plant in the coffee family. Flowers are abundantly produced over a long period, and occasional plants may be found in bloom even in the middle of winter. The flowers are followed by decorative red berries, which in combination with the attractive foliage produce a most ornamental effect. The berries are an odd shade of dull blood red and are not as colorful as the berries of our two other species of *Psychotria*. Wild-coffee is as hardy as it is beautiful and is widespread throughout peninsular Florida in both coastal and inland hammocks and thickets. Overall, it is an easy-to-grow plant that lends a decidedly tropical touch to our gardens.

217. *Psychotria sulzneri*

Common Name: Velvetleaf Wild-Coffee
Habit: Small shrub with intensely dark green leaves with a distinctive bluish green tinge.
Size: Plants growing 6–9 feet tall and about half to two-thirds as wide.
Season: Evergreen; flowering and fruiting year-round except during prolonged cold or dry spells.
Fruit: Small, attractive red berries.
Maintenance: None or else judicious pruning to maintain desired height and shape.

Motility: Abundantly establishing self-sown seedlings near the parent plant.

Growing Conditions: Dry to moist hammocks in partial to full shade; Zones 9–10.

Propagation: Seed; cuttings.

Comments: Velvetleaf wild-coffee is rather closely related to *Psychotria nervosa* and may be used in a similar manner in cultivation. However, velvetleaf wild-coffee has deep blue-green foliage with an unusual velvety texture that is difficult to describe. The foliage is unlike that of any other native plant and is quite striking and attractive. For the most beautiful, velvety foliage, the plant should be grown in rather dense shade. In the wild, *Psychotria nervosa* and *P. sulzneri* often grow together, and this is a combination that may be duplicated in cultivation to good advantage since the two plants contrast with and complement each other.

218. *Quercus chapmanii*

Common Name: Chapman's Oak
Habit: Colonial dwarf shrub to small tree.
Size: Highly variable, from about 6 to 30 feet tall.
Season: Briefly deciduous; new spring foliage attractive; fruit borne in the autumn.
Fruit: Small acorns.
Maintenance: None or essentially none.
Motility: Can sucker freely and form extensive thickets.

Growing Conditions: Deep, well-drained sandy soils; Zone 9.

Propagation: Seed (short-lived, sow as soon as mature).

Comments: Chapman's oak is a common component of scrub habitats throughout Florida from the Panhandle to Collier and Miami-Dade counties. Like many other oaks, it has a highly variable growth habit. After a fire or when growing under adverse conditions, such as on slopes with shifting sand, it grows as a colonial shrub, sometimes only a few feet high. In old, unburned scrub, it matures into a small tree with a broad, irregular open crown. It is quaintly attractive in the spring when adorned with the male flowers borne in pendulous, elongated catkins and when it produces a flush of new leaves. Later in the season, the tiny acorns, which are heavily produced every two to three years and are sought out by wildlife, add another interesting note. Other oaks with the same growth habit that live in scrub and have the same garden uses include myrtle oak (*Quercus myrtifolia*), dwarf forms of sand live oak (*Q. geminata*), and unthought-of-oak (*Q. inopina*). The last is unique in being the only oak restricted solely to Florida and occurring nowhere else on earth.

219. *Randia aculeata*

Common Name: White Indigoberry
Habit: Dwarf to midsized, often spiny, shrub or small tree with male and female flowers on separate plants.
Size: Highly variable from 1½ to 10 feet tall, depending on the form and growing conditions.
Season: Evergreen; flowering and fruiting whenever warm weather and soil moisture allow.
Fruit: Rather large, unusual white berries with dark purple flesh.
Maintenance: None or essentially none.
Motility: Some forms root suckering; spread by seed none or negligible in most gardens.
Growing Conditions: Coastal hammocks and rocky pinelands in full sun to moderate shade; Zones 9B–11.
Propagation: Seed.
Comments: White indigoberry is an evergreen shrub with rounded, leathery leaves and bearings small, fragrant, white flowers. These mature into rounded, marble-sized berries that take a long time to ripen from deep green to pure white. Mature berries contain several seeds embedded in a dark bluish purple or bluish black pulp, hence the common name. The berries have been used to obtain a blue dye. However, the plants are more useful as interesting, indestructible, and drought-tolerant additions to the wild garden than they are as dye plants. As a result of its neat, evergreen foliage and stiff branches, white indigoberry may also be utilized in formal gardens as a foundation plant or loose hedge.

220. *Rhus copallina*

Common Name: Winged Sumac; Shiny (or Shining) Sumac

Habit: Fast-growing but short-lived rhizomatous shrub or small tree.

Size: Variable, depending on growing conditions and form, from about 3 feet to 25 feet tall.

Season: Deciduous northward, nearly evergreen southward; flowering in the summer, the fruit borne in autumn and winter; foliage assuming brilliant autumnal colors northward.

Fruit: Small, reddish, one-seeded, rather dry berries relished by a variety of birds.

Maintenance: None in the wild garden; due to production of suckers, not suitable in formal gardens.

Motility: Tending to form thickets as a result of root suckers.

Growing Conditions: Rather dry, often sandy, soils in full or nearly full sun; Zones 8–11.

Propagation: Seed (scarify; northern clones may also need to be stratified); root suckers.

Comments: Winged sumac has attractive fernlike foliage, produces fruits eaten by a variety of songbirds, takes on spectacular autumn color (at least northward), and has an interesting form in winter. Additionally, it is a remarkably tough plant able to grow in a wide variety of open sunny areas ranging from the sand scrubs of central Florida to the rocky pinelands of Miami-Dade County. However, it is difficult to fit into most home landscapes since individual plants are short-lived and may sucker heavily over a wide area. On the other hand, it is perfect for large properties and native plant restorations where a fast-growing, thicket-forming shrub is needed to stabilize banks or cover road cuts and to provide shelter and food for wildlife. A related species, smooth sumac (*Rhus glabra*), occurs in the Panhandle and has a better-behaved, smaller-growing cultivar ('Laciniata') with deeply incised and extremely delicate ferny foliage. It is an exquisitely beautiful plant and is perhaps worth trying by gardeners in northern Florida.

221. *Sambucus canadensis* (Synonym: *Sambucus simpsonii*)

Common Name: Elderberry

Habit: Large suckering shrub or small tree with foliage divided into five to eleven leaflets.

Size: Mostly 6–10 feet tall, usually at least as wide as it is tall.

Season: Deciduous northward, evergreen southward; flowering and fruiting from early spring to midsummer (or into late autumn southward).

Fruit: Abundant masses of small, dark, edible purple berries utilized by birds and mammals.

Maintenance: Periodic removal of root suckers as necessary to constrain it.

Motility: Most forms generally spreading by way of root suckers.

Growing Conditions: Ditches, canal banks and pond margins in full or nearly full sun; Zones 8–10.

Propagation: Seed; cuttings; root suckers.

Comments: Elderberry scarcely needs an introduction as it is a common roadside shrub that occurs throughout a wide range from Canada to

Central America. As an ornamental, it is attractive for its ferny dark green foliage and large heads of innumerable white flowers, these contrasting beautifully with the foliage. Although native to wet areas, it readily adapts to average garden conditions and is able to spring back from even lengthy dry spells. Its principal faults are its suckering habit, which makes it unsuitable for formal garden situations, and the necessity of growing at least two plants of genetically different backgrounds if one is interested in securing good crops of berries. Elderberry is well-known for its edible flowers, which can be fried as fritters, and its edible berries, which have found their way into everything from elderberry pie to elderberry wine. It is nearly as well-known for its hollow branches, from which flutes and peashooters were made in days past.

222. *Schaefferia frutescens*

Common Name: Florida-Boxwood

Habit: Thin-branched leafy shrub or small tree with male and female flowers on separate plants.

Size: Reportedly up to 36 feet tall but commonly cultivated forms much smaller.

Season: Evergreen; flowering and fruiting all year with heaviest fruit set in late summer.

Fruit: Female plants bearing abundant quantities of small, bright red berries.

Maintenance: None or else light, judicious pruning.

Motility: None or occasionally self-sown seedlings appearing near the parent plant.
Growing Conditions: Tropical hammocks in deep shade to nearly full sun; Zones 10–11.
Propagation: Seed.
Comments: Florida-boxwood does have an overall superficial similarity to the true boxwood (*Buxus* species) and, like that species, can be pruned as a hedge. However, the two plants are wholly unrelated and belong to separate families. Our Florida-boxwood is a tough, resilient shrub that thrives in cultivation as long as it has well-drained soil. Related species occur in the desert Southwest and attest to its drought tolerance. Healthy female plants bear prodigious quantities of red berries and produce a highly ornamental effect over a long period. As with other shrubs with male and female flowers on separate plants, it is recommended that one male be grown for every three females for maximum berry production.

223. *Senna ligustrina* (Synonym: *Cassia ligustrina*)

Common Name: Privetleaf Senna
Habit: Small erect or spreading shrub, the latter forms as wide as or wider than they are tall.
Size: Variable from 3 to 12 feet tall, depending on the form and cultural conditions.
Season: Evergreen; flowering from early autumn to late spring, rarely also flowering during the summer.
Fruit: Long, thin, brown bean pods about 4 or 5 inches long.
Maintenance: Judicious pruning to maintain tidy appearance; removal of old flowering and fruiting stems.
Motility: Widely spreading by self-sown seedlings into open areas.
Growing Conditions: Rather dry to moist but well-drained sites in full sun or light shade; Zones 8B–11.
Propagation: Seed.
Comments: Privetleaf senna is usually a short-lived woody perennial or small shrub normally found in moist soil along the edges of hammocks. It is fast-growing, attaining 3–6 feet in height in a single growing season. It is a short-day plant that flowers when nights are long, beginning in the autumn, continuing through the winter if it is not too severe, and extending into spring. The bright golden yellow flowers fairly glow against the dark green foliage and are pollinated by large bees. Fresh new growth and flowers are among the favorite foods of the caterpillars of bright yellow sulphur butterflies. Other than being short-lived, the plant's only real faults are its unattractiveness when laden with mature, brown seed pods and the subsequent innumerable self-sown seedlings that are sure to follow if the fruiting branches are not pruned. Presently, there appear to be two forms in cultivation. One form is a dwarf plant rarely exceeding 3 feet high with very large flowers of a clear bright golden yellow. The second form is a larger plant usually 6–8 feet tall with smaller flowers in a softer shade of yellow. Both grow with equal vigor and lend a rather bold, tropical effect to the garden.

224. *Senna mexicana* var. *chapmanii* (Synonyms: *Cassia bahamensis* misapplied; *Cassia chapmanii*)

Common Name: Chapman's Senna
Habit: Dwarf shrub, its habit varying from erect to nearly prostrate, the latter forms wider than they are tall.
Size: Variable, usually 1–3 feet tall, reportedly up to 9 feet tall.
Season: Semidormant during prolonged dry or cold spells; variably and intermittently flowering depending on the form but most prodigiously flowering in autumn and spring.
Fruit: Thin, brown bean pods 3–4 inches long.
Maintenance: Judicious pruning to maintain tidy appearance; removal of old flowering and fruiting stems.
Motility: Self-sown seedlings moderately spreading into open areas.
Growing Conditions: Rather dry to moist but well-drained sites in full sun or light shade; Zones 10–11.
Propagation: Seed.
Comments: Chapman's senna is a spreading or erect shrubby plant found in the rocky pinelands and hammocks of southern Florida. The forms commonly cultivated in Florida are low, freely branching plants that may be used as single specimens or grouped to form an attractive groundcover. The leaves are divided into eight to ten dark green leaflets. The abundantly produced, large yellow flowers seem to glow against the background of the dark foliage, making this a highly ornamental plant. The flowers are pollinated by various species of bees and the foliage is a favorite food of sulphur butterfly caterpillars. Flowers are produced over a long period but tend to reach their peak in late summer or early autumn and again in late winter or early spring. Like *Senna ligustrina,* this plant adds a decidedly tropical touch to the garden.

225. *Solanum verbascifolium* (Synonym: *Solanum donianum*)

Common Name: Mullein Nightshade
Habit: Small rhizomatous shrub.
Size: Plant up to 3 feet tall, but mostly shorter.
Season: May be found in flower at any time of the year.
Fruit: Large, colorful red berries.
Maintenance: Occasional removal of older stems.
Motility: Colonial by way of underground rhizomes.
Growing Conditions: Moist areas in full sun to light shade; Zones 10–11.
Propagation: Seeds; cuttings; division.

Comments: Twenty-five species of nightshade occur in Florida; however, only six of these are native. None of the half dozen native nightshades boasts showy or colorful flowers, but mullein nightshade produces brilliant red berries that are beautifully complemented by the foliage, which is dark green above with silvery gray lower surfaces. The stems are mostly solitary and scarcely branch, but thin to dense colonies are sometimes formed from the widely creeping underground rhizomes. As a consequence, this is not a plant for formal gardens; it is best utilized in wild gardens where it adds variety and, when in fruit, a spot of bright color. A second native nightshade, the soda-apple (*Solanum capsicoides*), is also worth growing for its showy fruits. It is a densely prickly plant with large orange-red berries. Unlike mullein nightshade, soda-apple will grow in full shade and is a more widespread plant, extending north to USDA Zone 8B.

226. *Sophora tomentosa* var. *truncata*

Common Name: Yellow Necklacepod
Habit: Large, elegant, densely branched and densely leafy shrub with a natural rounded shape.

Size: Variable, but at full maturity usually about 6 feet tall and a little wider than it is tall.
Season: Evergreen; flowering all year except during prolonged cold or dry periods.
Fruit: Unusual bean pod 4–6 inches long, sharply constricted between the seeds and vaguely resembling a necklace.
Maintenance: None, but may be pruned annually to any desired height and/or to remove old seed pods.
Motility: Sometimes forming large numbers of seedlings in the vicinity of the parent plant.
Growing Conditions: Coastal strands and hammocks in full sun or light shade; Zones 8B–11.
Propagation: Seed.
Comments: Yellow necklacepod, along with beauty-berry and firebush, is part of an indispensable trio of fast-growing and easily cultivated ornamental native shrubs of great utility in the garden. As a plant of coastal habitats, yellow necklacepod is drought and salt tolerant. If grown where it gets even light from all directions, it naturally forms a large, symmetrical, rounded shrub of great beauty. As such, it may be utilized as a specimen plant. It may also be pruned to any desired height or shape and makes an excellent hedge

plant. The long stalks of beautiful yellow flowers are borne when the plants are scarcely more than seedlings. A large plant in full flower is extremely showy and attractive not only to people but to butterflies and hummingbirds as well. The curious, elongated brown seed pods add an interesting note but, in formal gardens, detract from the plant's overall tidy appearance. There are two forms available in cultivation. One has smooth, glossy, dark green foliage, the other has velvety, silvery gray foliage because of its dense covering of innumerable tiny hairs. Although they are dramatically different in their appearance, the plants are identical in every other respect and may be used interchangeably in the landscape.

227. *Styrax americana*

Common Name: American Snowbell
Habit: Shrub with elegant white flowers.
Size: Growing about 6 feet high and about as wide.
Season: Deciduous or weakly evergreen southward; flowering in the spring.
Maintenance: None or else judicious pruning to maintain shape and tidy appearance.
Motility: None or essentially none in most garden situations.
Growing Conditions: Moist to wet soil in swamps, floodplain forests, and on stream banks; Zones 8–9.
Propagation: Seed; cuttings; ground layering.
Comments: American snowbell graces a variety of moist habitats, both sunny and shady, with its attractive, slightly fragrant white flowers. Many other plants have flowers that more closely resemble bells, and the name snowbell is more appropriate for related Asiatic species. In any event, it is a charming and beguiling plant when in full flower, especially if planted along a trail or path so that its delicately beautiful and refined flowers may be enjoyed during spring walks. Like many plants of rich, moist soils, it is more easily established if planted during cool weather, and it is not wise to disturb the plant during the heat of summer. Propagation by cuttings and ground layers, while certainly possible, is rather difficult for the home gardener. This plant will grow from seed, but seeds should be sown as soon as they are fully mature and should remain exposed to natural variations in temperature and light. With such treatment, they usually sprout during the first spring following sowing. However, some batches of seed may wait until the second spring. A second, closely related species also occurs in Florida, *Styrax grandifolius*, the bigleaf snowbell. It is, in general, a larger, rather showier plant since the flowers are produced at the ends of short branches (in American snowbell, the flowers are borne at the bases of young leaves).

228. *Suriana maritima*

Common Name: Bay-Cedar
Habit: Densely leafy small-leaved shrub or small tree.
Size: Generally about 6–12 feet tall and about as wide, reportedly growing up to 24 feet tall.
Season: Evergreen; intermittently flowering in sporadic bursts all year.
Maintenance: None.
Motility: None in most garden situations.
Growing Conditions: Coastal beaches in full sun; Zones 9B–11.
Propagation: Seed.
Comments: With its innumerable, linear leaves of grayish green, bay-cedar presents a refined, delicate appearance quite unlike that of the tough, coarse-leaved plants one usually associates with coastal beaches. Bay-cedar does resemble a conifer, but it is more reminiscent of a podocarpus or yew than a cedar. The masquerade is over when it bears its pretty little yellow flowers like tiny gold stars shining against the foliage. Normally, it assumes a broad, rounded growth habit, although an occasional plant rarely takes on treelike proportions. Once established, it withstands wind, searing heat, blowing sand, and salt spray.

229. *Tetrazygia bicolor*

Common Name: Tetrazygia
Habit: Extremely ornamental tropical shrub with beautiful flowers and highly elegant foliage.
Size: Usually 6–12 feet tall and about as wide as or a little wider than it is tall.
Season: Evergreen; heavily flowering in the spring, sporadically in the summer and autumn.
Fruit: Rather large, juicy, edible, but bland berries maturing to dark purplish black.
Maintenance: None required; see Comments for notes on pruning.
Motility: None in most garden situations.
Growing Conditions: Rocky pinelands in full sun to light shade; Zone 10.
Propagation: Seed.
Comments: Tetrazygia ranks among the most beautiful native flowering shrubs in Florida, if not the entire United States. Its glossy, dark green leaves are tinged white or pink when young and have deeply impressed

veins, creating a marvelous sculptural effect. Complementing the striking foliage are profuse masses of pure white flowers accented by long yellow anthers. Flowers may be so abundantly produced that from a distance, a plant in full bloom resembles a mound of snow. These are followed by purple-black berries that are attractive to birds. In cultivation, flowers are borne from spring through autumn, although blooming is heaviest in the spring. Another of this plant's many charms is its self-branching habit: if it receives even light from all sides, it will grow into a perfectly symmetrical, rounded form with the foliage evenly produced from ground level to the top of the plant. Branches tend to die back to the main stem, or even to the ground, if the plant is pruned, so it cannot be used as a hedge plant or shaped through trimming of the branches.

230. *Vaccinium darrowii*

Common Name: Scrub Blueberry; Darrow's Blueberry
Habit: Dwarf, densely leafy shrub with tiny leaves covered with a silvery waxy coating.
Size: About 1–4 feet high depending on age and growing conditions.
Season: Evergreen; heavily flowering in early spring; fruiting in late spring.
Fruit: Relatively large blueberries covered with a silvery waxy coating.
Maintenance: None in most garden situations.
Motility: With age, will form small thickets from underground suckers.
Growing Conditions: Deep sandy soils in full sun to light shade; Zones 8–10A.
Propagation: Seed (sometimes difficult to germinate); ground layering; division.
Comments: Sometimes gardeners will scour the world for beautiful plants while failing to take account of worthy candidates on their own doorstep. Scrub blueberry is one such plant. It is a much-branched, suckering dwarf shrub forming tight patches with age. It is remarkable for two outstanding characteristics. First, it bears tiny leaves

rarely as much as half an inch long. This results in an unusual and highly graceful and delicate appearance. But perhaps even more remarkable is the color of the leaves, which come in indescribably beautiful shades of intense silvery blue, occasionally tinged with lavender, rose, or purple. Add to this the plant's small, charming white flowers, large edible blueberries, and common occurrence through much of Florida, and we have an outstanding horticulturally ornamental native plant worthy of cultivation in every garden that can support its growth. The successful cultivation of scrub blueberry requires but two things: well-drained sandy soil and, for the best appearance and most beautiful foliage, a spot in nearly full sun but with some protection from the hottest afternoon sun in summer.

231. *Vaccinium myrsinites*

Common Name: Shiny Blueberry
Habit: Dwarf, densely leafy shrub with tiny, glossy leaves.
Size: About 1–4 feet high, depending on age and growing conditions.
Season: Evergreen; heavily flowering in early spring; fruiting in late spring.
Fruit: Relatively large purplish black blueberries.
Maintenance: None in most garden situations.
Motility: With age, tending to form small thickets from underground suckers.
Growing Conditions: Flatwoods and scrubby sites in moist to very dry soils in full sun or light shade; Zones 8–10.
Propagation: Seed (can be difficult to germinate); ground layering; division.
Comments: Closely related to scrub blueberry (*Vaccinium darrowii*), shiny blueberry is essentially an identical plant but differs in having glossy, dark green leaves. Indeed, sometimes the leaves appear to have a coat of varnish on them. Also, shiny blueberry has dark purplish black berries as opposed to the silvery, waxy-coated berries of *V. darrowii*. In most respects, the plants may be used interchangeably. However, shiny blueberry often occurs in seasonally wet flatwoods and may be used as a substitute for *V. darrowii* in moist situations. Both plants produce edible blueberries that vary from bland and nearly tasteless to sweet and flavorful, depending on the particular plant. Isolated, solitary plants rarely form fruit; one needs two genetically unrelated plants for maximum fruit production.

232. *Viburnum nudum* (Synonym: *Viburnum cassinoides*)

Common Name: Possumhaw; Witherod; Appalachian Tea
Habit: Large shrub with a somewhat open crown.
Size: Growing 6–12 feet tall and about as wide.
Season: Deciduous; masses of white flowers in the spring; colorful fruit from late summer to autumn; red autumn foliage.
Fruit: Small dark blue or black berries.
Maintenance: None in the wild garden.

Motility: Rarely spreading in most garden situations.

Growing Conditions: Edges of moist woods and swamps in full sun to light shade; Zones 8–9.

Propagation: Seeds (sow as soon as ripe); cuttings (half ripe wood in summer with a heel).

Comments: Possumhaw is an extremely ornamental deciduous shrub native to north and central Florida. Its cultivation presents no particular problems so long as it is not planted in poor, dry soils or overly exposed to hot or excessively windy conditions. Plants are especially beautiful in the spring when they become clothed in frothy masses of innumerable little white flowers. A second show begins in late summer as the small green berries change to a striking pink, which gradually darkens to blue or purple and, at full maturity, to black. In late autumn, the foliage assumes various shades of red. There are several cultivars of possumhaw in the nursery trade, the most notable being 'Nanum' (with a dwarf growth habit and rich autumn coloring), 'Pink Beauty' (with especially beautiful pink berries that ripen to dark blue), and 'Winterthur' (with dark red autumn foliage). Propagation by seed requires much patience since seeds can take up to eighteen months to germinate.

233. *Viburnum obovatum*

Common Name: Walter's Viburnum

Habit: Densely branched and densely leafy large shrub or small tree with small, dark green foliage.

Size: About 12 feet tall and nearly as wide, old large plants reportedly to 30 feet tall.

Season: Briefly deciduous in winter, or evergreen in southern Florida; profusely flowering in spring; fruit maturing in the autumn.

Fruit: Somewhat flattened, elliptical berries ripening from red to black.

Maintenance: None in the wild garden; pruning to desired shape and height as well as periodic removal of root suckers in formal gardens.

Motility: Spread by seed rare in most gardens; forming thickets from subterranean suckers.

Growing Conditions: Moist soils in full sun to deep shade, but extremely adaptable in cultivation; Zones 8–10A.

Propagation: Seed; suckers.

Comments: Walter's viburnum is yet another widely useful Florida native. A single plant makes an attractive specimen, since if properly situated where it gets unobstructed light from all directions, it assumes a naturally rounded shape, with a much-branched crown densely clothed with small, glossy dark green leaves. In early spring, its tiny, pure white flowers, borne before the leaves are fully developed, are carried in such prodigious numbers that the plant resembles a mass of snow when viewed out of the corner of one's eye. Hence it may be utilized as a seasonal accent plant. The flowers are followed by small green berries that slowly mature over the course of the summer and early autumn to pink, red, burgundy red, purplish blue, and finally dark purplish black. These are useful to birds and assorted small wildlife. Since Walter's viburnum may be pruned to any desired height or shape, it is ideal for use along fence rows or as a hedge. Its one flaw is a marked tendency to sucker. To prevent the formation of a thicket, young plants should have their lower limbs removed to allow easy access to the base of the plant for removal of suckers. As Walter's viburnum becomes more popular, cultivars are beginning to appear on the market, including one with somewhat weeping, pendulous branches ('St. Paul').

Conifers and Cycads

There are thirteen species of conifers and one cycad native to Florida. Of these, the pines are the most common and most visible group with a total of eight distinct forms (seven species, one of which has two varieties). Since these plants have exceptional botanical and historical interest, as well as outstanding horticultural qualities, they are all included here for reference purposes, although not all species are illustrated.

Except for the Florida yew (*Taxus floridana*) and torreya (*Torreya taxifolia*), which are highly endangered, none of the plants in this section is listed as rare in Florida in the botanical literature. Yet, in spite of their apparent abundance, some of Florida's conifers are threatened. Mature trees are being adversely affected by a wide variety of factors, including wetland drainage, changes in grade, lower water quality, urbanization and other forms of habitat destruction, soil compaction, direct harvesting, competition from invasive exotics, pollution, and changes in the frequency and/or intensity of wildfires. These are serious problems, but it gets worse. Not only do the above factors adversely affect the mature trees; they often result in habitat alterations such that the recruitment of new plants into the population by the establishment of seedlings is low or even nonexistent.

Presently, southern slash pine (*Pinus elliottii* var. *densa*), longleaf pine (*Pinus palustris*), and coontie (*Zamia pumila*) are the most seriously affected. These are three of our most interesting and picturesque native plants and they once occurred throughout extensive areas of Florida in countless thousands. However, as wild, noncultivated plants, they may soon be reduced to relict populations restricted to nature reserves. To this list may be added pond-cypress (*Taxodium ascendens*) and bald-cypress (*Taxodium distichum*). Again, these are common plants that are commonly cultivated. However, wild stands are being harvested in a nonrenewable manner for use as wood mulch. And the aftermath of such harvesting—which often involves highly disturbed and compacted soils, drainage, and land development—is not conducive to the establishment of new cypress stands from seed.

On a happier note, except for the Florida yew (*Taxus floridana*), none of our conifers is difficult to grow in cultivation, nor is our single cycad. Coonties, for example, are now common landscape plants, and cultivated coonties vastly outnumber wild plants. The most important point to bear in mind when growing these plants is to avoid any disturbance to their root zone. If properly selected and placed appropriately in the landscape, conifers are essentially carefree and do not require the gardener's help. Richard Moyroud (1996b:12) put it well: "Almost any horticultural 'help' given to pines is harmful. Strong, usually alkaline fertilizers interfere with iron and manganese uptake and damage mycorrhizae [beneficial, symbiotic fungi that help pines survive harsh conditions]; supplemental watering (mostly alkaline) suffocates roots and also raises pH, further harming mycorrhizae; and fallen needles raked up and thrown away remove useful mulch."

Last, although conifers make up only a small percentage of the tree species occurring in Florida, they stand out as being among our noblest and tallest trees. Of Florida's ten tallest native tree species, three are pines. And the tallest tree native to Florida is loblolly pine, with the mean height of the seven champion-nominated loblolly pines being 122 feet (Ward and Ing 1995).

234. *Chamaecyparis thyoides*

Common Name: Atlantic White-Cedar
Habit: Large conifer growing as a slender column when young but conical or pyramidal with age.
Size: Growing at about 12 inches per year to about 50 feet tall and 20 feet wide.
Season: Evergreen; fruits ripening in the autumn.
Fruit: Small purplish cones.
Maintenance: None.
Motility: May grow from self-sown seeds if garden conditions are right.
Growing Conditions: Rich moist soils in full sun to light shade; Zones 8–9.
Propagation: Seed.
Comments: Atlantic white-cedar reaches its southernmost limit in Florida, where it occurs in the central and western Panhandle as well as northern peninsular Florida south to Lake County. It is superficially similar to eastern red-cedar (*Juniperus virginiana*) but may be distinguished by its branches, which grow in flattened sprays; its highly aromatic leaves with contrasting white margins; and its small, rounded cones that open tardily. A further distinction is that the two occur in completely different habitats: Atlantic white-cedar favors wet habitats, whereas eastern red-cedar is an upland species. Atlantic white-cedar is a beautiful and picturesque tree, reportedly long-lived and equally attractive as a single specimen tree or when massed as background in a large garden.

235. *Juniperus virginiana* (Synonym: *Juniperus silicicola*)

Common Name: Eastern Red-Cedar
Habit: Large conifer with small, scalelike leaves.
Size: Slowly growing to 30 feet or more in height, reportedly to 60 feet high in Florida.
Season: Evergreen; female trees with fruits ripening in the autumn.
Fruit: Tiny, fleshy, purplish cones resembling small berries.
Maintenance: None.
Motility: Spreading by bird-dispersed fruits far from the parent plants.
Growing Conditions: Well-drained sandy or rocky soils in full sun; Zones 8–9.
Propagation: Seed; cuttings.

Comments: Our red-cedar was formerly regarded as either a variety of the widespread eastern red-cedar (*Juniperus virginiana* var. *silicicola*) or as a distinct species in its own right (*Juniperus silicicola*). As such, it also had its own common name: southern red-cedar. However, recent publications treat it as identical with the red-cedar growing to the north of our area. In any case, it is a highly elegant and picturesque tree for sunny, dry situations. Young plants have prickly, needlelike leaves and offer protection for small animals. With maturity, the leaves become small overlapping scales. It makes an excellent specimen tree or may be massed as a background tree. It is also useful in coastal situations, where it will tolerate much adversity. Lone female trees sometimes bear abundant crops of berries. The berries are in that case sterile since there is no pollinating male, but this is of no consequence to the many birds that eat them.

236. *Pinus clausa*

Common Name: Sand Pine
Habit: Highly picturesque, fast-growing but short-lived small pine with distinctively small needles.
Size: Up to about 25 feet tall with a 12-inch trunk diameter.
Season: Evergreen.
Fruit: Small pine cones 1–3 inches long, in some forms opening only when very old or after a fire.
Maintenance: None.
Motility: None.
Growing Conditions: Deep, exceedingly well-drained soils in scrub or coastal dunes in full sun; Zones 8–10A.
Propagation: Seed.
Comments: Sand pine makes an attractive specimen tree in dry, sandy areas where it becomes more beautiful with each passing year. However, it lives a fast life for a tree, growing quickly and considered ancient if it survives more than seventy years or so. Since sand pines age so quickly, in a few decades they can assume a gnarled and elegant appearance of the kind usually characteristic of a

tree hundreds of years old. In addition to its ease of growth in difficult sandy situations, its short needles dry to an attractive reddish brown after they fall and in time make a wonderful mulch under the tree. This self-made mulch is a beautiful dark background against which to highlight colorful wildflowers also adapted to dry, sandy soils, such as dayflower (*Commelina erecta*), showy jointweed (*Polygonella polygama*), partridge-pea (*Chamaecrista fasciculata*), and sensitive-brier (*Mimosa quadrivalvis*).

237. *Pinus echinata*

Common Name: Shortleaf Pine; Yellow Pine
Habit: Large, taprooted tree with a tall, straight trunk and a small, oval to narrowly pyramidal crown.
Size: Growing 80–100 feet tall with a trunk 2–3 feet in diameter.
Season: Evergreen.
Fruit: Small reddish brown cones 1–3 inches long.
Maintenance: None.
Motility: None.
Growing Conditions: Dry sites in full or nearly full sun; Zone 8.
Propagation: Seed.
Comments: Shortleaf pine, like sand pine, is a moderately sized, fast-growing pine with similar uses. In Florida, it is restricted to the Panhandle with the exception of an occurrence in Columbia County. It is an ornamental tree but readily drops its needles, cones, and dead branches, and this should be taken into account when it is placed in the garden. In common with pond pines (*Pinus serotina*), but unlike most other pines, young shortleaf pines will resprout from the stump if the original trunk is cut or burned back.

238. *Pinus elliottii* var. *elliottii*

Common Name: Northern Slash Pine
Habit: Fast-growing, large, deep-rooted tree with a thin trunk and open groups of needles.
Size: Growing up to 100–120 feet tall.
Season: Evergreen.
Fruit: Lustrous brown cones 3–6 inches long with a glossy or varnished appearance; cones are produced abundantly and provide a large seed crop for wildlife.
Maintenance: None.
Motility: None in most garden situations.
Growing Conditions: Moist sites that do not regularly burn; Zones 8–9.
Propagation: Seed.
Comments: Slash pines produced crude pine gum for naval stores and were originally named for the marks left after turpentining. Two dramatically different varieties of this pine occur in Florida. The typical variety, *Pinus*

elliottii var. *elliottii,* is a fast-growing, common pine found in north and central peninsular Florida. It occurs in mesic, evenly moist areas and is neither fire adapted nor drought tolerant. Unfortunately, northern slash pine has been widely and indiscriminately planted outside its natural range in southern Florida. It is not suited to local conditions such as drought-prone sandy soils, rocky limestone soils, and frequent fires and becomes sickly and deformed when grown outside its natural range. When acquiring slash pines, homeowners should ascertain that they are indeed obtaining locally adapted plants native to their area.

239. *Pinus elliottii* var. *densa*

Common Name: Southern Slash Pine
Habit: Fast-growing, large, deep-rooted tree with a thick trunk and densely clustered needles.
Size: Growing up to 100–120 feet tall with a trunk diameter of 2–4 feet.
Season: Evergreen.
Fruit: Same as *Pinus elliottii* var. *elliottii.*
Maintenance: None.

Motility: None in most garden situations.
Growing Conditions: Wide variety of seasonally dry sites that regularly burn from Lake Okeechobee south; Zones 9–11.
Propagation: Seed.
Comments: True to its name, southern slash pine is the typical and common pine found in the Florida Keys, extending north about halfway up both coasts of Florida and through the middle of the state to Lake Okeechobee. In addition to the differences from northern slash pine in range, southern slash pine is slower growing, is extremely drought tolerant, and is highly adapted to fire. Young plants go through a "grass stage" in which there is no visible trunk and they form short, dense clumps of needles at or near ground level. The outer layer of needles may be scorched by a fire but the central growing bud will be unaffected. After passing several years in the grass stage, the tree shoots up many feet over a short period. If another fire should occur, the growing point is now held well above the fire. The combined ranges of both varieties of *Pinus elliottii* include every county in Florida. However, as noted, the two varieties have different ecological requirements and are adapted to different growing situations. For best results and to avoid genetic contamination between the two varieties, home gardeners should grow the kind that naturally occurs locally.

240. *Pinus glabra*

Common Name: Spruce Pine
Habit: Large tree.
Size: Growing 80–100 feet tall.
Season: Evergreen.
Fruit: Small cones 1–2 inches long, retained for three to four years on the tree and becoming gray.
Maintenance: None.
Motility: None.
Growing Conditions: Scattered among hardwoods in rich, moist sites in full sun or light shade; tolerates brief flooding; Zone 8.
Propagation: Seed.
Comments: Spruce pine has little commercial value, but it is common and grows to large size within its natural range in northern Florida. It has two noteworthy traits. First, it occurs in rich hardwood forests and moist bottomlands, habitats to which few pines are adapted. Second, it has smooth, pale gray bark that becomes tightly furrowed and noticeably darker at the base of older trees. Its attractive form, large size, and unusual bark make it one of Florida's more distinctive and interesting species of pine. Spruce pine has short needles, as does sand pine (*Pinus clausa*), but is distinguished by its different habitat, the unique bark, and needles that are always borne in bundles of two (sand pine usually has at least some needles in bundles of three).

241. *Pinus palustris*

Common Name: Longleaf Pine.
Habit: Large, taprooted tree with a tall, straight trunk and a small open crown; seedlings resembling coarse clumps of grass.
Size: Growing 80–100 feet tall, the trunk up to 3 feet wide.
Season: Evergreen.
Fruit: Very large cones 6–10 inches long, being the largest pine cones in the eastern United States.
Maintenance: None.
Motility: None.
Growing Conditions: Dry to moist but well-drained soils in full sun; Zones 8–9.
Propagation: Seed.
Comments: Like southern slash pine (*Pinus elliottii* var. *densa*), longleaf pine is also highly fire adapted and goes through an interim stage between seedling and sapling known as the grass stage. The grass stage may last three to ten years or so, depending on growing conditions, after which a trunk is developed and growth is fairly rapid. The

long, dense needles are another adaptation to fire since they hold much moisture and do not burn readily. Longleaf pine is the largest of the yellow pines and makes a majestic specimen tree in cultivation. It may also be utilized to create a magnificent background in large public gardens. Potted plants of both longleaf pine and southern slash pine may not develop a normal taproot when planted in the garden. For best results, obtain them as young plants and place them in the ground while they are in the grass stage and before the taproot has begun to elongate.

242. *Pinus serotina*

Common Name: Pond Pine
Habit: Medium-sized pine with an unbranched trunk and a small, open crown.
Size: Growing 40–70 feet tall, the trunk 1–2 feet wide.
Season: Evergreen.
Fruit: Sessile, light brown cones 2–4 inches long
Maintenance: None.
Motility: None.
Growing Conditions: Moist or even wet soil in full sun to light shade; Zones 8–9.
Propagation: Seed.
Comments: Pond pine is highly unusual among Florida's pines; if it were human, it might be the victim of gossip for its many eccentricities. First, it grows in habitats where few pines venture—bogs, wet pond margins, and the drier parts of swamps. It is regularly described as a crooked or twisted tree, so much so as to appear deformed. Although this certainly would not recommend the species to the timber industry, which insists on straight-trunked trees, it is a picturesque habit ideal for a wide variety of informal garden landscapes. Pond pine also has the unique habit of sprouting clumps of needles or dense branchlets along its trunk and major branches. Rounding off the list of unusual traits, the top-shaped cones persist on the tree for lengthy periods and may become embedded in the bark of older branches (Huegel 1995:73). As with shortleaf pine, young, vigorous saplings of pond pine will resprout following cutting or killing back by fire.

243. *Pinus taeda*

Common Name: Loblolly Pine; Old Field Pine
Habit: Tall pine tree with a large spreading crown.
Size: Growing 90–122 feet tall with a trunk diameter of 2–4 feet.
Season: Evergreen.
Fruit: Cones 3–6 inches long.
Maintenance: None.
Motility: None.
Growing Conditions: Pioneer species colonizing open, well-drained sites in full sun; in mature forests found scattered among hardwoods in moist areas and along streams; Zones 8–9.
Propagation: Seed.
Comments: Capable of growing up to 122 feet tall, loblolly pine is Florida's tallest and fastest-growing pine. It is usually likened to slash pine but is considered inferior both ornamentally

and as a timber tree. On the other hand, it is a common and highly adaptable tree that is easy to cultivate, although susceptible to pests and diseases if stressed. One of the more interesting and unusual features of loblolly pines is that "they have puzzle-patchy bark that exudes the fragrance of vanilla (or is it root beer?)" (Minno 1992). The tree is called old field pine for its habit of colonizing areas that have been cleared of trees, such as unused pastures and farmland. Yet, in spite of colonizing open, sunny areas, it is tolerant of shade and survives long after the open field has turned back into a hammock. As mentioned in the introduction to this section on conifers, our seven champion-nominated loblolly pines hold the record as the tallest native trees in Florida with a mean height of 122 feet.

244. *Taxodium ascendens*

Common Name: Pond-Cypress
Habit: Small to large conifer with tiny, scalelike leaves.
Size: Highly variable depending on conditions, from 10 to 50 feet tall.
Season: Deciduous in winter; attractive in the spring when young foliage is first developing.
Fruit: Rounded 1- to 2-inch-wide green cones maturing to reddish brown.
Maintenance: None or essentially none.
Motility: None in most home garden situations.
Growing Conditions: Moist soil in full sun to light shade; Zones 8–10.
Propagation: Seed.
Comments: Pond-cypress has tiny, awl-shaped leaves that provide a wispy covering of green so that the tree's branches and form are readily recognizable even from a great distance. For many, pond-cypress is an acquired taste and its leafy cover is too spartan to have much esthetic appeal. However, others are enchanted by its form. Dr. Kim Tripp (1996a) described pond-cypress as "one of the most gracefully beautiful trees on the planet, appearing in the landscape as a lost, silvered spirit of the mist ascending from the ground." It should be noted that Dr. Tripp was referring to pond-cypress growing in a botanic garden, and it is admittedly not easy to integrate the striking and unique form of the pond-cypress into most home garden landscapes.

245. *Taxodium distichum*

Common Name: Bald-Cypress
Habit: Large conifer with delicate, feathery green foliage; the crown pyramidal when young.
Size: Up to about 50 feet in cultivation, although huge, ancient plants reached 100 feet in height.

Season: Deciduous in winter; highly attractive in spring when the new foliage is just sprouting.

Fruit: Rounded 1- to 2-inch-wide green cones maturing to reddish brown.

Maintenance: None or essentially none.

Motility: None in most home garden situations.

Growing Conditions: Moist soils in full sun to light shade; Zones 8–10A.

Propagation: Seed.

Comments: Bald-cypress is attractive at every season of the year. In early spring, the new leaves are a bright shade of yellowish green and are highly decorative as they sprout along every branch. These slowly expand to produce a ferny, darker green mantle with a much softer effect than is found in any other native conifer. In autumn, the leaves assume various shades of reddish brown before falling. In winter, the leafless tree reveals its beautiful, narrowly pyramidal form and rich cinnamon brown bark exfoliating in long thin strips. Bald-cypress is a magnificent specimen tree, especially along pond margins on large properties. The so-called knees generally do not develop on upland sites. However, in wet sites, the gardener must factor in their presence as they may make walking in a grove of these trees difficult and mowing all but impossible. In many ways, bald-cypress is the "redwood" of the eastern United States; trees once grew to immense size with trunks of enormous diameters. Such giants are mostly gone, only a tiny handful remaining preserved in isolated pockets to give us a slight clue as to their former glory.

246. *Taxus floridana*

Common Name: Florida Yew

Habit: Small shrubby tree with horizontally spreading branches and soft, needlelike leaves.

Size: Older plants to about 15 feet high, rarely to 25 feet or taller.

Season: Evergreen; fruits maturing in the autumn or winter.

Fruit: Female plants bearing small red "berries" with a single black seed exposed at one end.

Maintenance: None or essentially none.

Motility: None in most garden situations.

Growing Conditions: Rich, moist, cool and usually shady woodlands; Zone 8B.

Propagation: Seed; cuttings.

Comments: Commonly a large shrub or small tree, Florida yew closely resembles and is easily confused with torreya at first sight. Florida yew has softer foliage that lacks the tiny but pungently sharp point present at the tip of torreya leaves. Also, torreya leaves have a distinctive odor (likened by one author to that of crushed tomato leaves) that is lacking in the Florida yew. Like all yews, it is an extremely attractive plant that may be utilized in a wide range of garden settings, from the wild garden to the most formal foundation planting. It is, however, a difficult plant to grow well outside its natural range as it greatly resents extended high temperatures, especially if conditions are dry or sunny. Florida yew is one of the world's rarest trees, occurring naturally only in a small area on the east bank of the Apalachicola River in northern Florida.

247. *Torreya taxifolia*

Common Name: Torreya; Stinking-Cedar; Gopherwood

Habit: Small to midsized conifer with stiff, sharp-pointed, pungently aromatic leaves, the branches with drooping tips.

Size: Mature height to about 35 feet tall with an 18-inch-wide trunk.

Season: Evergreen.

Fruit: Female trees bearing odd cones resembling large olives with a purple cast and whitish bloom.

Maintenance: None or essentially none.

Motility: None.

Growing Conditions: Rich, moist, usually shady hardwood hammocks; Zone 8B.

Propagation: Seed; cuttings.

Comments: Like Florida yew, torreya has a limited natural distribution in the Florida Panhandle. Factors such as burning, land clearing, and feral hogs have greatly diminished its numbers. Added to these woes, a disease that destroys the roots and blights the leaves has decimated the population. It is reported that at present no mature specimens remain in nature, only sprouts from afflicted trees and occasional saplings. Outside its natural range, where it is isolated from disease, torreya is remarkably resilient and will grow in rather sunny sites under ordinary garden conditions. It is an attractive and ornamental small tree but is also exceedingly slow-growing.

248. *Zamia pumila*
(Synonyms:
Z. angustifolia,
Z. floridana,
Z. integrifolia,
Z. silvicola,
Z. umbrosa)

Common Name:
Coontie
Habit: Highly unusual
and distinctive cycad
resembling a small,
leafy, stemless palm
with male and female
cones on separate
plants.

Size: Extremely variable from 1 to 4 feet tall and as wide as or wider than it is tall, depending on form, age, and growing conditions.

Season: Evergreen; flowering in the spring; fruit maturing in the autumn and winter.

Fruit: Large woody cones bearing numerous seeds covered with an attractive red or orange-red flesh.

Maintenance: None in the wild garden; overly large plants or plants infested with scale may be cut to the ground to produce fresh new foliage.

Motility: Occasionally producing numbers of self-sown seedlings near the mother plant.

Growing Conditions: Highly adaptable and growing in dry to moist soils in full sun to deep shade; Zones 8B–11.

Propagation: Seed; division.

Comments: Coonties have taken the Florida landscape by storm and are now being utilized in a wide variety of garden settings. The plants resemble large, leathery ferns or small, stemless palms, but they are neither ferns nor palms. Rather, coonties belong to an ancient lineage of cone-bearing plants that once were the dominant vegetation on earth; they might fairly be called living fossils. In cultivation, their principal enemies are continuously wet soil and a susceptibility to scale and sooty mold. Heavy infestations of scale are best dealt with by cutting the plant to the ground, to which it responds by producing a new crown of scale-free leaves. It is the larval food plant for the atala hairstreak (*Eumaeus atala florida*). Atala infestations are sometimes severe and can defoliate even large plantings of coontie. Coonties are extremely variable, with two primary forms available in cultivation: wide-leafed plants that ultimately form immense clumps and narrow-leafed plants of usually smaller size. Gardeners tend to love one form and hate the other. Both forms are at their best when producing a new crown of pale, lime green leaves, these forming an exquisitely attractive contrast with the older, dark jade green leaves.

Trees

Trees have enormous power in the landscape, both physically, as the backbone of the garden, and figuratively—they feed the soul. Large trees with their changing moods capture the imagination; they command a level of respect and awe not unlike that accorded to enormous animals, such as elephants and whales. Indeed, some trees are immense organisms reaching dozens of feet in length and weighing many thousands of pounds. Their selection and placement warrant serious consideration.

Properly selected and situated, trees provide shade and privacy and reduce dust, noise, and water runoff. Trees also diminish the effects of strong winds and reduce the need for irrigation. They conserve energy by reducing the need for air conditioning in summer and for heating in winter. They act as a sink for carbon dioxide and ameliorate global warming. Equally important, they also provide food and habitat for wildlife.

When improperly selected and badly situated, trees can wreak havoc. Water leaching from the foliage of a tree overhanging a roof has in it organic acids that shorten the life of the roof. Badly placed trees may interfere with utility poles and lines; they may block the view of homeowners, pedestrians, or drivers; and the branches of street trees may grow into the street and become a nuisance. Tree roots may invade and block sewer and water lines or tear up sidewalks or damage foundations. Certain trees and shrubs may increase the chances or severity of a fire when planted along the interface between a suburban or rural home and a fire-prone natural community. A tree that comes crashing down may pose an expensive threat to property or even to life. And if the tree is not native, it may escape to become a noxious, invasive, and ecologically disruptive pest plant. All these potential problems make it crucial that we select and situate trees with due regard for the long-term consequences of our actions.

It is worth repeating the observation made earlier that improper selection and placement of trees is a common gardening mistake, perhaps because most of us make such decisions only a few times in our lives; we do not have a chance to become expert at it. Frequently, poor decisions regarding trees are rationalized with the excuse that if a tree proves unsuitable, it can be cut down. But often the problem is ignored or left until the tree is so big that it costs hundreds of dollars to resolve.

Besides planting trees, homeowners often inherit trees, either planted by previous owners or naturally occurring on the site and left standing during home construction. The latter is frequently the case in Florida, where the rapid development of natural areas for home sites is a common occurrence. If possible, the owners of homes being built should work with the construction company to preserve as many native trees on the site as possible. Such trees may be of large size and many decades or even hundreds of years old. They are irreplaceable and add greatly to the value of the property. Bear in mind that during construction work, simply putting a fence around a tree may not be enough. Many factors can affect the trees: changes in grade and hydrology; soil compaction in the root zone by heavy machinery; direct damage to the roots by digging or trenching; and temporary lack of air to the roots during construction or permanent lack of air as a result of paving or new roads. Trees on a newly developed property may seem perfectly healthy at the end of the construction period but then slowly decline and die two or three years later. Fazio (1992) provides an excellent summary of steps to take to save trees before, during, and after construction.

249. *Acacia choriophylla*

Common Name: Cinnecord; Tamarindillo

Habit: Spineless tree with leaves divided into small, dark green, shiny leaflets and a broad, spreading crown.

Size: About 8–12 feet tall, reported to 36 feet tall; often as wide as or wider than it is tall.

Season: Evergreen; flowering in the spring; fruits maturing in late summer and autumn.

Fruit: Dark brown pods up to 4 inches long.

Maintenance: None or occasional judicious pruning.

Motility: None or essentially none in most garden situations.

Growing Conditions: Rocky pinelands and tropical hammocks in southern Florida; Zones 10–11.

Propagation: Seed (scarify).

Comments: Exceedingly rare in the wild, cinnecord is quickly becoming common in cultivation in southern Florida due to the remarkable beauty of the plant (including when not in flower), its tough, resilient nature, and the ease with which it may be propagated from seed. It is distinguished from other acacias by its large leaflets—up to twice as long as in our other native acacias—and by being spineless or nearly so at maturity. Plants are both drought and salt tolerant when fully established. They are transformed as they come into full flower in the spring with innumerable bright yellow flower heads. Cinnecord is perfect for growing at the edge of a tropical hammock garden and may also be utilized as a specimen or accent plant in more formal garden situations.

250. *Acer rubrum*

Common Name: Red Maple
Habit: Large, single-trunked tree of rugged constitution; easily grown under many conditions.
Size: Eventually to 45 feet high with a trunk diameter of about 2 feet.
Season: Deciduous in winter; attractive spring foliage; red fruits in spring; beautiful autumnal foliage.
Fruit: Female trees with pink-tinged or red, winged fruits in spring, these maturing to pale brown.
Maintenance: None or essentially none; do not plant in small gardens or near sewer systems where the invasive roots will cause problems.
Motility: Readily producing numerous self-sown seedlings.
Growing Conditions: Pioneer tree of open, moist areas but able to tolerate much shade and drought; Zones 8–10A.
Propagation: Seed (sown when fresh); cuttings.
Comments: Red maple has the widest north-to-south range of any tree native to the East Coast of the United States and occurs from Canada south to the everglades of Miami-Dade and Monroe counties. It is an outstanding ornamental shade tree characterized by a compact crown, freedom from pests, rapid growth, and ease of cultivation. Although it is a pioneer species of open moist or wet areas, it will grow in partial shade and is highly drought tolerant once established. However, for the most attractive appearance, plants should be grown in moderately moist sites where they will not suffer for lack of water. Red maple lives up to its name: in earliest spring it bears red flowers; in late spring, female trees bear reddish winged fruits; the spring foliage and new growth is often tinged burgundy red; and in the autumn, the foliage assumes a brilliant orange or red before falling. The foliage assumes only a hint of autumnal color when growing south of central peninsular Florida.

251. *Aesculus pavia*

Common Name: Red Buckeye
Habit: Small, sometimes shrubby tree with a single trunk, rather open crown, and attractive palmate leaves.
Size: Plant 6–12 feet tall, rarely to 20 feet tall.
Season: Deciduous; flowering in early spring; fruits borne in late summer.
Fruit: Brown capsules 2–3 inches wide bearing a few chestnut-like, but poisonous, seeds.
Maintenance: None or essentially none.
Motility: None in most garden situations.
Growing Conditions: Rich moist sites in partial shade; Zones 8–9.

Propagation: Seeds sown immediately upon ripening.

Comments: Red buckeye occurs in the southeastern portion of the United States, extending south to central peninsular Florida. Naturally occurring in a variety of moist or even wet situations, it adapts readily to average garden conditions. The red flowers are borne in early spring in large spikes at the ends of the branches as the new leaves unfold. As a result, red buckeye is an exceedingly attractive and ornamental plant. As with a great many other red-flowered plants native to the United States, the flowers are adapted to pollination by hummingbirds and are also attractive to butterflies. This is one of the first plants to drop its leaves; it is often completely leafless by the end of summer.

252. *Annona glabra*

Common Name: Pond-Apple; Alligator-Apple
Habit: Small tree with a swollen or buttressed base, short trunk, and broad, irregular crown.
Size: Usually 12–20 feet tall, reportedly to 35 feet tall.
Season: Evergreen; flowers borne in the spring; fruits maturing in late summer and autumn.
Fruit: Large, fleshy, pale yellow fruit with many seeds; the pale flesh is edible but bland and insipid.
Maintenance: None in the wild garden; choose location with care as fallen fruits are messy.
Motility: Producing large numbers of self-sown seedlings below the parent plant.
Growing Conditions: Pond edges, wet hammocks, and swamps in full sun to partial shade; Zones 9B–11.
Propagation: Seed.
Comments: Pond-apple is an attractive small tree with glossy, dark green foliage and a picturesque, enlarged trunk. The odd, subglobose, yellowish green flowers are borne in the spring and are followed by large fruits shaped like fat, rounded eggs. The fruits are filled with numerous large seeds surrounded by a pale creamy pulp that is edible but bland and flavorless. They are apparently utilized by mammals, but judging by the large numbers of rotting fruits to be found under the parent plants, even wild animals are not too enthusiastic about them. In cultivation, pond-apple will grow under average garden conditions, although plants grown in wet

soil are more densely branched and grow more rapidly. It will grow in considerable shade, but the heaviest flowering and fruiting occurs in plants growing in sunny areas. Propagation is effected only by seeds, which may be slow to germinate. The species' major drawback in cultivation is the messy fruits, which rot on the ground and produce numerous seedlings if not removed.

253. *Aralia spinosa*

Common Name: Devil's Walkingstick
Habit: Extremely spiny, rapidly growing small tree with large fernlike leaves borne near its apex.
Size: Variable, from 10 to 25 feet tall.
Season: Deciduous; numerous small white flowers borne in spring; fruits maturing in the autumn; spiny leafless stems provide interest in winter.
Fruit: Small dark purple berries carried on rose-colored stalks are attractive to birds and animals.
Maintenance: None in the wild garden or else removal of suckers as necessary; do not plant where its spiny stems may injure passersby.
Motility: Eventually forming thickets from root suckers.
Growing Conditions: Rich, moist but well-drained soils in partial shade; Zones 8–9.
Propagation: Seed (stratify for two to three months); suckers; root cuttings.
Comments: All parts of the devil's walkingstick, including the leaf stalks, are covered with sharp spines, and this is enough to dissuade most homeowners from giving it a try. However, for large properties where it may be accommodated along a woodland edge, there is much to recommend it. First is its unusual form, for the plant consists of clumps of spiny, unbranched stems that produce a crown of huge ferny leaves toward the apex of the stems. This growth habit is quite unlike that of any other plant native to Florida and results in a striking and highly exotic appearance. After the leaves have developed, and providing a sharp contrast to them, the tree bears large masses of tiny white flowers, resulting in a distinct flowering effect very different from that in other native woody plants. As the flowers mature into small berries, their stalks assume an attractive rose color. Last, after the leaves have fallen, the unbranched spiny stems provide a distinctive show of form and texture in the winter garden.

254. *Betula nigra*

Common Name: River Birch
Habit: Fast-growing, multistemmed tree with a broad crown and decorative exfoliating bark.
Size: Grows 40–70 feet tall and about two-thirds as wide.

Season: Deciduous; flowers borne in spring; autumn foliage yellow.

Fruit: Conelike catkins about 1 inch long.

Maintenance: None if properly situated.

Motility: Will readily self-seed in moist, sunny areas.

Growing Conditions: Banks of rivers and streams in full sun to light shade; Zone 8.

Propagation: Seed (sown as soon as it matures).

Comments: River birch is unique among North American birches for two traits: it is the only birch that flowers in the spring as well as the only one to occur in the southeastern coastal plain. As a consequence of this range, it has outstanding heat tolerance and is a common specimen or shade tree in the deep South. Its principal ornamental quality is its bark. Bark color and texture are highly variable both from tree to tree and as a single tree ages. Young, rapidly growing river birches have silvery gray to reddish brown bark that peels off in dramatic papery strips. Older trees tend to have darker, sometimes almost black bark broken into irregular scales. Other horticultural qualities are its graceful form; broad, open crown, which casts

such light shade that grass will grow beneath it; golden yellow fall color; and high resistance to the bronze birch borer. Although native to moist or wet areas, river birch is intolerant of prolonged flooding and readily adapts to regular garden conditions so long as it is provided with acidic soil up to a pH of about 6.5. Propagation is easily effected by seed, which germinates freely without any special treatment.

255. *Bourreria succulenta* (Synonyms: *Bourreria ovata* and *Bourreria revoluta*)

Common Name: Strongbark

Habit: Rapidly growing small tree bearing fragrant white flowers and ornamental fruit.

Size: Reportedly growing to 30 feet high but rarely even half that height in cultivation.

Season: Evergreen; flowering and fruiting whenever warm weather and soil moisture allow.

Fruit: Attractive orange berries of about H-inch diameter.

Maintenance: None; do not plant where falling flowers and fruits will be a nuisance.

Motility: None or essentially none in most gardens.

Growing Conditions: Full sun to light shade in well-drained sites, usually associated with limestone; Zones 10–11.

Propagation: Seed (sow immediately, can be slow or difficult to germinate).

Comments: Strongbark has nearly every desirable feature for a small garden tree: sturdy, dark green foliage; small but attractive pure white flowers with a strong, pleasing fragrance; and brilliant orange fruits. Additionally, it grows well in alkaline, rocky soils and is highly drought and salt tolerant. Its growth form is rather unusual since it has an irregular crown with slightly to strongly drooping branches. As a result, it does not lend itself well to highly formal settings, but it is excellent in semiformal and informal gardens. If well grown, it will produce (and drop!) flowers and fruits nearly throughout the year. However, since this is a plant of tropical affinities, the greatest number of flowers and fruits are produced in the summer and autumn. Its one major problem is that it can be difficult to propagate, and there are many accounts of gardeners sowing hundreds of seeds and getting only a few dozen to germinate. Two related species occur in our region, *Bourreria cassinifolia* and *B. radula*. They are dwarf shrubs or small trees that may be used in a similar manner as *B. succulenta* and are well-suited for smaller properties or gardens.

Special Note: Strongbarks are woody shrubs or trees of the genus *Bourreria* in the borage family. Do not confuse strongbarks with members of the genus *Borreria* (no "u"), a genus of small, often weedy annuals and perennials in the coffee family.

256. *Bursera simaruba*

Common Name: Gumbo-Limbo

Habit: Small to large, seasonally deciduous shade tree.

Size: Usually 15–30 feet tall in cultivation, reportedly growing to 60 feet tall.

Season: Briefly deciduous in late winter or spring, also deciduous during prolonged droughts.

Fruit: Reddish ½-inch capsules.

Maintenance: None or else judicious pruning to maintain desired height and shape.

Motility: None or essentially none in most gardens.

Growing Conditions: Full sun to part shade in well-drained soil; Zones 9B–11.

Propagation: Seed; cuttings.

Comments: One of southern Florida's most characteristic hammock trees, gumbo-limbo is best known for attractive, shiny, smooth bark that peels off in large, thin papery flakes. The color of the bark varies from silvery to deep mahogany red. It is a fast-growing, salt-tolerant tree resistant to high winds and drought. It is commonly used as a shade tree but such use has one minor drawback: the tree is briefly deciduous just before the onset of hot weather and does not provide shade for a few weeks at that time. Seed-grown plants are tall and rigidly erect, but cutting-grown plants tend to be shorter and to develop a wide, spreading canopy. Branches, even very large ones, will root if merely plunged into the ground or into a pot of moist sand. However, smaller branches, about the diameter of a nickel, develop the sturdiest root systems and have maximum wind resistance.

257. *Calyptranthes pallens*

Common Name: Spicewood
Habit: Small, shrubby tree with burgundy-tinged new growth.
Size: Reportedly to 25 feet tall but usually much smaller in cultivation.
Season: Evergreen; flowering in early summer; fruit maturing in the autumn.
Fruit: Small dark red to purplish black berries about ¼ inch in diameter.
Maintenance: None; may be pruned to any desired height or shape.
Motility: Self-sown seedlings establishing themselves near the parent plants.
Growing Conditions: Tropical and subtropical hardwood hammocks in full sun to partial shade; Zones 10–11.
Propagation: Seed.
Comments: Spicewood is the more common of our two species of *Calyptranthes,* both in the wild and in

cultivation. It is an attractive large shrub or small tree with dark green leaves nicely contrasting with the pink new growth. Flowers are tiny and have almost no ornamental value, although they are interesting when examined under magnification. The common name alludes to the aromatic foliage. However, this feature differs widely from plant to plant, some being richly aromatic and others nearly devoid of fragrance. Like so many Florida woody plants of tropical affinity, spicewood will grow in conditions from full shade to full sun but will not tolerate wet soils. Commonly grown in informal garden settings, it matures into a large shrub with a dense, rounded crown and would be useful in formal settings.

258. *Calyptranthes zuzygium*

Common Name: Myrtle-of-the-River
Habit: Small, shrubby tree with pale, pink-tinged new growth and showy, fragrant, white flowers.
Size: Reportedly to 40 feet tall but rarely even half that height in cultivation.
Season: Evergreen; flowering in early summer; fruit maturing in the autumn.
Fruit: Dark purplish black berries about ½ inch in diameter.
Maintenance: None; may be pruned to any desired height or shape.
Motility: Self-sown seedlings rarely establishing themselves near the parent plants.

Growing Conditions: Tropical and subtropical hardwood hammocks in full sun to partial shade; Zones 10–11.

Propagation: Seed.

Comments: Myrtle-of-the-river is native to extreme southern Florida, the Bahamas, Cuba, Hispaniola, and Jamaica. It is very rare in Florida, where it is listed as an endangered plant. It differs from spicewood in its olive green leaves, hairless inflorescence, and larger flowers. Like the stoppers in the genus *Eugenia,* myrtle-of-the-river is a "big bang" bloomer that opens all its flowers over a short period. Plants in full flower are among the most beautiful of flowering woody plants in Florida as a result of the sweetly fragrant, pristine white flowers with contrasting pink-tipped flower buds. Although native to the warmest part of the state, it is able to take light cold spells and is being successfully grown at least as far north as Palm Beach County.

259. *Canella alba*

Common Name: Cinnamon-Bark

Habit: Small, slow-growing tree with a dense, broad crown, thick aromatic leaves, and fragrant purplish red flowers.

Size: Reported to 30 feet tall but usually smaller in cultivation.

Season: Evergreen; flowering in the spring and summer; fruit maturing in winter.

Fruit: Small, round, bright to dark red berries.

Maintenance: None.

Motility: Self-sown seedlings establishing themselves beneath the parent plant.

Growing Conditions: Coastal, rocky hammocks in full sun to light shade; Zones 10–11.

Propagation: Seed.

Comments: Cinnamon-bark is a small native tree with outstanding horticultural attributes. Plants have a neat, tidy appearance and naturally grow with a broad, rounded crown requiring little or no pruning. Once established, the plant is extremely drought tolerant and will thrive in difficult coastal situations. The flowers are an intriguing shade of dark red and have a faint but sweet fragrance similar to that of daffodils. A second show is produced when the fruits mature to a pleasing red. Plants are essentially pest-free and, aside from the slow growth rate, are easily cultivated in a sunny, well-drained site. The inner bark does have a cinnamonlike aroma, but it is not at all closely related to true cinnamon, which is a plant in the avocado family native to the Old World. Except for the fleshy berry, all parts of cinnamon-bark are poisonous.

260. *Capparis cynophallophora*

Common Name: Jamaican Caper
Habit: Small, densely branched, shrubby tree naturally assuming a pyramidal shape.
Size: Growing up to 18 feet tall, often much smaller when growing in dry, rocky areas.
Season: Evergreen; flowering in the spring and summer; fruits ripening from late spring to autumn.
Fruit: An elongated, beanlike capsule 4–8 inches long.
Maintenance: None.
Motility: Self-sown seedlings often establishing themselves near the parent plants.
Growing Conditions: Well-drained sites in coastal hammocks, often in partial shade; Zones 9B–11.
Propagation: Seed.
Comments: Jamaican caper is an outstanding ornamental small tree highly recommended for both informal and formal gardens in southern Florida. Without any training or pruning, plants naturally tend to grow in a broadly pyramidal shape and are densely clothed with attractive leaves. The leaves are an extremely dark green and have a glossy surface. The effect is hard to describe—the plant appears both dark and bright at the same time. In flower, the plants are exquisite as each branch is tipped by a rather large white flower with long, pink anthers. As an added touch, the flowers are sweetly fragrant and are visited by many insects. Although they open in the evening and wither around noon of the following day, they are abundantly produced over a fairly long period. In addition to its ornamental qualities, Jamaican caper is extremely drought and salt tolerant once established and recommended for coastal and low-maintenance xeriscape gardens.

261. *Carpinus caroliniana*

Common Name: American Hornbeam; Musclewood; Ironwood; Blue-Beech
Habit: Small understory tree with a spreading crown.
Size: Variable from 10 to 30 feet tall.
Season: Deciduous; flowers inconspicuous in the spring; fruits maturing in the autumn; foliage color in the autumn variable, sometimes spectacular in shades of red and yellow.
Fruit: A small cone of tiny nutlets, each nutlet subtended by a large, three-lobed bract.
Maintenance: None.
Motility: Usually none under most garden situations.
Growing Conditions: Rich moist woodlands in partial shade; Zones 8–9.
Propagation: Seed (stratify for four months).
Comments: One can learn a great deal about this small shade-loving tree from its common names: "American hornbeam" tells us that it is the only North American representative of an otherwise Old World genus. "Musclewood" refers to the fluted, sinewy, undulating trunk and main branches, which might fancifully be said to resemble the well-muscled legs or arms of a body builder. "Ironwood" is an allusion to the very hard wood, traditionally utilized for mallets, golf clubs, and tool handles. And the name "blue-beech" relates to its attractive, smooth, bluish gray bark. As an understory tree, it is perfect for growing under taller trees and adding variety, texture, and form to the native woodland garden. If it is being purchased for its autumnal foliage, purchase it in the autumn in order to assess it autumnal color, since the intensity and beauty of the fall foliage display varies considerably from plant to plant. Horticulturally similar is the related eastern hop-hornbeam (*Ostrya virginiana*), another small understory tree, which differs from American hornbeam in having reddish brown bark that exfoliates into thin strips.

262. *Chrysophyllum oliviforme*

Common Name: Satinleaf
Habit: Small, often shrubby tree with arching branches gracefully displaying the beautiful foliage.
Size: Slowly growing up to 30 feet high but often smaller.
Season: Evergreen; flowering and fruiting whenever warm temperatures and adequate rainfall permit.
Fruit: Edible; gummy, dark purple olivelike fruits attractive to wildlife.
Maintenance: None.

Motility: Casually spreading by self-sown seedlings.

Growing Conditions: Tropical hammocks in full sun to rather deep shade; Zones 9B–11.

Propagation: Seed.

Comments: Satinleaf is one of the most beautiful small trees native to Florida with highly distinctive and ornamental foliage. The upper surface of the leaves is a rich, dark green and is so glossy as to appear coated with a heavy layer of varnish. The lower surface is densely covered with a thick felt of lustrous coppery hairs. Small, fragrant green flowers are produced year-round and they are followed by dark purple, edible fruits containing one or two seeds. All parts of the plant exude a gummy sap, and the fruits must be fully ripe before they may be eaten. Even then, they are still somewhat gummy. Satinleaf is easily propagated from seed, though this may take several months to germinate. It may be utilized in a wide variety of conditions from deep shade to full sun and tolerates

surprisingly dry situations. Seedlings are slow-growing and may take quite a while to get established. In hard freezes, plants may be cut back to the ground. However, they are tenacious and often sprout a new trunk from the cut stump.

263. *Coccoloba diversifolia*

Common Name: Pigeon-Plum

Habit: Small tree with a dense, narrowly rounded crown and attractive bark peeling in broad flakes.

Size: Growing to 30 feet high but often smaller, the trunk of bigger trees getting to 2 feet in diameter.

Season: Evergreen; flowering in the spring; fruits ripening in the autumn.

Fruit: Small, one-seeded, dark purple berries often borne in large numbers on female trees.

Maintenance: None; do not plant where the fallen fruit will be a nuisance.

Motility: Rarely spreading by self-sown seedlings.

Growing Conditions: Tropical hammocks in full sun to partial shade; Zones 9B–11.

Propagation: Seed.

Comments: *Coccoloba diversifolia* is a large shrub or small tree usually reaching about 23 feet tall. Although lacking attractive flowers and fruits, it is still a very decorative specimen plant. The branches are thickly clothed with leaves, and in full sun pigeon-plum forms a dense, dark green crown, noticeably taller than it is wide, of remarkably symmetrical

shape. Its compact, dense crown makes it an excellent candidate for "tight" areas such as parking lots or sidewalks. In older plants, the smooth bark forms large plates of cordovan brown that peel off to reveal an attractively contrasting whitish layer. Regarding the fruit, Workman (1980) notes that "the fruit are tart and astringent eaten raw but, if let set a few days, seem to lose the astringency. The Mikasuki Indians of the Big Cypress Swamp are reported to relish pigeon-plums and in Nassau they are sold in quantity at the outdoor market under the bridge to Paradise Island. Juice from the fruit is supposed to make very good jelly and a fine wine." This species is readily separated from *C. uvifera* by its smaller leaves, which are longer than they are wide. However, hybrids between the two species are known. Such plants are nearly exactly intermediate between the two parents, are sterile, and appear to posses hybrid vigor since they are even more robust than their parents.

264. *Coccoloba uvifera*

Common Name: Sea-Grape
Habit: Much-branched large shrub or small tree with a broad crown, fragrant flowers, conspicuous fruits, attractive bark, and a highly distinctive tropical appearance.
Size: Widely variable, a 3-foot shrub along coastal sand dunes to a 35-foot-tall tree in maritime hammocks.
Season: Briefly deciduous in early spring; flowering in the spring; fruit ripening in late summer or autumn.
Fruit: Female plants bearing numerous rather large, one-seeded, dark purple berries with a thin, pleasant, edible flesh.
Maintenance: None in a wild garden, raking of leaves in more formal situations; may be pruned to any desired height or shape; do not plant female trees where their fallen fruits will be a nuisance.
Motility: Self-sown seedlings establishing in the vicinity of female plants.
Growing Conditions: Coastal sand dunes and maritime hammocks in full sun or very light shade; Zones 9B–11.
Propagation: Seed; air layering; cuttings; veneer grafts.
Comments: Sea-grape is an amazing shrub or spreading tree quite unlike any other woody plant native to the United States. Along coastal dunes it grows as a low, dense shrub sheared by wind and salt spray. Farther inland, in maritime hammocks, it becomes treelike. Whether as a shrub or tree, it has a distinctive form since it branches close to the ground and has a broad rounded crown. The distinctive leaves are very nearly round, although the larger leaves tend to be wider than they are long. Of an amazingly thick and leathery texture, they are beautifully mahogany tinted when young, maturing to a dark sea green with contrasting reddish veins. The trees shed their leaves in the spring and replace them with a new set each year.

Before falling, the old leaves dry out and the plants look scorched. Fortunately, this phase does not last long.

Shortly after the new set of leaves is produced, the graceful, long white flower spikes are formed. The flowers contain copious amounts of nectar, and Workman (1980) reports that it is a locally important honey plant. The flowers are followed in the late summer and early autumn with clusters of pleasant-tasting fruits that do indeed resemble large grapes and can be used in exactly the same way to make jams, jellies, and wine. Although as a rule large-leaved plants make poor hedges, sea-grapes may be sheared to any shape and size. Sea-grape hedges are especially useful for estates along the coast that require a tall, sturdy hedge to protect against wind and salt spray.

265. *Conocarpus erecta*

Common Name: Buttonwood
Habit: Small, low-branching, often multitrunked tree with a spreading crown.
Size: Generally growing up to 20 feet tall and about as wide.
Season: Evergreen, flowering and fruiting throughout the year.
Fruit: Individually insignificant but aggregated into persistent, somewhat decorative, rounded cones.
Maintenance: None.
Motility: Very rarely establishing by self-sown seedlings.
Growing Conditions: Coastal shores and landward side of tidal mangrove swamps in full sun; Zones 8–11.
Propagation: Seed; cuttings.
Comments: Buttonwood is not spectacular but it has so many desirable features that it is widely grown throughout its natural range. Foremost among these is its iron constitution: it is a virtually indestructible tree that has few insect pests; produces very dense, strong wood; is highly drought and salt tolerant; and grows well in rocky, alkaline soils. With age, it develops a picturesque form that is complemented by beautiful deeply furrowed, flaking bark. It may be utilized as a specimen, shade, or street tree that is well-suited for difficult urban situations. Its fine-textured foliage makes it ideal for use as a clipped hedge or screen, and it is highly recommended as a patio tree. Normally bearing dark green leaves, it also comes in an extremely attractive form known as silver buttonwood (*Conocarpus erectus* var. *sericeus*), found in the Florida Keys. This variety is characterized by leaves densely covered with silky silvery white hairs. Occasionally, the foliage of buttonwoods becomes covered with black sooty mold (*Capnodium* species). Shady, humid conditions, frequent wetting of the foliage by irrigation, and the sugary secretions of sucking insects foster the growth of sooty mold, especially when buttonwoods are grown inland away from the saline influence of the coast.

266. *Cordia sebestena*

Common Name: Geiger Tree
Habit: Large shrub or tree with large, dark green leaves and extremely showy bright orange flowers.
Size: Reported to 33 feet tall.
Season: Evergreen; flowering and fruiting throughout the year.
Fruit: Single-seeded, white, egg-shaped fruit about 1 inch long.
Maintenance: None or essentially none.
Motility: None or essentially none.
Growing Conditions: Tropical hammocks in well-drained soil in full sun or very light shade; highly sensitive to cold and intolerant of frost; Zones 10–11.
Propagation: Seed.
Comments: Geiger tree has large leaves that have a rough, sandpaper-like texture due to a covering of short, coarse hairs. This is not apparent to the eye but is easily demonstrated by rubbing the leaves with one's fingers. The large tangerine-colored flowers are produced year-round in southernmost Florida. Dr. Henry Nehrling is quoted in Workman (1980) as follows: "Its flower bunches were so brilliant, so dazzling that I stood before it spellbound. I scarcely trusted my eyes whether this scintillating color was real or whether it belonged to a fairyland." Dr. Nehrling is not guilty of hyperbole; practically no other plant cultivated in Florida boasts flowers of such an intense orange. The flowers are followed by white fruits about the same size and shape as a small egg. The white flesh is made up of the highly modified sepals, which enlarge and enclose the true fruit as they age. Although edible, the fruits are not particularly tasty, having a bland banana-like flavor. The species' status as a native has been much debated; some have speculated that Geiger tree may perhaps be an early introduction to Florida from the West Indies.

267. *Cornus alternifolia*

Common Name: Pagoda Dogwood
Habit: Elegant large shrub or small tree with a wide, spreading crown and highly distinctive form, with the branches, and hence the foliage, carried in horizontal layers.
Size: About 12–15 feet high and nearly as wide.
Season: Deciduous; foliage carried in horizontal layers is interesting from spring through early autumn; innumerable tiny white flowers borne in the spring; fruit maturing in the summer; foliage assuming burgundy tones in the autumn; unusual branch structure interesting in the winter when the plant is leafless.
Fruit: Small blue-black berries on reddish or pinkish stalks are utilized by birds and wildlife.

Maintenance: None or else removal of suckers; selective pruning to train as either a single- or multitrunked tree.
Motility: Some forms tending to root sucker and forming a dense, multitrunked thicket.
Growing Conditions: Rich moist woodlands and swamps in partial to deep shade; Zone 8.
Propagation: Seeds (stratify); root suckers.
Comments: Pagoda

dogwood is so named because of its unusual branch structure, the horizontally layered branches resembling a pagoda. Its scientific epithet *alternifolia* means "alternate-leaved" and refers to the fact that this is the only species of dogwood native to the United States with alternate leaves, all other dogwoods having leaves borne in opposite pairs. Although widespread in the eastern United States, this is an extremely rare and endangered plant in Florida, limited to just four counties in the Panhandle. Nursery-propagated stock is becoming more readily available, and no doubt this highly ornamental small tree will prove popular for home landscaping in northern Florida. As indicated, it occurs in wooded habitats, but it readily adapts to either full sun or shade as long as it has ample soil moisture and is provided with a thick organic mulch to keep the roots cool. Hot, dry conditions are not to its liking and quickly lead to its demise.

268. *Cornus florida*

Common Name: Flowering Dogwood
Habit: Medium-sized deciduous tree with large opposite leaves with silvery green undersides.
Size: Grows 20–25 feet tall with spreading, horizontal branches borne low on the trunk.
Season: Large showy white flower clusters in the spring; fruit maturing in autumn; foliage assuming attractive autumn coloration.
Fruit: Rather large, brilliant red berries.
Maintenance: None or essentially none if properly situated.
Motility: None or nearly so in most garden situations.
Growing Conditions: Well-drained acidic soils along woodland margins in partial shade; Zones 8–9A.

Propagation: Seeds; cuttings.

Comments: Rightfully regarded as one of the most beautiful hardy trees in the world, flowering dogwood deserves to be grown in every yard that can accommodate its needs. Flower buds are set in the autumn and are dormant throughout the winter. In early spring, before the leaves have developed, the small, tightly packed flowers open. These would scarcely attract any notice were it not for the four large, white bracts (highly modified leaves) that subtend the actual flowers. Healthy, well-grown trees bear a flower cluster at the tip of every branch and form large masses of white. For a spectacular show of color, one cannot do better than to combine flowering dogwood with redbud (*Cercis canadensis*) and early-flowering azaleas. Dogwoods are at their best in well-drained acidic soils with a high level of organic matter. They should be mulched to maintain a cool, moist root run, and they appreciate some watering during summer. Dogwoods are intolerant of pollution and thus should not be planted along large streets with heavy traffic. Flowering dogwoods extend south only to central Florida. They may be grown south of their natural range, but the plants may not flower well. There are numerous cultivars of flowering dogwood, including forms that are abundantly flowering or have pink or rose bracts. One cultivar, 'Suwanee Squat,' is unique for its low, nearly prostrate growth habit. It was discovered by Bob Simons in Suwanee County, Florida.

269. *Cornus foemina*

Common Name: Swamp Dogwood
Habit: Large shrub or small, shrubby tree.
Size: Up to 15 feet high and often nearly as wide as it is tall.
Season: Deciduous, sometimes briefly so southward; flowering in the spring; fruit maturing in the autumn.
Fruit: Small blue berries about ¼ inch in diameter.
Maintenance: None.
Motility: May sucker under some conditions.
Growing Conditions: Wetlands in full sun to nearly full shade; Zones 8–10A.
Propagation: Seed (difficult to germinate); cuttings; suckers.

Comments: This is the most widespread species of dogwood in Florida, and locally adapted forms may be utilized throughout the state in a variety of garden situations. It is native to wet sites, often in shallow standing water such as along pond margins or the edges of swamps. As such, it is useful to gardeners who would like to beautify a wet area where most garden-center plants will not thrive. Swamp dogwood will also grow under ordinary garden conditions, doing best if established while dormant in winter. The masses of small white flowers are attractive, especially when viewed against a dark background. Two other species of dogwood that form multitrunked small trees occur in Florida: silky dogwood (*Cornus amomum*) and rough dogwood (*C. asperifolia*). Both may be utilized in the garden in the same manner as swamp dogwood.

270. *Diospyros virginiana*

Common Name: Persimmon

Habit: Relatively slow-growing tree with an oval crown and male and female flowers on separate trees.

Size: Growing 35–50 feet tall with a crown 20–30 feet wide.

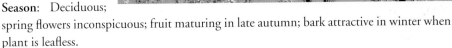

Season: Deciduous; spring flowers inconspicuous; fruit maturing in late autumn; bark attractive in winter when plant is leafless.

Fruit: Rather large, orange, one-seeded fleshy fruits; highly astringent when immature but pleasant tasting to the human palate when fully ripe and avidly sought by a broad range of animals.

Maintenance: None if properly situated; fallen fruit of female trees is messy.

Motility: Seeds spread by animals and germinate in open areas; will sucker and form thickets.

Growing Conditions: Moderately moist but well-drained soils in full sun or light shade; Zones 8–11.

Propagation: Seed (stratify for two months); suckers.

Comments: Large persimmon trees have thick, brownish black bark broken into a rather uniform series of small squares, frequently likened to alligator hide. This is especially noticeable in winter when the plants are leafless. The small creamy white flowers are borne in the spring and are not particularly showy, but they attract a wide range of pollinating insects. In the autumn, female trees are noticeable for the abundantly produced orange fruits with a whitish bloom. Unripe fruits are mouth-puckeringly astringent, but once ripe to the point of being soft and mushy to the touch, they lose the astringency, are surprisingly tasty, and may be used in a wide variety of recipes. Additionally, the roasted ground seeds may serve as a coffee substitute and the dried leaves may be used as a wild tea (Deuerling and Lantz 1993:18). Persimmons are easily grown under a wide range of conditions and occur in both rich, moist woodlands and dry, open fields. Their only drawbacks are a tendency to sucker, which limits their use in formal garden situations, and the necessity of having a nearby male tree to pollinate female trees.

271. *Dipholis salicifolia* (Synonym: *Sideroxylon salicifolium*)

Common Name: Willow Bustic

Habit: Small tree with glossy, dark green leaves and a narrow, upright crown.

Size: Growing up to 30 feet tall, but flowering and fruiting when much smaller.

Season: Evergreen; small whitish green, fragrant flowers are borne in dense clusters along the twigs in early to late spring; fruits ripening in the summer or early autumn.

Fruit: Small, rounded, one-seeded black berries.

Maintenance: None.

Motility: None in most garden situations.

Growing Conditions: Coastal hammocks under slightly moist to rather dry conditions in full sun; Zones 9B–11.

Propagation: Seed (sow as soon as possible after the fruit ripens).

Comments: Willow bustic is an easily grown, resilient tree that tolerates drought as well as alkaline or rocky soils. With some protection, it will grow well near the coast, where it exhibits moderate salt tolerance. Plants grown in very sandy soil without any supplemental watering were thriving two years later and their health was attested to by their profuse flowering and fruit set. Its narrow crown and long, thin branches with downward-hanging leaves give willow bustic a distinctive appearance that readily distinguishes it from other Florida trees. Another distinctive feature is the glossy, dark olive green foliage, with long leaf blades pointed at both ends. The narrow crown makes the tree useful for planting in tight places and close to buildings. Like all Florida members of the sapodilla family, willow bustic bears innumerable small flowers that are exceedingly attractive to insects and one-seeded berrylike fruits utilized as food by wildlife.

272. *Eugenia axillaris*

Common Name: White Stopper

Habit: Large shrub or small tree with pale whitish bark and distinctively aromatic foliage.

Size: Reportedly up to 21 feet tall but usually much smaller.

Season: Evergreen; flowering in midsummer; fruit maturing in the autumn.

Fruit: Rounded, purplish black berries about ¾–½ inch in diameter, these persisting on the plant for a long time.

Maintenance: None in the wild garden; may be pruned to any desired height and shape.

Motility: Occasionally some forms root suckering; occasionally spreading from self-sown seeds.

Growing Conditions: Maritime or tropical hammocks in full sun to dense shade; Zones 8B–11.

Propagation: Seed (sow immediately upon ripening).

Comments: White stopper has rapidly become well established in cultivation. The dense crown of dark green leaves is framed by milky-barked trunks and limbs and produces flushes of new growth tinged in shades of pink, deep rose, or burgundy. The plant has a neat, symmetrical growth habit and may be utilized for the most formal of garden effects, including hedges and foundation plantings. The small white flowers are individually insignificant but are produced in great numbers and make an interesting contrast against the dark foliage. They are followed by large, edible purple-black fruits, these being pleasantly aromatic and having an exotic, tropical flavor. The plants grow readily under varied conditions and are drought tolerant and somewhat salt tolerant. Additionally, plants are readily propagated from seed; young plants scarcely more than saplings 3–4 feet tall will flower and bear fruit. For its many valuable traits and ease of growth, white stopper is an indispensable addition to the wild garden in peninsular Florida. The unusual common name, stopper, is derived from the use of the leaves of this and related plants to make a tea to stop diarrhea.

273. *Eugenia confusa*

Common Name: Redberry Stopper
Habit: Large shrub or small tree with distinctive glossy leaves with an elongated, narrow tip.
Size: Very slowly growing to 18 feet tall, usually shorter.
Season: Evergreen; flowering in the spring or summer; the fruit maturing in autumn.
Fruit: Small scarlet or red berries.
Maintenance: None in the wild garden; may be pruned to any desired height and shape.
Motility: None in most garden situations.
Growing Conditions: Coastal hammocks; Zones 10–11 (also reported from Martin County in Zone 9B).
Propagation: Seed (sow immediately upon ripening).
Comments: Redberry stopper is one of the most beautiful shrubs or small trees native to Florida. It is densely clothed with attractive foliage that is exceptionally ornamental and elegant. The leaves have a long pointed tip that gives them a highly distinctive appearance when compared to other

stoppers. Further adding to its beauty, the bright green leaves have a smooth, glossy surface, as if each leaf had been heavily varnished. The brilliant scarlet fruits beautifully complement the leaves. Like all stoppers, this one is slow-growing, although redberry stopper seems to be slower than most, and plants do not flower or bear fruit until they reach a rather large size.

274. *Eugenia foetida* (Synonyms: *Eugenia buxifolia; Eugenia myrtoides*)

Common Name: Spanish Stopper
Habit: Large shrub or small tree densely clothed with small, rounded leaves.
Size: Reportedly to 36 feet tall but more commonly about half that height.
Season: Evergreen; flowering in the summer; fruits maturing in the autumn.
Fruit: Small purplish black berries.
Maintenance: None in the wild garden; may be pruned to any desired height and shape.
Motility: Self-sown seedlings rarely establishing near the parent plant.
Growing Conditions: Coastal hammocks; Zones 9B–11.
Propagation: Seed.
Comments: Densely clothed with small to medium-sized spoon-shaped leaves and often growing into a large, symmetrical, rounded shrub, Spanish stopper makes an excellent foundation or specimen plant in formal garden situations. With age, the plants eventually form small trees, but they may be pruned to any desired shape or size. Of all our stoppers, Spanish stopper has the smallest flowers and fruits, but it still has much wildlife value.
Special Note: Although the species epithet *foetida* means "malodorous" or "with a putrid odor," Spanish stopper does not have a particularly noticeable odor.

275. *Eugenia rhombea*

Common Name: Red Stopper
Habit: Large shrub or small tree with a warm, reddish brown bark.
Size: Very slowly growing up to about 9 feet.
Season: Evergreen; flowering in late spring or early summer; the fruit maturing in late summer or autumn.
Fruit: Round purplish black berries about ¾ inch wide.
Maintenance: None in the wild garden; may be pruned to any desired height and shape.
Motility: None in most garden situations.
Growing Conditions: Tropical hammocks; Zones 10–11.

Propagation: Seed.

Comments: Red stopper is a shrub or very small tree of refined appearance and with an elegant growth habit. Plants grow in a rounded, symmetrical shape and, when young, are often wider than they are tall. The branches are produced in flat sprays perpendicular to the main trunk, resulting in an interesting "layered" crown. It is slow-growing and does not flower or fruit as a young plant. Thus, large, fully mature red stoppers should be treated as cherished treasures. Red stopper is a rare plant native to Miami-Dade and Monroe Counties and has the most limited natural range of all the stoppers in Florida.

276. *Exothea paniculata*

Common Name: Inkwood

Habit: Tree with a wide crown and fragrant, white, male or female flowers borne on separate trees.

Size: Growing up to 40 feet tall, the crown about three-fourths as wide as the tree is tall.

Season: Evergreen; flowering in late winter or early spring; fruits maturing in early spring to midsummer.

Fruit: Female plants bear rounded reddish to blackish purple berries about ½ inch in diameter.

Maintenance: None or essentially none.

Motility: Self-sown seedlings occasionally establishing in the garden.

Growing Conditions: Tropical hammocks with moist but well-drained soil in full sun to partial shade; Zones 9B–11.

Propagation: Seed.

Comments: Inkwood is an exceptional ornamental tree with many excellent landscape features. It has a pleasing form and naturally grows with a dense, broad crown. The dark green leaves are attractive and nicely set off the abundantly produced fragrant white flowers. On female trees these are followed by berries useful to wildlife; where falling berries might be a nuisance, one can plant a male tree. The wood is reportedly strong and heavy, an important consideration in Florida, which is prone to tropical storms and hurricanes. Additionally, it will grow under a wide range of conditions and is tolerant of drought, salt, alka-

line soils, and shade. Finally, for a plant of tropical affinities, it is extremely cold tolerant, extending up the east coast of Florida as far north as Volusia County. Occasionally, young plants are plagued by leaf miner, but once established, the species is generally pest-free.

277. *Ficus aurea*

Common Name: Strangler Fig; Golden Fig
Habit: Usually epiphytic and somewhat vinelike when young, but a large terrestrial tree at maturity.
Size: Eventually reaching 40–60 feet in height.
Season: Evergreen; flowers insignificant; fruiting all year but tending to fruit most heavily in spring.

Fruit: Sweet, juicy rounded fruits may be red, brown, or yellow, are ⅓ inch wide, and are avidly sought by many birds and mammals.

Maintenance: None or essentially none; avoid planting where fallen fruits will create a problem.

Motility: Essentially no motility in cultivation; rarely an occasional seedling establishing itself in the boots of cabbage palms.

Growing Conditions: Hammocks in southern Florida, nearly always associated with cabbage palms; Zones 9B–11.

Propagation: Seed; cuttings.

Comments: *Ficus aurea* is the native strangler fig often found encircling cabbage palms. It begins life as a seed deposited on another plant and slowly grows as an epiphyte until its roots reach the ground. When this occurs, growth increases and the young fig envelopes the host plant in a series of roots. Eventually these coalesce into a woody trunk with the host plant ultimately dying in the fig's hollow core. Well-grown and healthy strangler figs are exceedingly ornamental as a result of the glossy, dark green leaves, these often provided with a pleasingly contrasting pale yellow midrib. Additionally, strangler fig is a fast grower under average garden conditions and is readily propagated from seed that germinates freely within a few weeks. Wild banyan tree, *Ficus citrifolia,* is our only other native fig but is a much rarer plant distinguished by its stalked figs, those of *F. aurea* being stalkless or nearly so. *Ficus citrifolia* has a neater, more formal appearance and is more tolerant of hot, rocky conditions than is *F. aurea.*

278. *Fraxinus pennsylvanica* (Synonym: *Fraxinus profunda*)

Common Name: Green Ash
Habit: Large, highly attractive, deciduous shade tree with opposite, hickory-like leaves.
Size: Grows 50–120 feet high with a trunk diameter of 18–30 inches.
Season: Deciduous in winter; small flowers in earliest spring; fruits in late spring; yellow autumn foliage.
Fruit: Winged, single-seeded fruits 1–2 inches long borne on female trees.
Maintenance: None or essentially none; do not plant where falling leaves and fruits will be a problem.
Motility: Self-sown seedlings appearing in the vicinity of female trees.
Growing Conditions: Moist, often seasonally flooded woodlands in full sun to light shade; Zones 8–9.
Propagation: Seed (stratify); cuttings (taken from seedlings or one-year-old stump sprouts).
Comments: Green ash is the most widely distributed of all American ashes and extends to Canada in the north and to Wyoming in the west. In Florida, it extends south to Hernando, Sumter, Lake, and Brevard counties. Although favoring deep, rich, moist soils, green ash is extremely adaptable and highly tolerant of stressful urban conditions, generally growing as a single-trunked tree with a large, dense, rounded to spreading crown. Its good form, resistance to insects and diseases, adaptability, and golden autumn color have made it a popular shade tree for large residential properties and parks. As with all of Florida's ashes, its leaves are utilized as the larval food of the eastern tiger swallowtail butterfly. White ash (*Fraxinus americana*) is a similar tree restricted to northern Florida and with leaflets having a whitish lower surface. Pop ash (*F. caroliniana*) is a smaller tree (to 50 feet high) with an open crown that casts light shade; it grows in very wet situations and extends south to southern peninsular Florida.

279. *Gordonia lasianthus*

Common Name: Loblolly-Bay
Habit: Highly ornamental large evergreen tree with an erect narrow crown, with older trees developing a deeply furrowed trunk of much character and beauty.
Size: Grows 65–80 feet tall with a trunk diameter of up to 20 inches.
Season: Flowers borne in the spring and early summer; some leaves often turning red in autumn.
Maintenance: None or essentially none if properly situated.
Motility: May establish itself from self-sown seedlings if moist, open areas are available.

Growing Conditions: Moist, acidic soils in nearly full sun to partial shade; Zones 8–9B.

Propagation: Seeds (stratify); cuttings.

Comments: Loblolly-bay is one of Florida's most attractive flowering trees. Loblolly-bays are large trees that seem even taller than they really are because of their narrow crown. They are densely clothed with dark green leaves and these serve as the perfect backdrop for the large, fragrant, pristine white flowers set off by a central ring of prominent yellow stamens. In the autumn, the oldest leaves assume a brilliant red, adding late-season color and interest. Additionally, plants make ideal specimen trees and flower at an early age. Established plants resent root disturbance, so plants should be situated with care. Loblolly-bays insist on moist acidic soil and have very poor salt tolerance. Thus, they cannot be grown throughout much of the southern third of peninsular Florida. Loblolly-bay grows under the same conditions as sweet-bay (*Magnolia virginiana*) and makes an ideal companion plant for that species in the garden. Besides stratifying the seed, it has been recommended that fresh seed be soaked in lukewarm water for two days, then air dried, and finally sown in a light mix; the seed germinates over a two-month period.

280. *Guaiacum sanctum* (the genus is sometimes spelled "Guajacum")

Common Name: Lignum-Vitae

Habit: Slow-growing large shrub or small tree with a broad horizontally spreading crown.

Size: Growing up to 25 feet tall with a crown as wide or wider.

Season: Evergreen; blue flowers in the spring; colorful fruit in the autumn or winter.

Fruit: Fleshy dark yellow capsule splitting open to reveal dark red seeds.

Maintenance: None.

Motility: None or essentially none in most garden situations.

Growing Conditions: Coastal, often rocky areas, dunes, and maritime hammocks in full sun or light shade; Zones 10–11.

Propagation: Seed.

Comments: Lignum-vitae (meaning "tree of life" in Latin) is an exceedingly slow-growing, shrubby plant while young but it eventually becomes a small tree with horizontally spreading branches. The dark green leaves have a delicate, somewhat fernlike appearance, and their dark color contrasts pleasingly with the pale, deeply fissured bark. In the spring, the plant bears attractive but rather small blue flowers that are utilized by a variety of bees. The flowers are followed by fleshy, yellow capsules that mature in the autumn or winter and open to reveal several seeds covered with a dark red, fleshy coat. Lignum-vitae is easily grown from seed, but some patience is required since the seeds are often slow to germinate. Its beautiful foliage, attractive growth form, and deep blue flowers make this a highly ornamental species that ranks as one of the most beautiful flowering trees in North America.

281. *Guapira discolor*

Common Name: Blolly
Habit: Small to medium-sized tree with a broad crown and leathery rounded leaves.
Size: Can grow up to 30 feet or higher but is usually much smaller.
Season: Evergreen; colorful fruit borne in the summer and autumn.
Fruit: Female trees bear brilliant red, single-seeded berries much relished by birds.
Maintenance: None or else periodic pruning to maintain desired height and shape.
Motility: Casually spreading from self-sown seedlings, often just below or near the parent tree.
Growing Conditions: Tropical and maritime hammocks in full sun to light shade; Zones 9B–11.
Propagation: Seed.
Comments: Blolly is a chameleon: a green, woody plant that melts into the background and frequently goes unnoticed. However, it is an important component of tropical hammock gardens and is often one of the first native woody plants acquired by budding native plant gardeners in southern Florida. This is not surprising since it is hardy, adaptable, and easily propagated from seed. It grows quickly and may be utilized in both formal and informal garden settings. The greenish flowers are small and inconspicuous, but female trees bear beautiful small berries in shades of intense red or rose-red. A plant in full fruit is a beautiful sight. Blolly is surprisingly variable; there are both smooth forms and forms with leaves coated with small, whitish hairs. There is also much variation in plant size, density of foliage, and size of the foliage. However, thus far none of the various forms has been given a cultivar name or become established in the general nursery trade, as has taken place with some of our other native trees, such as yaupon holly.

282. *Ilex × attenuata*

Common Name: East Palatka Holly

Habit: Vigorous, easily cultivated small tree able to grow under a wide variety of conditions.

Size: Grows 15–20 feet high and 10–15 feet wide.

Season: Evergreen; small, greenish white flowers in spring; abundant fruit in autumn, winter, and spring.

Fruit: Small, brilliant red berries borne in large quantities by female trees.

Maintenance: None or essentially none.

Motility: None in most garden situations.

Growing Conditions: Adaptable to a wide range of sites in full sun to light shade; Zones 8A.

Propagation: Cuttings.

Comments: The multiplication sign between the genus and the species epithet in the scientific name of this holly signifies that it is not a true species but is instead a hybrid. Its parents are dahoon holly (*Ilex cassine*) and American holly (*I. opaca*). This hybrid turns up spontaneously now and then throughout the southeastern United States wherever its parents occur together. Like other plants of hybrid origin, it is remarkably variable, some plants greatly resembling dahoon holly, others more like American holly, and most displaying an intermediate set of characteristics. The plants also possess hybrid vigor and, in general, are highly adaptable, fast-growing trees free from pests and diseases. Female trees are noteworthy for bearing enormous quantities of brilliant red berries. Numerous named forms have entered the nursery trade with 'East Palatka' being the most commonly grown cultivar in Florida. It resembles a dahoon holly but it has a neater, more regular appearance. Also, its dark green leaves often possess a few sharp teeth as a result of the influence of its American holly parent. Because of its vigor, this hybrid holly has been used as a street tree and in the medians of parking lots. Perhaps its most distinctive features are the large masses of red berries it produces and the ability to set berries without a male holly nearby.

283. *Ilex cassine*

Common Name: Dahoon Holly

Habit: Large shrub or small tree, often with an open, irregular crown.

Size: Growing 20–30 feet tall with a crown half or more as wide.

Season: Evergreen; flowering in the spring; female trees with red berries in autumn and winter.

Fruit: Small, one-seeded, brilliant red berries.

Maintenance: None or essentially none.

Motility: Rarely spreading in most garden situations.

Growing Conditions: Moist to wet soils in light shade to full sun; Zones 8–10.

Propagation: Seeds; cuttings.

Comments: Dahoon holly is a perfect holly for the beginning and advanced native plant enthusiast alike. The glossy, evergreen leaves make for an attractive plant that can be grown for the foliage alone. Yet, it is also a heavy bearer of bright red, orange-red, or sometimes yellow fruits late in the season, berries that can be utilized as holiday decora-

tions or to attract birds to the garden. The seed of this species lacks any dormancy requirements and germinates in a few weeks, with the young plants precociously blooming in their second year. A species of wet areas, it occurs throughout Florida and may be grown wherever sufficient moisture can be provided. However, established plants are remarkably drought tolerant. Myrtle holly (*Ilex cassine* var. *myrtifolia*) is a smaller plant with leaves less than 2/5 inch wide. It occurs in northern Florida and has often been treated as a distinct species

(*I. myrtifolia*). In any case, it makes an attractive shrub or small tree with a picturesque, somewhat gnarled habit. Since its leaves are so narrow, the berries are prominently displayed and are far more conspicuous and showy than would otherwise be the case.

284. *Ilex krugiana*

Common Name: Krug's Holly; Tawny-Berry Holly

Habit: Small tree adapted to South Florida's tropical conditions.

Size: Reportedly growing to 30 feet high, about half as wide as it is tall.

Season: Evergreen; small whitish flowers borne in the spring; fruit borne in late summer and autumn.

Fruit: Small reddish yellow berries ripening to black.

Maintenance: None.

Motility: Self-sown seedlings sparsely to abundantly produced, especially in the vicinity of the parent plant.

Growing Conditions: Tropical hammocks with alkaline, rocky soil in deep shade to full sun; Zone 10.

Propagation: Seed.

Comments: Krug's holly is a small shrubby tree that will stump your gardening friends, who will never guess it is a holly. It is Florida's only truly tropical holly and is quite distinct from its cold-tolerant cousins. Especially confusing is its foliage, which has been described as vaguely resembling that of certain wild cherries. The leaves are distinctive because of their long, pointed apex, deep dark green color, and highly glossy upper surface. Adding to its unusual appearance are the long, somewhat flexible leaf stalks, which cause the leaves to hang somewhat and to shake and bend freely with every breeze. When the tree is flourishing, flowers and fruits are borne in huge numbers, seemingly produced from the base of nearly every leaf. Although neither the flowers nor the fruits are particularly ornamental, their sheer abundance makes one take notice. In nature, Krug's holly is a plant of shady tropical hammocks. However, if given sufficient moisture, it appears adaptable to sunny sites. Interestingly, it is apparently highly resistant to wind. One South Florida native plant nursery reported that Krug's hollies were the only trees left standing at their nursery after the devastation of Hurricane Andrew.

285. *Ilex vomitoria*

Common Name: Yaupon Holly

Habit: Large shrub or small tree with attractive whitish bark, a densely branched crown, and small, evergreen leaves.

Size: Usually up to about 15–20 feet high.

Season: Evergreen; small inconspicuous white flowers borne in spring attract many insects; berries borne in the autumn on female plants.

Fruit: Small, brilliant red berries abundantly produced on female plants; plants with yellow fruits are also in cultivation.

Maintenance: None or plants may be pruned to any height or shape as desired.

Motility: None in most garden situations.

Growing Conditions: Extremely variable in a wide variety of moist to dry habitats in full sun to light shade; Zones 8–9.

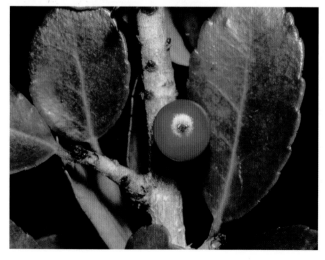

Propagation: Seed (double dormancy, may take two years to germinate); cuttings.

Comments: Yaupon holly has foliage containing a higher level of caffeine than in any other plant native to the continental United States. Native Americans made a potent, highly concentrated drink from the foliage as a cathartic purge. However, in small amounts the dried leaves make a pleasant tea that does not induce gastric distress. Horticulturally, there are few woody plants as adaptable as yaupon holly, for it withstands salty coastal conditions, can grow in highly alkaline soil, and is drought tolerant. The foliage resembles that of boxwood and, like boxwood, the plants may be utilized along fencerows or used as a hedge; they can be pruned to any desired height or shape. Yaupon holly is also remarkable in that many cultivars are available, which is unusual for most native plants. The cultivars fall into three main groups: (1) plants with a weeping habit; (2) female plants with especially heavy production of red or yellow berries; and (3) plants with a highly congested, dwarf growing habit. Weeping yaupon hollies make excellent specimen plants; heavily fruiting female cultivars are excellent accent plants; and dwarf-growing cultivars are utilized in foundation plantings, to make low hedges, and to demarcate boundaries. Not fitting into any of these categories is the cultivar 'Will Fleming,' which Kim Tripp (1996b) described as having an "incredibly formal, narrowly fastigate habit and gray-green foliage that resembles a small Italian Cypress from afar."

286. *Krugiodendron ferreum*

Common Name: Black Ironwood; Leadwood

Habit: Large shrub to medium-sized tree with dark green glossy leaves.

Size: Up to about 30 feet tall.

Season: Evergreen; flowers inconspicuous, borne in the spring and summer; fruits borne in the autumn and winter.

Fruit: Small, one-seeded black berries.

Maintenance: None; do not plant where fallen berries may be a nuisance.

Motility: Rarely spreading in most garden situations.

Growing Conditions: Tropical hammocks in full sun to light shade; Zones 9B–11.

Propagation: Seed (sow immediately upon ripening).

Comments: Black ironwood may be used in the landscape either as a background tree or highlighted as a specimen or accent tree. Its chief ornamental trait is the dark, emerald green leaves with a beautifully glossy upper surface. Their wavy margins add another interesting note. Its tiny green flowers attract many insects but go largely unnoticed by gardeners. These are followed by juicy, sweet berries avidly sought by birds and other wildlife and palatable to people. Because of its rather narrow crown, this tree is a good choice for street plantings. It is hardy as far north as Brevard County and, like all coastal hammock trees, has excellent drought tolerance and will grow in rocky, alkaline soils.

287. *Liquidambar styraciflua*

Common Name: Sweet-Gum
Habit: Tall handsome tree with a broad, spreading crown.
Size: Reaching 70–100 feet with age, the crown half to two- thirds as wide.
Season: Deciduous; spring flowers not showy but interesting and unusual; foliage assuming red or yellow autumn color in north and central Florida.
Fruit: Brown, prickly ball with approximately twenty seeds.
Maintenance: None; do not place it where the fallen prickly seed balls will be a nuisance.
Motility: Occasionally spreading by self-sown seedlings.
Growing Conditions: Rich, moist woodlands and clearings in partial shade to full sun; Zones 8–9.
Propagation: Seed (stratify).
Comments: Sweet-gum is so named for the gummy resin produced when the trunk of the tree is injured. In the past, children chewed this gum and it was believed to have medicinal properties. The foliage of sweet-gum is highly distinctive, closely resembling a five-pointed star. The only other trees with remotely similar leaves are the maples, but they have leaves borne in opposite pairs whereas sweet-gum leaves are alternate. In the autumn, the plants produce their boldest display as the foliage assumes various shades of yellow and red before falling. Horticulturally, sweet-gum requires average to moist soil with a thick organic mulch to keep the roots cool. Its principal flaws are the prickly seed balls, which can be a nuisance if the plant is not properly situated, and a susceptibility to insect pests toward the southern end of its natural range (Huegel 1995:44).

288. *Lysiloma latisiliqua*

Common Name: Wild-Tamarind
Habit: Fast-growing tree with a wide, spreading crown, delicate ferny foliage, and fragrant flowers.
Size: About 40 feet high or higher, reportedly reaching 60 feet.
Season: Evergreen southward, deciduous northward; intermittently flowers from spring to autumn.
Fruit: Thin, papery bean pods up to 6 inches long and 1 inch wide.
Maintenance: None in the wild garden or if properly situated.
Motility: Sometimes spreading by self-sown seedlings.

Growing Conditions: Grows in full or nearly full sun in pinelands, hammocks, and coastal situations; Zones 10–11.

Propagation: Seed.

Comments: Wild-tamarind plays an extremely important role in the ecology of South Florida hammocks. It is a fast-growing pioneer species. Seedlings establish themselves in open, sunny areas and quickly grow into large shade trees that serve as "nurse" trees for a wide array of hammock species needing such a canopy to become established. Because of its rapid growth and wide canopy, wild-tamarind is highly recommended as a shade tree. Generally, fast-growing trees

have weak or brittle wood. However, wild-tamarind is said to have strong wood capable of withstanding harsh winds (Scurlock 1987:108). Its small, pinnate leaves have a delicate ferny appearance and "melt" into the ground when they drop from the tree. Gardeners who do not like raking leaves will appreciate wild-tamarind. It will grow north of its natural range at least as far as Palm Beach County. Wild-tamarind is drought tolerant once established and is highly salt tolerant, with plants occasionally found growing on coastal strand.

289. *Magnolia grandiflora*

Common Name: Southern Magnolia

Habit: Large tree of noble appearance with a somewhat conical crown extending nearly or quite to the ground as a result of low sweeping branches.

Size: Growing up to 65 feet high, reportedly to 80 feet outside our range.

Season: Evergreen, the foliage attractive all year; huge, fragrant flowers borne in late spring and summer; attractive fruits maturing in the autumn.

Fruit: Prominent, conelike aggregation of fruits, each splitting open to reveal a single seed with a bright red, fleshy outer covering.

Maintenance: Old leaves dropping sporadically and difficult to rake up.

Motility: None in most garden situations.

Growing Conditions: Rich moist sites in full sun to light shade; sometimes growing in rather wet sites or, more surprisingly, in apparently dry sites such as coastal dunes; Zones 8–9A.

Propagation: Seed; cuttings; grafting (not recommended for amateur gardeners).

Comments: Southern magnolia is a noble, aristocratic tree renowned for its elegant form, beautiful foliage, and magnificent flowers. It is a stately, broadleaf evergreen with large leaves sometimes as much as 12 inches long. These have a dark green, highly glossy upper surface and an equally attractive lower surface covered by a dense, velvety layer of rich cinnamon brown hairs. The huge white flowers are richly aromatic and, in combination with the foliage, make this one of the most beautiful flowering trees native to the United States. In addition to its great beauty, southern magnolia is renowned for its tough, adaptable constitution. For example, in the Carolinas and the Florida Panhandle, there are small shrubby southern magnolias growing along coastal dunes. Research has shown that these are large, fully grown trees that have been covered by drifting sand such that only the branch tips appear above the ground! There are many "improved" cultivars that are propagated by way of grafting or specially treated cuttings. It is extremely difficult for home gardeners to propagate this magnolia vegetatively. Thus, plants traded among native plant enthusiasts are usually grown from seed and, once germination takes place, may flower in as little as two years or as many as ten.

290. *Magnolia virginiana*

Common Name: Sweet-Bay

Habit: Large shrub or, more often, a small to medium-sized tree.

Size: Normally a tree ranging from 20 to 30 feet high at maturity with a crown about half as wide as the tree is tall.

Season: Evergreen in all but the severest winters; fragrant white flowers borne in spring and summer; attractive fruits maturing in the autumn.

Fruit: Prominent, conelike aggregation of fruits, each splitting open to reveal a single seed with a bright red, fleshy outer covering.

Maintenance: None.

Motility: None or else suckering if shallow roots are disturbed.

Growing Conditions: Moist to wet acidic sites in partial shade to full sun; Zones 8–10.

Propagation: Seed (northern forms require three to five months' stratification); cuttings.

Comments: Sweet-bay is one of the few magnolias that can withstand "wet feet" and will thrive in permanently wet soil along the edges of shallow ponds. Plants also adapt readily to average garden conditions, their only requirement being acidic soils, otherwise the foliage becomes chlorotic and yellowish. Sweet-bay is a handsome tree even out of flower because the lower leaf surfaces are an attractive silvery green. This results in a graceful and especially pleasing display when the wind rustles the leaves and they shimmer dark green and silver. The flowers have a quaint charm and a crisp lemon scent. Since sweet-bay has a wide distribution throughout Florida, it is important to obtain locally adapted strains for your garden.

291. *Mastichodendron foetidissimum* (Synonym: *Sideroxylon foetidissimum*)

Common Name: Mastic; Jungle-Plum

Habit: Attractive large tree with a single trunk, dense, somewhat rounded crown, and yellowish green leaves.

Size: Reportedly growing 50–70 feet high but usually smaller.

Season: Evergreen; pale to bright yellow, fragrant flowers borne in the summer; fruits ripening in late winter and early spring.

Fruit: Rounded, yellow, one-seeded berry to 1 inch long, the flesh edible but unpleasantly gummy.

Maintenance: None if properly situated.

Motility: Rarely spreading in most garden situations.

Growing Conditions: Coastal hammocks in light shade to full sun; Zones 9B–11.

Propagation: Seed (sow as soon as possible after the fruit ripens).

Comments: Mastic is one of the more commonly cultivated trees in native gardens in southern Florida. This is due to three factors. Mastic has good form and grows as a straight-trunked tree with a broadly rounded, densely leafy crown. It is also easily grown near the coasts (where much of Florida's population is concentrated) and has excellent cold tolerance for a subtropical tree. As a wild plant, it ranges from the Florida Keys northward to Volusia and Manatee counties on Florida's east and west coasts, respectively. Third, and this is an important consideration if a plant is to become common in cultivation, it is easily propagated: lone plants will set abundant fruit, seeds germinate readily, and seedlings grow rapidly. Mastic has fragrant yellow flowers that are much sought after by insects, and the large yellow fruits add a bright accent touch late in the year.

292. *Myrcianthes fragrans*

Common Name: Simpson's-Stopper; Twinberry-Stopper

Habit: Extremely variable, highly ornamental small shrub to medium-sized tree with interesting flaky bark, a densely branched crown, attractive foliage, fragrant white flowers, and colorful fruit.

Size: Height varying from 6 to 20 feet or higher, the crown varying from narrow and subcolumnar to wider than the plant is tall.

Season: Evergreen; flowers and fruits borne intermittently in light to heavy flushes throughout the year, especially after heavy rains preceded by dry spells or warm weather preceded by cold weather.

Fruit: Rather large, bright orange to orange-red berries beautifully contrasting with the dark foliage.

Maintenance: None in the wild garden, may be pruned to any desired height or shape.

Motility: Self-sown seedlings sparingly to abundantly produced; some forms developing thickets by means of root suckers.

Growing Conditions: Coastal and tropical hammocks in partial shade to full sun; Zones 9–11.

Propagation: Seed (sow promptly as the seeds are green and will die if allowed to dry out).

Comments: Simpson's-stopper ranks as one of the most beautiful and ornamental woody plants native to Florida, and the list of all its virtues is a long one. It is a densely branched and densely leafy plant that varies from a small, spreading shrub to a rather large tree, depending on the plant's genetics and growing situation. The small leaves are a rich, dark green when mature and contrast beautifully with new growth, which may range in color from pale chartreuse to deep wine red. The foliage likewise handsomely complements the fragrant, pure white flowers as well as the ripe orange-red berries that promptly follow. Also attractive is the plant's flaking bark, revealing a mosaic of orange-brown, gray, pale green, and beige. Horticulturally, Simpson's-stopper may be used as a specimen or accent plant and it makes an excellent midsized to tall hedge or screen for privacy. However, when it is used as a hedge, flowering and fruiting may be curtailed if it is trimmed too frequently. This wonderful plant is as hardy and easy to grow as it is attractive, and it has been recorded as far north as St. Johns County, with cultivated plants reportedly hardy in Aiken, South Carolina (Zone 8). It often grows in coastal hammocks just behind the sand dunes, so it is also a good candidate for coastal properties. Because its dense crown provides excellent shelter for birds, the staff at Fairchild Tropical Garden recommend that Simpson's-stopper be grown near a feeder or birdbath to serve as a refuge for shy birds such as painted buntings and cardinals.

293. *Persea borbonia*

Common Name: Red Bay

Habit: Medium-sized tree with a broad, densely leafy, rounded crown.

Size: Variable from 20 to 60 feet high.

Season: Evergreen; inconspicuous yellowish green flowers borne in the spring; fruit maturing in the autumn.

Fruit: One-seeded purple berry about ¾ inch long.

Maintenance: None.

Motility: None or else sparingly spreading by self-sown seedlings.

Growing Conditions: Highly variable but usually in moist to dry wooded areas in partial shade to full sun; Zones 8–11.

Propagation: Seed (sow immediately upon ripening).

Comments: Red bay is a desirable broadleaf evergreen tree in the same genus as the avocado. It is known chiefly for its aromatic leaves, which

have been used as a substitute for true bay leaves; its adaptability and ease of growth; and as a larval food source for various swallowtail butterflies. The edges of the leaves are often characteristically swollen and deformed as a result of a tiny gall-forming insect. Heavy infestations detract somewhat from the plant's overall neat and tidy appearance. However, the galls cause absolutely no harm whatsoever to the plant and no steps should be taken to "cure" the tree. A number of bird-watchers report that small insectivorous birds have been observed opening the galls to get at the tiny insect larvae inside. A smaller variety of red bay (*Persea borbonia* var. *humilis*) is adapted to sand scrub and is a suitable alternative for homeowners with deep sandy soil. A closely related species (*Persea palustris*) occurs in wet habitats and is said to be far less prone to galls than is red bay.

294. *Piscidia piscipula*

Common Name: Jamaican-Dogwood; Florida Fishpoison Tree

Habit: Attractive tree with dark green leaves.

Size: Growing 30–50 feet high, the crown about half to two-thirds as wide.

Season: Deciduous; flowers borne in great numbers while the tree is leafless in spring.

Fruit: Distinctive four-winged pods about 1–3 inches long.

Maintenance: None if properly situated; do not plant where falling flowers, leaves, and fruits may be a nuisance.

Motility: None or self-sown seedlings sparingly establishing near the parent plant.

Growing Conditions: Tropical hammocks, rocky pinelands, and coastal sites in full sun; Zones 9A–11.

Propagation: Seed.

Comments: Jamaican-dogwood is an underutilized

tree native to southern Florida. Presently, it is grown principally by the most ardent of native plant enthusiasts in tropical hammock gardens. It is especially well suited for placement along the edges of a hammock. Situated in this manner, it makes an unusual accent plant when in full flower, with leafless branches adorned with masses of white flowers marked with pale green, lavender, or pink. The floral display of Jamaican-dogwood varies considerably: the best forms put on a subtly attractive display, while the poorest forms have dingy or muddy-colored flowers. In addition to their use in the wild garden, the plants may also be utilized as specimen trees in formal settings, such as urban parks, since they are very attractive when clothed with dark green leaves from spring to autumn. Jamaican-dogwoods grow in rocky soils and frequently occur in coastal areas just behind the sand dunes. Thus, the plants are tolerant of much adversity and are suitable for such difficult sites as rocky banks or dry, coastal situations with a saline influence. The wood is described as hard, heavy, strong, and durable. Formerly, the roots, bark, twigs, and leaves of this plant were thrown into small bodies of water where they stupefied fish, which rose to the surface and were easily caught, hence the common name Florida fishpoison tree. Such use is now prohibited by Florida state law (Scurlock 1987:123). The compounds present in the plant are also poisonous to people but, in small doses, have been used in herbal medicine for their sedative and soporific effects.

295. *Platanus occidentalis*

Common Name: Sycamore; American Sycamore; American Planetree

Habit: Fast-growing and long-lived specimen or shade tree.

Size: Grows 70–168 feet tall, with a crown 40–100 feet wide.

Season: Deciduous; bark attractive all year but especially in winter when the tree is leafless.

Fruit: Dense ball of tiny one-seeded fruits often remaining on the tree through winter.

Maintenance: None if properly situated.

Motility: None in most garden situations.

Growing Conditions: Deep, moist, but not flooded soils in full sun to light shade; Zone 8.

Propagation: Seed.

Comments: Although widespread throughout much of the eastern half of the United States, sycamore is restricted in Florida to the Panhandle and a few northern counties. In spite of this, it is such a distinctive and elegant tree that it is sometimes grown far south of its natural range. Its principal horticultural attributes are its great size, rapid growth, longevity, distinctive white exfoliating bark, and broad, dense crown. Additionally, it can withstand strong winds due to its robust and powerful root system. As a result of these qualities, it is an excellent landscape tree for use in parks and along boulevards and as a residential specimen or shade tree for large properties. No other American hardwood tree grows to a larger diameter than sycamore; an Indiana tree had a reported trunk diameter of 10.5 feet.

296. *Prunus caroliniana*

Common Name: Carolina Laurel Cherry
Habit: Small to medium-sized tree with a densely branched and densely leafy narrow crown.
Size: Grows 20–40 feet tall, the crown usually about half as wide.
Season: Evergreen; covered with masses of small white flowers in the spring; fruit inconspicuous, maturing in the autumn and winter.
Fruit: Small single-seeded black cherries with a large seed and a thin layer of flesh.
Maintenance: None; has been recommended as a hedge plant since, when young, it may be pruned to any desired height or shape, however, it is said that such hedges do not age well and become difficult to maintain.
Motility: Freely forming thickets and colonizing open areas as a result of self-sown seedlings and root suckers.
Growing Conditions: Found in a wide variety of wooded areas in light shade to full sun; Zones 8–9.
Propagation: Seed (sow immediately once the fruit ripens).
Comments: Carolina laurel cherry is an attractive tree with a neat formal appearance suitable for use as a specimen tree. Its foliage is dark green and glossy and has variably toothed margins; the most deeply toothed forms greatly resemble certain hollies. When crushed, the leaves give off a rich almond fragrance, and the plant is worth growing for this feature alone. However, do not attempt to use this plant for almond flavoring since the fragrance is due to cyanide-producing compounds! The small white flowers are scarcely noteworthy individually, but they are borne in huge numbers and contrast beautifully with the foliage. Flowers mature into small black cherries very late in the season, and Carolina laurel cherry has been recommended as a winter food source for birds and wildlife. Because of its many ornamental qualities, it is popular throughout the southern United States and has also been introduced into cultivation in southern California. West Indian laurel cherry (*Prunus myrtifolia*) is a related species that is a rare denizen of Miami-Dade County's tropical hammocks. It is better suited to the alkaline soils of southern Florida. It may be distinguished from Carolina laurel cherry by its untoothed leaves with undulate margins.

297. *Prunus serotina*

Common Name: Black Cherry
Habit: Medium-sized to large tree with a rather narrow crown.
Size: Fast-growing and reaching 40–60 feet with age, the crown half to two-thirds as wide.
Season: Deciduous; foliage dark green and glossy, attractive from spring through summer, turning yellow and red in the autumn; small white flowers are borne in innumerable elongated clusters in the spring; fruits ripening in late summer; plant interesting in winter for its attractive bark.
Fruit: Small cherries ripening from bright red to glossy black, eagerly eaten by birds and small wildlife; although poisonous when immature and bitter tasting at maturity, the berries have been used for making jelly and wine.
Maintenance: None.
Motility: Freely forming thickets and colonizing open areas as a result of self-sown seedlings.
Growing Conditions: Forests, clearings, and open fields in moist to average soil in partial shade to full sun; Zones 8–9A.
Propagation: Seed (stratify).
Comments: In the past, black cherry trees grew to be large forest trees to 100 feet high and were a source of high quality lumber. However, such trees are long gone and the species is now mostly seen as a smaller, often weedy tree springing up along fencerows, in clearings, and under power lines where birds visit and drop the seeds. Aside from these weedy tendencies, it is one of our premier trees and provides interest during every season of the year. In winter, it is noteworthy for the shiny reddish brown bark, which grows darker and develops a rough, scaly texture with age. In the spring, it becomes a luminous mass of white flowers contrasting beautifully against the dark green, glossy foliage. In late summer, it provides another show as its bright red berries mature to deep, shiny black. And in the autumn, it furnishes the garden with one last bit of color as its leaves assume a soft yellow glow, often with pinkish undertones. Generally, black cherry is pest- and disease-free, but occasionally it may suffer from heavy infestations of tent caterpillars.

298. *Quercus geminata* (Synonym: *Quercus virginiana* var. *geminata*)

Common Name: Sand Live Oak
Habit: Large, broad-crowned oak.
Size: Approximately 20–30 feet tall, occasionally taller, the crown nearly as wide or wider.
Season: Subevergreen; large numbers of fruits produced in the fall and avidly sought by a wide variety of wildlife.

Fruit: Small acorns about 1 inch long.

Maintenance: None if properly situated; tannin in the leaves and acorns will stain driveways and sidewalks.

Motility: Readily establishing itself in open, sandy ground by animal-dispersed acorns; some forms root suckering and forming thickets.

Growing Conditions: Well-drained sandy soil in scrub, sandhills, and coastal sites in full sun to light shade; Zones 8–10A.

Propagation: Seed (sow as soon as possible after the acorns mature).

Comments: Horticulturally, sand live oak may be utilized as a smaller version of live oak (*Quercus virginiana*), and it has similar wildlife and landscape value. Occasionally the two are confused in the trade, and homeowners are left wondering why their "live oak" is so slow-growing and small. When selecting sand live oak for a garden setting, bear in mind that it is highly variable. Some forms are more or less treelike and rarely sucker. Others are shrubby, sucker freely, and in time form extensive thickets. If the plants are in pots, study them carefully to select a growth form appropriate to your landscape needs. Inquire if the nursery owner has field-grown plants in the ground, as such plants will give you a better idea of the plant's mature form.

299. *Quercus incana*

Common Name: Bluejack Oak

Habit: Small to medium-sized tree.

Size: Variable from 15 to 40 feet in height depending on growing conditions.

Season: Deciduous, very briefly so southward; fruits borne in the autumn.

Fruit: Small acorns.

Maintenance: None or essentially none.

Motility: Sparingly spreading from seed.

Growing Conditions: Deep, well-drained sandy soils in full or nearly full sun; Zones 8–9.

Propagation: Seed.

Comments: Oaks have such outstanding wildlife value that they belong in every native plant garden capable of supporting their growth. But if the garden is too small for a large tree and there is concern over the suckering tendencies of

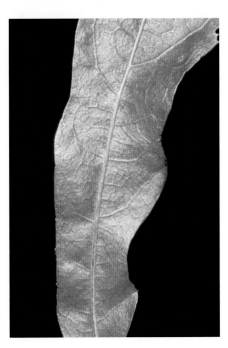

some of our smaller, shrubby oaks, then only a few oaks are suitable. One good candidate for this situation would be bluejack oak. It is a rather small oak that is normally treelike or easily trained into a tree, and it will not take over the garden. Its leaves are an elegant shade of grayish green and, depending on the plant and on weather conditions, they are often accented by a conspicuous pink or reddish central vein. This oak takes well to cultivation but will lose much of its character if grown in rich soils. Turkey oak (*Quercus laevis*) may also be suitable as a small oak tree in dry, sandy soils. Under regular or somewhat moist conditions, blackjack oak (*Q. marilandica*) might prove useful.

300. *Quercus laurifolia*

Common Name: Laurel Oak; Diamond-Leaf Oak
Habit: Beautiful, large tree with a broad, dense, rounded crown.
Size: Growing up to 100 feet tall with a trunk diameter of 3–4 feet.
Season: Briefly deciduous in late winter or early spring, or some forms essentially evergreen; large numbers of fruits produced in the fall and avidly sought by a wide variety of wildlife.
Fruit: Small acorns about 1 inch long.
Maintenance: None if properly situated.
Motility: Readily establishing itself in open, moist ground by animal-dispersed acorns.
Growing Conditions: Rich moist soil in wet hammocks in full sun to partial shade; Zones 8–10.
Propagation: Seed (sow as soon as possible after the acorns mature).
Comments: Laurel oak is a splendid landscape tree. It is most beautiful in very early spring when it drops many of its leaves and replaces them with new ones. The young foliage gradually expands and at first is thin, pale green, and translucent. These new leaves produce a remarkably ornamental effect, especially when backlit by the sun. Eventually they mature to dark green with a leathery texture, and the show is over until next spring. As a landscape or shade tree, laurel oak is valued for its straight trunk, fast growth, tolerance for wet soils, and dense, leafy crown, which naturally grows in a broad, rounded shape. It has superior wildlife value with large crops of acorns that are produced annually. On the negative side, laurel oak is commonly criticized as being short-lived—only 80–100 years!

301. *Quercus virginiana*

Common Name: Live Oak
Habit: Striking, large specimen tree with a very broad, spreading crown, stout trunk, and noble, majestic appearance.
Size: Growing 60–80 feet tall, the crown sometimes spreading to 100 feet wide.

Season: Subevergreen; large numbers of fruits produced in the fall and avidly sought by a wide variety of wildlife.

Fruit: Small acorns about 1 inch long.

Maintenance: None if properly situated; tannins in the leaves and acorns will stain driveways and sidewalks.

Motility: Readily establishing itself in open ground by animal-dispersed acorns.

Growing Conditions: Growing under variable conditions in moist to dry soil in full sun or light shade; Zones 8–11.

Propagation: Seed (sow as soon as possible after the acorns mature).

Comments: Live oaks have an undeserved reputation for being slow-growing. This is not the case; young plants that do not suffer for lack of water will grow with amazing rapidity to a huge size in just ten to fifteen years. Additionally, large trees are easily obtained and are not expensive. The notion that live oaks are slow-growing arises from rootbound, potted plants. These do not have a normal root system and, when planted in the ground, will often remain small for years before they show any real signs of growth. Compounding the problem is that live oak is sometimes confused in commerce with sand live oak (*Quercus geminata*), and the latter is indeed a small, slow-growing oak. In addition to their landscape and wildlife value, live oaks make elegant street trees. However, care should be taken not to plant them where their trunks and roots will damage sidewalks or where their broad crowns will obstruct traffic.

302. *Sapindus saponaria* (Synonym: *Sapindus marginatus*)

Common Name: Soapberry

Habit: Small to medium-sized tree with a leafy, densely branched, broad, rounded crown.

Size: About 20–30 feet tall, reportedly 45–60 feet tall in warm, tropical areas south of Florida.

Season: Deciduous northward, evergreen southward; masses of small greenish white flowers borne in spring, or all year southward; fruits mostly ripening in late summer or autumn.

Fruit: Round, rather hard, brownish berries to 1 inch wide, with translucent yellow flesh and a single large poisonous seed.

Maintenance: None if properly situated.

Motility: Rarely spreading by way of self-sown seed near the vicinity of the parent plant.

Growing Conditions: Coastal hammocks in well-drained soil in full sun or light shade; Zones 8–11.

Propagation: Seed.

Comments: The versatile, adaptable nature of soapberry is attested to by its incredibly wide range—from Kansas in the north to Argentina in the south as well as in the West Indies and,

as an escape from cultivation, in the Old World. Although not particularly ornamental, it was formerly a very useful plant, especially to aboriginal cultures. The flesh of the fruit forms abundant suds in water, and the crushed, poisonous seeds were used as an insecticide or thrown into small bodies of water to stupefy or poison fish (a practice now illegal in Florida). The seeds also found a place in jewelry, made good marbles, and were even made into buttons. Additionally, soapberry is a good bee plant and produces excellent honey. In spite of its poisonous nature, it was formerly used medicinally (a dangerous practice that is not recommended), and its hard, heavy wood was employed in carpentry. Horticulturally, soapberry is valuable as an indestructible, pest-free, drought- and salt-tolerant small shade tree.

303. *Sassafras albidum*

Common Name: Sassafras
Habit: Aromatic, root-suckering small shrub to large tree; male and female flowers borne on separate trees.
Size: Old trees on good sites reaching 60–90 feet in height but in Florida mostly short and shrubby.
Season: Deciduous; yellow flowers in spring; distinctively shaped foliage spring through

autumn; beautiful autumn color ranging from brilliant red to bright yellow or orange; deeply furrowed bark of large, old trees attractive in winter.
Fruit: Female trees bearing small, one-seeded, blue-black berries held in an orange-red cup.
Maintenance: None if situated properly.
Motility: Often forming dense thickets by root suckers.
Growing Conditions: Well-drained, often sandy soils in full sun to light shade; Zones 8–9.
Propagation: Seed (stratify three to four months); root suckers; root cuttings (large roots laid horizontally).

Comments: Sassafras is widely known for its distinctive leaves: some bear two side lobes, others resemble a mitten and bear a single lobe on one side, while still others are without any lobes. Particularly interesting and greatly facilitating its identification is that all three leaf shapes usually appear on a single plant. Other notable traits are its aromatic roots and leaves; the small but quaintly attractive yellow spring flowers, with male trees producing a showier display; and its rich autumnal color. Becoming a large, noble tree in rich woodlands, it is usually a compact, shrubby plant in Florida, where it extends south to Hillsborough County. The bark of large roots is especially aromatic and is made into tea and root beer; in Louisiana the powdered leaves are used to make a condiment called filé for flavoring and thickening stews and sauces. The aromatic agent, safrole, is a carcinogen of the liver, and sassafras has been banned for human consumption. However, to keep things in perspective, it should be noted "that a 12-ounce can of sassafras root beer is less than one tenth as carcinogenic for its safrole as a 12-ounce can of beer for its ethanol [grain alcohol]" (Duke 1992:18–19).

304. *Simarouba glauca*

Common Name: Paradise Tree
Habit: Highly ornamental, tall, elegant tree with beautiful foliage and a broad rounded crown; male and female flowers borne on separate trees.
Size: Growing up to 50 feet tall, but flowering and fruiting at a much lesser height when very young.
Season: Evergreen; flowers not showy, borne in the spring; female trees with fruits ripening in the summer.
Fruit: Rather large one-seeded, oval berries changing from green to red or reddish purple at maturity.
Maintenance: None if properly situated.
Motility: Self-sown seedlings often produced in the vicinity of female trees.
Growing Conditions: Well-drained soil in coastal hammocks in full or nearly full sunlight; Zones 9B–11.
Propagation: Seed (sow as soon as possible after the fruit ripens).
Comments: Paradise tree has leaves that are divided into ten to fourteen stiff, rounded leaflets. Their upper surface is extremely glossy and is a rich emerald to dark green, while the lower surface is pale lime green. The visual effect as the leaves rustle in the wind, first flashing glossy green and then pale, milky green, is extremely attractive and makes this

one of the most visually striking trees native to the United States. It is widely used as a specimen or accent tree in parts of southern Florida, even by gardeners who otherwise have little interest in native plants. It may also be used as a shade or street tree, but be aware of its large ultimate size and broad crown as well as the considerable litter produced by female trees dropping their fruits. The fruits are highly favored in South Florida by feral parrots, which crack open the seeds to eat the kernels. Although paradise tree has a reputation for being pest-free and thus still in paradise where pests do not exist, an insect sometimes seriously defoliates young trees.

305. *Swietenia mahagoni*

Common Name: West Indian Mahogany
Habit: Medium-sized to large tree with a stout trunk and a wide, densely leafy canopy.
Size: Growing 40–60 feet tall.
Season: Briefly deciduous, the old leaves falling just before or during the onset of new growth in the spring; flowers inconspicuous, borne in spring and summer; fruits ripening in late summer and autumn.
Fruit: Large, pear-shaped capsules to 4 inches long releasing many flattened, long-winged seeds.
Maintenance: None if properly situated; raking of fallen leaves and fruits when used as a street tree.
Motility: Occasionally establishing itself from self-sown seed, often at considerable distances from the parent tree.
Growing Conditions: Coastal hammocks, often in dry, rocky sites, in full or nearly full sun; Zones 10–11.
Propagation: Seed (sow as soon as possible after the fruit ripens).
Comments: Although mainly renowned as the finest cabinet wood on earth, mahogany is also a remarkably beautiful tree that is frequently planted along streets in southern Florida. It is sometimes planted as a shade tree, but it becomes massive and should not be planted too close to homes or other buildings. Mahogany has two principal faults: it is attacked by webworms that occasionally defoliate a tree, and its primary branches are prone to splitting. Plants repeatedly attacked by webworm should be replaced with more resistant forms. To prevent splitting, remove side branches that arise at a narrow angle to the main stem. The leaves assume a rich brown when they fall and are highly sought after by native plant gardeners as an attractive mulch. The wood of wild West Indian mahogany trees was extremely beautiful with a rich, intense color and heavy density that has never been matched in cultivated trees. Newly sawn logs were so dense that they sometimes sank in water. The trees were rapaciously harvested from the wild and the species is now endangered throughout its natural range, including in Florida.

306. *Tilia americana* var. *caroliniana* (Synonym: *Tilia caroliniana*)

Common Name: Basswood; American Linden
Habit: Medium-sized to large tree with a tall, straight trunk and a dense, oval crown.
Size: Highly variable, from 20 to 60 feet, depending on the plant's genetic background and growing conditions.
Season: Deciduous; small, fragrant white flowers borne in the spring; leaves turning various shades of yellow in the autumn.
Maintenance: None in the wild garden.
Motility: None under most garden conditions.
Growing Conditions: Rich, moist woodlands and dense hammocks in full sun to partial shade; Zones 8–9B.
Propagation: Seed (very difficult to germinate); grafting.
Comments: Basswood makes an elegant specimen, accent, or shade tree and is widely useful for planting in parks, along streets, or in formal allées. It bears innumerable small, fragrant white flowers and a tree in full bloom is quite attractive. Bees eagerly seek out the flowers, from which they make an excellent honey. The dried flowers have a mild sedative effect, and a pleasant and soothing tea is made from them. However, the web page of the University of British Columbia Botany Department indicates that "protracted use of this tea is thought to cause heart failure." In the past, basswood was important to aboriginal cultures for a wide variety of medicinal, culinary, and utilitarian purposes. Today, it is utilized for its easily carved, soft but strong, light-colored wood. Basswood seedlings are slow-growing, but once established, the plants grow fairly fast. Since they are shallow-rooted, they are not particularly drought tolerant. Cut or injured basswoods, as well as old plants in which the main trunk has died, sprout vigorously from the base and form clumps. Mulberries (*Morus* species) and basswood are sometimes confused as both have leaves that turn to various shades of yellow in the autumn. Basswood differs from mulberries in lacking a milky sap.

307. *Ulmus americana* (Synonym: *Ulmus floridana*)

Common Name: American Elm
Habit: Large, beautiful tree with a tall, straight trunk and an elegant vase-shaped crown.
Size: Reported to 70 feet tall in Florida (to 120 feet elsewhere).
Season: Deciduous; spring flowers and fruits insignificant; autumn foliage rich, golden yellow.
Maintenance: None in the wild garden.

Motility: Self-sown seedlings sometimes establishing themselves near the parent plant.

Growing Conditions: Rich, moist woodlands in full sun or light shade; Zones 8–10A.

Propagation: Seed (sow immediately upon ripening); cuttings.

Comments: American elm is fast-growing, has an extremely elegant form, and assumes bright yellow autumn color. This combination of characters has made it one of the most popular native trees in the United States, widely utilized in both private residences and public spaces. Before being devastated by Dutch elm disease and elm phloem necrosis, American elm ranked as one of the premier shade and street trees in eastern North America. Fortunately, these diseases do not appear to be a serious problem in Florida. Three other elms occur in Florida and are worth growing in gardens located within their natural ranges. Slippery elm (*Ulmus rubra*) is similar to American elm but has a rounded crown and occurs only in the Panhandle. Winged and cedar elms (*U. alata* and *U. crassifolia,* respectively) have smaller leaves than American elm. Their branches usually have decorative corky outgrowths, adding visual interest in winter when they are leafless.

308. *Vaccinium arboreum*

Common Name: Sparkleberry

Habit: Large shrub or small tree with reddish brown exfoliating bark, small glossy foliage, and a dense rounded crown.

Size: Growing 15–30 feet tall, with small shrubby forms nearly as wide as they are tall.

Season: Deciduous or sub-evergreen; fragrant white or pink flowers borne in the spring; fruit ripens in the autumn; older leaves assume reddish tints in the autumn.

Fruit: Small black berries, edible but bland.

Maintenance: None.

Motility: None in most garden situations.

Growing Conditions: Moist to very dry, usually acidic, sandy sites in full sun to moderate shade; Zones 8–9B.

Propagation: Seed.

Comments: Sparkleberry is one of Florida's most ornamental small trees and has tremendous horticultural potential. In nature, it occurs in many different situations, with the exception of coastal sites or areas with rocky, alkaline soils. With regard to soil moisture, it is said to occur in sand pine scrub at one extreme and the Fakahatchee Swamp at the other. Horticulturally desirable attributes include its graceful form with a densely leafy crown, exfoliating reddish bark, glossy leaves, and fragrant flowers. The flowers are individually small but have an exquisite shape, like delicate porcelain bells, and are carried in prodigious numbers. After attracting numerous, diverse pollinating insects, the flowers are followed by dark blue berries that are edible but have little flavor. This outstanding native plant deserves far wider cultivation and offers many rich opportunities for the selection of horticulturally valuable traits.

309. *Zanthoxylum clava-hercules*

Common Name: Hercules' Club; Toothache Tree

Habit: Small to medium-sized tree armed with stout prickles on the trunk, branches, twigs, and leaves.

Size: Variable from about 10 to 25 feet tall (reportedly up to 50 feet tall).

Season: Subevergreen, the leaves persistent; greenish white flowers borne in the spring; fruit maturing in the autumn.

Fruit: Female trees with small capsules that split open to reveal a hard, shiny, black seed.

Maintenance: None in the wild garden or else periodic removal of root suckers.

Motility: Rarely spreading by seed; some forms aggressively forming colonies by way of root suckers, other forms producing few suckers or none at all.

Growing Conditions: Hammocks on well-drained soil in full sun to moderate shade; Zones 8–10.

Propagation: Seed (germination sometimes poor); root suckers.

Comments: Hercules' club is a peculiar and oddly ornamental little tree. Its most striking feature is the innumerable stout prickles that cover much of the plant and are particularly noticeable on its trunk. Some people are put off by this and would not consider growing such a strongly armed plant in their garden. If one can look past its formidable armature, one will see an attractive plant with beautiful, glossy, dark green foliage carried in a broad, open crown. Nonsuckering forms are preferred in most garden situations but they are not easy to come by. Both male and female trees are needed to produce seeds, and propagation by seed is not always certain. Plants in the nursery trade have usually been propagated from root suckers. Since the resultant plant is genetically identical to its parent, this all but guarantees that it too will sucker. Hercules' club is often grown as an ethnobotanical curiosity because Native Americans and pioneers chewed the leaves to relieve the pain of toothaches. Today, it is an article of commerce in the herbal medicine industry.

310. *Zanthoxylum fagara*

Common Name: Wild-Lime

Habit: Large prickly shrub or small to medium-sized tree with a broad, densely branched crown.

Size: Growing up to 30 feet tall but usually substantially smaller in most gardens.

Season: Evergreen; flowers inconspicuous and greenish, borne in the spring; fruits ripen in the autumn.

Fruit: Female trees with small capsules that split open to reveal a hard, shiny black seed.

Maintenance: None in the wild garden or else periodic judicious pruning.

Motility: Self-sown seedlings sometimes numerous below the parent tree.

Growing Conditions: Hammocks with well-drained soil in full sun to moderate shade; Zones 9A–11.

Propagation: Seed.

Comments: Wild-lime is common in native plant gardens throughout its range in Florida. This is due in large part to the ease with which it may be propagated by potting up self-sown seedlings that appear below the female trees. It does not have any outstanding horticultural attributes but is easily grown, matures quickly, and is widely tolerant of adverse conditions, including rocky, alkaline soils and drought in both coastal and inland gardens. Additionally, its use is much advocated by butterfly gardeners since it is a larval food plant for both the giant swallowtail (*Papilio cresphonte*) and the endangered Schaus' swallowtail (*Heraclides aristodemus ponceanus*). This unassuming little tree has a wide distribution outside Florida, for it also occurs in the American Southwest, from where it extends southward into South America. Although it does not appear to be particularly adapted for long-distance dispersal, it also occurs in the Galapagos Islands.

Vines

All of the vines listed here are long-lived and, if well situated, vigorous and carefree. Nearly all are twiners that will climb anything capable of supporting them. Most may also be utilized as groundcovers as they will sprawl over considerable areas if not provided with anything to climb.

The following vines in this section will not form woody stems: bay bean (*Canavalia rosea*); butterfly-pea (*Centrosema virginianum*); swamp leatherflower (*Clematis crispa*); virgin's-bower (*Clematis virginiana*); tievine (*Ipomoea cordatotriloba*); beach morning-glory (*Ipomoea imperati*); railroad vine (*Ipomoea pes-caprae* subsp. *brasiliensis*); glades morning-glory (*Ipomoea sagittata*); sensitive-brier (*Mimosa quadrivalvis*); purple passion-vine (*Passiflora incarnata*); and corkystem passion-vine (*Passiflora suberosa*). All other vines listed here form thick, woody stems with age. As a result, care must be taken with their placement since twining, woody stems an inch or more in diameter are difficult to remove without damaging the underlying structures on which the vines are climbing. The vines that form woody stems may also be trained to grow as shrubs or small trees, or even as standards. Doing so is no simple matter and requires an artful eye and many years of diligent and dedicated pruning. However, the results can be spectacular, especially if a vine is trained to about six feet in height so that the flowers are all borne at or near eye level.

311. *Bignonia capreolata* (Synonym: *Anisostichus capreolata*)

Common Name: Crossvine
Habit: High-climbing vine attaching by tendrils with adhesive disks.
Size: Climbing to the top of the tallest trees with age.
Season: Partially deciduous northward, evergreen southward; flowering in the spring.
Maintenance: None in the wild garden; may be trained with frequent and persistent pruning.
Motility: Climbing over a vast area if allowed to do so.
Growing Conditions: Moist sites in full sun to light shade; Zones 8–9A.
Propagation: Seed; cuttings.
Comments: Found in northern and central peninsular Florida, crossvine is a large, robust vine that

climbs over trees in moist areas by means of tendrils bearing small adhesive disks. The leaves are divided into two leaflets, and in the spring the vine bears large, showy, trumpet-shaped red flowers. An especially attractive form has bicolored flowers with upper lobes of brick red and lower lobes of yellow. Robust plants grown in rich soil in a sunny location become covered with flowers and are absolutely irresistible to hummingbirds. Except for its large size, which precludes its use in smaller gardens, this plant presents few problems in cultivation and is readily propagated from cuttings or seeds. Occasionally, specialty nurseries offer cultivars of crossvine with dark red, pure yellow, or salmon-orange flowers and one of these, 'Tangerine Beauty,' has grown and flowered well as far south as Palm Beach County.

312. *Campsis radicans*

Common Name: Trumpet Creeper
Habit: High-climbing vine attaching by means of aerial rootlets.
Size: Climbing to the top of the tallest trees with age.
Season: Deciduous northward, evergreen or nearly so southward; flowering in the spring and summer.
Maintenance: None in the wild garden; may be trained with frequent and persistent pruning.
Motility: Will climb over a large area if allowed to do so.
Growing Conditions: Moist soil in full sun to light shade; Zones 8–9A.

Propagation: Seed; cuttings.
Comments: Trumpet creeper has soft, ferny, emerald-green foliage with a decidedly tropical appearance. Trumpet creeper is a fast-growing, tough-as-nails vine that will grow quite well under very harsh conditions. Plants have been observed growing on a reclaimed strip mine in soil consisting chiefly of seashells and sand. Although the plants were clearly stressed, they flowered regularly each spring. This is a remarkable feat in view of the fact that this vine is described as a species of floodplain forests! Of course, for the best appearance and most abundant flowers, it should be grown under somewhat better conditions. Trumpet creeper also grows well under shady conditions, but flowers are sparsely produced. Horticulturally, it is useful for its fast growth as well as the attractive and brilliantly colored flowers, which are readily visited by hummingbirds. The flowers are a bright reddish orange in the wild plant, but yellow and red forms are occasionally available in the trade. With age, trumpet creeper forms stout woody stems, and with diligent pruning, it may be trained as a shrub on small properties that do not have the space for a large vine.

313. *Canavalia rosea* (Synonym: *Canavalia maritima*)

Common Name: Bay Bean
Habit: Sprawling, groundcovering vine with large, rather coarse leaves.
Size: Small to very large, depending on age and conditions.
Season: Evergreen; flowering and fruiting all year.
Fruit: Stout bean pod 4–5 inches long.
Maintenance: None or else periodic pruning to keep it within bounds.
Motility: Eventually sprawling over as large an area as is given to it.
Growing Conditions: Coastal beaches in full sun; Zones 8B–11.
Propagation: Seed (scarify); cuttings.
Comments: Bay bean is a large, coarse plant with leaves divided into three leaflets and bearing rather large rosy pink flowers. The flowers are recognizably members of the pea family, with one important distinction: they are upside down! This vine makes a useful groundcover for harsh coastal sites, where it will withstand occasional salt spray, incessant winds, blowing sand, and intense sunlight. Although it is not a twining vine, the plants are able to clamber over low obstacles, and they are an important component of coastal foredunes, helping hold sand in place. The large bean pods add a further interesting note. As with so many other plants of coastal beaches, the seeds float in salt water and have served to disseminate bay bean to beaches throughout the tropics. Due to its robust nature, it is not recommended for smaller gardens.

314. *Capparis flexuosa*

Common Name: Limber Caper
Habit: Scandent shrub with large, fragrant white flowers.
Size: Growing from 12 to 25 feet high.
Season: Evergreen; flowers borne in spring and summer; fruits borne in summer or autumn.
Fruit: A beanlike capsule splitting open to reveal large seeds embedded in a red pulp.
Maintenance: None except for occasional pruning to keep it in bounds.
Motility: None in most garden situations.
Growing Conditions: Coastal hammocks, shell mounds, and the drier, landward side of mangroves in full sun to full shade; Zones 9B–11.
Propagation: Seed; cuttings.

Comments: Limber caper has been overshadowed by its relative, Jamaican caper (*Capparis cynophallophora*), an ornamental large shrub or small tree described in the tree section of this book. In general, most gardens cannot easily accommodate large, woody vines, and this accounts for limber caper's relative obscurity in cultivation. On the other hand, it is highly tolerant of salt and would be useful as a flowering vine in coastal gardens. Additionally, although its foliage is not as attractive as that of Jamaican caper, its fragrant, nocturnal, white or pink flowers are far showier and, in the best forms, much larger than those of Jamaican caper. Unfortunately, the flowers are short-lived, lasting but a single night and withering in the heat of the day. Although the plant is listed in various references as a shrub or small tree, those cultivated in Florida bear elongated, weak stems and are better described as straggling vinelike shrubs.

315. *Centrosema virginianum*

Common Name: Butterfly-Pea
Habit: Small twining or sprawling vine of delicate appearance with leaves divided into three linear leaflets.
Size: Variable from 3 to 12 feet, depending on age, form, and growing conditions.
Season: Winter dormant northward, evergreen southward; flowering in summer and autumn, or all year southward.
Maintenance: None or else periodic pruning to keep it within bounds.
Motility: Will cover small shrubs or climb to the tops of small trees if allowed to do so.
Growing Conditions: Growing in a wide variety of moist to dry sites in full or nearly full sun; Zones 8–11.
Propagation: Seed; cuttings.
Comments: Due to its ease of cultivation and beautiful flowers, butterfly-pea deserves to be more widely grown as a small, flowering vine. The plant is adaptable, occurring in a wide variety of habitats, including moist roadsides, flatwoods, sand scrub, and rocky pinelands. For the most compact growth and abundant flowers, it should be grown in full sun, although it will also grow in partially shaded situations such as woodland edges. Unlike some vines that flower only when they are climbing, butterfly-pea will flower when sprawling on the ground and may be trained to grow as an unusual groundcover. The showy and rather large flowers appear all year in southern Florida. They are short-lived, lasting but half a day and withering in the heat of the afternoon sun. However, a healthy, well-grown plant will produce numerous flowers nearly every day during the flowering season. Butterfly-pea also makes an unusual pot plant, flowering while still quite small.

316. *Clematis crispa*

Common Name: Swamp Leatherflower
Habit: Vine climbing by twining petioles (leaf stalks).
Size: Stems climbing to 6 feet or more.

Season: Dying to the ground in winter; flowering in the spring and summer, fruiting in the summer and autumn.

Fruit: A compact cluster of small, dry, one-seeded fruits, each with a prominent silky tail that aids dispersal by the wind.

Maintenance: None in the wild garden; removal of old stems in semiformal gardens.

Motility: Will cover small shrubs or climb to the tops of small trees if allowed to do so.

Growing Conditions: Rich, moist sites in full sun to light shade; Zones 8–9A.

Propagation: Seed (double dormancy, make take eighteen months to two years to germinate); division; cuttings.

Comments: A whole book could be devoted to the diverse ways

in which vines climb. Clematis have chosen a simple mechanism: the leaf stalk of young leaves twines around any object it encounters. It is an efficient way to climb but not a tidy one, and—more so than most vines—clematis tend to form hopelessly tangled masses of stems and foliage. If this is the case in your garden, cut back the main mass of the plant every few years. Then, thin out older, woody stems and cut down the remaining stems to about 2 feet. This treatment will result in a neater plant that will serve as an attractive background for the unusual flowers. Glaucous leatherflower (*Clematis glaucophylla*) is horticulturally similar, but the lower surfaces of the leaves are silvery white and the flowers have a magenta exterior. If you have well-drained soil, you may try reticulated leatherflower (*Clematis reticulata*), a plant similar to swamp leatherflower but found in partial sun along the edges of upland forests.

317. *Clematis virginiana*

Common Name: Virgin's-Bower

Habit: High-climbing vine with leaves divided into three leaflets.

Size: Forming large thickets if not given a support or else climbing up tall trees with age.

Season: Dying back to the ground in winter; flowering and fruiting from summer to autumn.

Fruit: A compact cluster of small, dry, one-seeded fruits, each with a prominent silky tail that aids dispersal by the wind.

Maintenance: None in the wild garden; cutting back to the ground in late winter in more formal gardens.

Motility: Able to cover a large area if allowed to do so.

Growing Conditions: Moist sites in full sun to moderate shade; Zones 8–9A.

Propagation: Seed (double dormancy, may take eighteen months to two years to germinate); division; cuttings.

Comments: Virgin's-bower is attractive both in flower and in fruit. Old, well-grown plants produce small white flowers in abundance and add a flamboyant touch to the wild garden. In fruit, the plant becomes covered with striking feathery clusters. These are most attractive when backlit by sunlight against a dark background—a common occurrence in nature since virgin's-bower often grows along the sunny edges of woodlands with the forest trees as a backdrop. Unlike most native clematis, virgin's-bower bears male and female flowers on separate plants. Therefore, only female plants bear the interesting seed heads, and only if a male plant is nearby. The silken seed heads have given rise to the less attractive common name of devil's darning-needles. Satincurls (*Clematis catesbyana*) is a closely related species with similar horticultural uses.

318. *Echites umbellata*

Common Name: Devil's-Potato; Rubber Vine
Habit: Twining vine with opposite dark green leaves and white flowers.
Size: Moderately sized, from about 6 to 12 feet long in nature, growing larger in cultivation.
Season: Evergreen; flowering all year, at least in southern Florida.
Maintenance: None or else periodic pruning to keep it within bounds.
Motility: Loosely growing over other plants but able to cover them with age.
Growing Conditions: Pinelands and coastal thickets in full sun; Zones 9B–11.
Propagation: Seed.
Comments: Rubber Vine is a beautiful native vine that deserves wider cultivation. It usually occurs in coastal situations where it tolerates much adversity, including occasional salt spray and drought. It is also a common component of some of Miami-Dade County's rocky pinelands. Plants may be grown from seed, which should be sown as soon as possible after ripening. When planting out rubber vines, select their position in the garden with care since they are difficult to move once established. If necessary, excessive growth may be controlled by cutting the plants to the ground. In pinelands, they are regularly burned to the ground by wildfires but soon sprout from the deeply buried root system.

319. *Gelsemium sempervirens*

Common Name: Carolina Jessamine
Habit: Twining vine bearing rather large, fragrant yellow flowers.
Size: Stems to 20 feet long; plant able to cover large areas with age.
Season: Evergreen; flowers borne in late winter and spring.
Maintenance: None in the wild garden, or occasional pruning to keep it within bounds.
Motility: Seed rarely formed in cultivation; some forms readily forming root suckers.
Growing Conditions: Occurs in moist, shady sites but, in cultivation, readily adapts to average garden conditions in full sun; Zones 8–9B.

Propagation: Seed; cuttings; suckers.

Comments: Carolina jessamine is a beautiful vine with glossy, dark green leaves that nicely set off the bright yellow flowers. The flowers first open in late winter when a spot of cheery color is most welcome. Floriferousness is directly proportional to the amount of sun the plant gets; in full sun, the vines can become nearly solid sheets of gold. This is not a small, shy, unassuming plant as it will grow up and over nearly everything in its path. Severe pruning will help constrain it, or it may be planted among large woody plants where root competition will help keep it in check. A double-flowered form ('Pride of Augusta') and a pale primrose yellow form ('Wood-

lander's Pale Yellow') are sometimes commercially available. Swamp jessamine (*Gelsemium rankinii*) is a nearly identical species that differs in having odorless flowers and a dual blooming season, flowering in the autumn and again in late winter and spring. Both species are occasionally utilized in herbal medicine. This is a dangerous practice since *all parts* of both Carolina and swamp jessamine are highly poisonous.

320. *Ipomoea cordatotriloba* (Synonym: *Ipomoea trichocarpa*)

Common Name: Tievine

Habit: Small, twining vine with rosy lavender or pink flowers with a darker throat.

Size: Variable, the stems 3–6 feet long or longer depending on growing conditions.

Season: Deciduous, or nearly evergreen southward; flowering in the autumn northward, continuing into the winter and spring southward.

Maintenance: None in the wild garden.

Motility: Perennial forms tending to root sucker with age; self-sown seedlings usually establishing themselves in the vicinity of the parent plant.

Growing Conditions: Moist, often disturbed, sites in full sun to light shade; Zones 8–11.

Propagation: Seed.

Comments: Although this vine is described as an annual in most references, Florida plants of this species are usually reliably perennial in cultivation. It is among the easiest of native vines to cultivate, the seedlings growing vigorously and flowering in the autumn of their first year. Healthy plants produce hundreds of flowers over a long period, which may extend from early autumn to late spring. Plants grow best in light shade. Avoid hot, dry conditions, which usually result in heavy infestations of spider mites. Select forms are worthy of greater cultivation; I once found a plant with nearly white flowers with a soft pastel pink throat in the West Palm Beach water catchment area.

321. *Ipomoea imperati* (Synonym: *Ipomoea stolonifera*)

Common Name: Beach Morning-Glory
Habit: Sprawling, nonclimbing vine with smooth, fleshy leaves.
Size: Rarely more than 6 inches high, but spreading to fill as much room as is available to it.
Season: Evergreen; flowers borne spring through autumn.
Maintenance: None or, when used as a groundcover or lawn substitute, an occasional mowing.
Motility: Quickly spreading from underground rhizomes.
Growing Conditions: Coastal shores above the high water mark; Zones 8B–10.
Propagation: Seed (scarify); cuttings.
Comments: Beach morning-glory is allied to the railroad vine (*Ipomoea pes-caprae* subsp. *brasiliensis*) and grows in the same habitat, coastal beaches, where it is subjected to relentless winds, scorching sun, and salt spray. Because its seeds float and are adapted for dispersal by sea, this species is a natural component of tropical coastal beaches nearly throughout the world. The leaves are rather small, variously lobed, and fleshy with a glossy surface. The magnificent flowers are produced from spring through fall. Large in comparison to the size of the foliage, they are brilliant white, shading to golden yellow in the throat. Cuttings root in a matter of days and, surprisingly, this vine makes an ideal pot plant. Rooted cuttings bloom in a few months, and they will do so even if grown in a tiny pot. Besides its use in beach and dune restorations, beach morning-glory can also be used as a groundcover or lawn substitute in open, sandy areas that are too poor to support lawn grasses.

322. *Ipomoea pes-caprae* subsp. *brasiliensis*

Common Name: Railroad Vine
Habit: Large, coarse, sprawling vine with smooth fleshy leaves and large rosy pink flowers.
Size: Plant rarely exceeding 6–8 inches in height but the stems growing 6–12 feet long or longer
Season: Evergreen; flowers borne in the summer northward to all year southward.

Maintenance: None or, when used as a groundcover or lawn substitute, an occasional mowing.

Motility: Quickly spreading from underground rhizomes.

Growing Conditions: Coastal shores above the high water mark; Zones 8B–11.

Propagation: Seed (scarify); cuttings.

Comments: Railroad vine lives up to its common name as it is a coarse, vigorous plant with elongated, crawling stems that grow in straight lines, rooting and helping to bind sand. As such, it is an important element of warm coastal beaches throughout the world. It is, of course, perfect for coastal gardens, where it will withstand adverse conditions such as blazing sun, constant winds, blowing sand, and occasional salt spray. In southern Florida, it is being utilized in coastal towns as a coarse groundcover in difficult situations such as parking lots and unirrigated street medians. If pampered by being given too much water, it will grow too exuberantly and overrun smaller and less aggressive neighbors. If it is given too much shade or overly rich soil, it becomes prone to insect pests. Like beach morning-glory (*Ipomoea imperati*), it grows readily from cuttings or seeds that have had the hard seed coat lightly chipped or filed.

323. *Ipomoea sagittata*

Common Name: Glades Morning-Glory

Habit: Vigorous twining vine bearing large, exquisitely beautiful pink flowers.

Size: Stems growing to 3–6 feet long or longer.

Season: Dormant or nearly so in winter; flowers borne in the summer northward, nearly all year southward.

Maintenance: None in most garden situations.

Motility: Vigorously spreading by underground rhizomes.

Growing Conditions: Moist situations such as roadside ditches, marshes, and wet flatwoods in full sun; Zones 8–11.

Propagation: Seed; division; cuttings.

Comments: Glades morning-glory is a magnificent native vine that occurs in moist sunny areas throughout Florida. It bears rather long but very

narrow arrow-shaped leaves that are dwarfed by the beautiful large flowers. These come in various shades of bright pink with a contrasting darker pink throat. Occasionally, one finds plants with pale, nearly white flowers. It readily adapts to garden conditions, where it produces abundant flowers. In northern Florida flowering occurs principally in the summer, but in southern Florida it may be found in flower in all but the very coldest months. Although vegetatively it has an exceedingly delicate appearance, glades morning-glory is an extremely tough plant that can spread with much vigor by means of underground rhizomes and is not suited to formal garden situations. Plant trivia buffs may be interested in knowing that this morning-glory has been introduced into the western Mediterranean and is now established there as a wild plant (Correll and Johnston 1979:1253).

324. *Jacquemontia pentanthos*

Common Name: Blue Jacquemontia; Key West Morning-Glory

Habit: Vigorous, twining or sprawling vine bearing sky blue or lavender-pink flowers.

Size: Stems growing 6–12 feet long or longer.

Season: Evergreen; flowering from early autumn to late spring.

Maintenance: None in the wild garden or else occasional pruning to keep it in bounds.

Motility: Widely sprawling or climbing and, in time, able to cover very large areas.

Growing Conditions: Well-drained, often rocky, soil in coastal situations or hammocks in full sun to light shade; Zones 10–11.

Propagation: Seed; cuttings.

Comments: Blue jacquemontia is one of the showiest flowering vines suitable for cultivation in South Florida. It is a fast-growing, generally pest-free plant. It quickly becomes a specimen plant when trained on a trellis or pergola. It may also be utilized as a groundcover for large areas since it will sprawl happily on the ground if there is nothing for it to climb. Unlike some other natives that occur in harsh coastal sites, it adapts readily to ordinary garden situations so long as it does not have to contend with overly wet soil. Blue jacquemontia begins to flower in the autumn and is covered with spectacular blue flowers throughout the winter, with continued flowering into the spring. Common names that designate flower color should not be taken too literally; this plant is not always blue-flowered—a pinkish lavender form is sometimes offered in the nursery trade and an occasional white-flowered form may be seen from time to time.

325. *Lonicera sempervirens*

Common Name: Coral Honeysuckle

Habit: Vigorous twining woody vine with attractive foliage, flowers, and berries.

Size: Stems up to 15 feet long; shorter when growing in dry, sunny areas.

Season: Deciduous northward, evergreen southward; flowering in spring and summer; fruits borne in autumn.

Fruit: Small, brilliant red berries attractive to birds and small animals.

Maintenance: None in the wild garden or occasional hard pruning to keep it in bounds.

Motility: Able to cover large areas if not constrained by root competition from other plants.

Growing Conditions: Forests, thickets, and low wooded areas in light shade to full sun; Zones 8–9A.

Propagation: Seed; cuttings.

Comments: Coral honeysuckle is a highly ornamental vine bearing attractive flowers from spring through summer and bright red berries from late summer through autumn. The foliage is also ornamental, having a glossy, dark green upper surface and a pale silvery green lower surface. It is easily cultivated under a wide variety of conditions. However, maximum flowering occurs in sunny situations. The flowers are irresistible to hummingbirds and will attract them to the garden. Because the plant is so showy and provides almost year-round interest, its cultivation has been taken up by regular gardeners and several cultivars are available from specialty nurseries. Some of the more common ones include 'Alabama Crimson' with bright red flowers, 'Magnifica' with 2-inch scarlet flowers with a yellow interior, and 'Sulphurea' with pure yellow flowers. Coral honeysuckle has poor salt tolerance but grows very well in poor soil subject to drought. As a result, it is highly recommended for planting on berms, medians, roadsides, and slopes (Chellman 1993).

326. *Mimosa quadrivalvis* (Synonyms: *Schrankia microphylla* and *Schrankia uncinata*)

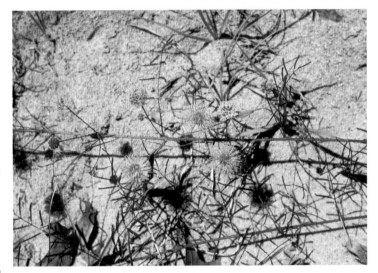

Common Name: Sensitive-Brier

Habit: Prostrate or straggling plant with delicate foliage and pink flower heads; stems liberally provided with hooked prickles and often climbing or vinelike.

Size: Variable, the stems growing 3–6 feet long or longer.

Season: Dying to the ground northward, evergreen southward; flowers borne from late spring to autumn.

Maintenance: None in the wild garden; not recommended for semiformal or formal gardens.

Motility: Rarely spreading from self-sown seed.

Growing Conditions: Found in moderately moist to very dry, often sandy soils in full sun; Zones 8–10.

Propagation: Seed (scarify).

Comments: This prickly vine is very resilient, often growing under harsh conditions where it has to contend with sandy soil, seasonal droughts, and intense sun. Yet, aside from its prickly armature, it is surprisingly delicate both in its finely dissected, feathery foliage and in its exquisite pink pom-pom flower heads. It is admittedly not a plant for formal gardens, but it does provide an interesting accent in sunny, sandy gardens. If the soil is very well drained and the plant has full sun, it will also grow well in less dry situations and is sometimes found in moist but sandy flatwoods. As with all members of the pea family, propagation is easily effected by lightly nicking the seeds with a file.

327. *Passiflora incarnata*

Common Name: Purple Passion-Vine; Maypop
Habit: Large, root-suckering, perennial vine climbing by tendrils.
Size: Stems growing 3–10 feet long or longer, depending on the growing conditions.
Season: Deciduous; flowering in the spring and summer; fruit borne in summer and autumn.
Fruit: Large yellow berry filled with numerous seeds, each surrounded by edible pulp.
Maintenance: None in the wild garden; can sucker aggressively and become a pest in gardens.
Motility: Colonial by way of root suckers, sometimes aggressively so.
Growing Conditions: Rather dry, well-drained soil in open, often somewhat disturbed areas in full sun or light shade; Zones 8–9 (with isolated occurrences in Zone 10).
Propagation: Seed (very slow to germinate); cuttings; root suckers.
Comments: Purple passion-vine is the hardiest passion-vine in general cultivation, extending as far north as southern Illinois. It is a large, robust vine with finely toothed three-lobed leaves, and it dies down to the roots in winter. It root suckers vigorously and, under ideal conditions, can cover large areas in a short time. The root suckers may be potted up while still small and provide a ready means of increasing one's stock. The intricately formed flowers are about 3 inches wide and are borne over a long period. Certainly, they are among the most magnificent and beautiful in our entire flora. The large, yellow fruits that follow are both decorative and edible. This vine may be grown in smaller gardens and its suckering controlled somewhat if it is grown under rather dry conditions and/or planted among fully established plants, where root competition will help keep it in check. For areas that are too moist or shady to support purple passion-vine, gardeners in south Florida may substitute *Passiflora pallens,* another vigorous species with large, showy white flowers that open in the late afternoon.

328. *Passiflora suberosa*

Common Name: Corkystem Passion-Vine
Habit: Deep-rooted, suckering, perennial vine.
Size: Stems growing 3–10 feet long or longer, depending on growing conditions.
Season: Evergreen; flowering and fruiting throughout the year whenever warm weather prevails.
Fruit: Purple-black berries about the size and shape of an olive.

Maintenance: None in the wild garden, or light to heavy pruning to keep it in bounds.

Motility: Casually spreading by self-sown seed; slowly spreading by root suckers.

Growing Conditions: Moist to dryish soils in full sun to deep shade; Zones 8B–11.

Propagation: Seed (may take months to germinate); cuttings.

Comments: This common—but often unnoticed—plant is a rugged, essentially everblooming vine that is easily grown in a wide variety of situations. The inconspicuous greenish flowers are about half an inch wide and are followed by purple-black berries that are attractive to various birds. Although lacking obvious horticultural appeal, this is a plant that becomes more and more pleasing with greater

familiarity. Its ease of growth, ready propagation from seeds and cuttings, unusual little flowers, and usefulness as a butterfly larval food source for gulf fritillaries (*Dione vanillae nigrior*), julias (*Dryas iulia largo*), and zebra longwings (*Heliconius charitonius tuckeri*) soon make it a favorite. Corkystem passion-vine is an extremely variable plant as regards its size and leaf shape. Rarely, dwarf forms occur with leaves scarcely 1 inch long. These are ideal for small gardens and make charming pot plants.

329. *Pentalinon luteum* (Synonym: *Urechites lutea*)

Common Name: Wild-Allamanda; Yellow-Mandevilla

Habit: Sprawling or twining vine with glossy leaves and large, bright yellow flowers.

Size: Stems growing 3–12 feet long or longer, depending on growing conditions.

Season: Evergreen; flowering from spring through autumn.

Maintenance: None in the wild garden or else occasional pruning to keep it in bounds.

Motility: With time, able to cover large areas if allowed to do so.

Growing Conditions: Growing in a variety of coastal situations from dry to rather moist in full sun; Zones 9B–11.

Propagation: Seed; cuttings.

Comments: Wild-allamanda is an outstanding and noteworthy plant that ranks as one of the showiest vines native to the United States. In common with

other coastal plants growing in southern Florida, it is an indestructibly tough plant able to withstand intense sunlight, strong winds, drought, and occasional salt spray. It has such high salt tolerance that it is one of the few plants able to grow in the vicinity of the salt flats of southwest Puerto Rico, where seawater is evaporated in order to harvest the salt. The plants are covered with an ashy coat of salt and are highly stressed, but they are able to grow and flower. The species readily adapts to ordinary garden conditions, where it thrives and flowers with wild exuberance. Although it may occur in moist, brackish situations along the edges of mangrove forests, it does not like overly wet soils in cultivation. Also, it requires a warm, protected niche when grown at the northern end of its natural range or if grown inland away from coastal sites.

330. *Rhabdenia biflora*

Common Name: Rubber Vine; Mangrove Vine
Habit: Robust, twining vine with dark green leaves and beautiful white flowers tinged with pink.
Size: Stems easily growing to 12 feet or longer.
Season: Evergreen; flowering all year whenever warm temperatures prevail.
Maintenance: None in the wild garden or else occasional pruning to keep it in bounds.
Motility: Colonial from subterranean suckers.
Growing Conditions: Moist, often brackish or saline areas; often associated with mangroves; Zones 9B–11.
Propagation: Seed; division (of suckers).
Comments: True to one of its common names, rubber vine is often found in association with mangroves, and it is usually at its best in moist, somewhat saline situations. However, it does not require such conditions and it readily adapts to average garden conditions. It will even grow in rather dry sites after it is established, if it is heavily watered when first planted. Plants tend to form a few stems that reach for the top of whatever they are climbing. As a consequence, cultivated plants should not be given tall supports as the flowers, which are borne mostly near the ends of the stems, will not be particularly visible. Plants that are regularly pruned produce more branches and tend to flower more freely. Rubber vine also makes an interesting potted plant, blooming while still small. Indeed, having its roots confined, as in a pot or by competition with other plants, actually seems to stimulate better flowering.

331. *Smilax* species

Common Name: Cat-Brier; Green-Brier
Habit: Sprawling or climbing, tuberous-rooted, tendril-bearing vines, often armed with recurved prickles, with male and female flowers borne on separate plants.
Size: Highly variable depending on species, age, and growing conditions from 3 to 12 feet long or longer; occasionally forming very large mounds.

Season: Deciduous northward, evergreen southward; flowering in the spring, summer, autumn, or all year, depending on species and geographic location.

Fruit: Female plants bearing small, purplish black or red berries, depending on the species.

Maintenance: None in the wild garden or an occasional hard pruning in more formal situations.

Motility: Some species colonial by way of subterranean runners; spreading by bird-dispersed seeds throughout the garden; certain species tending to be excessively weedy, especially in northern Florida.

Growing Conditions: Highly variable from rich, moist, shaded woodlands to dry sandy areas in full sun, depending on the species; Zones 8–11 (combined range for all twelve species native to Florida).

Propagation: Seed; division.

Comments: The majority of Florida's cat-briers are somewhat coarse, prickly vines of mostly botanical interest. They are rarely grown in gardens due to their weedy or aggressive tendencies. Five species, however, occur in rich, moist, shaded woodlands and are sufficiently ornamental to warrant further cultivation in wild gardens. Three of these are unarmed and lack prickles: *Smilax ecirrhata,* which lacks tendrils; *S. lasioneuron,* with long, functional tendrils; and *S. pumila,* with ornamental red fruits. The remaining two species are prickly vines with fruits that mature red: *S. smallii,* in which young leaves have distinctly red petioles; and *S. walteri,* with green petioles. *Smilax walteri* is especially useful for wet areas since it occurs in swamps and floodplain forests.

332. *Vitis rotundifolia* (Synonym: *Vitis munsoniana*)

Common Name: Muscadine; Wild Grape

Habit: Vigorous, fast-growing, tendril-bearing vine.

Size: Highly variable depending on growing conditions, the stems 3–50 feet long or longer.

Season: Deciduous northward, evergreen southward; flowering in the spring; fruit ripening in the autumn.

Fruit: Rather large, purplish black grapes; edible but with a thick skin and seedy.

Maintenance: None in the wild garden or an occasional hard pruning in more formal situations.

Motility: Plant covering large areas or climbing to the tops of tall trees with age; casually establishing itself from animal-dispersed seed.

Growing Conditions: Highly variable from dry, sandy areas to rich moist woodlands in full sun to deep shade; Zones 8–11.

Propagation: Seed; cuttings; ground layering.

Comments: Wild grape is a fail-safe native vine that grows in extremely varied habits throughout the whole of Florida. It will grow in deep shade but the plants prefer partial to full sun, and flowering and fruiting are poor in shade-grown plants. Normally it is kept in check by periodic fires, and if these are suppressed, it is quite capable of overrunning everything in its path, including trees, brush cover, and fences. Although it is sometimes regarded as short-lived, undisturbed hammocks that have not burned for decades often have old plants with woody stems 6 inches or more in diameter. If conditions are to its liking, Keller (1998) reports, it is capable of growing 50 feet in one year! Late in the year, it matures clusters of eight to thirty shiny black grapes. These are excellent for making jams and jellies, but they are extremely acidic and require lots of sugar and acid reduction in order to make a decent wine. Muscadine is easily distinguished from all other grapes by its simple, unbranched tendrils. The calloose grape (*Vitis shuttleworthii*) is horticulturally similar to muscadine, but it is far more ornamental since the lower surface of the leaves is permanently covered with a dense coat of white or rusty hairs.

Aquatic Plants

Detailed instructions for creating a water garden are beyond the scope of this book, but as a starting point, a few suggestions and caveats follow. First, we should categorize the different types of aquatic plants, most of which fall into one of three broad groups:

- *Marginals* are aquatic plants that grow in wet soil to several inches of water in wet ditches and along pond shores, stream banks, the edges of swamps, and the landward side of mangroves. They are always rooted in the substrate, and except during floods, the leaves emerge above the water's surface and flowers are always borne above the water. Many marginals will adapt to merely moist soil and may be grown under ordinary garden conditions. Others will not; they require constantly wet, boggy conditions to thrive.

- *Floating aquatics* have leaves that float on the water's surface and flowers that are borne just at or above the surface. They may or may not be rooted in the substrate.

This suburban home incorporates two aquatic gardens into its landscape scene. On the right is a small bog garden made from an earth-filled container sunk into the ground. Behind it is a stone-lined pond filled with water-lilies.

· *Submerged aquatics* bear all of their leaves below the water's surface. They may or may not be rooted in the substrate, and flowers may be borne under or above the water.

Of course, living organisms do not all fit neatly into artificial categories, and intermediates occur that cross the boundaries. For example, many species of pondweed (*Potamogeton*) are rootless, submerged aquatics that also produce floating leaves.

A water garden can be as simple as a small container or as complex as a large artificial pond carefully graded with "shelves" of varying height along its margins to accommodate plants that require different levels of water. In between these two extremes are large containers or small ponds in which marginal aquatics are grown in submerged pots. This last method saves on the amount of soil needed to fill the water garden and prevents plants from spreading. The principal problems associated with water gardens are leaking, algae, the accumulation of organic debris, mosquitoes, and wild animals.

Ponds may be lined with a variety of materials to prevent leaks: cement, fiberglass, polyethylene, polyvinyl chloride, or rubber. For most home gardeners, a liner made of EPDM (a synthetic rubber) is probably the best choice. EPDM synthetic rubber is sold in rolls or folded sheets, is extremely flexible, and is easily molded to the contours of the pond. Although usually guaranteed by manufacturers for about twenty years, EPDM normally lasts for forty years or more. Other materials commonly used to line ponds will require maintenance long before forty years have elapsed, and some, such as polyvinyl chloride, will barely last five years. EPDM is also manufactured for use by roofers; when purchasing it as a pond liner, look for the words "fish friendly" to avoid purchasing the roof-grade product.

Algae are present due to the amount of light and nutrients. If you are creating a natural water garden and eschew the use of chemicals, try the following recommendations to reduce algae:

· Plant a wide diversity of plants, including marginals and both submerged and floating aquatics.

· Use a nutrient-poor substrate in your water garden. Coarse sand or generic, unscented kitty litter is a good choice. For a neater appearance, either may be covered with a thin layer of pea gravel.

· Try to maintain a 60–75 percent cover of floating plants at all times. These reduce the amount of light entering the water garden and help to keep algae under control.

· Never use copper-based products to control algae since these may kill fish, and aquatic plants are sensitive to copper. Check also to make sure that the fittings on any hoses or ornaments used in the water garden are not made of copper.

Once a water garden is in place, it seems as if every bit of falling debris in the neighborhood finds its way there. As such material accumulates and decays, it may bring nutrients to excessively high levels. Leaves from oaks, maples, and other trees leach tannins into the water, which can affect some plants adversely and can kill fish. Tannins from such leaves can build up to lethal levels and kill your fish in as little as three days. Another problem rarely mentioned in water gardening books is birds that defecate in the water garden as they take a drink. Bird droppings quickly foul small water gardens. As for mosquitoes, these are easily controlled by placing small fish in the water garden. Always use native mosquito fish (*Gambusia* species) for control of mosquito larvae in water gardens. Exotic fish pose a serious aquatic pest problem in Florida and it is best to avoid non-native fish altogether.

In many parts of Florida, homes are built in wet areas and local zoning ordinances require the construction of a retention pond. In western Palm Beach County, homes are constructed on mounds of soil excavated from the home site, resulting in an instant pond. In order to minimize the size of such ponds, they are often built with steep sides, and the successful cultivation of marginal plants and aquatic plants rooted in the substrate is difficult or impossible. Natural ponds in Florida flatwoods have, on average, a very shallow grade: approximately one foot of vertical drop for every eight feet of horizontal distance from the shore. Further, the water level of ponds in the vicinity of drainage canals rises and drops as water in the canals is raised and lowered by water managers. The results for aquatic plants can be disastrous as they are variously and suddenly left high and dry or inundated.

Water plants, from the tiniest duckweed (*Lemna* species) to the largest water-lily (*Nymphaea* species), will attempt to fill as large an area as is given to them. The solution to this is to plant as wide a variety of plants as possible, both marginals and aquatics. Competition will keep them in check and they will soon reach a happy balance. Until they do, assiduously weed, prune, or constrain any overly aggressive plant—if you do not, it will soon be the only plant present in your water garden.

A bog garden is an interesting type of water garden distinctive in being completely filled with a low-nutrient substrate, such as sand, and planted with marginals and other plants that favor wet situations. It is somewhat easier to maintain than a water garden since there are no problems with algae, and concerns regarding water quality and chemistry are minimal. Bog gardens need not be fancy; some of the most successful bog gardens were made by slashing a few holes in a small wading pool, sinking it into the ground, and filling it with sandy loam.

In northern Florida, cold temperatures pose an additional problem. That cold temperatures pose difficulties may seem odd since many of our native aquatic plants extend as far north as the northeastern United States or even into Canada. However, most of such plants are cold hardy only so long as the body of water in which they are growing is sufficiently deep not to freeze solid.

Since Florida has so many easily accessible wetland areas and habitats, there is a strong temptation to procure aquatic plants from such wetland habitats. Resist the temptation at all costs! Remember that, as noted in the chapter on conservation, it is illegal to remove any plant, or part of a plant, without the express written permission of the landowner. Second, it is illegal to collect or transport *any wetland, marginal, or aquatic plant in Florida without a permit.* Why is this so important? Because Florida is plagued by numerous non-native and invasive aquatic pest plants. Many such plants are able to colonize new bodies of water from the tiniest fragment or from inconspicuous seeds clinging to other aquatic vegetation or even to your hands as you dip them into a pond.

When you collect aquatic plants, you may very well also be inadvertently collecting, transporting, and establishing new colonies of aquatic pest plants and aiding in their spread into other areas. Please support your local native plant nursery and do not add to Florida's pest plant problems by illegally collecting wetland, marginal, and aquatic plants from the wild.

One last note before proceeding to the plant descriptions: any area of the garden with water in it, including wet ditches and puddles where water stands after a rain, poses a drowning hazard for small children. As has been emphasized repeatedly in Florida news broadcasts, young children can drown in as little as two inches of water. Be a responsible gardener. If you have any area of water in your garden, ensure that it will not pose a threat to your own or neighborhood children.

333. *Azolla caroliniana*

Common Name: Mosquito Fern
Habit: Diminutive floating aquatic fern with a unique, unfernlike appearance.
Size: About ½–⅓ inch long.
Season: Evergreen or, toward the north of its range, dormant in winter.
Maintenance: None.
Motility: Spreading by fragmentation and forming large colonies.
Growing Conditions: Floating on quiet waters in full sun to light shade; Zones 8–10.
Propagation: Division.
Comments: Native plants are full of surprises and very few natives stretch credulity to the extent of the mosquito fern. Who would expect that this diminutive floating aquatic plant, about half an inch long and with a most unfernlike appearance, is indeed a true fern? South Florida botanist Doug Scofield aptly likens it to tiny, flattened juniper branches floating on the water's surface. With warm temperatures, it grows quickly and forms new plants by budding off small fragments, and by this means it can cover the entire surface of rather sizable bodies of water. This is a problem if one is growing submerged aquatic plants, since overly vigorous mosquito fern colonies can block out too much light. Also, this plant

is not recommended for water gardens with filtration systems, where it may become a nuisance when the tiny plant bodies clog the filter.

334. *Canna flaccida*

Common Name: Golden Canna; Bandana of the Everglades
Habit: Robust, erect perennial.
Size: About 3 feet tall, growing to nearly 6 feet in southern Florida.
Season: Winter dormant northward, evergreen southward; flowers borne from spring through summer.
Maintenance: Thinning of older stems; seed pods can detract from tidy appearance.
Motility: Forming large colonies by way of its widely creeping, stout, subterranean rhizomes.
Growing Conditions: Swamps and pond margins in full sun to light shade; Zones 8–10.
Propagation: Seed (scarify); division.
Comments: Cannas are large, robust plants with brightly colored and conspicuously showy flowers. Golden canna is the only species native to Florida, where it occurs throughout much of the state. It has large, pale green leaves reminiscent of a young banana and, throughout the summer, bears large, pure yellow, orchidlike flowers of exquisite and exotic form. The flowers are short-lived and wither in the heat of late morning. The plant grows from a tough, tuberous rhizome, a food store allowing it to spring back from adversity such as freezing weather, droughts, and even mowing. The rhizomes are wide-ranging; a single plant will freely sucker and quickly cover a surprisingly large patch of ground. Since it is such a bold and rapidly spreading plant, the golden canna can scarcely be recommended for small garden settings unless suitable means are found to constrain it. Cannas are easily propagated by removing young shoots with an attached portion of the rhizome, or they may be propagated from seed, which requires abrading the hard coat to allow water to penetrate.

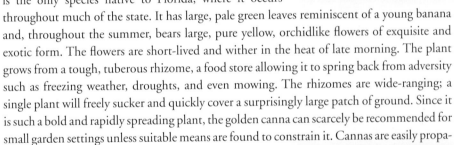

335. *Hydrolea corymbosa*

Common Name: Skyflower
Habit: Marginal aquatic plant.
Size: About 12 inches tall.
Season: Flowering in summer and autumn.
Maintenance: Essentially none.
Motility: Capable of filling as large an area of wet, open ground as is given to it, by way of underground rhizomes.

Growing Conditions: Pond shores and wet ditches in full sun to part shade; Zones 8B–10.

Propagation: Seed; division; cuttings.

Comments: Skyflower is a lovely plant that occurs from South Carolina to southernmost Florida. It is one of the showiest species of *Hydrolea* since it bears large inflorescences of good-sized, deep blue flowers throughout the summer and autumn. It is also attractive vegetatively, with its small, glossy, deep green foliage nicely complementing the exquisite flowers. Its only fault is its spreading, colonial nature. However, since it requires abundant moisture, it would not normally be planted in garden beds, where its rambling, underground rhizomes may cause problems. It is eminently suitable for growing in roadside ditches and other rough, wet areas, where the choice of flowering plant material is often limited. It should be utilized more often in wetland restorations, where it would add a welcome and novel patch of blue.

336. *Lobelia cardinalis*

Common Name: Cardinal Flower

Habit: Erect perennial, passing the winter as basal rosettes of foliage.

Size: Stems in full flower 3–6 feet tall, depending on soil and moisture.

Season: Flowering in late summer, autumn, or early winter.

Maintenance: Pruning to the ground of old flowering stems that have gone to seed.

Motility: Occasionally spreading by seed if conditions are favorable.

Growing Conditions: Wet sites in full shade to full sun; Zones 8–9.

Propagation: Seed; division of basal offshoots.

Comments: Cardinal flower is famous as one of the most beautiful red-flowered plants in all of North America. Young plants form basal rosettes, from which are borne in late summer, autumn, and early winter tall, many-flowered spikes of brilliant, pure red blossoms. The flowers are of exquisite form with a large lower lip. Hummingbirds find them irresistible and, when grown in large masses, this plant is useful for attracting these marvelous little birds to the garden. Cardinal flower has a wide range in Florida, extending from the Panhandle to Hillsborough County, but it is uncommon and is listed as threatened in the state. It can be grown south of its natural range and is being successfully cultivated as far south as Broward County. Its one fault is that it tends to be short-lived and often dies after blooming. In spite of such problems, it is worth every effort to cultivate. Additionally, seed germinates quickly if kept consistently moist, and if one's plants prove impermanent, a new batch is easily started from seed.

337. *Nymphaea odorata*

Common Name: White Water-Lily; Fragrant Water-Lily; Alligator Bonnet

Habit: Submerged aquatic plant, rooted in the substrate, with floating leaves.

Size: Floating leaves with a combined spread of 5 feet in diameter (2–3 feet in dwarf forms).

Season: Dormant during cool weather; flowering whenever warm temperatures prevail.

Maintenance: None.

Motility: Rapidly spreading vegetatively and able to fill small ponds completely.

Growing Conditions: Ponds, lakes, and slow streams in 3–60 inches of water; Zones 8–10.

Propagation: Seed; division.

Comments: White water-lily is one of the most strikingly beautiful aquatic plants in Florida and is much loved for its fragrant, pure white flowers with a contrasting yellow center. It is the most adaptable water-lily native to the United States, with a range that includes both cold-temperate and tropical zones. Not fussy as to growing conditions, it is able to grow and flower in shallow ditches as well as in deep ponds. Several cultivated forms of this species are available, including a large, robust form ('Gigantea'); a form with pink flowers ('Rosea'); and a delightful miniature form originally discovered in Palm Beach County, with white flowers fading pale pink ('Pride of Palm Beach'). Five other water-lilies are native to Florida and are worthy of cultivation: *Nymphaea ampla,* the only native water-lily with wavy-toothed leaf margins; *N. elegans,* a small plant with blue flowers; *N. jamesoniana,* with nocturnal flowers; *N. mexicana,* with bright yellow flowers and recommended for smaller ponds since it is less aggressive than *N. odorata;* and *Nymphaea × thiona,* a natural hybrid between *N. mexicana* and *N. odorata,* with soft yellow flowers.

338. *Nymphoides aquatica*

Common Name: Floating Hearts; Banana Plant

Habit: Submerged aquatic plant with floating leaves; greatly resembling a dwarf water-lily.

Size: Floating leaves to about 3 inches in diameter.

Season: Dormant during cold weather; flowering whenever warm temperatures prevail.

Maintenance: None.

Motility: Filling small, shallow bodies of water by vegetative spread and seeds.

Growing Conditions: Shallow water of ponds and swamps; Zones 8–10.

Propagation: Seed; cuttings; division.

Comments: Commonly regarded as "miniature water-lilies," floating hearts are not at all related to true water-lilies in the genus *Nymphaea*. Formerly, they were placed in the family Gentianaceae with the true gentians and rose-gentians (*Gentiana* and *Sabatia*, respectively). However, today they and a few close relatives are commonly relegated to their own family, the Menyanthaceae. The plants arise from a cluster of thickened roots that closely and remarkably resemble a tiny bunch of bananas. Although these are decorative, resist the temptation to try to grow the plant with the bananalike roots exposed since these must be buried if the plant is to survive and grow. At first producing submersed leaves, it eventually produces floating leaves that bear the exquisite little white flowers near their bases. Floating hearts are often recommended for even the smallest of water gardens but may take over if conditions are to their liking. Large, floating leaves may be cut, along with a bit of stem, and placed in water, where they will form a set of roots and in time form a new plant.

339. Pontederia cordata

Common Name: Pickerelweed; Pickerel-Rush

Habit: Vigorous marginal aquatic with attractive blue flowers.

Size: About 18–30 inches tall.

Season: Evergreen southward, dormant in winter northward; flowers borne whenever warm weather prevails.

Maintenance: None.

Motility: Has creeping rhizomes and can fill small, shallow bodies of water.

Growing Conditions: Shallow standing water in full sun to light shade; Zones 8–10.

Propagation: Seed (sow as soon as ripe); division.

Comments: Pickerelweed is easily grown and is one of the most common aquatic plants in cultivation. It may be grown in a wet area or it may be submerged in up to about 10 inches of water. Plants look their best, are more vigorous, and flower most abundantly when grown in full sun, but they tolerate light or partial shade. The medium blue flowers are produced over a long season and attractively complement the glossy, heart-shaped leaves. In addition to the typical blue-flowered plants, a form with pure white flowers (*Pontederia cordata* 'Alba') is commonly encountered in the nursery trade. In addition to its ornamental value, pickerelweed is much planted for its fruits, which are reportedly a valuable wildlife food, especially for waterfowl. Propagation is easily effected by division in the spring once vigorous growth has commenced or by seeds sown as soon as they are ripe. It is advised that the plants not be divided when dormant since they are prone to rot if disturbed at that time.

340. *Potamogeton* species

Common Name: Pondweed
Habit: Free-floating submerged aquatics, some species also with floating leaves.
Size: Variable but able to form large colonies.
Season: Dormant in cold weather.
Maintenance: None.
Motility: Spreading and colonial by fragmentation.
Growing Conditions: Lakes, ponds, and slow-moving streams with clean, unpolluted water; Zones 8–10 (combined range for all nine Florida native species).
Propagation: Division.
Comments: Florida has nine species of pondweeds, all of which are free-floating submerged aquatic plants. Six native pondweeds also have floating leaves, these usually being markedly different in their size, shape, and texture from the submerged leaves. Only the plants with floating leaves are of much horticultural interest, and of these, only two species (*Potamogeton diversifolius* and *Potamogeton illinoensis*) are common, the remainder being rare plants with highly localized ranges in Florida. Their successful cultivation requires clean, algae-free water. They also need open water that is neither shaded by nor crowded with larger or more vigorous aquatic plants.

341. *Sabatia bartramii*

Common Name: Bartram's Marsh-Pink
Habit: Aquatic marginal perennial with large pink flowers.
Size: 12–24 inches tall
Season: Dormant in winter; flowering from late spring to late summer.
Maintenance: None.
Motility: Forming small colonies from basal shoots borne on short rhizomes; spreading from seed if moist, open areas are available to it.

Growing Conditions: Very wet, usually seasonally flooded soils in full sun; Zones 8–10.
Propagation: Seeds; cuttings
Comments: Bartram's marsh-pink is among the most horticulturally attractive species in a genus filled with numerous gardenworthy plants. However, it is also fairly strict in its requirements and can be a difficult plant to grow well. Its favored habitats are shallow, sandy ponds or depressions that have accumulated a few inches of rich, black organic muck on their surface. During dry spells, the basal rosettes are exposed to the air, but during the rainy season they are covered with a few inches of water. These are conditions that are not easily duplicated in the average garden. An additional problem is that the plants are long-lived perennials that are not in a hurry to increase vegetatively, and they take an exceedingly long time to recover after any disturbance to their roots. Presently, attempts are being made to grow this very beautiful wildflower from seed in the hope of finding select forms that are more amenable to cultivation.

342. *Saururus cernuus*

Common Name: Lizard's Tail
Habit: Vigorous marginal aquatic with attractive spikes of white flowers.
Size: 12–36 inches tall.
Season: Flowering from late spring to late summer.
Maintenance: None.
Motility: Has creeping rhizomes and can fill small, shallow bodies of water.
Growing Conditions: Shallow standing water in full sun to partial shade; Zones 8–10.
Propagation: Division.
Comments: Lizard's tail is a vigorous, colonial plant that can fill wet ditches. When growing along pond margins and in swamps, it is controlled by competition with other plants and deep water. It takes readily to cultivation, where it will adapt to ordinary garden conditions if it is given extra moisture. It may also be utilized as an unusual pot plant, although it needs to be divided and repotted annually due to its vigorous growth. When grown as an aquatic along pond margins or in wet ditches, it will grow in up to 6 inches of water or so. The plant has dark green, heart-shaped leaves that make a pleasing background for the fragrant, creamy white flowers. These are carried in gracefully drooping spikes and provide a highly decorative and elegant accent in the water garden.

Epiphytes

Grouped together in this section are three very different types of plants: ferns, brome-liads, and orchids. All the plants listed here, however, have one thing in common: they are epiphytic plants that grow upon other plants, usually trees. These plants are not parasites like dodders or mistletoes. They utilize other plants merely for support and do not obtain any water or nutrients from the host plant.

Some of the rarest plants in Florida, with the greatest pressure from illegal collec-tion, are epiphytes, and it is with much hesitation that this section is included in this book. However, two considerations convinced me to include epiphytes.

First, Florida has far more epiphytic plants than any other state, and they are a conspicuous element of our flora even to the most casual of observers. Second, the epiphytes listed here are all common plants that generally take well to cultivation and are either readily available in the specialty nursery trade (including a selection of mail-order nurseries) or else have a long history of being traded among native plant garden-ers. Indeed, some of the epiphytes included here, such as strap fern (*Campyloneurum phyllitidis*) and golden polypody (*Phlebodium aureum*), have a tendency to become nursery and garden weeds, especially in the pots of cultivated exotic orchids.

The principal element in the successful cultivation of the epiphytes listed here is careful placement in the garden. If they are placed where they can get bright light, but no direct sun, in a humid but airy site, success is all but guaranteed. The second most important element in their cultivation is watering. Once established, they do not need to be watered except when there are prolonged periods of dry weather. Coddling these plants by constantly fussing over them, fertilizing them, and watering them will usu-ally kill them far more rapidly than simply ignoring them.

If you have never grown an epiphytic plant before, begin with non-native brome-liads in the genus *Tillandsia*. The more common kinds are available for a few dollars at most plant shows, none has ever shown any weedy or invasive tendencies, and if you make any mistakes, no native plants are affected. Once you can successfully grow non-native tillandsias, try your hand at the three native tillandsias listed here, followed by the three ferns. Only after you have mastered the cultivation of these plants should you attempt to cultivate either of the orchids listed. The epiphytes here are not especially difficult plants to grow, but neither are they beginners' plants. They do require careful placement in just the right microhabitat and a kind of calculated indifference that involves attending to their needs but not smothering them with too much coddling. Thorough knowledge of a garden's microhabitats and an appreciation for calculated indifference are often lacking in the beginning gardener but are soon acquired by growing the easier epiphytes before moving on to the more challenging plants.

It is well to repeat that under no circumstances should it be assumed that inclusion of a plant here is license or encouragement to remove native plants or plant parts from the wild in any form, including spore or seed.

343. *Campyloneurum phyllitidis*

Common Name: Strap Fern
Habit: Erect fern forming a large, vaselike rosette.
Size: 2½–3 feet high.
Season: All year.
Maintenance: Periodic removal of old fronds.
Motility: No vegetative spread; very rarely may spread from spore.
Growing Conditions: Commonly growing just above the high water mark on the trunks of large trees in swamps; Zones 9–11.
Propagation: Spore; division.
Comments: Strap fern has an arresting and unique look among our native ferns with its long, undivided fronds that gradually taper at both ends. The leaves are densely arranged near the tip of a very short rhizome, where they form a sizable vaselike rosette. The plant's growth form is utilitarian, serving as a funnel to direct water to the center of the plant and funneling organic matter, such as falling leaves, to supply nutrients to the roots. In spite of its decidedly dramatic and tropical appearance, strap fern adapts readily to cultivation as long as it is heavily mulched and kept evenly moist. It also makes an interesting pot plant that thrives if grown in a pot of bark mulch and fed occasionally with a high-nitrogen fertilizer.

344. *Phlebodium aureum* (Synonym: *Polypodium aureum*)

Common Name: Golden Polypody
Habit: Large, bold epiphytic fern with a prominent, densely hairy, golden brown rhizome; nearly always found on cabbage palms.
Size: Variable, forming large clumps with age; leaves up to 2 feet long or longer.
Season: Evergreen; provides year-round interest as a foliage plant.
Maintenance: None in the wild garden; periodic removal of old fronds.

Motility: Spreading by spore on cabbage palms if there are prolonged periods of high humidity; occasionally becoming a weed in potted epiphytic plants such as orchids.

Growing Conditions: Occurs in cabbage palm boots in hammocks and swamps in nearly full sun to dense shade; Zones 8B–10.

Propagation: Spore; division.

Comments: Golden polypody nearly always occurs in the boots of old cabbage palms (*Sabal palmetto*), especially in older palms, where the boots have had time to collect organic debris in the form of fallen leaves and twigs from nearby plants. Rarely, it can be found on the trunks of large and ancient saw-palmettos (*Serenoa repens*). Plants growing on the ground are rather common. However, the latter are apparently always the survivors of plants growing on cabbage palms that fell to the ground. Golden polypody is also commonly found on young, nursery-grown cabbage palms, the boots of which are kept moist as a result of overhead irrigation in the nursery. Such palms are the best source for young golden polypodies to transplant to one's yard, and they are often

free for the asking. Cultivation is usually as simple as inserting a young plant into a cabbage palm boot and keeping it moist until it is established. They may also be grown terrestrially if one has a partially shaded spot that is kept well mulched with a thick layer of organic material.

345. *Pleopeltis polypodioides* var. *michauxiana* (Synonym: *Polypodium polypodioides* var. *michauxianum*)

Common Name: Resurrection Fern

Habit: Small epiphytic fern growing on live oaks or, less frequently, on bald-cypress or other trees; may occasionally also grow terrestrially.

Size: Fronds usually 3–6 inches long, occasionally

longer; rhizomes long-creeping.

Season: Evergreen; provides year-round interest as a foliage plant.

Maintenance: None.

Motility: With age, able to clothe large oak limbs with a mantle of fern fronds.

Growing Conditions: Oak hammocks and cypress swamps where there is high humidity in partial shade; Zones 8–10.

Propagation: Spore; division.

Comments: This little fern never fails to attract attention when the dried, lifeless-looking fronds become fresh and green after a moderate to heavy rain. Under natural conditions, it is found growing on the branches of live oak. However, like several other epiphytic ferns, it is sometimes seen growing terrestrially, especially where a thick layer of fallen leaves and twigs has accumulated over well-drained sandy soil. Such plants are apparently always the survivors of bits and pieces that fell to the ground after a particularly heavy or windy rain storm. Young plants may be attached to a tree limb with fishing line and, for best results, should be watered at frequent intervals until they show signs of attaching to the new host. They also make highly unusual little pot plants and are easily grown in wide, shallow clay pots filled with bark chips.

346. *Tillandsia fasciculata*

Common Name: Cardinal Airplant

Habit: Large, rosette-forming epiphytic bromeliad found on cypress trees or, less frequently, on live oaks and pines.

Size: Variable, but well-grown plants with rosettes at least 12 inches wide and, in flower, 18–24 inches tall.

Season: Evergreen; provides year-round interest as a foliage plant; flowering in late spring and early summer.

Maintenance: None in the wild garden; removal of old flowering or fruiting spikes for a neater appearance.

Motility: Will spread in cultivation by way of wind-blown seed, often hundreds of feet from the parent plant.

Growing Conditions: Most luxuriant in wet hammocks with high humidity and light shade, but also occurring on isolated trees in full sun, although frequently appearing stressed and somewhat stunted under such conditions; Zones 9B–11.

Propagation: Seed (sow immediately upon ripening); division.

Comments: As long as the plant is allowed free drainage and is never in soggy conditions, cardinal airplant is remarkably easy to grow and can go from seed to flower in about five years. If you have rather dry, sandy soil with a layer of organic material on top, it may also be grown terrestrially, resulting in a novel landscape effect. Although at one time the cardinal airplant was generally free from pests and disease, this is no longer the case. The grub of a weevil now established in Florida eats out the heart of the plant, resulting in its death. Large numbers have been ravaged in southern Florida, and there is concern that cardinal airplant may become endangered if this pest spreads throughout the state.

347. *Tillandsia recurvata*

Common Name: Ball-Moss
Habit: Small, densely clumping epiphytic bromeliad forming rounded ball-like clusters on thin twigs, exfoliating strips of bark and utility wires.
Size: Variable depending on growing conditions, with clumps 3–6 inches in diameter.
Season: Evergreen; provides year-round interest as a foliage plant; flowering in late spring and early summer but flowers not particularly showy.
Maintenance: None.
Motility: Capable of forming colonies of many dozens of plants by self-sown seedlings.

Growing Conditions: Found in a wide range of both natural and artificial conditions, but always in sites with high air movement and bright light; Zones 8B–11.
Propagation: Seed (sow immediately upon ripening); division.
Comments: Ball-moss is perhaps the most common airplant in Florida and is found growing on a wide variety of hosts. It belongs to a highly adapted and particularly interesting group of epiphytes known as twig epiphytes, which indeed colonize thin branches and twigs; in these plants we see the epiphytic habit carried to an advanced level. With modern settlement of Florida, people strung power and telephone lines and this little plant became established on the wires; there is little difference between life on a thin twig and life on a utility wire. Ball-moss is extremely easy to cultivate. Successful establishment requires nothing more than tying it to a suitable twig with a short length of fishing line.

348. *Tillandsia usneoides*

Common Name: Spanish-Moss
Habit: Unique pendant epiphyte, especially common on cypress trees, oak trees, and pines.
Size: Variable but with age forming large pendant clumps at least 3 feet long.
Season: Evergreen; provides year-round interest as a foliage plant; flowering in the spring and summer, but flowers tiny, green, and inconspicuous.
Maintenance: None.
Motility: Capable of clothing large trees by way of wind-blown seeds or, more commonly, by way of wind-blown fragments; also spread by birds, which sometimes use it as nesting material.

Growing Conditions: Found under a variety of conditions but at its most luxuriant at the edges of wet hammocks, where it gets bright light and high humidity; Zones 8–11.

Propagation: Seed (sow immediately upon ripening); division.

Comments: Spanish-moss carries the epiphytic habit to its penultimate extreme. It has come as close to an aerial existence as a plant can get without sprouting wings and flying. Although it is anchored to its host plant, the bulk of its mass dangles freely in the air. Concomitant with its aerial existence is a reduction in all parts. The flower spikes, which are so conspicuous in most bromeliads, are here reduced to tiny, solitary green flowers that are scarcely ever noticed except by the most observant of naturalists and plant lovers. Yet, in spite of lacking showy flowers, its unusual and unique growth habit attracts much notice and many native plant gardeners like to grow it as a novelty evocative of the deep South and of untamed places such as cypress swamps. It is effortlessly grown, and its successful cultivation requires only that a small clump be draped over a suitable tree limb where it is exposed to rain, fresh air, and bright light. Nothing more is necessary to grow this amazing plant that, were it not so common, would rightly be considered one of the wonders of the plant world.

349. *Encyclia tampensis*

Common Name: Florida Butterfly Orchid

Habit: Epiphytic orchid commonly growing on oaks, cypress, pond-apples, buttonwood, or more rarely pine trees.

Size: Highly variable depending on growing conditions and age; most commonly 8–12 inches high (excluding the inflorescences), sometimes forming immense clumps consisting of a hundred or more growths.

Season: Evergreen; provides year-round interest as a foliage plant; flowering in early summer, sometimes with hundreds of flowers and extremely showy.

Maintenance: None or, in more formal gardens, removal of old flower stalks.

Motility: If conditions are exactly right, sometimes colonizing suitable sites by way of wind-blown seed.

Growing Conditions: Highly variable but usually at its best along the edges of wet hammocks and swamps, where the humidity is high and the plants get bright light; Zones 8B–11.

Propagation: Division.

Comments: More orchids are native to Florida than to any other part of the United States, with ninety-nine native species listed by Wunderlin (1998). This number is all the more astounding when one considers that the remaining forty-nine states, with a total land area far exceeding that of Florida, have a mere 107 native species of orchids (Luer 1975). However, despite Florida's diverse orchid flora, few native orchids are showy enough to be of interest to most gardeners. Florida's butterfly orchid is an exception. Not only is it our most common and widespread epiphytic orchid; it also is one of our showiest orchids. Among its many positive qualities are the small but pretty flowers, borne in large numbers. The flowers are fragrant with a sweet, honeylike aroma, although this varies—some populations have been described as having a fragrance resembling chocolate. Additionally, the flowers are rather long-lasting, yielding a display that remains at its peak for several weeks. The plants are easy to grow under a wide variety of conditions, from nearly full shade to nearly full sun. They look their best in partial shade but produce more flowers when exposed to bright light. If grown mounted onto a tree trunk or branch, their cultivation is essentially effortless. However, when a Florida butterfly orchid is grown in a pot, there is a tendency for beginners to pamper it to death by overwatering it. If potted, it must be allowed to become completely dry between waterings and should be grown in an extremely porous medium that dries out quickly. This beautiful plant has entered general cultivation and is readily available from a fair number of orchid nurseries throughout the United States; young seedlings two to four years from flowering may be purchased inexpensively. Thus, there is no excuse for plundering this plant from the wild.

350. *Epidendrum nocturnum*

Common Name: Night-Scented Epidendrum

Habit: Large, robust epiphytic orchid commonly growing on cypress and pond-apples.

Size: Forming small to large clumps, the stems 18–24 inches long or longer.

Season: Evergreen; provides year-round interest as a foliage plant; flowering intermittently throughout the year.

Maintenance: None.

Motility: Very rarely establishing itself on suitable sites by way of wind-blown seed.

Growing Conditions: Wet hammocks in partial shade where the humidity is high and the plants are sheltered from bright light and strong winds; Zones 9B–10.

Propagation: Division.

Comments: Night-scented epidendrum has an unusual growth form very different from that of most other native epiphytic orchids. First, it is a large plant with long, gracefully arching stems that may reach 3 feet in length. Second, it has broad, flat leaves so that it forms a conspicuous sight perched on its host tree. Last, it does not have the swollen bulbous bases or succulent stems or leaves commonly seen in other epiphytic orchids. This last characteristic is a clear indication that the plant is not adapted to hot dry conditions and provides important clues to its successful cultivation. Gardeners must provide it with shady, humid conditions as are found in mature hammocks and swamps. The yellowish or greenish flowers have a large, prominent, pure white lip and are highly fragrant at night. The flowers are gracefully attractive but not spectacular, although a large clump bearing many flowers at once is ornamental. Each stem produces only one flower at a time and the flowers are short-lived, but flowers are intermittently produced over a long period. Like Florida butterfly orchid (*Encyclia tampensis*), night-scented epidendrum is regularly available in the nursery trade at very reasonable prices, obviating the need to remove plants from the wild.

Appendix 1: Places to See Native Plants

Natural areas with plants growing wild are of interest since close observation of plants in their natural habitat often provides useful insights for growing the plants in garden settings.

Listing of a site in this appendix is for informational purposes only and does not imply endorsement. To the best of my knowledge, all of the sites listed specifically prohibit the removal or disturbance of any feature, whether vegetable, animal, or mineral. Removal of any plant material, including seed or spore, is a serious offense.

Federally Administered Lands

The National Park Service administers eleven sites in Florida, with the following six offering the greatest interest to native plant enthusiasts:

Big Cypress National Preserve
HCR 61, Box 110
Ochopee, Florida 33943
(941) 695-2000

Everglades National Park
40001 State Road 9336
Homestead, Florida 33034–6733
(305) 242-7700

Canaveral National Seashore
308 Julia Street
Titusville, Florida 32796–3521
(407) 267-1110

Gulf Islands National Seashore
1801 Gulf Breeze Parkway
Gulf Breeze, Florida 32561
(850) 934-2604

Dry Tortugas National Park
40001 State Road 9336
Homestead, Florida 33034–6733
(305) 242-7700

Timucuan Ecological and Historical Preserve
13165 Mt. Pleasant Road
Jacksonville, Florida 32225
(904) 221-5568

The USDA Forest Service administers the Apalachicola, Ocala, and Osceola national forests. Additional information on passive recreational uses of the national forests may be obtained from the USDA Forest Service, Woodcrest Office Park, 325 John Knox Rd, Suite F-100, Tallahassee, Florida 32303; (850) 942-9300.

State-Administered Lands

Presently, about 150 parks, preserves, recreation areas, trails, museums, and archaeological, botanical, geological or historic sites are run by the State of Florida. Of these, the state parks offer the greatest rewards for native plant enthusiasts as they are in a more or less natural condition, have well-marked trails, and often have trail leaflets that identify particularly prominent or conspicuous plants. Some of the state recreation areas have little to offer in the way of native plants, being intended primarily for recreational use by boaters, campers,

Local natural areas offer many opportunities to study native plants in their native habitats. For example, although it looks like a stretch of primeval wilderness, this scene was photographed at a nature preserve completely surrounded by residential development in a heavily populated area of Palm Beach County.

picnickers, and joggers. The *Florida State Park Guide* may be requested from Florida Department of Environmental Protection, Division of Recreation and Parks, 3900 Commonwealth Boulevard, Tallahassee, Florida 32399–3000; (850) 488-6131. This guide may also be requested at www.dep.state.fl.us/parks/emailus/parkguide.htm on the Internet.

Florida's state forests are administered by the Florida Department of Agriculture and Consumer Services and information may be obtained from Friends of Florida State Forests Inc., Florida Division of Forestry, 3125 Conner Boulevard, Tallahassee, Florida 32399–1650; (850) 488-7246.

Local Parks

A selection of local county and municipal parks, recreation areas, and nature centers offer excellent opportunities to observe cultivated or wild native plants. Local telephone directories include community guides that list local points of interest, and these guides are useful for tracking down sites with native plants. Additionally, most counties have a department of parks and recreation (look in the government section of the telephone directory), personnel of which can tell you if local parks have nature centers or trails.

Many local parks turn out to be little more than glorified playgrounds. However, do not be dismissive of local parks; some are real treasures. For example, a postage stamp–sized beachfront municipal park in Palm Beach County contains a fine example of coastal dunes and maritime hammock and boasts a population of a federally endangered morning-glory. Likewise, a Miami municipal park contains perhaps the finest example of subtropical rocky pinelands outside Everglades National Park. And perusal of the community guide in Tampa's telephone book reveals that Hillsborough County has many outstanding places to observe native plants, including a system of "wilderness parks."

Water Management Districts

Florida's water management districts manage many parcels of land that serve to protect water resources such as rivers, marshes, and floodplains. Most of these parcels are in a more or less natural state, have an abundance of native plants, and are open to the public for hiking. Contact your local district for a copy of their public use guide to land management areas:

Northwest Florida Water Management District
81 Water Management Drive
Havana, Florida 32333
(850) 539-5999
www.state.fl.us/nwfwmd/index.html

St. Johns River Water Management District
P.O. Box 1429
Palatka, Florida 37128–1429
(904) 329-4500
sjr.state.fl.us/index.html

South Florida Water Management District
3301 Gun Club Road
P.O. Box 24680
West Palm Beach, Florida 33416–4680
(561) 686-8800 or 800.432.2045
www.sfwmd.gov

Southwest Florida Water
Management District
2379 Broad Street
Brooksville, Florida 34609–6899
(352) 796-7211 or (800) 423-1476
www.swfwmd.state.fl.us

Suwanee River Water
Management District
Route 3, Box 64
Live Oak, Florida 32060
(904) 362-1001
srwmd@lo.gulfnet.com

Botanic Gardens

Nearly every botanic garden in Florida features native plants in one way or another, and a few botanic gardens are exclusively devoted to native plants. Even if a botanic garden does not strongly emphasize native plants, the garden can usually provide information on local areas to see native plants.

Alfred B. Maclay State Gardens
3540 Thomasville Road
Tallahassee, Florida 32308
(904) 487-4556

Bok Tower Gardens
1151 Tower Boulevard
Lake Wales, Florida 33853–3412
(941) 676-9412

Chapman Botanical Gardens
Apalachicola, Florida
(904) 653-8219

Eden State Gardens
P.O. Box 26
Port Washington, Florida 32454-0026
(904) 231-4214

This charming little garden artfully combines wildflowers with grasses against a background of native shrubs and small trees. It is located in Heathcote Botanical Gardens, one of many botanic gardens in Florida with prominent displays of native plants.

Eureka Springs Gardens
6400 Eureka Springs Road
Tampa, Florida 33610
(813) 744-5536

Fairchild Tropical Garden
10901 Old Cutler Road
Miami, Florida 33156
(305) 667-1651

Flamingo Gardens
3750 Flamingo Road
Davie, Florida 33330
(945) 473-2955

Florida Botanic Gardens
Clearwater, Florida
(813) 446-3356

Florida Tech Botanical Garden
150 West University Boulevard
Melbourne, Florida 32901
(407) 768-8000 or (800) 888-
    4348

Gulf Breeze Zoo and Botanical Gardens
5701 Gulf Breeze Parkway
Gulf Breeze, Florida 32561–9551
(904) 932-2229

Harry P. Leu Botanical Gardens
1920 N. Forest Avenue
Orlando, Florida 32803–1537
(407) 246-3668

Heathcote Botanical Gardens
210 Savanna Road
Fort Pierce, Florida 34982
(407) 464-4672

Jacksonville Botanical Garden
Florida Community College
Jacksonville, Florida

Kanapaha Botanical Gardens
4625 S.W. 63rd Boulevard
Gainesville, Florida 32608–3845
(352) 372-4981

Key West Botanical Garden
P.O. Box 2436
Key West, Florida 33040
(305) 296-6606

McKee Botanical Gardens
4871 North A1A
Vero Beach, Florida 32963
(561) 234-1949

Marie Selby Botanical Gardens
811 South Palm Avenue
Sarasota, Florida 34236
(941) 366-5730

Mead Botanical Gardens
S. Denning Drive
Winter Park, Florida
(407) 599-3334

Mockernut Hill Botanical Garden
Micanopy
(352) 466-4136

Mounts Botanical Garden
531 North Military Trail
West Palm Beach, Florida 33415
(561) 233-1700

Pan's Garden
386 Hibiscus
Palm Beach, Florida 33480
(561) 835-9442

Ravine State Gardens
P.O. Box 1096
1600 Twigg Street
Palatka, Florida 32178
(904) 329-3721

University of Central Florida Arboretum
4000 Central Florida Boulevard
Orlando, Florida 32816–2368
(407) 823-2141

University of Miami John C. Gifford Arboretum
Coral Gables
(305) 284-3974

University of South Florida Botanical Garden
4202 East Fowler Avenue (LIF 136)
Tampa, Florida 33620
(813) 974-2329

Washington Oaks State Gardens
6400 North Ocean Boulevard
Palm Coast, Florida 32137
(904) 446-6780

Willmot Memorial Gardens
University of Florida
Gainesville, Florida
(352) 392-4251

Appendix 2: Florida Native Plants on the Internet

There are substantial resources on Florida's native plants on the Internet and World Wide Web. The following list is not meant to be exhaustive and is included merely to provide starting points. Inclusion of a World Wide Web site in this appendix is for informational purposes only and does not imply endorsement of the site.

Wildflower Nirvana

wfnirvana.com
This is my own web site. Contents change periodically, and much information about Florida native plants is available, including many images of plants. The catalog section lists seeds of some of Florida's rarer or more unusual native plants available via mail-order. My web site also provides updates and changes to this book.

Aquaphyte **Online**

aquat1.ifas.ufl.edu/aquaph.html
Biannual journal of the Center for Aquatic and Invasive Plants is a must for anyone interested in wetland plants, both native and non-native.

Association of Florida Native Nurseries

www.afnn.org
AFNN's web site provides a complete listing of member nurseries, all of which specialize in Florida native plants. Additionally, one may search for a specific plant and see which AFNN member nursery carries it.

Atlas of Florida Vascular Plants

www.plantatlas.usf.edu
The Atlas of Florida Vascular Plants is an invaluable tool, providing distribution maps for every plant found growing in the wild in Florida, both native and introduced. In addition to the distribution maps, this site has hundreds of photographs of native plants.

Bok Tower Gardens

www.boktower.org/Default.htm
Botanical garden in Lake Wales, Florida, situated atop one of the highest points in peninsular Florida at 298 feet above sea level. Native plant features include scrub and sandhill restorations as well as extensive areas landscaped with native plants.

Carphephorus **Species**

epic38.dep.state.fl.us/weds/carpheph/carpheph.html
This is a subsection of Florida's Department of Environmental Protection Wetlands Evalu-

ation and Delineation section that describes species of *Carphephorus*, a genus closely related to the blazingstars (genus *Liatris*).

Center for Aquatic and Invasive Plants

(aquat1.ifas.ufl.edu/welcome.html)
Extremely thorough site with a broad range of resources pertaining to wetland plants, both native and introduced, including numerous photographs.

Center for Plant Conservation

www.mobot.org/CPC/welcome.html
Approximately one in every ten plants native to the United States is in danger of extinction. The CPC attempts to conserve such plants by a national collection housed at participating botanical gardens throughout the United States. Two such collections are housed in Florida, one at Bok Tower Gardens (www.boktower.org/Default.htm) and the other at Fairchild Tropical Garden (ftg.org).

Central Florida Wildlife Plants

www.wec.ufl.edu/extension/landscap/native.htm
Craig N. Huegel has prepared an excellent introduction to and thorough listing of trees and shrubs of value to wildlife in Central Florida.

Enchanted Forest Nature Sanctuary

www.nbbd.com/godo/ef/index.html
Brevard's County flagship nature sanctuary contains a variety of natural habitats from dry scrub to mesic hammock.

Enviroscaping to Conserve Energy: Trees for North Florida

edis.ifas.ufl.edu/scripts/htmlgen.exe?DOCUMENT_EH140
R. J. Black and A. W. Meerow provide a good introduction to the use of trees for passive climate control.

Everglades National Park

www.nps.gov/ever
Everglades National Park is the largest remaining subtropical wilderness in the continental United States and offers many opportunities for viewing and studying native plants.

Fairchild Tropical Garden

ftg.org
Located in Miami, Florida, Fairchild Tropical Garden is a large botanic garden housing several thousand kinds of plants, native and non-native alike. A large number of native southern Florida trees and shrubs are included in the collection.

Florida Department of Environmental Protection

www.dep.state.fl.us
Much of the information on this site is of a technical nature. However, the State Park Index (www.dep.state.fl.us/parks/maps/alpha.html) is useful since state parks provide a convenient and accessible means of studying, identifying and enjoying native plants.

Florida Exotic Pest Plant Council

www.fleppc.org

Invasive, non-native pest plants wipe out more natural habitat each year than does development. The EPPC's web site provides much useful information on invasive pest plants, including valuable directions on their control.

Florida Flora Picture Gallery

www.ftg.fiu.edu/lf

A site with approximately a hundred images of Florida native wildflowers and shrubs, with a strong focus on some rare and unusual north Florida plants.

Florida Game and Fresh Water Fish Commission

www.state.fl.us/gfc/gfchome.html

Although the focus of this site is on wildlife, there are several articles (www.state.fl.us/gfc/viewing/articles/articles.html) of interest to native plant enthusiasts.

Florida Native Plant Society

www.fnps.org

Visit the FNPS web site to locate a local chapter or, better yet, become a member and avail yourself of a range of benefits, including the quarterly bulletin and discounts on a wide variety of books.

Florida Natural Areas Inventory

www.fnai.org

The FNAI serves as a central depository for information on threatened or endangered natural habitats, plants, and animals in Florida.

Florida Plants Online

www.floridaplants.com

From the home page, click on the link labeled "Native Plants" for information on Florida's native plants and natural habitats.

Florida State Parks

www.dep.state.fl.us
www.abfla.com/parks/index.html

See the Florida Department of Environmental Protection's State Park Index for information on our state parks. The second address here is an alternate site from which to obtain information on state parks and other recreation areas.

Florida Wildflower Page

www.flwildflowers.com

Large collection of photographic images of a wide range of Florida native plants with a strong emphasis on northern Florida.

Florida's Endangered Species, Threatened Species, and Species of Special Concern

www.state.fl.us/gfc/pubs/endanger.html

This is the official list of Florida's endangered and threatened species as published by the Florida Game and Fresh Water Fish Commission.

Florida's Hollies

epic38.dep.state.fl.us/weds/ilex/Ilex.html
This is a subsection of Florida's Department of Environmental Protection Wetlands Evaluation and Delineation section, describing most of the hollies native to Florida.

Florida's Hummingbirds

www.mounts.org/mbglink.htm
Joe Schaefer and Craig N. Huegel have prepared an excellent introduction to creating a hummingbird garden with a strong focus on native plants.

Florida's Irises

epic38.dep.state.fl.us/weds/iris/iris.html
This is a subsection of Florida's Department of Environmental Protection Wetlands Evaluation and Delineation section that describes the irises, both native and introduced, that occur in Florida.

Florida's Pitcher Plants

epic38.dep.state.fl.us/weds/sarracen/sarracen.html
This subsection of Florida's Department of Environmental Protection Wetlands Evaluation and Delineation section describes the pitcher plants (genus *Sarracenia*) native to Florida.

Floridata

www.floridata.com
A "megasite" with much information on a large number of Florida garden plants, both native and non-native. It includes a detailed section on Florida scrub.

Forest Trees of Florida

www.fl-ag.com/forest/treeid.htm#TABLE
www.gate.net/~andykell/ftof/ftof_cov.html
The first site faithfully reproduces a handy little guide, first published in 1925 and still a valuable and interesting introduction to the forest trees of Florida. We are fortunate that it is available online as a resource for all Florida residents. The second site mirrors the preceding one but differs in the manner that the information is presented. Comparing the two is an interesting learning experience in web site design for beginning webmasters.

J. C. Raulston Arboretum

arb.ncsu.edu/Arboretum.html
An extensive site on the J. C. Raulston Arboretum at North Carolina State University. Much of the information is useful for gardeners in the Panhandle and northern Florida. Also, a series of articles titled "The Year in Trees" (arb.ncsu.edu/YearinTrees/YearinTrees.html) provides excellent information on a wide variety of woody plants suitable for the deep South, including numerous trees and shrubs native to Florida.

Mounts Botanical Garden

www.mounts.org
A thirteen-acre botanic garden in West Palm Beach, Florida, Mounts Botanic Garden has several displays of native plants. A small lake has had part of its shore planted with native wildflowers, and to the south of the lake are planted about three dozen native trees and

shrubs. Opposite the herb garden is a planting of mostly subtropical and tropical native trees and shrubs.

National Park System

www.nps.gov

Complete information, including maps, addresses, and telephone numbers, is provided for the eleven Florida sites in the national park system.

Native Florida Plants for Home Landscapes

edis.ifas.ufl.edu/scripts/htmlgen.exe?DOCUMENT_EP011

R. J. Black provides a good introductory list of native plants suitable for home landscapes.

Native Trees for North Florida

edis.ifas.ufl.edu/scripts/htmlgen.exe?DOCUMENT_EP007

This site provides a good introduction to native trees in north Florida, including a table that summarizes much information for each featured tree.

Northeast Florida's Native Trees and Shrubs

home.earthlink.net/~chouder/trees.html

Plants are broken out into three categories: large trees, small trees, and shrubs. There are lists of each category as found in northeast Florida with links to photographs of most species.

OmniCyber's Plant Family Key

www.omnicyber.org/Bio/Start.html

This is an online key to identifying a plant to the family level. Clicking on a particular character brings up a drawing that illustrates this character. This is an extremely useful feature for the amateur botanist. Although the site does not focus specifically on Florida native plants, it may prove useful in identifying a puzzle plant, at least to the level of family.

Plants, Bugs, Birds, Saving the World

www.mangonet.com/~doog

Doug Scofield's site focuses on southern Florida and includes much detailed information on native orchids and bromeliads as well as a database covering approximately one-ninth of Florida's native plants. Also included is information on invasive exotics.

Seed Germination Database

www.anet-chi.com/~manytimes/page52.htm

Extremely detailed information on every aspect of growing a wide variety of annuals, perennials, and woody plants from seed, including how to collect and store seeds.

Trees of Florida

www.sfrc.ufl.edu/Extension/ffws/tof.htm#menu

Comprehensive site that includes much detailed information on our state's trees.

Urban Integrated Pest Management

hammock.ifas.ufl.edu/en/en.html

An introduction by professors Philip G. Koehler and Donald E. Short of the University of Florida to the principles and practice of integrated pest management.

Urban Tree Identification for North Carolina

www.ces.ncsu.edu/depts/hort/consumer/Landscape/lands.htm

Dr. Alice B. Russell provides numerous high quality images and a wealth of information on many trees suitable for urban settings. Although the focus is on North Carolina, many of the trees listed have a native range extending into northern or central Florida. Beware, however: some of the non-native trees listed on this site are invasive pest plants in Florida.

USDA Forest Service

www.fs.fed.us

Information on Florida's three national forests (Apalachicola, Ocala, and Osceola) may be found at this site.

Wetlands Evaluation and Delineation

epic38.dep.state.fl.us/weds/weds.html

This site, a subsection of the Department of Environmental Protection site, contains a variety of images of Florida wetland plants. Click on the link labeled Previously Featured Plants (epic38.dep.state.fl.us/weds/previous.html) on the home page to get to the images.

Why Grow Native Plants

www.maxinet.com/garmour/cnps-ml2.htm

The Mount Lassen Chapter of the California Native Plant Society provides a succinct summary of the advantages and benefits of growing native plants, an assessment that is applicable to all parts of the country, not just California.

Wildflowers of Alabama

www.duc.auburn.edu/~deancar

Caroline R. Dean's site has numerous wildflower images of very high quality. The vast majority of the wildflowers appearing on her site are also native to Florida.

Wildflowers of Mississippi

WWW2.MsState.Edu/~jbyrd/wild2.html

This site features a selection of wildflower images organized by flower color. The majority of the wildflowers appearing on this site are also native to Florida.

Your Florida Backyard

www.nsis.org

Good all-around site focusing on native plants, birding, and butterfly gardening.

Bibliography

Austin, Daniel F. 1991. American Bays. *The Palmetto* vol. 11, no. 2 (summer): 12–13.

Bettinger, Edith. 1991. How to Know Some of the Common Ferns of Central Florida. *The Palmetto* vol. 11, no. 1 (spring): 6–8.

Brown, Elliott. 1995. Personal communication in a letter dated July 15, 1995.

Burrell, C. Colson (ed.). 1997. *The Natural Water Garden*. Brooklyn: Brooklyn Botanic Garden.

Buscher, Fred K., and Susan A. McClure. 1989. *All about Pruning*. San Ramon, Calif.: Ortho Books.

Chellman, Pat. 1993. You Won't Be Disappointed with Coral Honeysuckle. *The Palmetto* vol. 13, no. 2 (summer): 3.

Christensen, B. V. 1946. *Collection and Cultivation of Medicinal Plants of Florida*. Bulletin no. 14, New Series, Feb. 1946, State of Florida Department of Agriculture; reprinted and distributed by Micanopy Publishing Company, Micanopy, Florida.

Clewell, Andre F. 1985. *Guide to the Vascular Plants of the Florida Panhandle*. Gainesville: University Presses of Florida.

Coffey, Timothy. 1993. *The History and Folklore of North American Wildflowers*. New York: Facts on File.

Coile, Nancy C. 1992. Little-Leaf Redroot. *The Palmetto* vol. 12, no. 1 (spring): 10–11.

Conrad, Roseanne D. 1998. *An Owner's Guide to the Garden Pond*. New York: Howell Book House.

Correll, Donovan S., and Marshall C. Johnston 1979. *Manual of the Vascular Plants of Texas*. Dallas: University of Texas at Dallas.

Cronquist, A. 1980. *Vascular Flora of the Southeastern United States: Asteraceae*. Chapel Hill: The University of North Carolina Press.

Deuerling, Richard J., and Peggy S. Lantz. 1990. Native Wild Foods: Nuts to You! *The Palmetto* vol. 10, no. 4 (winter): 13.

———. 1991a. Native Wild Foods: Catttails. *The Palmetto* vol. 11, no. 1 (spring): 11.

———. 1991b. Native Wild Foods: Water Lilies. *The Palmetto* vol. 11, no. 2 (summer): 7.

———. 1991c. Native Wild Foods: Indian Lemonade. *The Palmetto* vol. 11, no. 3 (fall): 7.

———. 1991d. Native Wild Foods: The Pleasures of Sassafras. *The Palmetto* vol. 11, no. 4 (winter): 8.

———. 1992. Native Wild Foods: Wild Onions and Garlic. *The Palmetto* vol. 12, no. 2 (summer): 10–11.

———. 1993. *Florida's Incredible Wild Edibles*. Orlando: Florida Native Plant Society.

Donselman, Henry. Undated. Lethal Yellowing of Palm Trees in Florida. Florida Cooperative Extension Service Department of Ornamental Horticulture Fact Sheet. Internet: http://www.floridaplants.com/horticulture/ly.htm.

Doukas, Annette. 1993. Trumpet Creeper. *The Palmetto* vol. 13, no. 4 (winter): 24.

Duke, James A. 1992. *Handbook of Edible Weeds.* Boca Raton, Fla.: CRC Press.

Fazio, James R. 1992. Building *with* Trees. *The Palmetto* vol. 12, no. 2 (summer): 12–13.

Fernald, Merritt L. 1950. *Gray's Manual of Botany.* New York: D. Van Nostrand Company.

Foster, Steven, and James A. Duke. *A Field Guide to Medicinal Plants.* Boston: Houghton Mifflin Company.

Gerberg, Eugene J., and Ross H. Arnett, Jr. 1989. *Florida Butterflies.* Baltimore: Natural Science Publications.

Gibbons, Euell. 1966. *Stalking the Healthful Herbs.* Putney, Vt.: Alan C. Hood and Company.

Godts, Jose E. 1990. The Upside-Down Flower. *The Palmetto* vol. 10, no. 4 (winter): 3.

Hall, David W. 1991. Common Beggar's Tick. *The Palmetto* vol. 11, no. 1 (spring): 15.

Hill, Lewis. 1986. *Pruning Simplified.* Pownal, Vt.: Storey Communications.

Howell, John T. 1970. *Marin Flora.* Berkeley: University of California Press.

Huegel, Craig. 1992. Bumelias. *The Palmetto* vol. 12, no. 3 (fall): 6–7.

———. 1993a. Hawthorns. *The Palmetto* vol. 13, no. 2 (summer): 4–5.

———. 1993b. Selecting Food Plants for Wildlife. *The Palmetto* vol. 13, no. 4 (winter): 6–7.

———. 1995. *Florida Plants for Wildlife.* Orlando: Florida Native Plant Society.

Jewell, Susan D. 1993. *Exploring Wild South Florida.* Sarasota, Fla.: Pineapple Press.

———. 1995. *Exploring Wild Central Florida.* Sarasota, Fla.: Pineapple Press.

Kartesz, J. T. 1998. A Synonymized Checklist of the Vascular Flora of the United States, Puerto Rico, and the Virgin Islands. Full Text Index—July, 1998. Internet programming by Hugh Wilson and Erich Schneider. Internet: http://www.csdl.tamu.edu/FLORA/b98/check98.htm.

Kartesz, J. T., and J. W. Thieret. 1991. Common Names for Vascular Plants: Guidelines for Use and Application. *Sida* 14(3):421–34.

Keller, Jack. 1998. Requested Recipe: Muscadine Grapes. Internet: http://www.geocities.com/NapaValley/1172/reques15.html.

Kilmer, Anne. Undated. *Gardening for Butterflies and Children in South Florida.* West Palm Beach: Pine Jog Environmental Education Center, Florida Atlantic University.

Kral, Robert. 1983. *A Report on Some Rare, Threatened, or Endangered Forest-Related Vascular Plants of the South.* 2 vols. U.S. Department of Agriculture Forest Service, Technical Publication R8-TP 2. Atlanta: USDA Forest Service.

Little, Elbert L., Jr., and Frank H. Wadsworth. 1964. *Common Trees of Puerto Rico and the Virgin Islands.* U.S. Department of Agriculture Forest Service, Agriculture Handbook no. 249. Washington, D.C.: U.S. Government Printing Office.

Long, Robert W., and Olga Lakela. 1971. *A Flora of Tropical Florida.* Coral Gables: University of Miami Press.

Luer, Carlyle A. 1972. *The Native Orchids of Florida.* New York: New York Botanical Garden.

———. 1975. *The Native Orchids of United States and Canada (excluding Florida).* New York: New York Botanical Garden.

Martin, H. W. 1994. More on Beautyberry. *The Palmetto* vol. 14, no. 1 (spring): 5–6.

McCartney, Chuck. 1998. Florida's Aquatic Orchids. *The Palmetto* vol. 18, no. 2 (summer): 20–23.

Meerow, Alan W. 1992. *Betrock's Guide to Landscape Palms.* Cooper City, Fla.: Betrock Information Systems.

Meerow, Alan W., and Jeffrey G. Norcini. 1998. *Native Trees for North Florida.* Circular 833, Department of Environmental Horticulture, Florida Cooperative Extension Service, Institute of Food and Agricultural Sciences, University of Florida.

Minno, Maria. 1992. Florida Pines: Evergreens for the Christmas Season. *The Palmetto* vol. 12, no. 4 (winter): 9–11.

Morrison, Ken. 1991. Boycott Mulch! *The Palmetto* vol. 11 no. 2 (summer): 16.

Moyroud, Richard. 1996a. Cabbage Palms: Can We Continue to Transplant from the Wild? *The Palmetto* vol. 16, no. 3 (winter): 11–12.

———. 1996b. South Florida Slash Pine. *The Palmetto* vol. 16, no. 4 (winter): 11–12.

Mullins, Stephen. 1993. Moving Joewood Trees. *The Palmetto* vol. 13, no. 2 (summer): 8–9.

Munson, June. 1991. Oshibana. *The Palmetto* vol. 11, no. 1 (spring): 4–5.

Nash, Helen. 1996. *Low-Maintenance Water Gardens.* New York: Sterling Publishing Company.

Nash, Helen, and C. Greg Speichert. 1996. *Water Gardening in Containers.* New York: Sterling Publishing Company.

Nelson, Gil. 1994. *The Trees of Florida.* Sarasota, Fla.: Pineapple Press.

———. 1996. *The Shrubs and Woody Vines of Florida.* Sarasota, Fla.: Pineapple Press.

———. 1999. Personal communication by e-mail dated July 12, 1999.

Norwood, Mary Lou, and Craig Huegel. 1992. Gardening for Hummingbirds. *The Palmetto* vol. 12, no. 4 (winter): 14–15.

Osorio, Rufino. 1990. *Pectis linearifolia. The Palmetto* vol. 10, no. 4 (winter): 4.

———. 1991a. *Stenandrium dulce* var. *floridana. The Palmetto* vol. 11, no. 1 (spring): 3.

———. 1991b. *Lindernia grandiflora. The Palmetto* vol. 11, no. 2 (summer): 6.

———. 1991c. Three Pine Rockland Shrubs. *The Palmetto* vol. 11, no. 3 (fall): 8–9.

———. 1993a. Lyre-leaved Sage. *The Palmetto* vol. 13, no. 3 (fall): 9.

———. 1993b. Goldenrod Fern. *The Palmetto* vol. 13, no. 4 (winter): 18.

———. 1994a. Sweetspires. *The Palmetto* vol. 14, no. 1 (spring): 12.

———. 1994b. Sundrops and Friends. *The Palmetto* vol. 14, no. 2 (summer): 9.

———. 1996. Ornamental Bunchgrasses. *The Palmetto* vol. 16, no. 1 (spring): 5–6.

Pais, David. 1991. Loblolly-Bay: *Gordonia lasianthus. The Palmetto* vol. 11, no. 1 (spring): 10.

Radford, Albert E., Harry E. Ahles, and C. Ritchie Bell. 1968. *Manual of the Vascular Flora of the Carolinas.* Chapel Hill: University of North Carolina Press.

Rataj, Karel, and Thomas J. Horeman. 1977. *Aquarium Plants: Their Identification, Cultivation and Ecology.* Neptune, N.J.: T.F.H. Publications.

Reich, Lee. 1997. *The Pruning Book.* Newtown, Conn.: Taunton Press.

Riach, J. 1993. The Florida Cedars. *The Palmetto* vol. 13, no. 1 (spring): 5–7.

Riefler, Steve. 1993. Grafting. *The Palmetto* vol. 13, no. 3: 16.

Schaefer, Joe, and George Tanner. 1998. *Landscaping for Florida's Wildlife: Re-creating Native Ecosystems in Your Yard.* Gainesville: University Press of Florida.

Scheper Interactives L.C. 1999. Floridata: *Myrica cerifera.* Internet: http://www.floridata.com/ref/M/myrica.cfm.

Scurlock, J. Paul. 1987. *Native Trees and Shrubs of the Florida Keys: A Field Guide*. Pittsburgh: Laurel Press.

Seaman, Paula A., and Ronald L. Myers. 1992. Propagating Wiregrass from Seed. *The Palmetto* vol. 12, no. 4 (winter): 6–7.

Small, John K. 1933. *Manual of the Southeastern Flora*. 2 parts. New York: Hafner Publishing Company.

Smith, Elizabeth. 1993. Natural Dyes. *The Palmetto* vol. 13, no. 3: 12–15.

———. 1995a. Butterfly Orchid. *The Palmetto* vol. 15, no. 2 (summer): 3

———. 1995b. Firebush. *The Palmetto* vol. 15, no. 3 (fall): 3.

Stout, Jack. 1990. Pigmy Fringe Tree under Fire. *The Palmetto* vol. 10, no. 4 (winter): 5.

Tasker, Georgia. 1984. *Wild Things: The Return of Native Plants*. Winter Park: Florida Native Plant Society.

Tomocik, Joseph. and Leslie Garisto. 1996. *Water Gardening*. New York: Pantheon Books.

Tripp, Kim. 1996a. Bald Cypress: A Coniferous Cure for Gardener-Wilt. Internet: http://arb.ncsu.edu/YearinTrees/List/Taxodium.html.

———. 1996b. Yaupon: Versatile Southern Ladies and Gentlemen of the Garden. Internet: http://arb.ncsu.edu/YearinTrees/List/Ilexvomitoria.html.

USDA, NRCS. 1999. The PLANTS database. National Plant Data Center, Baton Rouge, La. Internet: http://plants.usda.gov/plants.

Vanderplank, John. 1991. *Passion Flowers and Passion Fruit*. Cambridge, Mass.: MIT Press.

Ward, Daniel B., and Robert T. Ing. 1995. Florida's Ten Tallest Native Tree Species. *The Palmetto* vol. 15, no. 3 (fall): 6–7.

Wasowski, Sally. 1991. *Native Texas Plants: Landscaping Region by Region*. Houston: Gulf Publishing Company.

Wasowski, Sally, and Andy Wasowski. 1994. *Gardening with Native Plants of the South*. Dallas: Taylor Publishing Company.

Watson, Craig. 1991. Ponds in the Backyard Habitat. *The Palmetto* vol. 11, no. 2 (summer): 4–5.

Wettstein, Fritz. 1992. A Future for Gopher Apples. *The Palmetto* vol. 12, no. 1 (spring): 8–9.

Workman, Richard W. 1980. *Growing Native: Native Plants for Landscape Use in Coastal South Florida*. Sanibel, Fla.: Sanibel-Captiva Conservation Foundation.

Wunderlin, Richard P. 1982. *Guide to the Vascular Plants of Central Florida*. Gainesville: University Presses of Florida.

———. 1998. *Guide to the Vascular Plants of Florida*. Gainesville: University Press of Florida.

Wylly, Molly. 1992. Audubon's Wild Poinsettia. *The Palmetto* vol. 12, no. 4 (winter): 8.

Zona, Scott. 1994. Beautyberry, an Underused Native. *The Palmetto* vol. 14, no. 1 (spring): 3–4.

Index

Bold indicates a page with a photograph.

Rufino Osorio is past president of the Palm Beach chapter of the Florida Native Plant Society. He is a freelance writer, photographer, and proprietor of Wildflower Nirvana, a rare plant nursery.

Books of related interest

Landscape Plants for Subtropical Climates, by Bijan Dehgan

Landscaping for Florida's Wildlife, by Joe Schaefer and George Tanner

Florida Gardening by the Sea, by Mary Jane McSwain

Common Coastal Plants in Florida, by Michael R. Barnett and David C. Crewz

Florida Wildflowers in Their Natural Communities, by Walter Kingsley Taylor